Nabokov in Motion

Nabokov in Motion

Modernity and Movement

Yuri Leving

BLOOMSBURY ACADEMIC
NEW YORK · LONDON · OXFORD · NEW DELHI · SYDNEY

BLOOMSBURY ACADEMIC
Bloomsbury Publishing Inc
1385 Broadway, New York, NY 10018, USA
50 Bedford Square, London, WC1B 3DP, UK
29 Earlsfort Terrace, Dublin 2, Ireland

BLOOMSBURY, BLOOMSBURY ACADEMIC and the Diana logo are trademarks of
Bloomsbury Publishing Plc

First published in the United States of America 2022

Cover design by Daniel Benneworth-Gray
Cover image; Zig-zag passenger and freight train by an unknown artist. Original from
Library of Congress. Digitally enhanced by rawpixel. Image is in the public domain.

Bloomsbury Publishing Inc does not have any control over, or responsibility for, any third-
party websites referred to or in this book. All internet addresses given in this book were
correct at the time of going to press. The author and publisher regret any inconvenience
caused if addresses have changed or sites have ceased to exist, but can accept no
responsibility for any such changes.

Library of Congress Cataloguing-in-Publication Data
Names: Leving, Yuri, author.
Title: Nabokov in motion: modernity and movement /
Yuri Leving; translated from the Russian by Keith Blasing
Description: New York: Bloomsbury Academic, 2022. |
Includes bibliographical references and index. |
Identifiers: LCCN 2021040027 (print) | LCCN 2021040028 (ebook) |
ISBN 9781501386534 (hardback) | ISBN 9781501386541 (paperback) |
ISBN 9781501386565 (pdf) | ISBN 9781501386558 (epub) |
ISBN 9781501386572 (ebook other)
Subjects: LCSH: Nabokov, Vladimir Vladimirovich, 1899-1977–Criticism and
interpretation. | Literature and technology.
Classification: LCC PG3476.N3 Z7283 2022 (print) |
LCC PG3476.N3 (ebook) | DDC 813/.54–dc23
LC record available at https://lccn.loc.gov/2021040027
LC ebook record available at https://lccn.loc.gov/2021040028

ISBN: HB: 978-1-5013-8653-4
          PB: 978-1-5013-8654-1
          ePDF: 978-1-5013-8656-5
          eBook: 978-1-5013-8655-8

Typeset by Integra Software Services Pvt. Ltd.
Printed and bound in the United States of America

To find out more about our authors and books visit www.bloomsbury.com
and sign up for our newsletters.

CONTENTS

List of Figures   x
Acknowledgements   xv

1   Chaos and Order   1
On the Poetics of Urbanism   1
Bodies and Texts   8
From Chaos to Order   11
The Urban Infrastructure, or "What Lies Beneath the Asphalt of the Text?"   14
The Resurrection of Electricity   17
Buildings, Stairs, Elevators   23
The Life of Things   29
The Telephone: A Conduit to the Other World   33
The Street Advertisement   38
The Shop Window of Metatexts   44

2   The Train as a New Locus of Myth Creation in Literature   51
The Topos of the Beginning   51
The Railroad as a Metaliterary Device   56
The Railroad Metaphor   59
Childhood and the Locomotive: A Model of the World   61
Toys and Reasons   67
The Station/Depot   70
The Hierarchy of Classes   82
The Existential Nature of the Journey by Rail   88
The Killing Power of the Train and Engine   95
The Train Wreck   98
Conductor to Immortality   102

The Mythology of the Train   104

The Esoteric Language of Trains   109

Train. Love. Fate   113

The Boredom of the Road   117

An Erotic Encounter   122

Violence and the Railroad   127

The Poetics of Description   135

Personification and Animation   139

Clichés: Russians and the Railroad   143

On the Road and Longing for Russia   146

Nabokov and Tsvetaeva: Synoptic Chart of a Dialog   149

The Beckoning Distance   151

Telegraph Poles   155

The View from the Train Window   159

The Underground   165

3 The Automobile in the Works of Nabokov: The Semantics of Driving and the Metaliterary Process   175

Auto vs. Train   175

The Ride to School   177

The Nabokovs' American Cars   181

Driving Experience   186

The Model   189

Car Controls (a Novel on Wheels)   194

"Crossroads of Life": The Symbolism of Driving   197

Worlds Unknown to Each Other   200

Metaphysics of the Garage   203

The Route Through the Text   208

The Automobile in the Landscape   211

Vehicular Mimicry   218

Sex in a Car   221

An Incident on the Street   229

Forewarnings   232

The Car Accident   235

Death of the Hero   239

The Furniture Truck   243

4   Symbolism of the Airplane: Breakthrough to Another Dimension   251

The Airplane Schematic   251
Flight in the Russian Periodical Press in the 1910s   254
"And the Steel Bird Will Fly": The Airplane in Russian Poetry in the Early Twentieth Century   257
The Magic of Names   262
Insects, Birds, and Fish   266
On the Genesis and Context of Nabokov's Poem, "The Airplane"   271
The Music of Flight   275
Flight and Performance   276
The Aesthetics of Public Death   279
Death of the Pilot   283
War in the Air   288
The Futurist Thesaurus   292
Overcoming Gravity: Hymn to the Airplane   299
Flights, Dreaming, and Waking   302
The Last Station   309

Bibliography   313
Index   328

FIGURES

1.1   The Blagoveshchensky (Annunciation) Bridge which was called the Nikolaevsky Bridge from 1855 to 1918 in honor of Tsar Nicholas I. It was the first permanent bridge built across the Neva River in St. Petersburg, Russia. Glass negative, between *c.* 1900 and 1907. George Grantham Bain Collection, Library of Congress   5

1.2   Drawing by V. Nabokov to his son Dmitri in a letter to Véra Nabokov, June 9, 1944. Henry W. and Albert A. Berg Collection, The New York Public Library   9

1.3   Currier & Ives. *The Progress of the Century—The Lightning Steam Press, the Electric Telegraph, the Locomotive, and the Steamboat.* New York: Published by Currier & Ives., *c.* 1876   12

1.4   Photograph shows cars driving along Bowery in New York City. To the left Comet Hotel is visible. Photographer: Angelo Rizzuto, 1956. Gelatin silver print. Anthony Angel Collection, Library of Congress   16

1.5   Aerial view of Times Square lined with pedestrians and automobiles, looking north from the Times Building. New York, 1952. Photographer: Angelo Rizzuto. Anthony Angel Collection, Library of Congress   24

1.6   Miss Harriot Daley supervises a staff of thirty-seven operators as they answer calls from 1,200 extensions at the United States Capitol switchboard. Washington, D.C., July 30, 1937. Harris & Ewing collection, Library of Congress   33

1.7   Charles H. Woodbury. Advertisement for Trolley trips on a Bay State Triangle. Boston, 1897. Heliotype Printing Co. Prints and Photographs Division, Library of Congress   39

1.8   James Fuller Queen. *Design for advertisement, Charles Oakford & Sons, furrier and hatter, located at 104 Chestnut.* Philadelphia,

Pennsylvania, 1843. Drawing shows a street view of the façade of a storefront with entrances; windows with merchandise displays; awning over an entrance; and lightly sketched pedestrians; across the top are samples of lettering and designs. Marian S. Carson collection, Library of Congress   45

2.1   *The Express Train*. United States, *c.* 1870. New York, N.Y.: Published by Currier & Ives. Lithograph. Library of Congress   53

2.2   Drawing by V. Nabokov to his son Dmitri in a letter to Véra Nabokov, February 7–8, 1937. W. Henry and A. Albert Berg Collection, The New York Public Library   59

2.3   J. N. Swartzell and daughter Margaret seated with parts of electric train, on porch of home, Washington, D.C. Between 1909 and 1932. National Photo Company Collection, Library of Congress   61

2.4   Toy factory. Stephanie Cewe is assembling locomotives for toy trains. Photographer: Howard R. Hollem. New Haven, C.T., 1942. Office of War Information, Photograph Collection, Library of Congress   67

2.5   Design for a Railroad Station. Nineteenth century, Anonymous, French. Graphite heightened with white on heavy wove paper. The Elisha Whittelsey Collection, The Metropolitan Museum of Art   71

2.6   Group at Train Station. United States, 1929. Photographer: Harris & Ewing. Prints and Photographs Division, Library of Congress   78

2.7   Honoré Daumier. "Mr. Prudhomme: Long live the third-class compartments …," from "On the train," published in *Le Charivari*, August 30, 1864. Lithograph on newsprint. The Metropolitan Museum of Art   83

2.8   *On Woman's Train*, 1916. Photograph: Bain News Service. George Grantham Bain Collection, Library of Congress   86

2.9   *Train Accident*. United States, 1932. Photographer: Harris & Ewing. Prints and Photographs Division, Library of Congress   99

2.10   Fixing the locomotive. 1930s. National Photo Company Collection, Library of Congress   110

2.11   Two women bathers standing by bushes along a river as a train passes over a bridge spanning the river in Edward Hopper's illustration, *Train and bathers* (1920). Etching. Prints and Photographs Division, Library of Congress 114

2.12 Train interior with men. 1930s. National Photo Company Collection, Library of Congress 118

2.13 Illustration by artist Bernhard Gillam showing a man hoping to cause the oncoming train labeled "N.Y. City Reforms" to derail. Cover illustration from *Puck*, vol. 17, no. 427 (13 May 1885) 128

2.14 Train rounding a curve. Dry plate negative, between 1910 and 1920. Detroit Publishing Company photograph collection, Library of Congress 142

2.15 Telegraph poles. Photographer: Paul Strand. Illustration appeared in *Camera Work*, no. 48 (October 1916) 156

2.16 Berlin's new subway, 1920. A new crosstown subway designed to relieve the downtown congestion after the manner of subway building in New York. Heavy steel girders form the foundation for the street, the subway being directly under it. Glass negative. American National Red Cross photograph collection, Library of Congress 166

3.1 Automobile travel in the tsarist era. This photograph is from an album produced by the artistic studio of the *Obrazovanie* (Education) association in Moscow that documents the construction of the western portion of the Amur line of the Trans-Siberian Railroad in 1908–13. Russian State Library 176

3.2 Vladimir and Véra Nabokov, and Dorothy Leuthold (Dasha), VN's student who drove the Nabokovs from New York to the American West, 1941, with Leuthold's 1941 Pontiac ("Pon'ka") 178

3.3 and 3.4 Vladimir Nabokov and Dmitri at a tennis court in front of the family's 1950 Buick Special. Ithaca, N.Y., 1951 183

3.5 Véra Nabokov next to Dmitri's Bizzarini GT, Montreux, 1969 186

3.6 Véra Nabokov with Dmitri's 1977 Ferrari 308 GTB, 1978 187

3.7 Dmitri Nabokov and his first car, a Mercedes Benz. Berlin, 1937 190

3.8 Dmitri Nabokov in his racecar, Alfa Romeo GTZ. Monza, Italy, 1964 190

3.9   Dmitri Nabokov and Viper GT2 at Moroso, 1998   193

3.10   Men fixing tire. Glass negative, between *c.* 1920 and *c.* 1925.
        George Grantham Bain Collection, Library of Congress   195

3.11   Famous Sequoia tree in California. Véra Nabokov, Dmitri Nabokov,
        and family friends, Bertrand and Lisbet Thompson with their
        Studebaker, 1940s   198

3.12   Véra, Dmitri, Vladimir Nabokov, and Vladimir Sikorskii (the son of
        the writer's sister Elena). The car is a Triumph TR3-A. San Remo,
        December 1959   202

3.13   Assembly. Detroit Publishing Co., 1923. Dry plate negative possibly
        made for Ford Motor Company   204

3.14   Cover of the Soviet magazine *Motor*, No. 2, 1929   209

3.15   Dmitri Nabokov and his 1957 MG-A. New York, *c.* 1959   213

3.16   Horace Allen Gasoline Station, San Jose, C.A., 1933. This structure
        is an excellent example of the so-called "domestic style" that
        characterized gasoline station design in the late 1920s and early
        1930s. With its massive brick chimney, steep shingled roof, and
        full-arched multi-paned windows, the station closely resembled the
        English Cottage style house. Historic American Buildings Survey
        Collection, Library of Congress   219

3.17   Two ladies in a convertible automobile. *Automobility*, 1906.
        Campbell, Metzger & Jacobson. Popular and applied graphic art
        print filing series, Library of Congress   222

3.18   Edith and Irene Mayer, daughters of Louis Mayer, head of the
        Metro Goldwyn Mayer Corp., posing next to the automobiles and
        wearing fur-trimmed coats. National Photo Company Collection,
        Library of Congress   226

3.19   Automobile accident recreation with miniature cars, between 1915
        and 1923. Harris & Ewing photograph collection, Library of
        Congress   229

3.20   "Don't blame the motorist for all the automobile accidents in city
        streets. Look at some of the things he is up against," by artist Will
        Crawford. The illustration shows an automobile driver trying to
        negotiate workmen in the roadway, children playing ball in the
        street and darting in front of automobiles, absentminded pedestrians
        stepping off the curb, and people exiting streetcars into oncoming

traffic (New York, N.Y.: Keppler & Schwarzmann, Puck Building, January 29, 1913)   236

4.1   Russian aviator Mikhail Efimov (1881–1919) seated on airplane, *c.* 1910. George Grantham Bain Collection, Library of Congress   252

4.2   Cover of a magazine, *Global Panorama*, published in Petrograd (formerly St. Petersburg), showing a British spy hydroplane. August 29, 1914   255

4.3   "Airships are getting so dreadfully commonplace." Illustration by artist Will Crawford shows a two-panel cartoon with pedestrians looking with amazement at an airplane flying over a city (on the left); and on the right, citizens no longer take notice of all the airplanes crowding the sky above the city. Appeared in *Puck*, vol. 70, no. 1799 (August 23, 1911), centerfold   258

4.4   Aviators Vsevolod Abramovich (1890–1913) and Russian princess Eugenia Mikhailovna Shakhovskaya (1889–1920). In 1913, the two aviators were in a plane crash in which Abramovich was killed. Glass negative, between *c.* 1910 and 1913. George Grantham Bain Collection, Library of Congress   263

4.5   Continental Can hangar, Morristown Airport, New Jersey. April 9, 1952. Gottscho-Schleisner Collection, Library of Congress   268

4.6   South American aviator Juan Domenjos with his wife, 1915. Harris & Ewing photograph collection, Library of Congress   277

4.7   A photograph of Louis Blériot's aeroplane after an accident at Reims, August 1909. George Grantham Bain Collection, Library of Congress   280

4.8   "The discovery of the law of gravitation." Illustration by artist Louis Glackens shows a Wright Brothers airplane crashed into a tree with Sir Isaac Newton and another man in the wreckage on the ground. Published on the cover of *Puck*, vol. 68, no. 1753 (October 5, 1910)   284

4.9   Russian poster showing fighter plane in flight, with man standing to fire mounted machine gun. The caption reads: "Sign up for a military loan, help achieve victory!" Petrograd, 1916. Color Lithograph   290

4.10 Farman airplane, 1908. George Grantham Bain Collection, Library of Congress   293

ACKNOWLEDGEMENTS

This book is a modified version of a Russian monograph that appeared in 2004, with the St. Petersburg publisher, Ivan Limbakh Press. I am grateful to my translator, Keith Blasing, for handling the Russian text with such care and grace; to Haaris Naqvi, my editor at Bloomsbury Academic, who has now guided me successfully through two publications; to my friend and colleague, Frederick H. White, for helping to settle on the new title; and to my two anonymous peer-reviewers whose wise suggestions I tried to adopt while adapting the Russian original to its new linguistic and cultural domain.

The original monograph came out under the title, *Train Station – Garage – Hangar. Vladimir Nabokov and the Poetics of Russian Urbanism* [*Vokzal – Garazh – Angar. Vladimir Nabokov i poetika russkogo urbanizma*]. The Russian and English versions are not identical: besides pruning the text and updating the bibliography to make it more relevant to a contemporary English-speaking readership, I also selected new images for this edition. Similar to the Russian layout, the photographs are meant to provide a parallel visual narrative to my story of modernity and movement through the prism of Nabokov's writings. All photos of the Nabokovs and cars were generously provided by the late Dmitri Nabokov, who was a racing driver himself and took a great deal of personal interest in this project in its nascent stage. Dmitri supported my scholarship in more ways than one and his presence is greatly missed in Nabokov studies today.

I dedicated the Russian version of this book to my teachers, some of whom have departed since then to the other, more ephemeral world. Now, as I myself have had an opportunity to teach Nabokov in the classroom for many years, I wish to dedicate this edition to my students, past and future, for it is their continuous curiosity that drives me to reconsider the ubiquitous movement of modernity. In that amazing company of mentors and pupils, I navigate the literary maze built by Nabokov, even if this is just one long mental trip, as Professor Timofey Pnin used to think while "wiggling [his] toes and shifting phantom gears."

October 2021,
Rome – Halifax

1

Chaos and Order

On the Poetics of Urbanism

I am writing these lines by electricity,
And at the gate sits an automobile, humming;
Starry flags flew up at the terminals;
The "Titanic" class rocks the ocean;
Submarines cut open its depths,
And into the blue flew an airplane rattling.
                              —Valery Briusov, *Under Electricity*

The complex process of urbanization left its mark on our cultural codes, warped the fabric of our language, created new motifs, and gave the literary world a great many unexpected conflicts for plot material.

This book examines and interprets the personal mythology of Vladimir Vladimirovich Nabokov in a broad context of prose and poetry limited by time (1837–1977) and thematic constraints, in a synchronic cross-section, and from the point of view of what we will call *the poetics of urbanism* in literature. In contemporary literary studies, "urbanism" is generally understood to mean the interaction of technological innovations and the "corporeal world" with human culture, and the subsequent mapping of this process onto an artistic text.

When presenting a description aimed at the "urbanistic code" as a whole (an attempt to track the motif by modeling a "single" railroad or aviation topos in Russian literature), one cannot avoid smoothing over the idiosyncrasies of specific authors and works to a significant degree. The paradox is that the genius of the artist relies on the transformation of this "predetermined" paradigm. Consequently, as Hanzen-Leve has observed, the more an artist conforms to a general artistic system, the less "effective" he becomes and the more relevant his work is for uncovering the model structure and the typical features of his epoch or period. Hence the large number of marginal prose writers and poets quoted in this book; no effort was made to restrict the field of authors analyzed to those that were within Nabokov's sphere of awareness or that he engaged with in open or concealed polemics.[1] In the decision to include in the textual analysis various documentary sources (newspaper items, correspondence, archival materials, etc.), we are making an *a priori* assumption that a text is the product of cultural conventions, and constitutes a palimpsest of the collective memory and mythology (Gasparov, *Literaturnye leitmotivy*, 279–282).

Nabokov is the ideal subject for structuralist analysis. The world of his fiction is riddled with the qualities that Roland Barthes was fascinated by in the work of Jules Verne (Barthes, *Mythologies*, 401–412), whom Nabokov named as one of his favorite authors when he was a child: both Nabokov and Verne were able to create a self-enclosed "cosmogony," with its own space and time, replete with recurring motifs and with its own operating principles. The specific nature of Nabokov's texts and subtexts, and his orientation toward a thoughtful, "interactive" reader and interlocutor are characterized by certain didactic features of the texts. Nabokov's works, as has been noted a number of times, are tutorial in nature. In figuring out the laws inherent to a particular text, the reader is able on his own to gather the keys that unlock the solution to the "mysteries" presented by a work at all of its different levels.

It is worth saying a few words about the poetics of movement in Russian literature as a whole by way of introduction. A brief but precise overview of the topic was presented in the wide-ranging work by Jerzy Faryno, who noted that, in real life, vehicles and machines are categorized based on prestige and on function (ceremonial/ritualistic or commercial/economic): in other words, by their purpose—transporting passengers or freight, a corpse to a cemetery or a bride and groom to their wedding (Faryno, *Vvedenie*, 357). Similar meanings, Faryno suggests, must be activated and realized in art as well: in literature, painting, and cinematography. Because the differentiation and symbolism of vehicles are developed in art at a deeper level than in everyday life, artistic space will catalyze and strengthen the mythologizing potential of the mechanisms introduced into the text.[2] In Mandel'shtam's "Concert at the Railway Station" and Pasternak's *Safe Conduct*, the locomotive is associated with the archetype of the psychopomp, who leads souls to the next world. The same function is performed by the steamship

---

[1] Regarding the "strong" and "weak" points of this method, see the introductory chapter to Hanzen-Leve, *Russkii simvolizm*, 11. I present similar intertextual analyses in previous works that examine the specific nature of some presupposition or another (see Leving, *Keys to* The Gift).

[2] See the useful section entitled "The Feeling of the Railroad" ("Chuvstvo zheleznoi dorogi"), in Yangirov, "'Ekran zhizni'."

in Bunin's "The Gentleman from San Francisco" and by the bus in the eponymous narrative poem by Tsvetaeva. In Slavic cultures, and Russian culture in particular, the locomotive or tram took on, Faryno states, the older symbolism of the horse of folk tales that carried souls across. The horse for avant-garde artists was not merely a domesticated animal, but rather an ancient psychopomp, the "verse-producing Pegasus," and even a redeemer and savior (in Maiakovskii's "On Being Kind to Horses"; ibid., 358). The airplane had a similar fate, and additionally acquired the functions of the dragonfly, the mosquito, the soaring and ascending "heavenly spirit": a new Icarus or Hermes. Modernism's system of vehicles also mythologized not only bicycles, motorcycles, automobiles, and the metro, but also, less obviously, ice skates (Tsvetaeva's "Ice skaters," Nabokov's "The ice skater," and poems by Otsup, Sadovskoi, and Mandel'stam, as well as Lyovin's famous skating scene in *Anna Karenina*), and skis (Akhmatova's poem "I know, I know – the skis again," Nabokov's "Ski jump," and *Doctor Zhivago*). With their special brand of movement and sliding, these also belong to a paradigm such that they occupy the position of "winged" footwear and perform the function of Hermes' sandals. The position that Nabokov formed early on regarding the evolution and origin of the poetics of movement in human culture[3] is most clearly expressed in the final chapter of his autobiography. Instead of "corrupting" Freudian experiments, the author advises that psychologists attempt to explain "the phylogenetic aspects of the passion male children have for things on wheels":

Of course we know what the Viennese Quack thought of the matter. < ... > Rapid growth, quantum-quick thought, the roller coaster of the circulatory system – all forms of vitality are forms of velocity, and no wonder a *growing child desires to out-Nature Nature by filling a minimum stretch of time with a maximum of spatial enjoyment.* Innermost in man is the spiritual pleasure derivable from the possibilities of outtugging and outrunning gravity, of overcoming or re-enacting the earth's pull.

(*Speak, Memory*, 300–301)[4]

---

[3]As early as 1923, Nabokov composed a three-poem cycle under the general title "Movement," which concludes the poetry collection *The Cluster* (*Grozd'*) (*Russian Collected Works*, 1:465–467); in 1924 he conceived a series of plots for presentation at the "Blue Bird," a Berlin cabaret, united under the English title, "Locomotion" (Boyd, *American Years*, 272).
[4]Cf. Erenburg's "10 horsepower" (1929): "The automobile is a new divinity ... Mr. Citroen sells toy cars for advertising ... Wooden horses have long been out of fashion. Children are now playing with shifting speeds. But besides that, children are also growing" (Erenburg, *Sobranie sochinenii*, 7:27; 30). Here and elsewhere, the italics in quotations are added—Y.L. English quotations from Nabokov's autobiography are quoted from *Speak, Memory* in cases where an adapted version of the passage appears close enough to its Russian precursor; in all other cases I use the Russian, *Drugie berega* [*Other Shores*], in my English translation.

A mechanical means of movement in a literary text is a tool for transporting not only the characters, but also the whole of the literary baggage, seen or unseen, that is affixed by tradition or by the author himself to a particular image. In the chapters to come, we will focus on three modes of transportation that represent the urban idea in literature, and outline the general semantic and symbolic context in which they operate in an artistic system. To leave the topic open for other scholars, we must emphasize that all means of locomotion are important for understanding the structure of a text and its contextual ties, including those to which this book will not devote special attention, such as the bus, bicycle, ship, etc.[5]

As often happens with Nabokov, a stock image ends up metamorphosing and becomes covered over in metaliterary connotations.

Using the example of the *tram*, I will show how a universal poetics works in a particular case. The first tram in Petersburg left the Admiralty building on September 16, 1907. Within a year, there were already nine routes operating in the capital city, and by 1913 there were hundreds of cars in the tram fleet. The tram lines were laid beginning in 1905 by the American Westinghouse company, which won the bidding competition for the project. (A scandal surrounding the tram lines in the capital city almost made a widow of Nabokov's mother, and the writer himself sustained significant psychological trauma.[6]) The tram, whose appearance on the city streets was immediately reflected in the city's mythopoetic space (Timenchik, "K simvolike tramvaia"), is among the text-producing symbols capable of reproducing themselves, forming a semantic well where crossover meanings are condensed and associations with other texts arise. Alexander Dolinin has found at least two possible references in *The Gift* from Soviet poetry of the 1920s in the description of Fyodor working his way to the platform of the tram car: "Just then the wind searched him cruelly after which Fyodor drew the belt of his mackintosh tighter and adjusted his scarf, but the small amount of tram warmth had already been taken away from him" (*The Gift*, 84). One phrase echoes Maiakovskii's *About This* (1923), "The boy was searched by the thief wind," and another recalls Mandel'shtam's "You, with the square windows and short houses" (1924): "The absurd final tram warmth!" (see the comment in *Russian Collected Works*, 4:662). It may be demonstrated that Mandel'shtam's poetics suffuse the novel further, to the sentence that follows shortly after the previous one: "The tram came out on the square and, braking excruciatingly, stopped, but it was only a preliminary stop, because in front, by the stone island crowded with people standing by to board, two other trams had got stuck, both with cars coupled on, and this inert agglomeration was also evidence somehow of the

---

[5]For more on this, see Iozha, "Avtomobil' versus tramvai," 116–124.
[6]N. Snessarev, "Urok insinuatsii gg. Miliukovu, Gessenu, i Nabokovu," *Novoe vremia*. October 16 (29), 1911. № 12786; Leving, "Antipatiia s predystoriei," 154–190.

disastrous imperfection of the world" (*The Gift*, 84). The tram grinding to a halt seems to refer back to Mandel'shtam's children's book, *Two Trams* (1924–25), about two trams named "Tram" and "Klik" that are separated and suffering ("And Tram finds Klik on the platform"). The fact that this refers to a Petersburg event is reinforced by the phrase "stone island"—a strange designation for a tram stop in Berlin, until we realize that this is in fact a mention of a Petersburg site, "Kamennyi ostrov" ("Stone Island").[7]

The theme of Petersburg childhood saturates the opening of the second chapter in *The Gift*, as Fyodor hurries to class, but memories of Russia confuse his accustomed path through Berlin—until something finally returns him or,

FIGURE 1.1 *The Blagoveshchensky (Annunciation) Bridge which was called the Nikolaevsky Bridge from 1855 to 1918 in honor of Tsar Nicholas I. It was the first permanent bridge built across the Neva River in St. Petersburg, Russia. Glass negative, between c. 1900 and 1907. George Grantham Bain Collection, Library of Congress.*

[7]Cf. Mandel'shtam's *The Egyptian Stamp*: "The trams on Kamennoostrovskii prospekt are developing unheard-of speed. Kamennoostrovskii is a flighty handsome one, with his only two stone shirts starched, and the wind whistling through his trammy head" (Mandel'shtam, *Sobranie sochinenii*, 2:67).

more accurately, pushes him back into the flow of the novel's events. The bit of realia that breaks through the nostalgia for "the hothouse paradise of the past" is in this case an everyday tram ("a dim yellow blotch approaching, which suddenly came into focus, shuddered, thickened and turned into a tramcar"; *The Gift*, 79). The tram "transports" Godunov-Cherdyntsev from the world of the sharply defined images living in his powerful memory into the excruciating pallid reality to which he is traveling to teach French lessons. Additionally, along the way there is a vexing misunderstanding: the failure to recognize a compatriot whom Fyodor secretly blames for all the ills among banal burghers, until this "German" opens up a Russian newspaper. For our purposes, it is important not so much that the mistake is narrated by Nabokov while contemplating the idea of "how essentially good life is" (ibid., 80), but that here we can trace a literary leitmotif in the "tram plot"—misrecognition in an émigré setting was a common punch line in humorous émigré literature from the middle of the 1920s.[8]

The tram, after gathering up a great number of associated motifs and images in the 1910s, begins in the 1920s (and not only in Nabokov) to play an additional, meta-descriptive function. In a letter to Aldanov dated January 29, 1938, Nabokov admits that he was doing a favor by "taking along on this journey [through time] the images of several contemporaries of mine, who otherwise would have had to stay home forever" (Dolinin, "Plata za proezd," 15). In presuming to classify the significance of writers and scientists by using as a "weight measure"[9] the tramcar matrix,[10] Nabokov is in essence repeating the tram symbology of his colleagues.[11] As Georgii Ivanov wrote in his memoirs:

Someone has compared literature to a tram car. Some have been seated for a long time; others are standing and waiting for a seat to open up; still

---

[8]See, for example, the short story signed by "Ivan Krolik" (Zhan Lapen), "Liamur v metro i Nord-Siude (Franko-russkii roman iz podzemnoi zhizni Parizha, v 5 chastiakh, s prologom i epilogom)" (*Illiustrirovannaia Rossiia*. January 15, 1927. № 3, 17.

[9]"The weight of authors compared to machines / They were measuring in a discussion: / A 'genius' was a long ZIL / And a mere talent was a 'Pobeda'." ("Mery vesa" ["Measures of Weight"]), 1954; Marshak, *Stikhotvoreniia i poemy*, 401). ZIL stands for "Likhachev Plant," which has produced high-end luxury cars and limousines, as well as military and off-road vehicles in the Soviet Union and Russia, and "Pobeda" refers to a model of Soviet car produced in the 1940s and 1950s that was fairly nice, but quite a bit more accessible to the average consumer than a ZIL.

[10]Cf. "We will leave him <Freud> and his fellow travelers to jog on, in their third-class carriage of thought, through the police state of sexual myth" (*Speak, Memory*, 300).

[11]In a poem entitled "Literary Hell" ("Literaturnyi ad") (*Volia Rossii*. 1929. № 1, 23), Boris Poplavskii constructs an image of a vulnerable author traveling on a tram and taking on fellow passengers and passersby as participants in the literary process ("thought-recruits," a "pitiful pupil," etc.).

others have packed the platform, and some are hanging on the running board, while still more are vainly attacking the packed car ... The literary hierarchy is complicated, and the farther one gets from the prized running board the more complicated it becomes.

(*Kitaiskie teni*, 1924–1930; Georgii Ivanov,
Sobranie sochinenii, 3:269)

The "someone" that Ivanov refers to is most likely Nikolai Gumilev, author of the tram image that has become a commonplace in Russian literature. The idea of the literary tram hierarchy is developed in a somewhat revised version of the quotation from Ivanov in the memoirs of Vassily Ianovskii, entitled *The Elysian Fields* (*Polia Eliseiskie*):

Georgii Ivanov, a man intimately connected with all manner of everyday nastiness, but quite smart in his own way, joyfully repeated the words of Gumilev: "Making one's entry into literature is like squeezing into an overcrowded tram car ... And after finding a place, you in turn want to shove away whoever latches on."

(Ianovskii, *Sochineniia*, 2:198)

And finally, Adamovich in his review of Levi's *Novel with Cocaine* remarks that in literature there is a "law that Gumilev once called the 'tram law' based on observations of Soviet streets: the last person who caught on to the running board pushes away the next person who wants to squeeze in behind him"[12] (cf. Mandel'shtam's passenger bumped from the running board: "And they curse me for my eyes / In the language of tramway quarrels," 1931; Mandel'shtam, *Sobranie sochinenii*, 1:178). Not the least important source for Nabokov's image was the essay by Ilf and Petrov, "The Literary Tram," published in *Literary Gazette* in 1932 (August 11. № 36) and later included in all editions of the authors' collected works. This piece cleverly compares the society of authors with embittered passengers in a stuffy and crowded tram car:

[S]omeone is sitting stubbornly, pretending to admire the asphalt pavement, while in fact thinking only of how to avoid surrendering his seat to the woman with a child.

Someone is digging in his pocket, raking out dropped commas along with the bread crumbs. Someone, in keeping with the decisions, is calling unprecedented attention to himself. And of course, someone has been forgotten again.

It's hot.

---

[12]*Poslednie novosti*. December 3, 1936. № 5732, 3.

But it's good that the tram is moving, that impressions are being exchanged, and that the travelling differentiation of the tram is, with our characteristic quarreling and jostling, prepared to enter into the great and necessary argument on the means of maintaining the Soviet literary economy.

(Il'f & Petrov, *Sobranie sochinenii*, 3:175)

This brief excursion into the history of the tram image and the methods of maintaining the "literary economy" demonstrates how a means of transportation becomes the subject of an association game, carrying into new contexts the functional reasoning that has attached to it.

Bodies and Texts

The life of the city has long been compared to the way an organism works (cf. Nekrasov's *Physiology of Petersburg*, Zola's *Le Ventre de Paris*, Joyce's *Ulysses*, etc.). Those who have commented on this typological similarity have been struck by the clear analogies made with human anatomy: cities have lungs, arteries, blood vessels, intestines, and hearts, and they perform the corresponding functions.[13] Phil Cohen has developed the less-studied parallel between the city and the text. Cohen believes that the European city in its development process turned into the equivalent of an unintelligible manuscript or text in a foreign language (Cohen, *Out of the Melting Pot*, 79). The task of the researcher of urbanism is to decipher the local codes (dialects), figure out the structure of sentences (streets), and translate the local idioms into a comprehensible language. In the case of professional *flâneurs*, what is required is an ability to "read through" the exotic signs as hidden signals expressed, as in Nabokov's short story, "A Guide to Berlin," in the chaos of the urban infrastructure.[14] In *The Real Life of Sebastian Knight*, the world surrounding the attentive traveler offers itself up for perusing in the form of a search for answers to questions of life and death:

[T]he wild country he surveys is not an accidental assembly of natural phenomena, but *the page in a book where these mountains and forests,*

---

[13]In the Russian humanities tradition, the paradigm of "textualization" of an architectural landscape has led to the notion of the "Petersburg text" in Russian literature. As this pertains to Nabokov, see Malikova, *Nabokov: Avto-bio-grafia*, 68–69.

[14]Dolinin notes the similarity between Nabokov's position on Berlin and that of Baudelaire's *flâneur* on Paris: the "passionate observer" of city life at once dreams of simultaneously, "seeing the world, being in its center, but remaining invisible to it" (a quote from Baudelaire's essay "*Le peintre de la vie modern*") (Dolinin, "Clio laughs last," 201). As Walter Benjamin defines it, the *flâneur* is one who seeks cover in the urban crowd (Benjamin, *Reflections*, 156).

and fields, and rivers are disposed in such a way as to form a coherent sentence; < ... > the windings of a road writing its message in a round hand, as clear as that of one's father. (*The Real Life of Sebastian Knight,* 150)

Thus the traveller "spells the landscape and its sense is disclosed, and likewise, the intricate pattern of human life turns out to be monogrammatic, now quite clear to the inner eye disentangling the interwoven letters."

(ibid.)

The bodily model, more appropriate for the preindustrial understanding of the city as an organic community, reflected the growth of the urban space with its center (boulevards for promenades, open spaces designated for commerce and entertainment) and periphery (areas for the poor). The analogy between the city and an enormous body has often been used to depict the processes by which characters fall and perish because certain parts of the city stop functioning and become mere parasites, compromising the integrity of the whole. Discourses on different types of space ("healthy" and "sick") can also be discerned: some come in the form of analyzable text where the plot unfolds more or less teleologically, with heroes and villains, and bearers of good and bad news (cf. the novels of Hugo, Balzac, Dickens, and Nabokov's short story, "Breaking the News"); others absorb the quality of *incompleteness*[15] from their subjects and become process-oriented: the incompleteness of the text

FIGURE 1.2 *Drawing by V. Nabokov to his son Dmitri in a letter to Véra Nabokov, June 9, 1944. Henry W. and Albert A. Berg Collection, The New York Public Library.*

[15]Cf. the complicated semantic and syntactic injection of the sense of apathy in the description of the complex hierarchical structures of the city in the short story, "The Potato Elf" (1924): "Drowse < ... > looked, indeed, so somnolent that one suspected it might have been somehow mislaid among these misty, gentle-sloped fields where it had fallen asleep forever. It had a post office, a bicycle shop, two or three tobacconists with red and blue signs" (*Stories,* 240–241).

becomes a means for artistic activation of its structure (Lotman, *Struktura*, 363). What is it about bodies and texts that makes it so easy to turn them into metaphors for urban subjects, and what do cities contain that makes it possible for them to take on such metaphorical configurations?

The body and the text are similar in that they are both finite. However, as Cohen observes, the results of their physiological and narrative existence differ: the body has a physical end at the finale of the plot of life, but the text does not die with the typographical dot on the final page (Cohen, *Out of the Melting Pot*, 80). Books may go out of circulation more quickly than bodies, but usually they outlive not only their authors, but, when one becomes canonical, entire generations of readers. As concerns boundaries as such, the body is limited by the end of life, as the printed page is limited by the book margins, with the difference being that the audience can read his own interpretations into the white margin and between the lines, and in this sense the potential dialog between the text and the reader is infinite. The intensity of the dialog depends on the receptive horizons of the reader, which may vary based on ideologies, politics, and aesthetic conventions. Texts, just as bodies, have "erogenous zones," which usually suggest an external—real or imagined—source of agitation (Cohen, *Out of the Melting Pot*, 80; Barthes, *Mythologies*, 468). The caveat, however, is that in bodies these zones may be taboos, unlike the text, where the main task if to draw the reader into the inner mental world of the author.

Physical contact with urban spaces gives rise to an erotic set of metaphors. Though in Nabokov's novel, *The Real Life of Sebastian Knight*, the main character spends most of the day writing, his girlfriend manages to type out no more than two pages a night, and those too await further corrections, "for Sebastian used to indulge in an orgy of corrections" (*The Real Life of Sebastian Knight*, 70). Movement through a text of the writer Sebastian Knight is overtly compared to movement through a virtual space or the gradual building of a city:

> His struggle with words was unusually painful < ... > *the bridging of the abyss* lying between expression and thought < ... > *and the shudderings of the still unclothed thought* clamouring for them [words] on this side of the abyss.
>
> (ibid.)

Bodies have internal organs and an outer covering; the text presumes a surface covered with signs, and tunnels of meaning hidden "between the lines."[16] At the point where the surface meets the depths, the urban space

---

[16]Cf. the sniping characteristic of émigré reviews of Nabokov's prose: "Sirin's prose is reminiscent of Chinese shadow puppets ... Just try to peer into the intervals, into the cracks, and what gapes wide open in between them: there's nothing there; the eye gets lost in milky white emptiness" (G. Adamovich, "Sirin," *Klassik bez retushi*, 196).

harbors a repository of plots and hidden possibilities, a transparent world where the characters move around in whatever directions the author needs through whatever means the author's imagination has devised. Each analogy assumes its own strategy in marking desires on the map of the urban expanse:

"At the next corner his approach automatically triggered off the doll-like mechanism of the prostitutes who always patrolled there. One of them even tried to look like somebody lingering by a shop window, and it was sad to think that these pink corsets on their golden dummies were known to her by heart, by heart" (*The Gift*, 296–297); "there [in the shop window] flashed by in turn an orgy of glossy footwear, < ... > a sunny paradise of sports articles; then Franz found himself in a dark passageway where stood an old man < ... > next to a slender-legged woman in furs" (*King, Queen, Knave*, 68).

The final point of intersection between the inner and outer covers in this metaphorical city atlas is the realm of interaction between the center and the periphery: the dominant and subservient spaces of the city.

In the final sentence of *Other Shores/Speak, Memory*, Nabokov describes the pier on the outskirts of the city, whence his family was to abandon inhospitable Europe for decades. Entering this border space, the character/author/reader encounters a different pole of meaning: the center and periphery change places. As he approaches the harbor, as if on a child's map, the smokestacks of a transatlantic steamship miraculously show through the "broken row of houses" (*Speak, Memory*, 309).

The solved cryptogram attains composition and rhythm at the time when a picture appears in the chaos, i.e., the disorder acquires a form. The chaos remains (the text remains unchangeable), but the rereading becomes a stage in the process of understanding and, in the final analysis, makes it possible to uncover the author's intent. This would seem to be what Khlebnikov had in mind when he wrote about the rules of interchange, in an ideal structure, between the nature of stone and air ("substance and emptiness"). For the sake of clarity Khlebnikov resorts to the language of meta-description, characterizing the ordered urban structure as if it were subject to the laws of poetry. Using the example of the relationship between stressed and unstressed syllables in a poem, Khlebnikov declares: "Streets have no pulse. Continuous streets are as hard to see as words with no spaces are hard to read, and as words without stress are hard to speak. We need a broken street with the stress on the height of buildings, the vacillation in the breath of stone" ("My i doma" ["Houses and Us"], 1915; Khlebnikov, *Tvoreniia*, 596).

From Chaos to Order

As we see in Russian literature from the early twentieth century, especially decadent and symbolist literature, the technological innovations relentlessly becoming part of everyday life, and gaining the status of urban realia, were as much as anything interpreted as a dangerous violation of a spiritual status quo. Poets, observing the fabric of the city being torn apart to accommodate tram depots and parking lots, and the language taking on foreign calques and inventing neologisms, were led by the dual nature of technologies to a particularly active mythologizing process. Poetry simultaneously underwent a revision of the technical lexicon, formed a special brand of poetics, and developed a new layer of metaphors and subjects (death on the rails under a tram car or a car's wheels as an adaptation of the fatal function of the horse carriage).[17]

The city, the road, and modes of transportation, which run throughout the entirety of human culture and take on branching complexes of meaning at every cultural level, were supplemented by complicated associative connections: introducing these into the text created multiple opportunities for the appearance of narrative meanings outside the primary plot itself

THE PROGRESS OF THE CENTURY.
THE LIGHTNING STEAM PRESS.   THE ELECTRIC TELEGRAPH.   THE LOCOMOTIVE.   THE STEAMBOAT.

FIGURE 1.3 *Currier & Ives.* The Progress of the Century—The Lightning Steam Press, the Electric Telegraph, the Locomotive, and the Steamboat. *New York: Published by Currier & Ives., c. 1876.*

---

[17]On the paradigm of events taking place in the street in pre-symbolist and symbolist literature, see Langleben, "Korobkin i Bashmachkin," 27–33.

(Lotman, *Pushkin*, 787). The early symbolists saw the city as a place of death and captivity[18] (Minskii's "City of Death"), and the city was demonized by Bal'mont and Sologub.[19] In the persecution of the "little man" in Bely's poem, "On the Street" (1904), one cannot help but see reflections of the scene in which Evgenii is chased down in Pushkin's *Bronze Horseman*, the difference being that three-quarters of a century later the urban labyrinth is filled with the openings of factory furnaces belching out flames.[20] It is no accident that Pushkin is called to mind here: the consolidation of city motifs in Russian poetry began with *The Bronze Horseman*, and it was this narrative poem that laid the foundation for a city theme in opposition to the tradition that considered only bucolic nature suitable for poetry (Tomashevskii, *Pushkin*, 247). By surrounding Falconet's monument to Peter the Great with the new features of the modern city in the twentieth century, "shrouding it in urban fumes and the smell of gasoline," poets have extended the life of the myth (Ospovat & Timenchik, "*Pechal'nu povest'*," 142). Creative work on the edge of recognition, an emphasis on the "quotability" of a text, make it easier for the features of other texts to work their way in at the turn of a line—as in the composition of verse itself, compared to the shadows cast onto a wall by a candle:[21]

> there was a smile: *"After a ball*
> *It's easy to sleep through all the trains"*.
> *And the music once again resounded,*
> *And we danced another round.*
> ("University Poem" ["*Universitetskaia poema*"], 1927; *Russian Collected Works*, 2:585)

The enjambment between the first and second lines emphasizes the title of Lev Tolstoy's short story, "After the Ball," and refers the reader of Nabokov's "University Poem" back to Baratynskii's narrative poem, *The Ball*; the image of the train placed immediately afterwards "shifts" the intertextual

---

[18]See the chapter entitled "The Diabolical City and Anti-Nature" ["*Diabolicheskii gorod i Anti-priroda*"], particularly subchapter 14.1, "Diabolical Urbanism" ["*Diabolicheskii urbanizm*"] in Hanzen-Leve, *Russkii simvolizm*.

[19]"The smell of asphalt and the rumble of wheels, / Walls, stonework and slabs ... / O, if only the wind would suddenly blow in / The rustle of a coastal willow!" (Sologub, *Stikhotvoreniia*, 161).

[20]"Through the dusty, yellow clubs / I run ... / And the smoke of factory pipes / I spit out into the fiery horizon" (Bely, *Sochineniia*, 1:134).

[21]An increasingly fragile separation between thinning prosaic and poetic textures lead to their mutual shift and mixing: "Enormous, alive, a metrical line extended and bent; at the bend a rhyme was coming deliciously and hotly alight, and as it glowed forth, there appeared, like a shadow on the wall when you climb upstairs with a candle, the mobile silhouette of another verse" ("Torpid Smoke"; *Stories*, 400).

orientation on nineteenth-century Russian literature, if only to give the
reader a chance one line later to recognize a paraphrase from Pushkin's
"Autumn" ("Osen'"): "The hulking mass [*gromada*] has stirred and now
cuts through the waves":

> The thunderous [*gromovaia*] shaking of the motor –
> The wheels have stirred

In this half-joking pastiche Nabokov parodies the entire young tradition of
negative Russian urbanism, which had reached its pinnacle in the image of
the city as vampire in Sergei Solov'ev ("The sky has long been empty, while
under it / Just the screech of machines, the rumbling of cars ... / You are
made of screeches and knocks, / Vampire city!"), with clear signs of influence
by Verhaeren.[22] The stylistic updating also affected the mythopoetics of
Petersburg, moving the symbolism of Pushkin and Gogol in the direction of
urbanism. Verhaeren and his numerous imitators took one last look at the
dying, hallucinating city. Many of these, struck by what they saw as a crisis
in life and art, caught in the magnetic field of the mythology of industry,
could not write their way into the new landscape and themselves became the
victims of the new way of living.

   As one proponent of Russian urbanism put it (Toporkov, *Tekhnicheskii
byt*, 58–60), the generation that was born in big cities found itself in an entirely
different position: the short-lived crisis bypassed them, and they viewed the
city as a chaotic megalopolis. The eclectic visage of the contemporary city,
contrasting in one block an old cathedral and a new tall building, no longer
evoked revulsion in people close to Nabokov's generation in age.

The Urban Infrastructure, or "What Lies Beneath the Asphalt of the Text?"

In chapter 5 of *The Gift*, Godunov-Cherdyntsev goes to the apartment of his
former landlady Frau Stoboy, but within a few pages we understand that his
father's return and the meeting with him are happening in Fyodor's dream.
Descending into the journey through the depths of his own subconscious,
Fyodor sees a Berlin city scene: "Some night workers had wrecked the
pavement at the corner, and one had to creep through narrow passages
between planks, everyone being given at the entrance a small lamp" (*The Gift*,

---

[22]Cf.: "There / Braided bridges of steel are cast / By jumps through air. / Blocks of stone,
pilasters, columns / Raise the visage of the Gorgon; / The outskirts are oaked with towers, /
Pipes, and platforms, and spires – / In broken ascents over roofs" (translated from French by
M. Voloshin: *Stikhotvoreniia i poemy*, 468).

321). In the history of contemporary Russian literature of the time, at least after the appearance of Russian formalism, the technical instrumentation in a work of literature almost always emphasizes the meta-descriptive semantics of the text. As the novel approaches its resolution, its experimental chaos grows: the minor characters patch the holes in the fictional landscape, and on the way to the train station whence the Shchegolevs are to depart Berlin in order to leave the city in the hands of the enamored couple, Zina and Fyodor, the latter remarks on Potsdam Square, "always disfigured by city work" and "the pseudo-Parisian character of Unter-den-Linden" (*The Gift*, 326–327).[23]

In his work on the subtexts from Shklovskii in Nabokov's short story, "A Guide to Berlin," Omri Ronen writes of the pipes in the first part:

> "lying innocently in front of the house where the narrator lives, the enormous black pipes clearly represent an instance of 'baring the device,' i.e., jokingly bringing into relief a particular element of the formal structure, without any external stimulus or else overcoming the stimulus, self-sufficient and (in Sirin) taking precedence over the 'masked,' concealed, motivated, and subservient technique of more traditional narration: 'iron intestines, still idle, still not plunged into the depths of the earth beneath the asphalt.'"
>
> (Ronen, "Puti Shklovskogo," 169)[24]

Ronen goes on to suggest that Shklovskii himself used a similar metaphor at the beginning of the final (1927) version of his essay on Andrei Bely and ornamental prose, in order to illustrate the struggle between separate aspects of literary form: "Imagine that water pipes are laid under the earth" (ibid.).[25]

It should be noted that such "baring of the device" did not go unnoticed among the émigré derivatives of the formal method, who interpreted this method through the experiments of Sirin perhaps more than anyone else. In Bronislav Sosinskii's short story, "His Death," part of a cycle with the sonorous title, "Guests of Time," there appears a description of a modern city in which

> under the smooth asphalt is an entire network of water and sewage pipes. The inhabitants of this underground kingdom – in large, heavy boots up over their knees, with faint lights in their hands – have grown accustomed

---

[23]Cf. the German street scene in Remarque's novel, *Three Comrades* (1938), placed (unlike in *The Gift*) in the novel's opening pages (Remarque, *Three Comrades*, 32). The voyeuristic episode serves for the narrator as an impetus to change his life completely.

[24]Cf. the aggressive poetics of imaginism: "From the hewn sidewalk crawled out the intestines of pipes" (Shershenevich, *Stikhotvoreniia i poemy*, 82).

[25]Cf. Rozanov's *Fallen Leaves*: "Torn up ties. Shrapnel. Sand. Stone. Potholes. What is this? Sidewalk repair? No, this is 'The Works of Rozanov.' And the tram is moving steadfastly on the iron rails" (Rozanov, *Opavshie list'ia*, 113).

FIGURE 1.4 *Photograph shows cars driving along Bowery in New York City. To the left Comet Hotel is visible. Photographer: Angelo Rizzuto, 1956. Gelatin silver print. Anthony Angel Collection, Library of Congress.*

to their work. Through the tunnels, screeching at every turn, trains move through pipes that are the same, but of a different size for a different purpose. Not long ago, before making it to Edgar-Quinet station, an old workman died in a train car, apparently from heart failure.

(*Volia Rossii*. 1929. № 12, 39)

Whether as a conscious device or a simple coincidence, this excerpt would likely be of little interest in adding to our understanding of Nabokov's prose if not for the curious ending. In the circular composition of the story, the plot returns to the beginning, and the author describes the execution of the protagonist, contaminating the medieval guillotine with the trivial accident on the metro tracks:

He was being taken to execution …
    A thug in tall boots emerges from the round opening onto the sidewalk, and in his hands, as if it were a lantern, dangles a bloody human head …
    As a matter of fact, it is not even worth thinking about this.

The execution was performed. The corpse was tossed out of the metro car onto the filthy platform – the train, not delayed in the slightest, tears on further. It surfaced at Pasteur and flew on along the rail embankment, past forests and steppes, leaving on the horizon the phantoms of Russian churches, the vague ridges of the Urals – to meet the Siberian snows.

(ibid., 43–44)

The surreal finale of this work by Sosinskii, a little-known (though not unnoticed by Nabokov) author in the Paris Russian émigré community, may have been carved up and used in two very important scenes. The first is in the conclusion of "The Aurelian" (1930), where the soul of the butterfly collector, who has just died from a stroke, is let go in a westerly direction ("Most probably he visited Granada and Murcia and Albarracin"; *Stories*, 258), i.e., in the exact opposite direction to that described by Sosinskii. The second is in the much-discussed ending of *Invitation to a Beheading*.

The type of iron pipes not hidden under the asphalt of the text invites us in to a hermeneutic construction process: was there an execution or not? What direction, and to which voices, did Cincinnatus go? And would the unfortunate predecessor of Cincinnatus described by Sosinskii not be one of the creatures similar to him? An unambiguous answer is not only not forthcoming, but would even seem to contradict the immanent logic of the text—while the literary genealogy of a particular turn in the plot or, to borrow the language of the formalists, the coupling of a particular pipe, must be established.

The Resurrection of Electricity

By the 1910s, world literature, not yet feeling the intense competition from film, would once and for all transform itself into a laboratory for the creation of urban mythology, and the reader into a mass consumer of its production. The representatives of Russian literature did not arrive at a single, uncontroversial interpretation of city themes. In the opinion of one author, all of contemporary culture, "newspapers, railroads, the telephone and telegraph, resist the creation of myths and legends. For myth is not merely a newspaper hoax. A myth requires not just mere credulity, but reverence as well" (Tan, "Wells i sovremennaia utopia," 1:40). Nevertheless, in the early twentieth century, when the city finally became acknowledged as a source of lyrical strivings as rich as nature, "urbanist" poetry becomes predominant.[26]

---

[26]In *Novel with Cocaine* (1934), M. L. Levi (M. Ageev), the schoolboy Shtein, based on the fact that his "amenities now include automobiles, and airplanes, and central heating, and an international society of sleeping cars," lets everyone around him know that he considers himself entirely justified in looking down at "people from the horse-and-buggy days" (Ageev, *Roman s kokainom*, 33).

An experiment in combining the two principles, the country (in its easier "dacha" version) and the city, is presented in *The Gift*, a novel that is part of the "Petersburg text" in Russian literature (a model in which the refraction is shifted and a Russian topography is projected onto a Western European one). As strange as it may seem, it fell to Nabokov to defend the material culture of his age against the attacks of his contemporaries, exhorting the reader in a paean to the urban century to enjoy "the marvelous machines and huge hotels, whose ruins the future will cherish, as we cherish the Parthenon; with its most comfortable leather armchairs, unknown to our ancestors; with its extremely refined scientific investigations; with its smooth speed" ("On Generalities"; Nabokov, *Think, Write, Speak*, 58).[27]

The most amazing thing is that Nabokov, as many of his characters, "never had been on intimate terms with the secret fraternity of man-made things that goes under the name of technology" ("Perfection"; *Stories*, 340) and, like Krechmar (Albinus in the English version, *Laughter in the Dark*), was not one of those people who, "without possessing any expert knowledge, are yet able to readjust an electrical connection after the mysterious occurrence known as a 'short circuit'; or, with the aid of a penknife, to set a watch going again" (*Laughter in the Dark*, 232). We need not see a contradiction inherent in this combination of helplessness in practice and openly declared ecstasy at the wonders of technology. The former comes from the everyday world, while the latter is from the realm of metaphysics. John Shade's poem, "The Nature of Electricity" in the novel *Pale Fire* may provide an explanation:

> The dead, the gentle dead – who knows?
> In tungsten filaments abide,
> And on my bedside table flows
> Another man's departed bride.
>
> (*Pale Fire*, 192)

Kinbote comments on the otherworldly theme with the following reference: "Science tells us, by the way, that the Earth would not merely fall apart, but vanish like a ghost, if Electricity were suddenly removed from the world" (*Pale Fire*, 193). Light is existential order; chaos is total darkness. The electric lamp where the spirit of a dead body might dwell operates on a metaphysical voltage in Nabokov's texts. The problem of true light resembles the riddle of life and death that troubles the passerby who suddenly freezes, dazzled by the deceptive abundance of lighting in a Berlin shop window: a lampshade store "with all bulbs aglow, so that one could

---

[27]The admonition, characteristically Nabokovian in tone: "One should not speak ill of our own times. They are spiritually wonderful and physically comfortable" (*Zvezda*. 1999. № 4, 9) resonates with Maiakovskii's call "to tear happiness away from future days" ("To Sergei Esenin," 1926; Maiakovskii, *Sobranie sochinenii*, 4:14).

not help wondering which of them was the workday lamp belonging to the shop itself" ("Torpid Smoke"; *Stories*, 397). The sacred nature of light shines through even in its most base form, the street advertisement, which in Nabokov's poem, "Electricity," evokes associations with the blazing inscription from Belshazzar's feast:[28]

Play, fiery ad,
Over the mirrors of the squares,
Ascend, manual lightning,
Words setting this alight.
Not those, with a holy threat
Appearing in a letter form,
That the sweetness had been briefly
Removed from the wine of Babylon.[29]
In flowers of magical fire
Write something a bit simpler,
In praise of marketable goods,
To comfort a burgher's soul.
And in a lacquer box,
In a ventriloquistic grave,
Obeying the plug and switch,
Sing, I say, toot the horn.
And not a cataclysm, but the weather
You bring us through the megaphone.
Heat our water with your life,
And light the pages of our books.
Run through the wires of the tram,
Rustling like a Bengal sparkler,
And the damp night of the city
Is made strangely nice by you.
But sometimes, when the sky
Is pouring in a storm, sometimes
The earth suddenly quiets and draws in,
As if from some secret shame.

---

[28]According to legend, Belshazzar, the last king of the Babylonians, gathered his close friends at a feast. Wine flowed freely and the revelers praised the gods, when suddenly a fiery hand appeared on the wall and inscribed: "Mene Tekel Peres." A wise man is called in and explains that "Mene" means "God hath numbered thy kingdom, and finished it"; "Tekel" means "Thou art weighed in the balances, and art found wanting"; and "Peres" means "Thy kingdom is divided, and given to the Medes and Persians." That same night Belshazzar dies in combat with the Persians, who have sacked the city, and Babylon ceased to exist.

[29]Cf.: "There is the entrance, and long inscriptions, / – And all the street is cloaked in blood – / And two-foot letters blaze / In a light unbearably red" ("Tale," 1924; Shakh, *Semia na kamne*, 105).

And then, as before, unearthly,
Not ours, you fly past,
Showing the blue fissures
Of the inscrutable bareness.
Again the world, as many hundreds
Of hazy ages now long past,
Is unsteady and permeable,
Encircled by the fire of God.[30]

The electric advertisement makes Eros and Thanatos burn together—blazing letters are written on the naked body of the heroine of *Transparent Things* immediately before her death (the light of an advertising slogan fell on her body such that "Giulia, or Julie, wore a Doppler shift over her luminous body"). At the beginning of chapter 20 of the novel we are told as an aside that "an electric sign, DOPPLER, shifted to violet through the half-drawn curtains and illuminated the deadly white papers he had left on the table" (*Transparent Things*, 77).

Electricity animates a dead text with an injection of light,[31] but for the characters themselves it is fatal at too high a dose. The paradigmatic death from electrical voltage is achieved by the young wife of Chorb, who carelessly touches a live wire that has fallen from a utility pole in a storm. The protagonist thinks that this is "a most rare, almost unheard-of occurrence; nothing, it seemed to him, could be purer than such a death, caused by the impact of an electric stream, the same stream which, when poured into glass receptacles, yields the purest and brightest light" ("The Return of Chorb"; *Stories*, 148). Contamination of biblical Light and Word[32] can also be hazardous to one's health: Person, acting according to the program inserted into him by the author's will, smothers his beloved in her sleep:

<Giulia> prostrated herself on the sill, with outspread arms < ... >. He glanced down across her, and there, far below, in the chasm of the yard or garden, the selfsame flames moved like those tongues of red paper which

---

[30]This poem was not included in the *Russian Collected Works*, nor does it appear in most poetry anthologies published in Russia (including Nabokov, *Stikhotvoreniia*). Here it is quoted from Nabokov, *Stikhi*, 176–177.

[31]Cf. "And silently over the buildings / Meander flashes of distant lightning. / Life and death are scratching each other" ("Corner of the City"; Chekhonin, *Stikhi*, 16).

[32]In practice, the aura of the "divine nature" of electricity faded quickly, but in the literary world there was resistance to this poetic amnesia for some time; as Kuprin reproached in 1917: "In our time, electricity began shining in the streets, the telephone began to speak, the phonograph began to sing, animated figures began to move on the screen, and trams and automobiles started to run ... And here we are, having ceased to be amazed at most discoveries. When we flip that copper switch, at the moment when the room becomes illuminated with a clear, even light, we no longer say to ourselves with a smile: 'Let there be light!'" (Kuprin, *Sobranie sochinenii*, 9:263).

a concealed ventilator causes to flicker around imitation yule logs in the festive shopwindows of snowbound childhoods.

(*Transparent Things*, 80)

The "transparent thing" in this case is none other than the book of memory—a model remarked on earlier in the description of childhood in *The Gift*,[33] where the adult Fyodor recalls the cardboard palace "with celluloid windows the color of raspberry jelly through which painted flames like those on Vereshchagin's picture of the Moscow Fire flickered when a candle was lighted inside—and it was this candle which < ... > eventually caused the conflagration of the entire building" (*The Gift*, 19). The final dream of the main character of *Transparent Things* is "incandescence of a book < ... > completely transparent and hollow" (*Transparent Things*, 104). In Nabokov's version of the Prometheus myth, the "resurrection of electricity" becomes "resurrection by electricity": the element of fire is reunited with its original cosmogonic meaning.

The brother of Sebastian Knight tries to use electricity to resurrect the inner life of the desk in the former office of the late writer. In a world of "bookshelves densely peopled," the lamp on the table is taken for a living witness of the secrets of its deceased owner: "I *found its pulse* and the opal globe melted into light: that *magic moon* had seen Sebastian's white moving hand. < ... > I took the key that had been bequeathed me and unlocked the drawers" (*The Real Life of Sebastian Knight*, 31–32). The lamplight is called upon to sanction this intrusion into the private life of the former inhabitant; shortly after this the light falls on a page that has accidentally flown away from a packet of letters destined for the fire, "lying alone on the blue carpet, half in shade, cut diagonally by the limit of the light" (ibid., 32). Nabokov inherited the mystical survival of the phenomenon of electricity from Russian symbolism, and specifically Briusov ("We cannot dream of future ages ... Electrical light is the harbinger of their coming")[34] and Blok:

You are taking revenge, electrical light!
You are not the light of dawn; you are a dream from earth,
But on dark days with a ray you pierce
      The eternal deception of the ocean[35]
        ("The Ships Are Coming," 1906; Blok, *Polnoe sobranie sochinenii i pisem v 20 tt.*, 2:50)

---

[33]Memoirs, like a box, framing reminiscences of childhood placed in a display window} the display window into snow} the display window in snow into a garden} the garden with a display window into a window frame, and so on.

[34]From lines that were not included in the final version of the long poem, *The Shut-ins* (1900–01).

[35]See also Toporkov, "Iz mifologii."

The sources of the philosophical dialogs in one of Nabokov's last works
from in the Russian period, "Ultima Thule" (1939) should also be sought in
symbolist metaphysics; among these subtexts is Gippius's poem, "Electricity"
(1901):

> Ends will touch ends –
> Another "yes" and "no,"
> And "yes" and "no" will awake,
> Intertwined, will flow together,
> And their death will be – Light.

(Gippius, *Stikhotvoreniia*, 111)

Falter warns his interlocutor, who recently lost his wife, that there is very
little chance of him posing a question that he, Falter, could answer with a
simple "yes" or "no." Sineusov thinks a moment and then asks: "Let me ask
you: does God exist?" (*Stories*, 517). The widower wants to know "is there
even a glimmer of one's identity beyond the grave, or does it all end in *ideal
darkness*"[36] (ibid.). In the rumination he gives by way of a response, Falter
compares both states of being with light and darkness, pointing out that
everyone has experienced the total darkness of deep sleep—a state in which,
as the symbolists would have it: "so peaceably are merged the strands ...
/ Of sleep, and dark, and forgetting" ("Electrical Light in an Alley," 1904;
Annenskii, *Stikhotvoreniia i tragedii*, 62): "Round-the-clock lighting and
the black inane. Actually, despite the difference in metaphysical color, they
greatly resemble each other. And they move in parallel. They even move at
considerable speed" (*Stories*, 519). The meeting of two parallel lines leads
to a dazzling burst of light, which, in order to convey adequately, Nabokov
needs to make use a verbal balancing act on the model of Joyce's *Finnegan's
Wake*: an electrical street ad for a music hall, with letters vertically arranged
in steps, which then fall dark and then repeat the whole process again.[37]
Fyodor Godunov-Cherdyntsev wonders what sort of Babylonian word
might reach all the way to the heavens, and thinks up "a compound name
for a trillion tints: diamondimlunalilithlilasafieryviolentviolet" (*The Gift*,

---

[36]Cf. Ol'ga Chiumina's poem, "In the Fog" (1907): "The light of the street lamps – trembling,
reddish – / Recalls the shadow of the tomb" (*Serebrianyi vek*, 42).

[37]Cf. the short story, "A Letter That Never Reached Russia": "And beyond the bend, above the
sidewalk—how unexpectedly!— the front of a cinema ripples in diamonds" (*Stories*, 138) and
the novel *Glory*: "Lighted advertisements went running up dark-red façades and dissipating
again" (*Glory*, 50).

296).[38] The existence of the young Luzhin is depicted as an esoteric descent into darkness, where the only ray of light is a game of chess: "in April < ... > did that inevitable day come for Luzhin when *the whole world suddenly went dark, as if someone had thrown a switch*, and in the darkness only one thing remained brilliantly lit, a newborn wonder, a dazzling islet on which his whole life was destined to be concentrated" (*Defense*, 39). The usual progress of time is cut off, and the "switch" controls not so much an electrical light as a metaphysical one, transposing Luzhin into a new system of space-time coordinates—into a world organized on the basis of the rules of chess.

Buildings, Stairs, Elevators

And perhaps when we turn cold
and move from life to naked paradise,
we will regret what we forgot on earth,
not knowing how to furnish our new home.

—Nabokov, "A Room"

Elevators and staircases in literature are rarely just a matter of interior decorating. In the hierarchy of symbolism, the elevator competes with the stairway as a moving link connecting the earth and the sky. Thus, apparently based on the presumption of the permanence of marriage consecrated in the heavens, "one afternoon in the spring of 1871" one of the ancestors of Van Veen in *Ada* proposes marriage to the title character "in the Up elevator of Manhattan's first ten-floor building, was indignantly rejected at the seventh stop < ... >, came down alone" (*Ada*, 5). The elevator, as the closest quarters where strangers of the opposite sex might meet in the same space, automatically heightens the erotic tension between the passengers.[39] The possibilities of flirting in a "moveable pantry" were not lost on the futurists:

You read in darkness, like a cat,
A tiny font,

---

[38]When we peel back the layers of this dense text, we find at least two biblical references. The first relates to the tower of Babel and the confounding of the speech of the people; the second has to do with the image of Lilith ("lunaLILITH"), a beautiful night demon in the Kabbalah tradition. The forbidden relations between Humbert and Lolita will later be characterized as "a cinematographic still" (*Lolita*, 43). The light show brings the advertisement into the realm of the mystery of the starry sky; cf. Eisner's short story, "Romance with Europe": "The constellation of streetlights and the colorful fogginess of advertisements made for serious competition with the sun" (*Volia Rossii*. 1929. № 4, 15).

[39]Even to the point of a possible rape: "An elevator / They unbuttoned the soul's bodice. / Hands burn the body / However much you cry 'I didn't want to!'" ("From Street to Street," 1913; Maiakovskii, *Sobranie sochinenii*, 1:67–68).

Our common road precipitous –
A songbird-lift.
Two of us in this moveable pantry.
Let's play at flirting!
But oh dear God!
I just forgot that you get off on three,
And I'm on eight.
            (S. Tret'iakov, "Elevator," 1913; *Poeziia russkogo futurizma*, 442)

The central character of *The Eye* is tormented by "a most violent desire that the elevator carrying Evgenia and Uncle Pasha get stuck forever" (*The Eye*, 70), making reference to the banal desire of a jealous character to eliminate outsiders from the narrative who might hinder his courtship.[40]

FIGURE 1.5 *Aerial view of Times Square lined with pedestrians and automobiles, looking north from the Times Building. New York, 1952. Photographer: Angelo Rizzuto. Anthony Angel Collection, Library of Congress.*

---

[40]Eric Naiman writes about the resemblance "between moving towards the heavens and agonizing withdrawal from the plot" with regard to the role of the elevator in *The Defense* (Naiman, "Litlandiia," 183).

In *The Gift* the situation is somewhat more complicated: Fyodor travels to the editorial board of "Gazeta," located on the ninth floor, specifically the little room of the "moonlike" secretary, who has repeatedly saved the paper from the hounding of "Jakobins" in "the strange emptiness of an enormous elevator" (*The Gift*, 62).[41] It is perhaps no accident that Yakov falls in with the radical revolutionaries known as "Jakobins" under the moonlike gaze of the phlegmatic newspaper employee. The symbolism of the heavens (outside the window of the editor's office there are repairs going on "so high in the sky that it seemed as though they might as well do something about the ragged rent in the gray cloud bank") updates the allegory of Jacob's dream (Genesis 28:11) of a ladder standing that reaches to heaven. Angels ascend and descend the ladder, expressing the living interaction of God and man. But this is not the case with Godunov-Cherdyntsev, whose poetry is being evaluated on the eighth floor in a narrow little room "smelling of the 'decaying corpse of actuality'."

More often, however, the operation of elevators is associated with less happy events than a marriage proposal—a fatal crash, for example.[42] An elevator that had hitherto served its purpose for the protagonist, once that character falls into a dramatic set of circumstances, also begins to act up out of solidarity, even to the point of losing all capacity to move. On the evening when Krug returns from the hospital where his wife has just died, it is not only his accustomed former life that is broken but the mechanical devices that surround Krug in his home also begin to fail him. Krug

> entered the elevator which greeted him with the small sound he knew, half stamp, half shiver, and its features lit up. He pressed the third button. The brittle, thin-walled, old-fashioned little room blinked but did not move. He pressed again. Again the blink, the uneasy stillness, the inscrutable stare of a thing that does not work and knows it will not.
>
> (*Bend Sinister*, 23)

Krug is forced to ascend the "neglected but dignified stairs" (ibid.) of his building and enter into interactions with its inhabitants.[43] The staircase

---

[41]In the English version: "German Trotskyists hired locally, or some robust Russian Fascist, a rogue and a mystic" (*The Gift*, 62). The semantic shift in the subsequent revision is discussed in my monograph, *Keys to* The Gift, 405–406.

[42]Cf. the poem by Shershenevich: "Arrived at the skyscraper in a simple carriage, / I asked the gray-haired operator / To take me up in the lift to you on six ... / And suddenly the lift capriciously stopped, / And I was stuck between two floors, / Pounding and crying, tiresomely yelling, / Resembling mice in a mousetrap" ("A year I forgot, but I recall it was Friday," 1913; Shershenevich, *Stikhotvoreniia i poemy*, 54).

[43]Cf. the functioning of the architecture in rhythm with the sufferings of the character in "A Letter That Never Reached Russia": "At night one perceives with a special intensity the immobility of objects—the lamp, the furniture, the framed photographs on one's desk. Now and then the water gulps and gurgles in its hidden pipes *as if sobs were rising to the throat* of the house" (*Stories*, 137).

may be slower than the elevator, but is more reliable. Timofey Pnin, in an untenable position without a prepared text, as any defenseless speaker, has his own technique for overcoming his audience's resistance. Nabokov provides a comic detail in his monotonous style of reading, which is compared to a person clambering up "one of those interminable flights of stairs used by people who dread elevators" (*Pnin*, 15).

In *Mary*, in a stalled elevator, Alfyorov continues a conversation struck up over lunch—"the sense of this émigré life of ours"—and sees a deep symbolism in the fact that the elevator broke down:

> By the way, the floor is horribly thin and there's nothing but a black well underneath it. Well, as I was saying, we stepped in without a word, still not knowing each other, glided up in silence and then suddenly—stop. And darkness.
> "What's symbolic about it?" Ganin asked gloomily.
> "Well, the fact that we've stopped, motionless, in this darkness. And that we're waiting."
>
> (*Mary*, 3)

"And darkness," Alfyorov's rhetorical flourish, takes on a significance in opposition to the biblical "And there was light," not only because of the because of the momentary resemblance of Alfyorov's face to that of an evangelist when the lights are turned on ("something about his features reminded one of a religious oleograph"), but also because of the epithet from Ganin when Alfyorov steps on his foot: "Hell" (*Mary*, 1; on the role of the elevator in *Mary*, see Buks, *Eshafot*, 33). The black well of the elevator shaft destroys characters both in a literal and in a metaphorical sense. The son of Eugenia Isakovna in "Breaking the News" falls into one ("the poor young man had fallen into an elevator shaft from the top floor, and had remained in agony for forty minutes: although unconscious, he kept moaning horribly and uninterruptedly, till the very end"; *Stories*, 390); in *Laughter in the Dark*, Margot (Magda) flings the tatters of a picture by Rex (Gorn) into the darkness, thus symbolically bidding farewell to childhood:

> The light went out with a thud, and Margot leaned against the grating of the lift crying afresh. < ... > She wiped her nose on her sleeve, groped in the darkness and pressed the switch again. The light calmed her a little. She examined the sketch once more < ... >; tore it into fragments and flung these through the grating into the well of the lift. This reminded her of her early childhood.
>
> (*Laughter in the Dark*, 138)

Elevators play a special role in *The Defense*, where Luzhin recalls his Petersburg home with its old-fashioned water-powered elevator. Little Luzhin was often left at the bottom and

> listened to the elevator, high up and behind the wall, struggling, upwards—and he always hoped < ... > that it would get stuck halfway. Often enough this happened. The noise would cease and from unknown, intermural space would come a wail for help: the janitor below would move the lever, with a grunt of effort, then open the door into blackness

which resulted in the elevator eventually descending, but empty; the governess, the happy child presumed, had perhaps "traveled up to heaven and remained there with her asthma, her liquorice candies and her pince-nez on a black cord" (*Defense*, 165). The theme of the heavens is seen in the dark spots of moisture visible through the glass of the elevator as it slowly climbs along "its thick velvet cable," and among which, "as among the clouds in the sky" (ibid., 164) the outlines of the Black Sea or Australia predominate. Here Nabokov shares with his character, along with the unfortunate woman, a portion of the interior of his own house at 47 Bol'shaia Morskaia:

> In our Petersburg mansion there was a compact water elevator which was climbing on its velvet cable up to the third floor along the slowly descending stains and cracks on an inside yellowish wall < ... > Insultingly hinting at her heaviness, this elevator would often strike, thus forcing Mademoiselle to ascend the staircase with numerous asthmatic pauses.
> (*Russian Collected Works*, 5:217; this passage is absent from *Speak, Memory*; transl. is mine—Y.L.)

The "stairway to heaven" also appears in the house where the newlywed Luzhins rent an apartment: "on the fifth floor, it is true, but that did not matter—there was an elevator for Luzhin's shortness of breath, and in any case the stairs were not steep and there was a chair on every landing beneath a stained-glass window" (*Defense*, 172). The disruptions in Luzhin's daily life correspond to the malfunctions of the elevator at the end of the novel. The house is a giant organism working in tandem with Luzhin's body: "The elevator *proved to be out of order* but Luzhin made no complaint. < ... > He began to climb the stairs and since he lived a very long way up his ascent continued for some time; he seemed to be climbing a skyscraper" (*Defense*, 250). Nabokov intentionally adds stories to the house, extending it vertically, just as Luzhin's apartment is capable of telescoping horizontally: the extension effect will be essential in the suicide scene, where the reader in essence never finds out whether his falling body ever reached the earth.

On the night after their nuptials, Luzhin stands in the elevator "smiling and blinking, somewhat dazed but not in the least drunk," looking at the row of buttons, one of which his wife presses. Having looked at the elevator ceiling, "as if expecting to see the summit of their journey," Luzhin says "hic," and then, already inside the flat: "Where's the little place?" (ibid., 181). This short passage is important for the idea of the novel as a whole, though the key to understanding it is found in a different text: a poem by Pushkin. Coming out of the elevator, Luzhin gets locked in the bathroom from whose window he will fling himself at the end of the book, while the elevator (the link to the author) ceases to work. Asking where the "little place" is, Luzhin subconsciously makes his way back to the elevator, which is connected to the creator of the text. Isolation of the grandmaster at a "familiar height" refers us to the game of chess in *Eugene Onegin* (4, XXVI):

> Retiring far from everybody,
> *Over the crossboard they,*
> Leaning their elbows on the table,
> At times sit deep in thought,
> And Lenski in abstraction takes
> With a pawn his own rook.
>
> (Nabokov, *Eugene Onegin*, 1:194)

While "retiring" metonymically stands for a game of chess, retiring for Luzhin ultimately means literally dropping out of the game of life. At the end, Luzhin musters the last bit of strength he has that is required for him to merge with the chess board of eternity.[44] Similarly, but more explicitly, the end of one of Nabokov's short stories decodes the meaning of a metaphor that was carefully encased in what would seem at first reading to be nothing more than a description of a character's the mechanical movement:

> When, at last, late as usual, he went up in the elevator, he <Ivanov> would have a sensation of slowly growing, stretching upward, and, after his head had reached the sixth floor, of *pulling up his legs like a swimmer*. Then, having reverted to normal length, he would enter David's bright room.
>
> ("Perfection"; *Stories*, 340)

A few pages later Ivanov, who has a heart defect, drowns in the sea.

---

[44]Another code might be seen in the name of the piece that Lenskii takes absent-mindedly: the rook (which can be called *"tura"* in Russian). According to Nabokov's logic, this should refer the reader to the name, Turati. It is worth noting that as a child Luzhin was not fond of Pushkin—a fact that keeps him from taking advantage of the "elevator" clue provided by the author.

The Life of Things

As the members of the LEF group asserted, the "biography of a thing" should serve as a "cold shower for literature workers," useful for a writer—the age-old "anatomist of chaos" (as Tret'iakov put it)—primarily because it "puts the human soul, inflated by novels, in its place."[45] Nabokov never stopped being captivated by the poetics of objects, and he professed their inherent anthropomorphism, speaking of this several years before Tret'iakov's manifesto:

> I don't like hearing when people talk of machines: oh, our mechanical age; oh, robots; or, this and that. ... In this sense, the penknife is no different from some very complicated factory machine. ... When a man looks at a steam engine, its mechanism seems to him unbelievably intricate, because in his notion of it he has disconnected the object from the mind that conceived it.[46] < ... > *Man is God's likeness; a thing is man's likeness. ...* An automat is in many ways most similar to man.[47]

Nabokov's championing of technology was not shared either by his friends[48] or even by his most perceptive readers. In Sirin's work, complained one critic,

> *the city is never old and full of tradition, but is solely modern, reminiscent of a chess board*, measured only by the count of taxi meters, adorned on

---

[45]S. Tret'iakov, "Biografiia veshshi," *Litertura fakta: Pervyi sbornik materialov rabotnikov Lefa.* Moscow: Federatsiia, 1929 (cited from *Literatura fakta*, 71). Cf.: "not a solitary man moving through the order of things, but a thing passing through the order of men—this is the methodological literary device that we believe is more progressive than the devices of classical belles-lettres. Books such as *Forest, Bread, Coal, Iron, Flax, Cotton, Paper, Locomotive, Factory*—have yet to be written. We need them, and they can best be written by using the methods of the 'biography of the thing'" (ibid., 72).

[46]Cf. the passage from Platonov's *Chevengur*, similar in tone: "The road foreman took a long look at the locomotive and was filled with accustomed joyous sympathy. The locomotive stood noble, enormous, warm, on the harmonious inclines of its tall body ... *Man is the beginning for any mechanism ... Any devices, especially metal ones, on the other hand, existed animate and were even, in their structure and strength, more interesting and more mysterious than man*" (Platonov, *Chevengur*, 54–55).

[47]From the essay, "Man and Things" (Nabokov, *Think, Write, Speak*, 71).

[48]After reading the manuscript of his book on Gogol, the Harvard professor M. Karpovich advised Nabokov in a letter dated October 18, 1943 to remove the "eccentricity," the "literary escapades, of a sort": "I must openly confess that while reading it I found all of these things distracting and even annoying. Indeed, why must you *settle your own accounts* (these must, of course, be understood internally) with Faust, with Germans, with *American advertising*, and so on, at the expense of Gogol and your readers?" (cited from Bongard-Levin, "Vladimir Nabokov i russkie uchenye-emigranty v SShA").

street corners by restaurants, cafes, and cinemas, enmeshed in a net of telephones, which inevitably participate in all events. *The feelings and passions, the virtues and vices – all is of the city, not to say of Berlin; die-pressed, obligatory, apartment-hotel-ish*, hidden by walls, until – for exceeding the limit – it ends up in the newspaper, in the listing of events and crimes.[49]

The "soft quickness" of which Nabokov wrote in his essay, "On Generalities," was deeply ingrained in his sense of time and space: it is the sign of a traveler, a person from a mobile culture. At the same time, Nabokov was seeking a new pivot in the theme, and was turned off both by the mannerism of the futurists and the puritanism of critics such as Osorgin, who yearned for a bucolic landscape. The exaggerated image of the latter appears in *Glory*, where the metaphysical menagerie of Martin's stepfather, Uncle Henry, included "a little black beast, and that *bête noire* was to him the twentieth century" (*Glory*, 126).

Despite a seeming fascination with mechanical bestiary, Nabokov never forgot about the universe densely populated with little, unnecessary things that would more often than not go completely unnoticed. His characters experience "piercing pity < ... > for the tin box in a waste patch, for the cigarette card < ... > trampled in the mud" (*The Gift*, 152), stare endlessly at an "old-fashioned, hut-shaped cuckoo clock" that "unhurriedly < ... > kept breaking off dry little sections of time" ("The Fight"; *Stories*, 143), or as Lik does, discover in agony that he had lost the crystal but that his wristwatch "was still alive, defenseless and naked, like a live organ exposed by the surgeon's knife" ("Lik"; *Stories*, 466).

The task of the author is to provide a momentary snapshot of the world of objects (cf. Lev Lunts's 1923 screenplay, *Things in Revolt*), to bring a recording device into a dark room, as the *Kinoki* planned to leave a camera undetected in a crowd of workers. Others thought it necessary for life to flow "into the cinema through the channels of literature, refreshing, updating, and enriching the formal fabric of our cinema."[50] Nabokov combined these two elements: "It is amusing to catch another's room by surprise. The furniture froze in amazement when I switched on the light. Somebody had

---

[49]Osorgin, *Pro et contra*, vol. 1, 240–241. The critic is riding his favorite hobby horse; cf. his piece, "Saturday Train" ("Subbotnii poezd"), where dacha life is described as the complete antithesis of that "complicated, urban, contrived life in which even the passage clouté [crosswalk] and the *alternate glancing left and right does not save one from inexplicable accidents because a truck might also mount the sidewalk*" (*Novyi zhurnal*. 1943. № 6, 9).
[50]Piotrovskii, "Kino i pisateli," 6.

left a letter on the table; the empty envelope lay there like an old useless mother, and the little sheet of note paper seemed to be sitting up like a robust babe" (*The Eye*, 61). Similarly, Anton Petrovich, the protagonist of "An Affair of Honor" who ducks a duel, comes to the understanding that indifferent objects will continue to live even after he is dead: "The furniture, the bed, the wash stand seemed to awake, to give him a frowning look, and go back to sleep" (*Stories*, 220).[51]

Nabokov's entire world is objectified, right down to a forest path (along which the protagonist of *Despair* walks), where "tree roots and scrags of rotting moss stuck out of its earthen walls like the broken springs of decrepit furniture" (*Despair*, 6). The inside-out-ness of objects suggests that these are the springs in the device of the artistic text, intentionally concealed by Nabokov, but also not quite fully, so as to provoke his critics.[52]

Nabokov is haunted not only by longing for the "lost paradise" of childhood, but also by suffering over the broken connection with objects forever lost:

> At a fair, in a remote little town, I won a cheap porcelain pig at target shooting. I abandoned it on the shelf of the hotel when I left town. And in doing so, I condemned myself to remember it. I am hopelessly in love with this porcelain pig. I am overcome by an unbearable, slightly silly tenderness when I think, won, and unappreciated, and abandoned.
> (From the presentation Nabokov delivered at the Russian Writers' circle in Berlin; Nabokov, *Think, Write, Speak*, 70)

The loss of a porcelain pig is compensated for in *Bend Sinister* by a porcelain donkey on the table set with other objects that are dear to Dr. Alexander: "a glass ashtray, a porcelain donkey with paniers for matches, a box made to mimic a book" (*Bend Sinister*, 42). It's a cozy farce perhaps taken from Pushkin's *The Queen of Spades*: "Every corner was crammed with porcelain shepherdesses, table-clocks by the celebrated Leroy, little boxes, bandalores, fans, and sundry ladies' playthings" (Pushkin, *The Queen of Spades*, 85).[53]

---

[51]The secret night life of objects was described in detail by the Soviet poet Nikolai Berendgof in his poem, "The Life of Things": "When all are asleep, / And night is trembling, / Things move noisily / About the room. / The old chair grunts, / It must have dried up" (Berendgof, *Beg*, 12).

[52]M. Tsetlin was shocked by the physiological nature of Nabokov's tropes, stating in a review of *Glory* that the phrase, "the motley innards of the wardrobe had spilled onto the carpet," in his opinion, "borders on the tasteless" ("Sirin, V. 'Podvig,' Fel'zen, Iu. 'Schast'e'." *Sovremennye zapiski*. 1933. Book LI, 458–459); cf. in the short story, "A Russian Beauty": "the silken insides of her handbag were in tatters" (*Stories*, 387).

[53]The theme of letter-writing and objects is developed in "Spring in Fialta" when Ferdinand buys at a souvenir shop an inkwell that becomes a leitmotif in the story (due to its depiction of St. George Mountain, the emblem of Fialta) (*Stories*, 423).

Not only tools and toys have their own lives; toiletries do as well. No commentators on *The Gift* seem to have remarked on why Fyodor, in the scene where he rents the Berlin apartment, is strangely drawn to the wondrous dress of the owner's daughter (which, as we later learn, did not belong to her), forcing him to agree not only to a high rent, but also to the agonizing presence of the repellent vulgarian Shchegolev. It is not just the case that Fyodor seems to feel in the gauzy dress the aura of a future love. Nabokov also outfits the situation with a strong literary allusion that Godunov-Cherdyntsev himself might even grasp, but he cannot quite recall its origin. Meanwhile, the author drops a hint—such dresses as were "worn then at dances":

> "Here is my daughter's room, here is ours," he <Shchegolev> said, pointing to two doors on the left and right. "And here's the dining room," and opening a door in the depths, he held it in that position for several seconds, as if taking a time exposure. Fyodor passed his eyes over the table, a bowl of nuts, a sideboard. ... By the far window, near a small bamboo table, stood *a high-backed armchair: across its arms there lay in airy repose a gauze dress, pale bluish and very short* (as was worn then at dances), and on the little table gleamed a silvery flower and a pair of scissors.
>
> (*The Gift*, 135)

The view that opens up to the lodger is in fact a shift in focus to the suite in the 1830s Petersburg house from Gogol's "Diary of a Madman" (which appears before the narrator when he comes for his boss's daughter):

> I'd like to peek into their drawing-room, where sometimes you can see an open door leading into yet another room. Lord, the richness, the finery! The mirrors and the fine china! I'd like to have a look in there, in her Ladyship's half of the house, that's what I'd like! I'd sneak into the boudoir, where she has all her little pots and phials, and such exquisite flowers that you wouldn't dare breathe on them, *I'd see her dress lying there, so ethereal it is more like air than dress.* Oh, for a look into the bedroom .... In there I reckon you would see something truly wondrous, you would find a paradise to surpass even that in heaven.
>
> (Gogol, *Plays and Petersburg Tales*, 164)

Thus it stands to reason that Nabokov's passage ends with this sentence: "The distance from the old residence to the new was about the same as, somewhere in Russia, that from Pushkin Avenue to Gogol Street."

The Telephone: A Conduit to the Other World

Nabokov by nature could not stand telephones, and all calls were answered by his wife.[54] It would seem that this attitude is telling and deserves a certain amount of attention.

Telephone communications, as a social conduit and a means of conveying information, reduced distances in space and time in the twentieth century. In everyday life its location is always a point of emphasis (a dedicated place on an end table or a desk), determined by accessibility within the dwelling space. For

FIGURE 1.6 *Miss Harriot Daley supervises a staff of thirty-seven operators as they answer calls from 1,200 extensions at the United States Capitol switchboard. Washington, D.C., July 30, 1937. Harris & Ewing collection, Library of Congress.*

---

[54]Cf. the memoirs of Dmitri Nabokov, the author's son: "My father hated electricity and could not stand the telephone. As an alternative to the latter he devised [in *Ada*] the so-called 'dorophone,' which operates using water. He did not even like to plug things into a wall" (Dzhaginov, "Interv'iu," 13). See also in *The Real Life of Sebastian Knight*: "I dislike telephoning as much as I do writing letters" (17).

Nabokov, with his heightened sense of personal independence, the telephone represented first and foremost an acceleration in the erasing of boundaries between public and private life.[55] In the earliest telephone books for Moscow and Petersburg, when the number of users amounted to just a few thousand, anyone who wanted could easily find the telephone number associated with the apartments of Lev Tolstoy or Aleksandr Blok. The telephone number for Nabokov's father, a member of the parliament, was 24–43.

Despite a number of disadvantages (an invisible interlocutor, background noise, the need for loud conversation audible to bystanders), the telephone also has a number of virtues, which were picked up by people and their literature: from the ability to remain anonymous to the permissibility of looking how one wanted and doing what one wanted because no one could see you.[56] Meanwhile, the receiver is unable to convey the true feelings of the speakers regarding each other or the subject matter of their conversation.[57] Without face-to-face contact, the sense transmitted by a living person is lost: the temperature of his palms, the rhythm of his breathing, and the pattern of pupils dilating and contracting. It is another matter, notes Faryno, that in actual contact interlocutors either conceal their feelings or convey them in a culturally acceptable range of expression (Faryno, "O semioticheskoi tipologii," 3).

In 1875 when Alexander Graham Bell first used two membranes to control electromagnets, allowing him a year later to transmit sound signals at a distance, he could hardly have assumed that his invention would revolutionize bourgeois life and become a focus of debate in the early twentieth century: the new communications device not only did away with geographical attributes, but also equalized classes, men and women, the rich and the poor, and at the same time increased the risk that they would be brought together in communication (Marvin, *When Old Technologies Were New*, 4–5).[58] The unreliability of communications technologies was made use of in literature and became the subject of a multitude of jokes

---

[55]Cf. in *The Gift*, where a ring distracts Fyodor from his composition, interrupting the harmony and shifting the agonizingly arranged chain of rhymes back into chaos: "From the hall came the jangling peal of the telephone. < ... > The ringing went on and on, with brief pauses to catch its breath. It did not wish to die; it had to be killed. Unable to hold out, with a curse Fyodor gained the hall phantom-fast" (*The Gift*, 146).

[56]Jerzy Faryno makes a differentiation in the pragmatics of telephone communication of sounds and body language: one behavior is "obligated and required by convention with the caller, and the other (like an 'aside' on the stage) is spontaneously emotional ... Only that which is controlled and urgently desired by both interlocutors is allowed into the receiver" (Faryno, "O semioticheskoi tipologii," 3).

[57]Cf. Nabokov's poem "Telephone" (April 24, 1921; Nabokov, *Stikhotvoreniia*, 16).

[58]If Nabokov missed school to meet Liusia Shul'gina then he must first have bribed the porter, Ustin, who answered the phones at the house on Morskaia and duly informed V. V. Gippius that Volodia was not well (*Russian Collected Works*, 5:288).

and complaints in the media. In the 1910s, Russian parlance even gained the term "plug into" (*brat' na shtepsel'*), meaning to connect to a telephone station and thereby become a user of it:

> My simple-hearted story about the strange, Hamletesque things that began to follow me around from the time the telephone exchange gave me the number 165–43, had a magical effect ... a new savior appeared before me. He pressed one button, then another, and then both together, giving me ample opportunity to enjoy the rings. I in turn showed him how one has to wait for the languid voice to be heard from the exchange.
>
> < ... > *But about half an hour after my savior left, my telephone went silent.* The noise when one pressed the button was quite weak and monotonous, but no answer from the exchange was forthcoming.
>
> *Tu l'as voulu, Georges Dandin, I said to myself. If someone publicly complains that they've been plugged into must be happy when they get unplugged. It's true* that this makes it impossible to use the telephone now, but on the other hand there are no more annoying noises.
>
> (Skeptik, "Sniali so shtepselia (O telefonnykh poriadkakh)," *Rech'*. July 3 (16), 1911. № 179)

The carnivalesque nature of telephone communications provides a mask instead of an interlocutor, a molded cast from his voice; Dreyer, the good-natured German burgher who is cheated on by his wife, "for he was extremely fond of hearing his wife's soft, smooth, formal voice over the phone < ... > in a kind of early Florentine perspective" (*King, Queen, Knave*, 122). In face-to-face conversations, Dreyer's wife is far more piercing. The telephone distorts her voice beyond recognition (cf. the synesthetic reception of the voice of Luzhin's fiancée: "Three different people came to the telephone in turn and replied they would get him immediately, and then the operator cut her off and she had to start all over again. < ... > Finally a yellowy, worn little voice informed her dejectedly that Valentinov was not there"[59] [*Defense*, 239]); the perspective changes a human voice into a zoomorphic sound, and for Nabokov this is a persistent association with the barking of a dog. In the short story "A Nursery Tale," Erwin walks around the city seeking women for the "harem" given to him by the devil. The protagonist finds one of his captives sitting in a restaurant next to a telephone. The female devil had promised to give Erwin a sign of confirmation each time the deal had been done. The reader in turn is delighted to note the diversity of these little hints. In this instance, the telephone is approached by a man in a bowler hat who "called a number and started to jabber as

---

[59]Cf. "Do not talk on the phone from a Petersburg pharmacy: *the receiver peels off and the voice becomes colorless.* Remember that Proserpina and Persephone did not have phones installed" (Mandel'shtam, *Sobranie sochinenii*, 2:71).

ardently as a hound that has picked up the scent of a hare" (*Stories*, 167). The hunting motif is appropriate, because as this background conversation occurs Erwin's wandering gaze settles on a girl by the bar. Erwin decides to choose her, and just as he does he hears: "'All right, all right!' barked the man into the mouthpiece" (ibid.). The canine burst into the telephone receiver produced by an imperfect phone connection is repeated in "Spring in Fialta": "I remember talking to her on the telephone across half of Europe (on her husband's business) and not recognizing at first her eager barking voice" (*Stories*, 425).[60] In *King, Queen, Knave*, Franz is called to the phone and, as he approaches, he sees "the gleam of the telephone at the end of the corridor. Owing perhaps to his being unaccustomed to telephones, he could not identify at first the voice barking in his ear" (*King, Queen, Knave*, 60).

The metaphysical fear of the telephone and the role it played in communicating with the dead in early-twentieth-century literature and culture has been studied in some detail (Ball, "Toward Sociology of Telephone," 59–75; Timenchik, "K simvolike telefona," 155–163; Gorelik, "Kommunikativnost'," 56). In the case of Nabokov, the use of the telephone paradigm as a conduit to the other world is complemented by a biographical intonation. As we know from a diary entry, the author was informed of the death of his father, Vladimir Dmitrievich Nabokov, by telephone. The device unites the two worlds through a telephone code as described in the poem, "The Room" (1950), which appeared in the collection, *Poems and Problems*:

> The room a dying poet took
> At nightfall in a dead hotel
> Had both directories – the Book
> Of Heaven and the Book of Bell.

Among the belongings of the late Sebastian Knight, his brother finds an old notebook full of "an old notebook (1926) filled with dead telephone numbers" (*The Real Life of Sebastian Knight*, 33); trying to reach a colleague, Adam Krug in *Bend Sinister* glances at a telephone book with numbers handwritten by his late wife: "the telephone might not work. But from the feel of the receiver as he took it up he knew the faithful instrument was alive. < ... > Here is the back of the telephone book on which we used to jot down names and figures, our hands mixed, slanting and curving in opposite directions" (*Bend Sinister*, 27–28). The device is not always "faithful"; in its symbolic connection with the spirit world it more often acts as a hostile and

---

[60]Nina's husband, Ferdinand, on the other hand, "was particularly fond of long distance calls, and particularly good at endowing them, no matter what the distance, with a friendly warmth" (*Stories*, 428).

even dangerous creature.[61] A false death is reported by telephone in "The Potato Elf." Shock, the magician, takes revenge on his unfaithful wife by simulating her poisoning. Suspecting from the start that this is just another trick, Nora soon understands that this is a matter of life and death:

> Then Nora with a wild gesture dashed into the next room, where there was a telephone, and there, for a long time, she joggled the holder, repeated the wrong number, rang again, sobbing for breath and hammering the telephone table with her fist; and finally, when the doctor's voice responded, Nora cried that her husband had poisoned himself, that he was dying; upon which she flooded the receiver with a storm of tears, and cradling it crookedly, ran back into the bedroom,

where the magician is calmly tying his necktie in front of a mirror (*Stories*, 240). In the story, "Signs and Symbols," two calls to parents whose son is in a psychiatric ward and has already been stopped twice from committing suicide turn out to be false alarms: "the telephone rang. It was an unusual hour for their telephone to ring" (*Stories*, 602). As the story ends, a third call is heard from what might be the hospital where their son is a patient, but the mystery of the call remains unsolved within the boundaries of the text. In that case there remains at least a glimmer of hope, but the heroine of the story, "Breaking the News" is not so fortunate. As the deaf old Madame Mints walks around the elegant streets of Berlin, her friends spread the terrible news of her son's death by telephone.

However, telephone communication is not limited to a social and cultural level; it also has an existence as a linguistic phenomenon. It is telling that Roman Iakobson, in analyzing the functions of language and its emphasis on the addressee and the interpreted message, was so quick to use examples from telephone conversations. At first glance there is some strangeness in the association of language exercises in Professor Pnin's introductory Russian course, where the phrases are arranged as follows: "Mama, telefon! Brozhu li ya vdol' ulits shumnykh" (*Pnin*, 67). Thus subtle cento in fact follows the model of the interaction between texts and intertexts as such: one party from (non-)artistic work X connects with another party from work Y, with the connection often being totally arbitrary, but the random association creates an unexpected additional meaning that can be designated Z. Such randomness of juxtaposed acts of communication applies not only to the written text, but to the entire cultural and communications atmosphere of the era in which the author was immersed. Nabokov wrote that he was subject

---

[61]In *The Gift* the telephone trumpet resembles "a huge, slightly crushed ant" (*The Gift*, 152). We do not know whether at this time Nabokov was familiar with Salvador Dali's kitsch collage with a lobster claw in place of a telephone's receiver, *Téléphone-homard* (1936), but he had undoubtedly read Mandel'shtam's "telephone receivers in beer halls, terrible as crayfish claws" (Mandel'shtam, *Sobranie sochinenii*, 2:76).

to auditory hallucinations for his whole life, which in his case amounted to "something one happens to hear *between lifting and clapping down the receiver of a busy party-line telephone*" (*Speak, Memory*, 33). As he drifted off to sleep, the writer heard "a kind of one-sided conversation going on in an adjacent section of my mind, quite independently from the actual trend of my thought. It is a *neutral, detached, anonymous voice*" (*Speak, Memory*, 33; in the Russian original, the telephonic metaphor is more obvious since an "anonymous voice" clearly belongs to some "unknown caller," *Russian Collected Works*, 5:156). This seems to refer to the archetypal mechanism of artistic creation, as Shklovskii wrote about in his book on Tolstoy:

> The thoughts of one person and the thoughts of society cross-pollinate each other. Topics merge, and the person who begins to write and enters into communication with the Muses becomes connected to the telephone exchange of general human interaction. When he picks up the receiver, he hears the hum of his epoch.
>
> (Shklovskii, *Lev Tolstoy*, 341)[62]

The Street Advertisement

Signage heightens the textuality of urban space, engages the material of the native language in everyday circulation, and turns words and phrases into parts of the landscape. The life of language, as Mandel'shtam wrote, is open to all: everyone speaks and participates in the movement of language, and every word spoken leaves on the language a "living furrow"; and a wonderful opportunity to observe the development of picturesque language is provided by urban signage ("Something about Georgian Art," 1922; Mandel'shtam, *Sobranie sochinenii*, 2:262). The city, as described by Max Weber in his now-canonical work of that name, is chiefly an economic and commercial concept (Weber, *The City*, 71–72). Recalling the Petersburg of his childhood, a contemporary of Nabokov exclaimed:

> What streets! Nevskii Prospekt. You can't see it for the tram poles and street ads. Among the advertisements are some pretty ones; they climb up whole stories of buildings, up to the third floor, all over downtown: on Liteinii and Vladimirskii. The squares, however, do not have ads, and they are all the more enormous and deserted for it. On the small streets

---

[62]Cf.: "And I will be long dead when, / Tired of everything, on a sleepless night / The future ages pick me up / Like a telephone receiver, / And start to hear, like surf, / The hum of a bygone world through the receiver" ("But no!.." 1933; Shengeli, *Inokhodets*, 168–169).

above the sidewalks hang golden bakery pretzels, golden bulls' heads, enormous pinces-nez, and so on. It's rare, but occasionally there are boots or scissors hanging there. All gigantic. These are also advertisements.

(Likhachev, *Vospominaniia*, 38)

The praises of bakery pretzel signs were also sung in Russian art (see M. V. Dobuzhinksii's lithographs[63]) and poetry (in Blok's "The Unknown Woman": "the bakery pretzel shines slightly golden," and Zabolotskii: "The iron pretzel, friend of nights, / Brighter than the lights of heaven" ["Pekarnia," 1928; Zabolotskii, *Polnoe sobranie*, 86]), to say nothing of countless mentions in memoirs.[64] The adventures of a character looking in shop windows was made into its own topos in European literature from

FIGURE 1.7 *Charles H. Woodbury. Advertisement for Trolley trips on a Bay State Triangle. Boston, 1897. Heliotype Printing Co. Prints and Photographs Division, Library of Congress.*

[63]See the chapter, "The Petersburg of My Childhood," in his memoirs: "and the gold jackboot with a spur ... on Vladimirskaia, and *the gold pretzels, so familiar, under the crowns of German bakers*" (Dobuzhinskii, *Vospominaniia*, 6–9).

[64]As Sergei Gornyi (A. A. Otsup) writes in his article, "Signs (On a Russian Street)": "Sign painters loved life. They knew that *pretzels and cream puffs, and bars and pastries spilled out of the horn of plenty at a bakery* ... Hang it on the corner and you can see it from both streets" (*Zhar-ptitsa*. 1922. № 9, 133–134); Andrei Bely observed the mysticism of the advertisement, calling the "*golden 'bakery' pretzel*" "a symbol of the final boldness," which the mystical realists describe such that "one's hair stands on end" (*Vesy*. 1907. № 5, 52).

the time of Hoffmann and Gogol, and in émigré literature acquired a sense
of mnemonic "wanderings" in recollections of Petersburg. Looking around
him, a perceptive city-dweller might find himself immersed in a colorful,
contradictory world of images and texts:

> Colored ads,
> Golden letters,
> Bathed in sunshine,
> A row of stores
> With brisk sales,
> The thunder of horses, –
> The city's glad to see the sun.

> (Sologub, Stikhotvoreniia, 160)

The advertising poster is its own kind of language, which the streets
use to speak with strangers: "Letters along the walls wove tales as they
waved: 'The Brothers Geschwinder' ... must be quite fat" ("V Berline" ("In
Berlin"), 1911; Chernyi, *Sobranie sochinenii*, 1:251). In a new city, one can
learn much about the nature of the locality based on advertising even before
talking to passersby.[65] Even a native provincial street, if one looks closely
enough, offers "the shop signs – top hat, a fish, the copper basin of a barber"
(*King, Queen, Knave*, 2). The fact that a traveler in an urban space can read
a city as if it were a book was first noted by the French symbolists, who
recognized in these call signs a message to the city and the world—the *Urbi
et Orbi* blessing of the late nineteenth century:

> *copper letters*
> *Along the rooftops, ledges, and walls*
> *Try to inscribe the universe.*

> (E. Verhaeren, "La Ville"; Russian translation in
Voloshin, Stikhotvoreniia i poemy, 469)

Soon after, a new understanding of space, planarity, perspective, and physical
form in artistic works was arrived at in painting by the futurists and primitivists,
and in literature by a constellation of young poets with a renewed interest in the
elevated sensitivity of words and the almost electric excitement of metaphors.
When the rethinking of artistic values broadened into the world of poetry at
large, these "iron books" had faded into the past:[66] in the 1910s, the era of

---

[65]Cf. Nina Berberova's story, "The Black Disease" ("Chernaia bolezn'," 1959): "in an
unfamiliar city about which one now knows nothing, it always seems like the city center is
wherever you are currently located. Then, *the beauty of the ads, the blue, pink, and green
world, resembling nothing real because they are too well fabricated* " (Berberova, *Biiankurskie
prazdniki*, 426–427).

[66]In his "Signs" ("Vyveski," 1913), Maiakovskii invited: "Read iron books! / To the tune of a
flute of gilded letters" (Maiakovskii, *Sobranie sochinenii*, 1:71).

electricity and fluorescent lights, the hellish stream of advertising described by Shershenevich is what becomes relevant: "at the edges of rooftops, through the numbers and letters of ads, / Laughs a bloody electro-electrical current" (Shershenevich, *Listy imazhinista*, 106).[67] Illuminated advertisements filled with electrical power acted as a link between everyday goods and that which was at an inscrutable, taboo, and almost cosmic level[68]:

And a lush lighted advertisement,
Sparkling behind a grid of rain,
To the singing of the evening tram
Insisting on dazzling happiness,
Golden advertising raptures,
Golden raptures without end;
And the smiles of a valuable face
Drenched with the shine of stores.

(Nal'ianch, "Stolitsa," 28)

With the expansion in commercial language, signs begin to self-replicate, particularly from the center of the city to the periphery, and multiply themselves to match the standardization in public tastes and the growing demand of urban monopoly culture for the instant message-placard, the advertisement in letters. In some sense, the phenomenon of the urban Text, read as some kind of integral work, a "novel in signs," we might say (or a narrative poem, or lyric poem, or any literary genre for that matter), falls within the framework of the language's grammatical philosophy, which regards "writing" as a continually developing process with no beginning, ending, or discrete phases: each new utterance, like a palimpsest, is "written" over the previous ones (Derrida, *De la grammatologie*, 16).

The advertising text/image is secondary by nature; it does not simply describe an object, but rather rewrites it anew, cloaking it in a modeled covering, such that the original image is muted, like the woman in Nabokov's early story, "Revenge" (1924), reincarnated as a worm whose body, a "plump, taut cadaver consisted entirely of narrow, circular bands of skin, as if it were all bound evenly and tightly by invisible strings, something

---

[67]Cf. Andrei Bely in an advertisement tantalizing as the fruit of paradise: "Evenly towering apples of electric lights in the middle. On the sides the flickering light of signs plays; there fires of rubies suddenly flame up, and here emeralds" (Bely, *Sochineniia*, 2:38).

[68]In the pre-war years Nevskii Prospekt had an electric advertisement for Maggi bouillon cubes, which made an appearance in a poem by Maiakovskii: "And if with canine happiness / Turn the Maggi constellations" ("Signs" ["Vyveski"], 1913; Maiakovskii, *Sobranie sochinenii*, 1:71). See also, "Electric gnomes climbed up facades, endeavoring to tempt even the moon with 'bouillon in cubes'" (Erenburg, *Sobranie sochinenii*, 2:408).

like that advertisement for French tires, the man whose body is all tires"
(*Stories*, 71). This refers to the emblem of the French company Michelin,
specializing in the production of automobile tires; the repellent ad made such
an impression on Nabokov that twenty years later he uses it to help describe
the personality of Gogol's Chichikov: "I am reminded of a certain poster
in old Europe that advertised automobile tires and featured something like
a human being entirely made of concentric rings of rubber; and likewise,
rotund Chichikov may be said to be formed of the tight folds of a huge
flesh-colored worm" (*Nikolai Gogol*, 74). The rubber Frankenstein used
for commercial purposes disgusts Nabokov, as does the vulgar advertising
inherent in the depiction of the "ideal family":

> Open the first magazine at hand and you are sure to find something of
> the following kind: a radio set (or a car, or a refrigerator, or table silver –
> anything will do) has just come to the family: mother clasps her hands in
> dazed delight, the children crowd around, all agog.
>
> (ibid., 66)[69]

There are other satirical depictions of the idyllic family in Nabokov: "a family
had enjoyed the coolness at nightfall, clumsy children had colored pictures
by the light of a lamp" ("Spring in Fialta"; *Stories*, 429); in an interview
with *Vogue* (1972): "I think [the airline companies'] *publicity department,
when advertising* the spaciousness of the seat rows, should stop picturing
impossible children fidgeting between their imperturbed mother and a gray-
templed stranger trying to read" (*Strong Opinions*, 203); and "Small boys
and girls in ads are invariably freckled, and the smaller fry have front teeth
missing" (*Lectures on Russian Literature*, 311). The protagonist of *The Gift*
notices advertising boards and signs which he noticed as a child but which
now represent a transformation, and degeneration, of humanity over time:

> Those same children have now grown up and I often run across them
> in advertisements: he, with his glossy, sleekly tanned cheeks, is puffing
> voluptuously on a cigarette < ... > she is smiling at a stocking she herself
> is wearing, or, with depraved delight, pouring artificial cream on canned
> fruit; and in time they will become sprightly, rosy, gormandizing oldsters.
>
> (*The Gift*, 20)

Nabokov also reacted negatively to the latent sexism of advertising
as in the "one of those bold-eyed, humid-lipped Berlin beauties that one
encounters mainly in liquor and cigarette advertisements" (*King, Queen,*

---

[69]Cf. Mandel'stam's essay, *The Tenishev School*: "*He was an old man ruddy as a child with a jar
of Nestle*" (Mandel'stam, *Sobranie sochinenii*, 2:25).

Knave, 14). The advertisement gives erotic connotations to the advertised product, as conveyed by the key words, "puffing *voluptuously*," "*a stocking she < ... > is wearing*," "with *depraved* delight." However, in Nabokov's view, "a world of handsome demons" still has a secret disadvantage: "the glamorous glutton of the advertisement, gorging himself on gelatin, can never know the quiet joys of the gourmet, and his fashions (lingering on the billboard while we move onward) are always just a little behind those of real life" (*The Gift*, 20); "the black of the asphalt, the truck tires leaning against the railings by the shop for motorcar accessories, the beaming young bride on a poster displaying a packet of margarine" (ibid., 151).

Placards, brochures, and posters were printed in Germany as early as the mid-fifteenth century. The first newspapers appeared in England in the sixteenth century, and over time advertising became an important part of this, growing by the twentieth century into a fully fledged genre of visual art. And yet the content of advertising discourse has and continues to exist in a realm only remotely related to high culture. Moreover, the commercial text is generally associated with a lack of sincerity and an attempt to tempt the consumer with goods and services that are not necessarily required and do not always correspond to the virtues described. An advertising circular in *The Defense*, in which "an almost indecently blue gulf, and a sugary white hotel with a multicolored flag waving in the opposite direction to the smoke of a steamer on the horizon" (*Defense*, 187),[70] embodies a surrogate of a tourist's impressions. Equally superficial is the connection between Margot and Axel (Magda and Gorn in the Russian version) in *Laughter in the Dark*, the model of true but unachievable happiness—as unreachable as the girl sunbathing against the blue background of the water, reminiscent of resplendent beach poster ("a young girl lying asprawl on a hot lonely beach," 17). And if the impoverished émigré Olga is made uneasy by the "the luxury of certain advertisements, written in the saliva of Tantalus" ("A Russian Beauty"; *Stories*, 387), another of Nabokov's characters, Godunov-Cherdyntsev, reacts to commercial advertising as a mechanism for intentional deceit ("unscrupulous advertisements for patent medicines, which cure all illnesses at once"; *The Gift*, 228). Nabokov's sympathies are with the latter, and he sincerely praised a real émigré poet on the grounds that a collection of his poetry was modestly entitled "Poems," since "a perfume catalog is the proper place for sonorous titles" (from a 1927 review of a collection of poems by Andrei Blokh; *Russian Collected Works*, 2:649).

---

[70]Cf. Erenburg's *The Summer of 1925*: "I found the posters oppressive. The promised everything: the sea, a girl in a bathing suit, valleys full of narcissus and hygiene, milk chocolate, the ruins of castles, Africans, and a roulette wheel at a casino pale from excitement. I sucked on little bits of ice, alone and outside of this world, without a ticket, without flowers, and without pillows" (Erenburg, *Sobranie sochinenii*, 2:410).

And yet Nabokov's attitude toward advertising is not entirely uniform. He was occasionally forced to admit that advertising per se could be quite good—images were raised to true artistic heights (Nabokov, *Lectures on Russian Literature*, 386). Advertising, as one poet friendly with the futurists put it, is "the engine of life,"[71] while the space of the city is ordered by the advertising constellations of the universe,[72] where the moist earth imitates the sky, rhyming with it, reflecting it imprecisely but magnificently: "Again, as on the previous night, the sky swarmed with stars and the asphalt glistened like smooth water, absorbing and lengthening *the magic lights of the town*" ("A Nursery Tale"; *Stories*, 169). In *Other Shores/Speak, Memory*, Nabokov flatly confesses that in his youth, "the blue evenings in Berlin, the corner chestnut in flower, light-headedness, poverty, love, *the tangerine tinge of premature shoplights*, and an animal aching yearn for the still fresh reek of Russia – all this was put into meter, copied out in long-hand and carted off to the editor's office" (*Speak, Memory*, 281). The city streets serve as readily usable material for poetic emotions poured into easy rhymes,[73] and the more visually appealing the product in the shop window, the more informative its future literary fortunes turn out to be.

The Shop Window of Metatexts

The enormous glass facades on new buildings constructed in the early twentieth century shifted the emphasis of advertising to the shop window. Because of growing literacy, painted signs were increasingly replaced by print ads, and shop owners in old buildings turned the lower floors entirely into shop windows (Povelikhina & Kovtun, *Russkaia zhivopisnaia vyveska*, 115). The shop window gradually becomes a narrative space—a frame in which a micro-plot can be inserted and played out. At first these were static scenes with toy figures, but later, as technology progressed and more money was put into advertising, and as fashions changed and retailers were in increasing competition for consumers, the scenes became

---

[71]Cf. P. D. Shirokov's poem, "Long Live Advertising!" (1914): "A broad line in the evening clouds, / Letters of electric light: / Buy the poems of / The great poet Shirokov!" (*Poeziia russkogo futurizma*, 374).

[72]The sign at Dreyer's shop: "In sapphire letters with a diamond flourish prolonging the final vowel, a glittering forty-foot sign spelled the word D*A*N*D*Y" (*King, Queen, Knave*, 67–68).

[73]We see an example of "semantic rhyming" with advertisements in Nabokov's prose in the following montage: the "the beaming young bride" in a margarine ad, which flashes before Godunov-Cherdyntsev, "rhymes" with a toothpaste ad pasted to the side of a Berlin city bus, which Fyodor soon enters ("Along this side and along the toothpaste advertisement upon it swished the tips of soft maple twigs") (*The Gift*, 152).

FIGURE 1.8 *James Fuller Queen.* Design for advertisement, Charles Oakford & Sons, furrier and hatter, located at 104 Chestnut. *Philadelphia, Pennsylvania, 1843. Drawing shows a street view of the façade of a storefront with entrances; windows with merchandise displays; awning over an entrance; and lightly sketched pedestrians; across the top are samples of lettering and designs. Marian S. Carson collection, Library of Congress.*

dynamic, moved by electricity. In Berlin, in front of the drug store at the corner of Potsdamerstrasse and Privatstrasse, young Nabokov's attention was drawn by "a mechanical manikin in the pharmacy window [that] was going through the motions of shaving, and tramcars screeched by, and it was beginning to snow" (*Speak, Memory*, 162). In *The Gift*, Godunov-Cherdyntsev finds a shop window striking for a mismatch in its contents and the objects representing it, while a character from the ad seems to come out of it, transposed outside the shop window:

> [T]he Christmas tree lights burned dully in the windows, and here and there at street corners a commercial Santa Claus in a red stormcoat and with hungry eyes was distributing handbills. In the windows of a department store some villain had had the idea of setting up dummy skiers on artificial snow beneath the Star of Bethlehem.
>
> (*The Gift*, 87)

The blasphemous juxtaposition in the shop window nativity scene is created by the artificial lighting and the wrapping of the product in bright, shiny packaging. As Levinson suggests, the ancient symbols of the divine sun and light, which were at one point appropriated by Christianity, and which

were such an important part of occult symbolism and, later of the aesthetics
of Church rituals, are transformed at the level of urban life into mirrors,
tinsel, glass beads, foil, and clear plastic in the packaging of products and
delicacies (Levinson, "Zametki," 109). In their coloration, their abundance
of light sources, their silver and gold reflectors, shop windows become
an imitation of paradise,[74] for which the primary model is the temple (a
subconscious reconstruction of this "altar" is the crystal cabinet or kitchen
buffet in a society apartment, devoid of any religious significance just as the
icon traditionally placed in the corner of a Russian house).[75] The dialectic
between the sacred and the worldly is characteristic of the festive sweets and
fizzy drinks in urban life, in which the attributes of brightness are forced out
into the street, retaining, in the aesthetics of sequins, the ritual features of
the urban holiday (ibid., 109).

The shop-window-gazing characters created by Nabokov, an author
with a cinematographic way of thinking, lean toward anthropomorphizing
a static picture that, like a medieval mystery, sets in motion a secret
mechanism or the hands of the Master of Puppets. Nabokov devotes an
entire novel to the problem of Hoffmannesque automatons (*King, Queen,
Knave*), and he frequently returns to the motifs of advertising and machines
throughout his oeuvre. However, what intrigues us more is a case when the
picture must be set in motion when the springs of allusion are activated at
the moment the reader succeeds in figuring out the inner mechanism and
inserts the right key.

In the famous scene of Fyodor's childhood illness in *The Gift*, the narrator
lives through a moment of clairvoyance:

> I was, let me tell you, weak, capricious and transparent—*as transparent
> as a cut-glass egg*. Mother had gone to *buy* me < ... > one of those freakish
> things that from time to time I coveted with the greed of a pregnant
> woman < ... >. Suddenly the door opened and Mother came in, smiling

---

[74]Cf. Briusov's poem, "Evening Tide" (1906), which describes a street illuminated with electric
advertisements and the sparks and lights of city transport ("trams throw out blue lightning, /
Automobiles – a sheaf of fire"): "Posters scream, lushly colored, / And the words of signs begin
to moan, / And the sharp lights of stores / Taunt like cries of celebration. // Matters sleep there
behind the windows, / Diamonds pour vibrant poison ... // 'Dust, we praise Your Excellency,
/ We dance and sing for you, / Around altars of electricity, / That plunge their spears into the
heavens!'" (Briusov, *Sobranie sochinenii*, 1:516–517).

[75]Compare this with the situation in the comfortable Berlin apartment where the family of
Luzhin's fiancée lives: "Her parents, rich once more, had first decided to start living in strict
Russian style which they somehow associated with ornamental Slavic scriptory, postcards
depicting sorrowing boyar maidens, varnished boxes bearing gaudy pyrogravures of troikas or
firebirds" (*Defense*, 104). Handing Luzhin a box of chocolates, his fiancée utters the key words:
"'Just like a little idol,' she laughed. 'Sitting in the middle while sacrificial gifts are brought
to him'" (*Defense*, 130). Here the "idol" takes the place of a king in chess and plays on the
common use of the Russian verb "est'" (to eat) in chess.

and holding a long, brown paper package like a halberd. From it emerged *a Faber pencil a yard long and of corresponding thickness*: a display giant that had hung horizontally in the window as an advertisement and had once happened to arouse my whimsical greed.

(The Gift, 28)

As Omri Ronen demonstrated, the phrase "as transparent as a cut-glass egg" is a reference to the magic crystal from H. G. Wells's fantasy story, "The Crystal Egg" (Ronen, "Nine Notes to *The Gift*," 20–21). A Russian subtext for this scene is found in an excerpt from Goncharov's story, "May in Petersburg," in which a character "during Holy Week, *somewhere on Nevskii Prospekt, in a foreign store, bought an egg of such monstrous size* that the entire building gasped. He filled the egg to the top with candies and gave it to his little sisters along with the traditional Russian Easter greeting of three kisses" (Goncharov, *Polnoe sobranie sochinenii*, 11:262).

In both cases, the motivation and its realization coincide: a large, unnecessary purchase in downtown St. Petersburg (on Nevskii Prospekt), at a *foreign* store, in order to wheedle out a gift. The customer is tantalized by the enormity of the item, i.e., its incidental advertising function.[76] The brand name of the pencil was likely chosen by Nabokov to resonate with the famous maker of Easter eggs, Faberge (Leving, "Six Notes to *The Gift*," 36).

The unguessed reference is an integral part of the text, existing as a given in its world. The laws of the text are such that until the reader recognizes the strangeness of a particular detail in the fictional world, the world is perceived as an order created by the author. The change comes when the reader identifies a stylistic wrinkle left deliberately by the author, an imprecise joint between plot points, a repeated motif, a hint, etc. Simply put, the Faber pencil, before and after it is recognized as the bearer of a literary allusion, plays a carefully determined role in the narrative, which has progressed and continues to progress on its way regardless of any fact established by a researcher. The conditions for the transition from one state to the other can be defined as a state of chaos, either in full or in part. The mind's reaction to chaos is almost always sharply negative, and yet in chaos lurk the conditions for creative potential, and these conditions must be of interest to us in the study of the arts—at the same level as that which is opposed to this creative principle (Likhachev, "Cherez khaos k garmonii," 5).

* * *

---

[76]We might consider the window of a train car a sort of moving shop window through which the protagonist looks on as "the brick rear walls of houses went gliding past; one of them displayed the painted advertisement of a colossal cigarette, stuffed with what looked like golden straw" ("A Matter of Chance"; *Stories*, 53).

This introductory part of this book has examined the mechanics by which the "material world" is translated and transferred into the literary world, where a marginal object, be it a piece of furniture or an outdoor scene, comes into focus through an artistic description refracted by literary awareness. Any automated technology, from the telephone to the electric lift, that becomes part of industrial progress takes on heightened signification in twentieth century poetics. The semiotics of objects gives rise to the mythology of things—a process accompanied by a radical transformation in the state of the language and its place in society.

In addition to the characters, mechanical modes of transportation in a text also carry the literary genealogy of an image. The structure of the text in many ways resembles a human body: beginning with the model of the body projected onto the literary appropriation of the city, we then moved on to examine the array of technological devices in works of literature, proposing that in recent literary history this is often a marker for a meta-descriptive semantic field in a text.

Electric lights, with their sense of the religious dichotomy of light and darkness; the elevator, vying with the mythology of the ladder or stairway connecting the earthly and heavenly realms; symbols of telephonic communication; advertising signs in the textualized space of the city; and many other such items from the "material world" (from the radio to the piano) that were not addressed in this introductory overview, but that would be worthy of analysis, rarely appear as mere decorative objects in an artistic text.

The microscopic narrative details in the literary optics of the twentieth century also play an important auxiliary role in decoding the text. The novel or poetry anthology (be it a handmade work or, until relatively recently, a *handwritten* work) begins to be perceived as part of the world of objects. In its published form an author's work belongs to the ordered universe of the bookshelf, but during the creative process the writer must contend with the chaos of language, and in the process also identify with an object: the *typewriter*. Iurii Olesha provided a meta-descriptive characterization of this technology in his article, "The Literary Craft" (the noun in the title is significant): "*when you write, you feel within yourself the operation of this complicated, enormous, and mysterious machine. Levers of some sort in this machine draw out memories. Writing with a pen and following the syntax, let's say, you also feel that memory is arising from the depths before your mind's gaze*" (Olesha, *Izbrannye sochineniia*, 429). Attempts to penetrate not only the essence of objects, but also the secrets of their construction, were made by authors and readers alike. A. A. Bestuzhev compared a physiological experimentation that would now be called "deconstruction" with the desire a child feels to eviscerate a doll: "We are like children experiencing their first power over toys by breaking them open and curiously examining what is inside" ("Vzgliad na russkuiu slovesnost' v techenie 1824 i nachale 1825 godov," *Dekabristy*, 118).

Sergei Rudakov used machine metaphors to describe the creative process of Osip Mandel'shtam, one of the twentieth-century Russian poets who was most willing to reveal the mechanics behind his writing:

> *I stand before the working mechanism (or body, which is the same thing) of poetry* ... It sees nothing and understands nothing. It walks around and mumbles: "black fern as green night." For four lines four hundred are uttered. This is literally the case ... *I study the wondrous structure whose secret is hidden for mortals. I study the living Mandel'shtam.*
> (entry from 1935, cited from Gershtein, *Memuary*, 189)

We may compare this to a note written by Lidiia Ginzburg in 1933, in which Mandel'shtam's composition of poetry approaches the status of a physiological process:

> [Mandel'shtam] is full of rhythms, thoughts, and words in motion. He practices his craft on the move, unashamed and indifferent to furtive onlookers. *It was uncanny, as if you were spying on a biologically precise process of creation.*
> (Ginzburg, *O starom i novom*, 414)

A proponent of a morphological approach in his literary practice, Nikolai Gumilev as a theorist posited the poetic text as an object for anatomical vivisection, and he compared poetic psychology with physiology. For Gumilev, any theory of poetry must be deductive, analogous to the way in which mechanical theory explains various structures rather than simply describing them ("Anatomiia stikhotvoreniia" ["The Anatomy of a Poem"]; Gumilev, *Izbrannoe*, 191). Vivisection of an organism transposed as analysis of a poem's structure was appropriated by an attentive reader of Gumilev, Sirin, in his Cambridge period poem "Biology":

> The Muse does not accuse me: in the science of the tremors of life / all is beauty ... with a lively heart I admire a crucified frog: / my heart flushes sweetly, as a sticky, ripe cherry. / I cut, dismember, enter; I see the hidden muscles, / the branches of countless veins ... The precise labor is joyous, and *I joyously think that at home / a little volume of verse awaits me.*
> (*Russian Collected Works*, 1:549).

The poet-machine is a new phenomenon, but it inherits the imagery of spiritual verse with its metonymy of laboring in a craft. The Bible itself was the source of poems about the weaving loom as a metaphor for artistic creation in this new time, later developing into a biological organic system or the full automation of the writer's laboratory.

Moving on from the narrative stage props to a listing of motifs, we must emphasize that the construction of an operating model for the literary text and the metaphorical description of the artistic process as a mechanical one demonstrate not only the workings of Nabokov's individual narrative structures, but, more broadly, the mechanics of the creative process. Despite the fact that we are speaking of the works of specific authors, analysis shows that the person of the author is often a somewhat nominal thing. To put it in a simplistic way, we might say that the existence of universal poetic laws in culture that dictate a particular writing process for an author is what organizes the text independently of the level of talent given to an individual author, and what fills it (the text) with topoi that are relevant at a given point in time.

In the ensuing parts of this book, I will present a systematized view of the theme of movement in the poetics of urbanism. Texts dealing with rail, motor vehicle, and air transport in Russian literature offer a rich body of material with a relatively homogenous composition and stable stock of literary motifs. These three topics have been selected as the pivot to illustrate a synchronous approach in the study of urban consciousness in literature.

2

The Train as a New Locus of Myth Creation in Literature

The Topos of the Beginning

The first rail line in Russia was officially opened ten months after the death of Pushkin, on October 30, 1837, when a train consisting of ten cars made the trip from St. Petersburg to Tsarskoe Selo in twenty-eight minutes. By the following summer the line had been extended to Pavlovsk, and it was initially served by four locomotives, three manufactured in England and one in Belgium. The railroad was a smashing success in Russia: in the first full year of operation (1838–39), trains carried 725,626 passengers and the total profit from their operation was more than 265,000 rubles (Westwood, *A History of Russian Railways*, 24). "Bless the railroads!" exclaimed one aristocratic woman[1] at about the same time Tolstoy was finishing his story of Anna Karenina, and just over three decades before his own death at the station house of a small rail stop.[2]

Osip Mandel'shtam, looking back at it, summarized the development of Russian literature in the first quarter of the twentieth century in his own

---

[1]From the diary of M. Bashkirtseva, October 26, 1876 (Bashkirtseva, *Dnevnik Marii Bashkirtsevoi*, 146).

[2]The irony of Tolstoy being "killed" by a Russian railroad was noted by Shklovskii, who dwelt at length on the design of the railcar in which the author spent the last hours of his life: "Lev Nikolaevich decided that he would take third class from the Gorbachevo station. ... It turned out that this was a train carrying both freight and passengers, with one third class car that was overfilled. Over half of the passengers were smoking. ... Many were standing in the aisles and on the vestibule platform. ... It is quite likely that Tolstoy ended up in the car that was then referred to as 'fourth class.' These cars had benches only on one side. The inside of the car was painted a dull gray. When the upper bunks were raised, they stuck together" (Shklovskii, *Lev Tolstoy*, 818–819). See also: "It was somehow natural that Tolstoy came to rest ... as a pilgrim, near the through tracks of that Russia about which his heroes and heroines continued to fly and circle and looked through the train windows at the paltry stations around them" ("Liudi i polozheniia," 1967; Pasternak, *Sobranie sochinenii*, 4:322).

way: "The railroad has changed the entire flow, the entire structure, the entire cadence of our prose" (Mandel'shtam, *Sobranie sochinenii*, 2:87).[3]

It was fashionable in the late nineteeth and early twentieth centuries to begin a novel with a scene in a railroad car. The stream of such openings created a relatively consistent topos that essentially permitted no deviations from the plot structure depicting the protagonist setting out on his journey (Vladimir Propp's "absentation" ["*otluchka*"] function) or his arrival at a train station (the means of entering the plot).[4]

Despite their artful ability to bring their characters into their works on trains (cf. Dostoevsky's *The Idiot*), Russian writers seem not to have produced a single novel that takes place entirely in the enclosed space of a train car.[5] Generally speaking, a train appears in a text for one of the following purposes, which may intersect: approaching a train, the character passes through the threshold territory of the station in order to be subjected to a test or an unexpected/unavoidable meeting;[6] in the railcar, narrowed to the space of a compartment, the protagonist and antagonist are brought together; the time of the journey is used as a pretext for a conversation to develop between fellow travelers (Tolstoy's *The Kreutzer Sonata* or, a markedly simplified version, Teffi's short story, "In the Train Car" (1912), which in its entirety presents the paradigm of the train car dialog [Teffi, *Sobranie sochinenii*, 5:142–145]); or, as a symbol of the mythology of the road, extreme situations arise and develop, including even the death of a character (Tolstoy, *Anna Karenina*).

---

[3]Late in his life Mandel'shtam described his own role in Russian letters with the help of a transportation metaphor. In a letter to Iurii Tynianov (dated January 21, 1937), he wrote: "For a quarter century now I have been dissolving into Russian literature, mixing the important with trifles, but soon my verse will merge with it, *changing something in its structure and composition*" (the Russian word *sostav* refers to the composition or make-up of something, but also refers to a railroad train) (*Novyi mir*. 1987. № 10, 222). And yet Mandel'shtam, at the beginning of his career path, embarked for fame in the capital cities practically without a ticket (*zaitsem*, in Russian, literally "to ride rabbit," figuratively "to ride without a ticket"). Cf. the diary of S. P. Kablukov (October 24, 1910): "Iosif Mandel'shtam came to see me today, having arrived at his homeland in the middle of October after many long wanderings with great adventures (one of these adventures was the loss of his wallet in Dvinsk, which had his rail ticket, and thus 'riding rabbit' to Petersburg in the 'crew' compartment for 3 rubles 50 kopeks paid in Petersburg). I asked Zinaida Gippius to have a good look at his poems and recommend him to the *Russian Thought* journal, i.e. to Briusov" (Mandel'shtam, *Kamen'*, 242).

[4]See Bezrodnyi, "Rossiia na rel'sakh," 94–97. He also wittily called Emelya's traveling stove from the Russian folk tale, "Emelya and the Pike," "the first version of the steam engine and the wagon-lit as well" (ibid., 94).

[5]In the twentieth century, Andrei Sobol' (in the novella, *Parlor Coach*; *Oblonki. Tret'ia kniga rasskazov, 1920–1923*) and Venedikt Erofeev in the "narrative poem," *Moskva-Petushki* (translated in English as *Moscow to the End of the Line*) approached this task.

[6]This plot was given heightened attention in Russian poetry relatively early, beginning in the early 1870s. In Apukhtin's long lyric poem (105 lines) "With an Express Train" describes the train station meeting of a man and woman who were in love when they were young (Apukhtin, *Stikhotvoreniia*, 196–199). See also "*Only a distant train in a steel voice / Sings at night of an inevitable meeting*" (Shuvalova, "Bessonitsa" ["Insomnia"], 144).

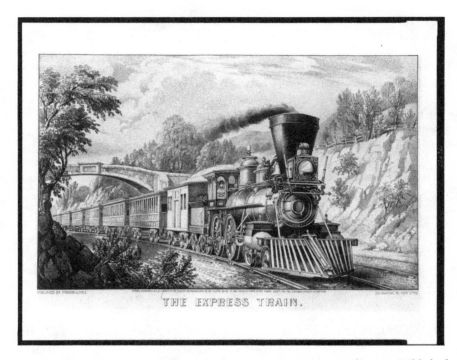

FIGURE 2.1 The Express Train. *United States, c. 1870. New York, N.Y.: Published by Currier & Ives. Lithograph. Library of Congress.*

We will look at the evolution of these motifs in the context of the Western Modernist tradition (Émile Zola,[7] Thomas Mann,[8] and others), but our main focus will be the railroad mythos in Russian literature,[9] examined through the prism of Nabokov's fiction.

The tradition of opening a novel with a railroad scene passed with only minor modifications from the decadent era to the Russian Silver

---

[7]Cf. the function of the railroad in Zola's novel, *La Bête Humaine* (1890), as described by Matthews: "The function of the railway in this novel comes to be that it serves as a contrast to the elementary tendencies of the beast in man. ... As the story unfolds, and the role of the railway is more clearly appreciated, it becomes evident that the personages are living in a world apart and that contact with different society – constantly evoked in the image of passing trains – is unlikely, impossible even" (Matthews, "The Railway ...," 55–56); see also Carter, *Railways and Culture*, 121–123.

[8]In 1951, Nabokov devoted a lecture to analyzing Thomas Mann's *The Railway Accident*, which he subjected to harsh criticism paragraph by paragraph (Boyd, *American Years*, 196).

[9]As far as was possible to tell, the only Russian attempt at putting together a compendium of texts on the rail theme was an anthology with an ideologically loaded foreword but no analytical commentary whatsoever: Leites et al., *Zheleznodorozhnyi transport*. As the anthologizers promised in the foreword, "now the Soviet railway man will know in what unbearable conditions the steel tracks were laid ... how horribly the menial transport laborers lived in the clutches of fearsome exploitation and police tyranny in autocratic, bureaucratic Russia" (*Zheleznodorozhnyi*, 3).

Age and on into Soviet stylizations (as in Sergeev-Tsenskii's novel, *The Brusilov Offensive*,[10] whose tone is largely reminiscent of Pasternak): in reminiscences, the boundary between the two centuries is symbolized by a train whose type alliterates with the train's origin: "On a hot summer morning in 1900, an express train (*kur'erskii poezd*) pulls out of Kursk station (*Kurskii vokzal*)" (Pasternak's *Safe Conduct*). The exotic nature of the journey for a young protagonist initiates his entry into a new world, be it a city full of the temptations of society, or the idyllic countryside, contrasting with the malaise with which the experienced passengers approach the trip. This is the case in a short story by Leonid Andreev,[11] and this is acted out by Mikhail Kuzmin, who from the first lines of his novella sets the rhythm of the narrative with an entry into Petersburg:

> Everything became brighter in the railcar, somewhat deserted in the morning ... *At the frequent stations, each of them different, new local passengers packed into the car with their briefcases, and it was clear that the train and the railroad were not an epoch for them, not even an episode in their lives, but a normal part of the daily agenda.*[12]
>
> (*Kryl'ia* [*Wings*]; Kuzmin, *Proza*, 1:184)

The starting point of the narrative in *King, Queen, Knave* (1928) also corresponds to a train's moment of departure. Nabokov's innovation, however, is to depict the traditional departure by looking out from within a character who has not yet been introduced:

> The huge black clock hand is still at rest but is on the point of making its once-a-minute gesture; that resilient jolt will set a whole world in motion.

---

[10]The threshold symbolism in the opening sentences of *The Brusilov Offensive*—war and revolution—is introduced deliberately, through mechanistic memory, like the pace of a train: "The southern day in late March 1916 beamed and shone. Rattling on the rail joints, locomotive conscientiously puffing, but not hurrying too much, a passenger train was moving westward, made up almost entirely of fourth class red cars. The compartments of the single yellow car were packed tight" (Sergeev-Tsenskii, *Brusilovskii proryv*, 3).

[11]"The station with its discordant commotion, the noise of trains arriving, the whistles of engines ... *first appeared before Pet'ka's dazed eyes and filled him with a feeling of excitement and anticipation.* ... When they boarded the train and departed ... *everything there was strikingly new and strange for him*: and the fact that you could see so far, that the forest looked like grass and the sky, which in this world was amazingly clear and wide, you could see right from the roof ... some gentleman, reading a newspaper and constantly yawning, either because he was extremely tired or because he was bored, shot two hostile glances at the boy, and Nadezhda hurried to apologize: *First time riding on a train, he's interested ...*" ("Pet'ka na dache" ["Petka at the Dacha"]; Andreev, *Sobranie sochinenii*, 1:66).

[12]Regarding Nabokov's familiarity with this novella, see Skonechnaia, "'People of the Moonlight'," 33–52.

The clock face will slowly turn away, full of despair,[13] contempt, and boredom, as one by one the iron pillars will start walking past, bearing away the vault of the station like bland atlantes. < ... > not only did the station depart removing its newsstand, its luggage cart, and a sandwich-and-fruit vendor < ... > not only did all this fall behind; the entire old burg < ... > moved as well.

(King, Queen, Knave, 1)

The exterior panorama, momentarily shifted to a bird's-eye view by the author's perspective ("tilled fields had long been unfolding their patchwork past the railway car window"), is folded up into the close confines of a third-class compartment.

In the aspect of the railroad topos that we are examining, Nabokov was a virtuoso, gathering an extensive arsenal of metaliterary moves over his years of writing. His American novel *Pnin* also begins with a scene in a railcar. The first sentence presents the character using the classic device of an English novel, presuming that the reader already knows the character as a matter of course (it later turns out that the narrator has been indeed familiar with the protagonist): "The elderly passenger sitting on the north-window side of that inexorably moving railway coach, next to an empty seat and facing two empty ones, was none other than Professor Timofey Pnin" (*Pnin*, 7).

The variability of the railroad topos and its metaliterary potential can be used to illustrate the grammatical quirks of one's native language: as a teacher, Nabokov compared the morphological changes in Russian nouns to a service railcar, or the extension of a train, or the loss of the greater part of a train somewhere in a dark tunnel, or the replacement of the last passenger car with a restaurant car (Nabokov, "On Learning Russian"). Khodasevich himself remarked that Sirin not only does not conceal, but actually displays his literary devices, like a magician "who on the spot, after dazzling the audience, shows them the laboratory where his tricks are developed" (*Pro et contra*, vol. 1, 247). Using the vocabulary of the formalists, he "lays bare" his devices (*obnazhaet priem*). In Nabokov's artistic "laboratory of tricks" the devices based on railroad themes take on the features of a literary game, and the railroad becomes one of the principles underlying the structure of the texts, as well as a factor in the dynamics of the plot.

---

[13]The meaning of the metaphor "The clock face < ... > full of despair" helps explain Nabokov's comment from his essay, "Man and Things," where he speaks of the physiological associations evoked by the position of the hands on a clock; for example, "a clock with its hands at twenty past seven brings to mind a face with whiskers turned down Chinese-style" (Nabokov, *Think, Write, Speak*, 72).

The Railroad as a Metaliterary Device

As people became used to the new means of transportation, the railroad broadened its metaphorical range in the literature of the twentieth century. To convey the state of a writer during his creation, Zamiatin, in his essay "Behind the Scenes" ("Zakulisy"; 1930), resorts to the complex imagery of controlling the lighting machinery in a section of a train:

> In each compartment in the sleeping cars there is a little handle of bone: if you turn it to the right you have full light, and to the left is dark, and if you leave it in the middle a blue light turns on and you can still see everything, but the light does not keep you from falling asleep or wake you up.

Zamiatin goes on to explain that when he is asleep and dreaming the handle of consciousness is turned to the left, when he is writing it is in the middle, and "consciousness is lit in blue" (Zamiatin, *Litsa*, 261).

The three positions of the "handle," corresponding to the various mental states of an artist and a passenger, are illustrated by Nabokov in the first chapter of *King, Queen, Knave* (all twenty pages of which are taken up by the description of a train ride), baring the narrative mechanism in the process. "The first chapter of a journey," digresses Nabokov from the narrative flow, "is always detailed and slow. Its middle hours are drowsy, and the last ones swift" (*King, Queen, Knave*, 16). And the meta-descriptive analogy is supported by a plot point: "The train, as if it were already within the magnetic field of the metropolis, was now travelling with incredible speed" (ibid., 18).

In the short story "Cloud, Castle, Lake" (1937), the poetic consciousness of the unhappy Vasili Ivanovich, who in a train car is not permitted to join with his little volume of Tiutchev, finds what is not being read from the scenery zooming by: "The badly pressed shadow of the car sped madly along the grassy bank, where flowers blended into colored streaks" (*Stories*, 432). The speed of the train, which affects the visual perception of the landscape,[14] contributes to the literalizing of the metaphor, "read the world like a book," and the reading of Tiutchev in particular is made, motivated by the statement of the poet himself, who after his first train journey through Europe wrote that from now on, "cities will reach out to each other to shake hands": space has contracted, the distances between cities have been

---

[14]The noise of poetic inspiration is similarly audible to Kuprin's character, who is deeply engaged in the poetry of Afanasii Fet: "And, accompanied by the measured sounds of the speeding train, Shakhov heard the hum of the sonorous verses: 'Light of night, shadows of night, shadows without end'" (Kuprin, *Sobranie sochinenii*, 1:220).

shortened, and one can "be carried to one [city] without saying goodbye to the others" (*Starina i novizna*. St. Petersburg, 1914. Book 18, 20; see Lotman, *Pushkin*, 539). Sharing his literary plans with his addressee in the same year (1937), Nabokov states that "a new idea is shining like a mountain in my train car window, now from the left, now from the right – and soon I leave the train and begin climbing – already I hear the little clatter of rockslides" (Shakhovskaia, *V poiskakh*, 31).

The author/character in the short story, "The Passenger" (1927), before sharing the secrets of his art, confesses his passion for the railroad in general: "I happened to be traveling in the sleeping car of an express. I love the process of settling into viatic quarters—the cool linen of the berth, the slow passage of the station's departing lights as they start moving behind the black windowpane" (*Stories*, 183). Then, as if on the basis of Zamiatin's theory, the handle of consciousness is turned to the middle position and the "blue light" is turned on:

> After some private musings—at the time I was anxious to write a story about the life of railway-car cleaning women—*I put out the light* and was soon asleep. And here *let me use a device cropping up with dreary frequency in the sort of story* to which mine promises to belong. Here it is—that old device which you must know so well: "In the middle of the night I woke up suddenly." What follows, however, is something less stale.
>
> (ibid., 184)

The conversation between the writer and the critic (for whom the prototype seems to have been Iurii Aikhenval'd), who has prior knowledge, gives Nabokov the chance to leave open the doors of the laboratory so that the reader can observe the implementation of literary devices.[15] Such openness on the part of Nabokov is not a rarity; all his prose is aimed at the supersensory reader, and anyone who falls outside of this category becomes the subject of cruel derision. Three critics who were unable to perceive the secrets of what

---

[15]Here we see a three-layer frame: the real author writing about the fictional author shares an excerpt of a work planned as a novella *with a train car as the setting*. The plot involving an author sharing the secrets of his trade with a random fellow traveler is also seen in Chekhov's sketch, "On the Train (A Conversational Shootout)" (1885): "Say what you like, *our work as writers is a difficult one*! (Grand sigh.) Our colleague Nekrasov was right to say that our fate can be a matter of life and death" and so on; the interlocutor eventually reveals that the "writer" composes newspaper articles on the Jewish question (Chekhov, *Polnoe sobranie sochinenii i pisem*, 4:346).

Chekhov's stylistics seem to be invoked in an episode from Gor'kii's *Mother* where a "blind" detective, complaining about his fate to the revolutionary he is seeking, and not recognizing that she is the very person in the train car with him, disguised as a nun: "he was certain that she was on this train in a second class car, and at every stop he got out and said to her upon returning: 'I don't see her. She probably went to bed. They get tired too – *life is hard, just like ours*!'" (Gor'kii, *Mat'*, 164).

was "behind the scenes" of Nabokov's art figure into *The Gift*. Imitating the reviewing style of the journalist Linyov, Nabokov concentrates the railroad allegory: with a poor understanding of the opening pages of the work he is analyzing, "thereafter energetically pursuing a false trail," Linyov "would make his way to the penultimate chapter in the blissful state of a passenger who still does not know (and in his case never finds out) that he has boarded the wrong train" (*The Gift*, 157). The stipulation in parentheses hints that, as far as Nabokov is concerned, there is as little hope of correcting the émigré critic's errors as there is of resisting the movement of a train. The author is fixated not so much on the idea of the train speeding in the opposite direction as on the impossibility of stopping this fateful movement.

But we must not overestimate Nabokov's professional good will. The "wrong path" can not only tempt a critic, but also become a trap for an attentive reader. After the Linyov scene, the author summarizes a chess problem that conceals the model structure of an ideal novel and in the process mentions that "perhaps the most fascinating of all was the fine fabric of deceit, the abundance of insidious tries < ... > and of *false trails carefully prepared for the reader*" (*The Gift*, 160). Another meta-descriptive model, transparent in every sense of the word, for the structure of a novel using the railroad trope is seen in the description of a nighttime journey: "a small structure, *brightly lit inside and housing a row of levers*, appeared and also passed. The train rocked gently as it switched tracks, everything grew dark beyond the window, and once again there was only the rushing night" (*Glory*, 21–22). Like the wrong direction of the train, the path to a dead end is set up in advance for the critic, for the reader, and for the protagonist planted by Nabokov on the wrong train (cf. *Pnin*). True, in *Transparent Things*, the main character meets Armande in a Swiss train precisely as a result of this sort of confusion. And here also there is a metaliterary dimension: the acquaintance happens solely because the *book* in the hands of the female passenger "randomly" turns out to be one edited by Person himself: "He had boarded a slow train by mistake. < ... > Hugh unfolded the 'Journal de Genève'. < ... > A book lay in her lap under her black-gloved hands" (*Transparent Things*, 25). The character can also simply be left standing alone on the platform ("That in Aleppo Once ..."),[16] while the moving machine remains the unwavering instrument of fate, with all, including the author, powerless to stop it. In the final analysis, it was only in his own prose that Nabokov could experience the superiority of a demigod, a controller of trains. In actual life he himself was victimized by just such incidents. In a

---

[16]The protagonist looks out at the "the atrocious void" gaping before him: "coal dust glittering in the heat between naked indifferent rails, and a lone piece of orange peel" ("That in Aleppo once ..."; *Stories*, 563).

letter to Zenzinov dated May 28, 1944 he wrote: "On the way from Cornell to New Iork *<sic>* I was half-asleep and got off in Newark instead and then, through some kind of nightmare, made it to my destination by local trains" ("Dorogoi i milyi Odissei ...," 98).

The Railroad Metaphor

With stanza joints,
To the beat of rhymes,
History drives its
Locomotive

—V. Narbut, "The Railroad"

An exceptionally wide range of metaphors can be inserted into the railroad template, comparing the rail tracks to a walkway, chains of rectangular garden beds to a train, and the metaphysical sense of "winds from the past" (as Nabokov himself called it in his Russian poem meaning something along the "transparent things") with the mental state of a nervous passenger. In *Speak, Memory*, Nabokov writes that when he and his family began traveling in Europe he had a sense that the parks were traveling with them: "Le Nôtre's radiating avenues and complicated parterres were left behind, like side-tracked trains" (*Speak, Memory*, 306). Earlier on in his memoirs he admits that he has been interested in his parents' age all his life and inquired about it "*like a nervous passenger* asking the time in order to check a new watch" (ibid., 22).

What interests Nabokov in the symbolism of railroads is the variability in the boundaries between the mundane and the fantastic, mythological, and folkloric. Nabokov differs in this sense from Mandel'shtam, who brilliantly

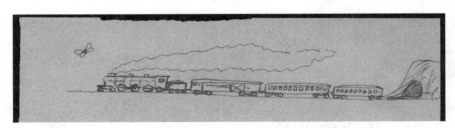

FIGURE 2.2 *Drawing by V. Nabokov to his son Dmitri in a letter to Véra Nabokov, February 7–8, 1937. W. Henry and A. Albert Berg Collection, The New York Public Library.*

pecks at the metaphorical keyboard of the railroad, but does not delve into
its philosophical implications.[17] It is clear that for Nabokov the train unites
certain incompatible properties. A *long-distance* train easily becomes a
"train with fabulous destination" (*Glory*, 133). A character emerging in a
foul mood into the hallway from a room knocks on a doorjamb "as if he
were a clumsy passenger in a speeding train" (*King, Queen, Knave*, 229).
In the pyric poem, "To Prince S. M. Kachurin," the author provides this
explanation: "all life / stopped, like a train / in the rugged silence of the
fields" (*Russian Collected Works*, 5:429). It is as if we are being reminded
that we are in constant motion[18] and that on the journey called "life" we
are each given a ticket with an origin and a destination: "He reflected what
a strange, strange life had fallen to his lot, it seemed as if *he had never left a
fast train, had merely wandered from car to car*"; this is then followed by a
list of relatives, friends, and acquaintances from various points in Martin's
life, who are sitting in various cars on the train (*Glory*, 157).

The inertia of life's journey requires that the text contain the appropriate
cosmic discourse: "We partake of food at predetermined hours because the
planets, like trains that are never late, depart and arrive at predetermined
times" ("La Veneziana"; *Stories*, 105). The astrological focus on trains
reached Soviet writers as well—Pil'niak: "The Troskyist Akim was late for
the train, just as he was for the train of time" (Pil'niak, *Rasplesnutoe vremia*,
137) and Samoilov in "The Wooden Railcar":

> It seemed to me the car was not moving, but standing,
> And the earth on some creaking axis
> Turned past our doors,
> *And above it turned the heavens,*
> *The sun, stars, the moon,*
> The days, years, and ages
>
> (Samoilov, *Izbrannye proizvedeniia*, 59)

The author can manipulate the schedule according to his own artistic ideas.
But for the success of his operations, Nabokov needs to shift the scale, to
convert the proportions of adults to the playground of a "child's text."

---

[17]Cf. *The Egyptian Stamp*: "The open railroad cars poorly obeyed the steam and, after
fluttering the curtains, played bingo with the chamomile summer. *The locomotive in its top-
hat, with its chicken-leg pistons,* was indignant at the weight of the opera hats and the muslin"
(Mandel'shtam, *Sobranie sochinenii*, 2:72).

[18]See Vladimir Shuf's lyric poem, "On the Way": "I go by the steppe, the night is mute, / Can't
see in the darkness … / The colored flame lit, / Extinguished the mile post. // Is it far? Yes, still
far! / *Just like life, my path distant*" (*Sovremennye russkie liriki*).

Childhood and the Locomotive:
A Model of the World

FIGURE 2.3 *J. N. Swartzell and daughter Margaret seated with parts of electric train, on porch of home, Washington, D.C. Between 1909 and 1932. National Photo Company Collection, Library of Congress.*

At almost thirty-eight years of age, struck by what he saw in the shop windows, Nabokov wrote to his wife from Paris: "What a luxurious toy store on the Champs-Elysees, incomparably better than our Czech stores – what trains! (*'le plus rapide train du monde des jouets,'* with a streamlined engine and wonderfully decorated light blue cars)" (Nabokov, *Selected Letters*, 20). Nabokov retained his passion for models throughout his life: in his seventies, he recounted the following in an interview with *Vogue* (1972):

In the early years of this century, a travel agency on Nevski Avenue displayed a three-foot-long model of an oak-brown international sleeping car. In delicate verisimilitude it completely outranked the painted tin of my clockwork trains. Unfortunately it was not for sale. One could make out the blue upholstery inside, the embossed leather lining of the compartment walls, their polished panels, inset mirrors, tulip-shaped reading lamps,[19] and other maddening details. Spacious windows alternated with narrower ones, single or geminate, and some of these were of frosted glass. In a few of the compartments, the beds had been made.

(Strong Opinions, 201–202)[20]

As we know, Nabokov generally answered interview questions in writing. In this case he quoted his own works, published long before, with the insertion of additional details. Compare the above to the corresponding excerpts from *Glory*:

[T]he magnificent model of a brown-paneled sleeping car in the window of the Société des Wagons-Lits et des Grands Express Européens on the Nevsky Avenue.

(Glory, 6)

And from *Speak, Memory*:

In the early years of this century, a travel agency on Nevski Avenue displayed a three-foot-long model of an oak-brown international sleeping car.[21] In delicate verisimilitude it completely outranked the painted tin of my clockwork trains. < ... > One could make out the blue upholstery inside, the embossed leather lining of the compartment walls, their polished panels, inset mirrors, tulip-shaped reading lamps < ... >. Spacious windows alternated with narrower ones, single or geminate, and some of these were of frosted glass. In a few of the compartments, the beds had been made.

(Speak, Memory, 141)

Nabokov, whose mother tried to buy the model from the agency ("Unfortunately it was not for sale"), was able to compensate for his childhood railroad obsession in prose. The European origins of the intricate model were conditioned by the historical preeminence of the Western

---

[19]The Nord-Express in *The Defense* is likewise equipped with the "tulip-shaped lamps in the sleeping car" (*Defense*, 74).

[20]Ganin's mania in *Mary* is redacted and converted from a train model to watercraft: he gazes for some time at the "splendid model" of the RMS Mauretania transatlantic liner in the shop window of a Berlin steamship company (*Mary*, 18).

[21]Cf. "Extended railcars painted like oak" ("The Express"; *Russian Collected Works*, 1:466).

masters in this field.[22] The first toy trains, made primarily from tin plate, began serial production in France as early as 1835 (Freeman, *Railways and the Victorian Imagination*, 212). The distinguishing feature of toy train design in the last third of the nineteenth century was its restrospective nature. Windup engines generally reproduced the look of models from the first few decades of railroad history (Pressland, *Great Book of Tin Toys*, 6), and it was only around 1900 that the fashion evolved from the archaic to the modern. The turn to modern miniatures was helped by the English manufacturing company W. J. Basset Lowke, whose 1904 catalog was 252 pages long; a catalog issued by A. W. Gamage in London (1906) presented 150 models, most of them produced in Germany (Carson, *Toy Trains: A History*, 56; 59). Accompanied by more and more accessories, the toy train gradually begins to become not simply an isolated object, but part of the world in miniature.[23] In *Ada*, the fifteen-year-old Van Veen "studied with a poet's passion the timetables of three great American transcontinental trains that one day he would take" (*Ada*, 345): the dark red New World Express, the dark blue African Express, and the brown Orient Express. In terms of luxury, Nabokov's fantasies outdid any catalog models: "Those three admirable trains included at least two carriages in which a fastidious traveler could rent a bedroom with bath and water closet, and a drawing room with a piano or a harp" (ibid., 333).

Nabokov held any author to rigorous standards for accuracy, and he recreated the historical particulars of Tolstoy's *Anna Karenina* based on an 1892 guidebook published by Karl Baedeker and Collignon's *Les Chemins de Fer Russes* (*Russian Railroads*) published in Paris in 1868. He justified this by saying that "trains and coaches play a significant part in the novel: we have Anna's two journeys in the first part, from Petersburg to Moscow

---

[22]Model railroads originated in England in the mid-nineteenth century, when there was a boom in rail construction. By the end of the century English model train enthusiasts began forming clubs that began producing trains and operating miniature railroads, with the models reproducing in full the impression upon seeing the engines and cars of actual railroad trains. And yet at the 1900 Paris World's Fair, the model of the Siberian Express produced by Russian craftsmen took the gold medal. As demand for their products increased, small shops that made simple toy trains were transformed in the first third of the twentieth century into large model railroad companies. In Europe the most famous company was Marklin, Fleischmann, Rivarossi. "The focus of model manufacturers, which had initially been on the mechanical reliability of the toy trains, reacted to customer interest in a resemblance to specific engines and cars by gradually shifting to the external appearance and the improvement of their processes using special equipment, new craft techniques, fine die-casting, and so on. In this way a spring-driven toy was turned into a miniature model with precise mechanical and electrical design, mimicking a specific type of engine or car" (Barkovskov et al., *Modeli zheleznykh dorog*, 5; 7).

[23]The glimmering Petersburg shop windows were also recalled by a younger contemporary of Nabokov's: "Children tug on their moms, holding their hands, and demand to have a look in the toy stores at the tin soldiers and *the little engines with attached cars riding along the rails*" (Likhachev, *Vospominaniia*, 38).

and back to Petersburg," and "great, clanging, and steaming trains are used
to transport and kill the characters" (*Lectures on Russian Literature*, 198).
Nabokov provides his students with a dozen minor details on the specifics
of journeys by rail in Russian in the second half of the twentieth century:
how many rings were given before a train departed and what they signified
to passengers, the design of the Moscow–Petersburg night train (with a
drawing!), and how much time this journey took.[24]

Modeling as a reproduction of reality in a small-scale format, or by
creating the text of a novel, has an additional aesthetic aspect for Nabokov.[25]
The construction of an alternate reality produces a secondary model of the
copied object in the realm of art. In other words, the master model builder
and the artist are faced with similar tasks. The difference is that the model
builder requires the precise art of imitation, while the artist also needs to
have his own angle of vision.[26]

A model, by definition, must correspond to the original as much as possible
on its own scale—in the case of the shop window on Nevskii described in
Other Shores/Speak, Memory the length of the car was between 90 cm and
1.5 mm (Nabokov's estimates varied). The modeler must be particularly
accurate when it comes to details, and Nabokov left an interesting example
of this punctiliousness. As a child he asked his drawing teacher to depict
an international express train and watched "his pencil ably evolve the

---

[24]"A fast train covered the distance between Petersburg and Moscow (about 400 miles) in
twenty hours in 1862. Leaving Petersburg around 8 p.m., Anna arrived in Moscow a little after
11 a.m. the following day" (*Lectures on Russian Literature*, 225–226). Westwood presents
similar data, stating that by 1880 there were five trains traveling in each direction between
Moscow and Petersburg, the fastest of which could make the journey in fifteen hours (this train
had only first and second class for passengers) with eight stops along the way and an average
speed of 42 km/h (Westwood, *A History of Russian Railways*, 89–90).

[25]We see a real-world example of such "modeling" in a borrowing in *The Gift* from Dostoevsky's
Demons (also translated as *The Devils* or *The Possessed*), first noted by B. Maslov. Dostoevsky's
novel has a minor character, Governor von Lembke, a lover of models who glued together
"*an entire railroad train*" and then began to work on a church with a pastor and his flock.
The "bifurcated" scene from *Demons* involving this church twice figures in the description
of the crematorium model in the shop window of the Berlin funeral office and the funeral of
Alexander Yakovlevich in *The Gift*. For more on the mechanics of this allusion, see Maslov,
"Poet Koncheev," 183–184.

[26]Cf. the memoirs from the Petersburg childhood of A. N. Benua, a family friend of the Nabokovs,
describing the last quarter of the nineteenth century (a period that determined the reality of the
1900s as seen in Nabokov's memoirs and in *The Gift*): "I cannot fail to mention two more
categories of 'toys' – that which I would call the 'dwarf world' and that which might be united
under the term 'optical toys.' Both of these types catered, if you please, still more to the nature
of my personality; both are connected to the theatre and *with any art that reproduces life* ...
[My father] had on the bookshelf, next to an entire village of wonderful little houses he brought
from Switzerland in the 1840s, a *model of the Sterlinskii Station*, which Papa had glued together
to present to Tsar Nikolai I himself" (Benua, *Moi vospominaniia*, 1:212). This refers to a model
of the Strel'na station of the Baltic Railway, which was built based on a design by N. L. Benua.

cowcatcher and elaborate headlights of a locomotive that looked as if it had been acquired secondhand for the Trans-Siberian line after it had done duty at Promontory Point, Utah, in the sixties" (*Speak, Memory*, 93).[27] But the five carriages following the engine were bitterly disappointing to the future memoirist in their plain simplicity: "When he had quite finished them, he carefully shaded the ample smoke coming from the huge funnel, cocked his head, and after a moment of pleased contemplation, handed me the drawing. I tried to look pleased, too. *He had forgotten the tender*" (ibid.).

It is possible that this locomotive features again in *Lolita* in a work by an artist seen in the shop window of an antique store: "a splendid, flamboyant, green, red, golden and inky blue, ancient American estampe[28] – a locomotive with a gigantic smokestack, great baroque lamps and a tremendous cowcatcher, hauling its mauve coaches through the stormy prairie night and mixing a lot of spark-studded black smoke with the furry thunder clouds" (*Lolita*, 27). In his American period, Nabokov does not limit himself to simple depiction, but rather uses a piece of it as a spark to change the narrative register and shift the spotlight to a new perspective on the plot: "These [clouds] burst" (ibid.). This "burst" turns out to be the death of his uncle abroad, who left Humbert a large inheritance.

Nabokov uses a similar recollection, but with a tender, to create an actual engine in *Glory*: "Snow and frost met one on the Russian side of the border, a whole mountain of logs swelled up on the tender, the crimson Russian locomotive was equipped with a fan-shaped snowplow, and *abundant white steam flowed, curling, from the huge smokestack*" (*Glory*, 24). The tufts of

---

[27]In the commentary on *Anna Karenina*, Nabokov digresses at length about the history of engine building in the nineteenth century: "The famous photograph (1869) of the first two intercontinental trains meeting at Promontary Summit, Utah, the engine of the Central Pacific (building from San Francisco eastward) is seen to have a great flaring funnel stack, while the engine of the Union Pacific (building from Omaha westward) sports but a slender straight stack topped by a spark-arrester. Both types of chimneys were used on Russian locomotives. < ... > the seven and a half meters long locomotive < ... > of the fast train connecting Petersburg and Moscow had a straight funnel two and a third meters high, i.e., exceeding by thirty centimeters the diameter of its driving wheels whose actions is so vigorously described by Tolstoy" (*Lectures on Russian Literature*, 227).

[28]There was a tradition in America of producing gravures on railroad themes: "Initially the illustration of the railways was dominated by the work of print-makers, sketchers, and engravers rather than painters. It is estimated that some 2,000 different railway prints were published in the twenty years after 1830, mainly in form of lithographs. .... Many of these prints were commissioned directly by the railway companies to promote a positive and attractive image of train travel and dispel the many fears that people entertained about the new form of locomotion. Without exception these prints stress the engineering miracles achieved by the railway builders and highlight the grace, symmetry, and formal order of the railway system" (*The Station in Painting and Poetry, Postcard and Poster*; Richards & MacKenzie, *The Railway Station*, 316). "In the 1920s the actual trains and their engines began to figure much more and the posters drew attention to the speed, comfort, and punctuality of their services, as the railways began to feel the effect of competition from road transport" (ibid., 338).

smoke and the infernal crimson reflections (which may be internal, from the stove, or external, e.g., from the sun) remain unchanged in this description: "It smelt of soot. Out of the *locomotive* smokestack one could see, like giant clumps of cotton, *smoke* emanating and freezing motionless in the air. Closer to the engine these clumps flashed and were colored dark purple" (A. Kuprin, *Na raz"ezde*; *Sobranie sochinenii*, 1:226); "a reddish sun ray, flashing in an uneven glow through the clumps of locomotive steam" (*Kryl'ia*; Kuzmin, *Proza*, 1:182).[29]

Moving back from Russian poetry to *Lolita*, which is full of references to world literature, it is worth taking another look at the traditional American engraving. The image of a locomotive there is not simply a figment of Nabokov's imagination, but rather another "hypogram"—a version, recast in prose, of Walt Whitman's poem, "To a Locomotive in Winter" from *Leaves of Grass* (1891–92)[30]:

Thee for my recitative!
Thee in the driving storm even as now—the snow—the winter-day declining;
Thee in thy panoply, thy measur'd dual throbbing and thy beat convulsive;
Thy black cylindric body, golden brass and silvery steel;
Thy ponderous side-bars, parallel and connecting rods, gyrating, shuttling at thy sides;
Thy metrical, now swelling pant and roar, now tapering in the distance;
Thy great protruding head-light fix'd in front;
Thy long, pale, floating vapor-pennants, tinged with delicate purple;
The dense and murky clouds out-belching from thy smoke-stack;
Thy knitted frame, thy springs and valves, the tremulous twinkle of thy wheels;
Thy train of cars behind, obedient, merrily following,
Through gale or calm, now swift, now slack, yet steadily careering:
Type of the modern! emblem of motion and power! pulse of the continent!
For once, come serve the Muse, and merge in verse, even as here I see thee[31]

---

[29]Just a century ago the householder took / A kettle that for a thousand centuries / Had boiled soup, and put it on wheels / And, raising a coupler, / Harness it to a cart. / *The steam ejected a piston, made a lever bend, / And the locomotive, breathing haltingly, /* Started moving, belabored, / And dragged along the rails / A giant train of people and belongings (M. Voloshin, "Par" ("Wings"), 1922; *Stikhotvoreniia i poemy*, 318–319).

[30]In his own time Whitman was translated into Russian by the author's uncle, Konstantin Nabokov (S. Nabokov, "Profili," 157–158).

[31]Whitman, *Leaves of Grass*, 476. For more on the Whitman reference, see Leving, "Come serve the Muse ...," 11–12.

Following Whitman's interweaving of the engine motif into the industrial fabric of verse ("Roll through my chant, with all thy lawless music! thy swinging lamps at night"), Nabokov illuminates the text of *Lolita* with a foreign word: the strong visual image hints at where to find its original artistic incarnation, and the "stormy prairie night" and "furry thunder clouds" (in its own way a translation of Whitman's "Launch'd o'er the prairies wide" and "free skies") confirm the originating depot of this old engine.

Toys and Reasons

The Child's Toys and the Old Man's Reasons
Are the Fruits of the Two Seasons.
                    —*William Blake*, "Auguries of Innocence"

FIGURE 2.4 *Toy factory. Stephanie Cewe is assembling locomotives for toy trains. Photographer: Howard R. Hollem. New Haven, C.T., 1942. Office of War Information, Photograph Collection, Library of Congress.*

The "passportless shadow" of the poet, which visits the Petersburg home of his childhood, finds there sleeping children who dream of the "toys, ships and trains" belonging to the previous inhabitant ("Dlia stranstviia nochnogo mne ne nado"; 1929; *Russian Collected Works*, 2:597). Of his toy trains, Nabokov was most fond of the passenger trains. A fictional uncle giving his nephew little *freight cars* made of tin leads to secret tears of disappointment (*Glory*, 35). Martin wants a train meant not for cargo but for people, united under one roof by the will of fate, placed on a single unsteady foundation. Shaken by a common rhythm, speeding in the direction of a common goal, they embody the power of fate, and this was prosaically destroyed by the uncle's gift. The compartment serves to feed the imagination, with each of them holding an invented drama ("The trouble is that I did not learn, and shall never learn, why the passenger cried"; "The Passenger"; *Stories*, 187). Martin recalls how the toy animals and diminutive bonbonnières that were arrayed for them in the children's room on Christmas morning were in some way just an "introduction" to the big gift: "an engine with carriages and tin rails (of which huge eights could be constructed) waiting for him in the drawing room" (*Glory*, 179). In narrative time the toy train is a catalyst for the appearance of the real one: "Today also a train was waiting for him; it would be leaving Lausanne toward evening" (ibid.).

The author is concerned about detailed accuracy in connection with metaliterary reflection: the design of a secondary model or a verbal duplicate. A prose writer tries to reproduce reality in a small scale while adhering in a fundamental way to the important details. The model train is a medium representing someone else's creation; the toy train is a stimulus for creation. The model requires study; the toy requires interaction.

Nabokov is not an author who mechanically bestows on a sympathetic character the passions of his own youth. Martin, for example, has no creative impulses whatsoever. It is a different matter in the realm of aesthetics. Martin cherishes his childhood memories of journeys abroad, during which the thing he remembers most clearly are the "marvelous toy shops (locomotives, tunnels, viaducts)" in Berlin (ibid., 23). The toy store, concentrating a number of favorite objects, is retrospectively conceptualized as an Edenic space. From out of the rich assortment in the big-city store, the grown-up Martin's gaze picks out the objects with a focus that is decidedly Nabokov's. In the process of remembering, his childhood recollections appear more stark than in reality, and it seems to Martin that "the toy shops on the once elegant Friedrichstrasse had thinned out and lost their sparkle, and the locomotives in their windows looked smaller and shabbier" (ibid., 134). The splendor would seem to be fleeting and vanishes with the loss of childhood. The same "demythologizing" fate is shared by real means of transportation, which lose all of their former charm as the narrator grows up.[32] Going to a toy store means temporarily returning to the lost paradise of childhood, as Nabokov describes in *Speak, Memory*, writing that everything "had fallen through, like my toy trains that < ... > I tried to run over the frozen puddles" (*Speak, Memory*, 27), referring to the toy engines that he tried to set loose across frozen puddles in the yard of a Wiesbaden hotel in the winter of 1904–05.[33]

Only select representatives of the adult world were allowed access to the closed territory that Nabokov calls "the world of my windup trains." In the author's "real life," one of the few exceptions who was given a "pass" into the intimate world of childhood was his uncle, V. I. Rukavishnikov. Interacting with him gave Nabokov a feeling similar to that which he had when entering the "world of toys" of some elegant foreign city (ibid., 68). The language of windup trains is a kind of password into the heart of the child.[34] The perceptive Krug, in David's kindergarten, notices the "brilliantly painted cardboard bricks and mechanical trains" (*Bend Sinister*, 160). Wanting to cheer up his own son during an extended absence, Nabokov draws railcars and engines for young Dmitri in a number of letters addressed to his wife in 1936–37 (unpublished letters to V. E. Nabokova from the author's archive, Berg Collection, New York Public Library). The repeated railcars form an endless train, compensating in part for the separation, and deploying the motif of anticipation of his father's return.

In *The Defense*, a green toy locomotive makes two appearances in the novel. In the first it "peep[s] out" from under the flounces of an armchair in the nursery (*Defense*, 33), and in the second it is in a flashback ("the clockwork train with its tin car painted to look like paneling went buzzing under the flounces of the armchair, and goodness knows how this affected the dummy engine driver, too big for the locomotive and hence placed in the tender"; ibid., 165). The prototype for Luzhin's train is "a toy engine lying

---

[32]The ostensible reason for the loss of enchantment is the decision by the Nabokovs' tutor to implement a "more democratic" regime for the growing boys, but the true conflict for the author is seen in his reaction not to the deprivation of the lawful rights given to him by his social standing, but rather to the lost connection to *childhood*, which had meant a continuation of his journeys on the Orient Express cars: "the beloved Northern Express and Orient Express, elegant, thickly carpeted, with lacquer and mirrors, full of memories of childhood were replaced by the foul dirty floors and cigar stench of the noisy and swaying *Schnellzugs* [German express trains] or the faded comfort of Russian state-owned trains with some sort of servers instead of conductors" (*Other Shores; Russian Collected Works*, 5:250).

[33]The metaphor is significant, particularly if we consider the date: the year of the Russo–Japanese War. The same chapter also describes the drawings of Japanese correspondents from the war, depicting the destruction of "Russian locomotives which, because of the Japanese painting style, looked entirely like child's toys." For more on the semantics in the context of this drawing, see Leving, "Vladimir Nabokov's Japan," 1–9.

[34]"Grandma waved / and just then a locomotive / came up to the children and said / drink your porridge and trunk" ("Sluchai na zheleznoi doroge" ["Incident on a Railroad"], 1926; Kharms, *Sobranie sochinenii*, 1:59).

on its side with its wheels still working gamely" that Nabokov describes in a dream in *Speak, Memory* (145). The same toy engine figures in the poem "Childhood" ("Detstvo"; 1918), where it appears as part of a complex structure mixing reality and fiction, past and present:

> *silently, by myself, I played on the floor alone;*
> *in innocent imagination, with a sacred freedom from care,*
> *I imitated life with childish inspiration;*
> *from thick dictionaries I created bridges,*
> *and the windup train ran true*
> *along the tin rails...*
> *And strange it is: it seems to me my dream extended long*
> *... that now, just now I'll wake up as a child again*
> *and find in the corner by ball and engine*
> (Russian Collected Works, 1:515–516)

The solipsistic experience of the lyrical narrator in the poem resonates with the idea of the eternal quest in the most important characters from Nabokov's prose; they search for people (a father, a brother, an ideal conversation partner) and elusive places (Russia, Tibet, "Zembla," "Terra/Antiterra") and heroically try to return to a "lost time."[35] The processes of thought and memory in Nabokov are saturated with railroad metaphors; time, as one contemporary aptly put it, begins to hum in a locomotive boiler.[36] In *Bend Sinister*, Krug finds himself thinking that, while he is working on urgent matters, his consciousness is being bombarded by flashes of memory, "an air bubble from the past," which Nabokov expressively calls: "two parallel passenger trains of thought, one overtaking the other" (*Bend Sinister*, 179).

The Station/Depot

Our artists must feel the poetry of train stations as their fathers understood the poetry of forests and rivers.

—Émile Zola

---

[35]Cf. the childhood impressions of the narrator in *The Real Life of Sebastian Knight* after a meeting with his father, who lifts his son "up from the floor, one half of my *toy train* still dangling from my hand and the crystal pendants of the chandelier dangerously near my head" (*The Real Life of Sebastian Knight*, 7).

[36]The wind, chased, seeing the station, / Falls in the gray flickering of rail ties. / Time hums in the engine boiler. / Like a forest choked by air ("Ballada o mashiniste" ["Ballad of an Engineer"]; Berendgof, *Beg*, 42–43).

FIGURE 2.5 *Design for a Railroad Station. Nineteenth century, Anonymous, French. Graphite heightened with white on heavy wove paper. The Elisha Whittelsey Collection, The Metropolitan Museum of Art.*

The train station as temple of the urban epoch is the embodiment of the high point of a dynamic aesthetic. The station is full of sounds, day and night.[37] As Theophile Gautier, struck by the agglomeration of glass and iron in contemporary stations, put it, "they are the churches of a new civilization, where nations come together" (Richards & MacKenzie, *The Railway Station*, 3). The religious ritual in the ceremonial adherence to the schedule and the architectural features of stations, reminiscent of cathedrals, were remarked on by Chesterton ("The Prehistoric Railway Station") and Karl Čapek (*Intimate Things*, 1935), and in Russian poetry by Boris Pasternak:

There, like an organ, in an ice of mirrors
The station sparkled as an enigma,
Did not close its eyes and nursed its sorrows
And argued in wild beauty

---

[37]The etymology of the Russian word for trains station, "*vokzal*," reveals its connection with places of merriment: it is from the English Vauxhall, originally a park and pavilion near London named after the owner, Jane Vaux. The Tsarskoe Selo and Pavlovsk train stations of the 1830s and 1840s really were "Vauxhalls" for entertainment, including the performance of concerts (Haywood, *The Beginnings of Railway*, 136–139).

With the conservative emptiness
At times of repairs and holidays.
("Vysokaia bolezn'" ["High Disease"], 1924; Pasternak,
Sobranie sochinenii, 1:556–557)[38]

The temples of the train station become inevitable locations on the route of new European incarnations of Odysseus, as in the 1902 poem, "Cities" by Émile Verhaeren (from *Les Forces tumultueuses*):

En aimas-tu l'effroi et les affres profondes
O toi, le voyageur
Qui t'en allais triste et songeur
Par les gares de feu qui ceinturent le monde?
... Avez-vous vu, le soir, leurs couronnes de feu,
Temples de verre et d'or assis sur les collines,
D'où se braquent vers les étoiles sybillines
Les monstrueux regards des lentilles d'airain?

Rail station architecture produces the effect of grandiose design, and the enormous glass surfaces, something that became technologically feasible only relatively recently, emphasize a connection to heaven. We see this in the description of the train station in *Glory*: "through the opening of the iron-and-glass arch a pale-blue sky and a gleam of rails, and in comparison to this luminosity all was drab under the station vault" (*Glory*, 183), which calls to mind the color palette of Monet's series of paintings of the Gare Saint-Lazare (1876–77).

The industrial/quasi religious space knows no conflict with the higher realm because it is in of itself confirmation of their existence: "And not a single star speaks, / But, God sees, there is music above them, / The station trembles form the song of the Aonian sisters, / And again, with locomotive whistles / Torn, the violin air is merged" ("Kontsert na vokzale" ["Concert at a train station"], 1921; Mandel'shtam, *Sobranie sochinenii*, 1:139). Compare this to Nabokov's poem, "The Express" written two years later (1923): "In the dusky train station at night / solemn and empty, as in a cathedral" (*Russian Collected Works*, 1:467). The lexical and semantic parallels between these texts, reveal Mandel'shtam's influence not only on Nabokov's prose, but also on the poetry of the young Sirin (Maslov, "Poet Koncheev"):

The iron world is spellbound again.
To a sonorous feast in foggy Elysium
The railcar solemnly zooms away
(Mandel'shtam, *Sobranie sochinenii*, 1:139)

---

[38]Cf. another of his poems, "Prostranstvo" ("Space"; 1927): "And the track of rails stretches / In the anguish of glass and cement. / On Tuesday a prayer and exercise. / But is that all they are worried about? / Not for that and not so / Along the ties they lay the road" (Pasternak, *Sobranie sochinenii*, 1: 232–233).

The transcendental aspect of railroad poetics is typical to both Mandel'shtam and Nabokov:

> And in a moment the wheels began to shake
> and the panels of the buffers to resound –
> and the extended cars, fiery and smooth,
> stretched into the yawning well of darkness
> ... And soon
> The station forgot their ringing and their magic,
> And under its roof it became
> Solemn and empty as in a cathedral.
>
> (*Russian Collected Works*, 1:467)

The sources of this ritual pathos in the railroad theme are seen in an early Nabokov poem from the almanac, *Dva puti* (*Two paths*; Prague, 1918):

> I love unfamiliar train stations,
> I love the cars of long-distance trains.
> The engine whistle is a mighty roar.
> Night. Light rain. I hurry, I'm late.
> And at midnight again in alien cities
> I enter along, anxious and exhausted,
> The deserted, anguished halls,
> With no familiar icons in the corners.
>
> (*Russian Collected Works*, 1:441)

As the poem continues there is no prospect of contact with sacred space—in the expected location of the iconostasis there is only emptiness: "I love the phantoms of train stations: sadness, / The echo of farewells, perhaps deceits" (ibid.). (In imperial Russia, waiting rooms were often furnished with Orthodox icons; in Greece, train stations had a special section of a room where a passenger could place a candle, a common Orthodox religious tradition, in prayer for a safe journey.)

In the summer of 1918, in Yalta, Nabokov met Maksimilian Voloshin with whom he discussed his early verse (Boyd, *American Years*, 180). Little is known about the content of these conversations, but we can assume that among the topics of discussion was the notion of fateful shifts, which was of great importance in poetry during that pivotal time, and about which the elder Voloshin wrote in his poem, "Na vokzale" ("At the train station"; 1919). The train station embodies the disorder of human life which merges with the otherworldly:

> In the dim light of faded
> Electric lamps
> On bundles, bales, and blankets

Among the baskets, trunks, and bins ...
They suffocate in the reeking
Vapors of body and soul.
As it in the world beyond the grave,
Where each carries in himself
The balances and weights
Of daily passions and concerns.

This is how they sleep in train stations,
Cars, platforms, halls,
Markets, squares,
At walls, and in latrine pits

(Voloshin, *Stikhotvoreniia i poemy*, 237–238)

The world beyond the grave and the threshold symbolism of the crossing, overlaid on a scene of parting (albeit not forever), produce a "tragic departure" complex. The religious rhetoric of parting was united with the railroad theme as early as Bashkirtseva's "Dnevnik" ("Diary," 1876)[39] (then echoed in Tsvetaeva's poems dedicated to Bashkirtseva in her book, *Vechernii al'bom* [*Evening album*]).[40] Meanwhile, the arrival of the train is described with the pomp and circumstance almost fitting for the anticipation of a messiah:

And suddenly three eyes of salvation
Burn, shining in the darkness.[41]
The train approaches, closer, closer ...
Dotting the darkness with splashes of sparks,
Moving its wheels ever quieter,
It's stopped. All run to it.

("Pribytie poezda" ["Arrival of a train"];
Gorodetskii, *Stikhotvoreniia*, 2:316)

---

[39]A pivotal point in the life of the narrator is presented as a religious revelation: "Grandfather ... *blessed me and gave me an icon of the Mother of God.* ... But, I thought as I looked at her [the narrator's mother] through the window of our train car, I had been cruel not out of spite, but out of grief and despair; and now I am leaving in order to change our life. When the train began to move I could feel that my eyes were filled with tears. And I unwittingly compared that departure with *my final departure from Rome*" (Bashkirtseva, *Dnevnik Marii Bashkirtsevoi*, 97). (Regarding Bashkirtseva in *The Gift*, see *Russian Collected Works*, 4:691, notes.)

[40]"Evening smoke arose over the city, / Railcars humbly went to some far-off place, / There suddenly flashed, more transparent than an anemone, / A half-child face in one of the windows. ... With that girl at the dark window – / *A vision of paradise in the station commotion* – / I've often met in the valleys of my dreams" (Tsvetaeva, *Stikhotvoreniia i poemy*, 39).

[41]Cf. the poem by the Berlin émigré poet Dzhanumov: "The engines screamed like birds at night / Their straining eyes glowed yellow in the haze. / Sacred memory preserved forever / The trunks, kisses, kerchiefs, and voices" (*Antologiia poezii russkogo zarubezh'ia*, 1:204).

The revolution liberated the train station from its religious and symbolic baggage for a short time, but at night the mystical aspect of the site would come to life with the same force as before. In the darkness the station was repellent with sickening putridity and deviance,[42] an experience which stunned Voloshin's impressionable passenger.[43]

Given such poetic misoneism, it is understandable that several members of the Russian avant-garde attempted to resist imposing these connotations of decay on a key symbol of a New Era. In his manifesto, "Architecture as a Slap in the Face to Ferroconcrete" (1918),[44] the Suprematist artist Kazimir Malevich attacks the creator of the eclectic design for the Kazan railway station,[45] who decided to cover this "roiling spring of rapids ... with the roof of an old monastery": "the locomotives will blush with shame at seeing an almshouse before them." Malevich's invective is delivered expressively and is comparable to the rail station anthems written by many of his contemporaries:

Did the proprietors of the Kazan railroad understand our age of reinforced concrete? Did they see the beautiful figures for iron musculature – the twelve-wheeled locomotives?

Did they hear the living roar? The calm of even breath? The moaning in motion? Did they see the living semaphore fires? Did they see the shapeless and formless – the race of the moving?
...
Did the builder ask the question: what is a train station? Clearly not. Did he stop and think that a train station is a door, a tunnel, the nervous pulse of trepidation, the breath of the city, a living vein, a trembling heart?[46]

Like meteors, iron 12-wheeled express engines enter there; gasping, some enter into the larynx of the reinforced concrete throat, and others

---

[42]"from sadness / the stations turned white / as lunar lime / the worn inscriptions / in the cooling steam / jump into the porcelain nests / of telegraph poles ... / the red semaphore peacock / knocks in the back of the head / tossing here and there / the junction attendants ... / the somnambulism of train stations / undressing a fiery spirit / to the sounds of a timber cog / frightening at night / in an invisible pirouette ... / the nervous whistle of a yawn" (A. Kruchenykh, "Lunatism vokzala," 1920; *Poeziia russkogo futurizma*, 233).

[43]"Again the road. And with a magic force / All of this again surrounds me: / The roar, the porters, electric light, / Shouts, farewells, whistles, bustles" (Voloshin, *Stikhotvoreniia i poemy*, 71).

[44]The title of this article references the attention-grabbing compilation by the Russian Futurists, *A Slap in the Face of Public Taste* (1912).

[45]The Kazan Station in Moscow, constructed between 1913 and 1926, was based on a design by the architect A. V. Shchusev, and it combined elements of pseudo-Russian décor with the Italianate palace architecture that was the norm in Russia.

[46]Cf. the biological morphology of the train station in Francis Ponge's poem, "La Gare" (1942): "*Un quartier phlegmoneux, sorte de plexus ou de nodosité tubéreuse, de ganglion pulsatile, d'oignon lacrymogène et charbonneux*" (Ponzh, *Na storone veshchei*, 96).

flew the jaws of the city, carrying with them a multitude of people who, like microbes, rush about in the body of the train station and the railcars.

The whistling, clanging, and groaning of the engines, the heavy, proud breathing, like a volcano, throw the sighs of the engines; the steam amid the elastic roofs and trusses cleaves its lightness; the rails, semaphores, bells, signals, piles of suitcase, porters – all of this is connected by the movement of rapid time, and the shockingly slow clock drags its hands along, making us nervous.

(Malevich, Chernyi kvadrat, 61–62)

The railroad station is not just a crossing of paths; in the late nineteenth and early twentieth centuries it was also a place of urban life intensified, where the telegraph, post office, stores, buffets, restaurants, and police precinct offices were located together. The train station, this "blind giant" (Gordon, *Ottepel'*, 21), amounts to a symbolic city gate (as expressed in the "jaws"[47] and "larynx" of Malevich). Russia's contemporaries viewed the future as the erosion of this gate, envisioned, for his example, by H. G. Wells in his novella, *A Story of the Days to Come*:

Nineteenth Way was still sometimes called Regent Street, but it was now a street of moving platforms and nearly eight hundred feet wide. The middle space was immovable and gave access by staircases descending into subterranean ways to the houses on either side. Right and left were an ascending series of continuous platforms each of which travelled about five miles an hour faster than the one internal to it, so that one could step from platform to platform until one reached the swiftest outer way and so go about the city.

(Wells, Tales of Space and Time, 240)

The city's transformation into the likeness of a colossal train station, resulting from the complete erasure of the boundary between the static urban space and the dynamics of movement, is a typical feature of utopian fiction from around the turn of the century.

---

[47]E. Shakh: "But the city is close, the rails multiply / In the distance hung a cloud of smoke. / There on the ad a funny face / Looks at us tormented by anguish. // Factory buildings flashed / And pipes straight as pines ... / The train station and inseparable people; / And the knocking of the wheels broke off. // Caught and strangled by the flow, / And thrown into the light beyond the walls, / I see a column, presented for the crowd, / And the jaws of the city subway. // And once again there is no pure sky. / Taxis and trams rush past, / Automobiles honk furiously ... / The whole city, alien and beloved" ("Nesetsia poezd, mel'kaiut stantsii," 1924; Shakh, *Semia na kamne*, 49).

On a metaphysical level, the train station acts as a liminal area, the final locus of the earthly, pedestrian, element. Separation is a commonplace in the lyric poetry of the railroad: "Train station, the fireproof box / *Of my separations, meetings, and separations*" (Pasternak, "Vokzal" ["Train Station"], 1913; *Sobranie sochinenii*, 1:55); and from the literary grande-dame Mineeva in the same year: "*To forget the mourning of separation and the cry of heavy suffering* ... / O, dear meeting, o cherished meeting!" ("Na stantsii" ["At the station"])[48]; by the future Soviet favorite, then a budding poet, I. Sadof'ev: "*In separation my heart sank, / Dewdrop tears fall* ... / Rage, fury of the son, / To the measured knocking of the wheels!" ("Provody" ["Wires"]; Sadof'ev, *Izbrannoe*, 11)[49] and, a decade later, the "a heavy toll" it takes on Anna Akhmatova.[50] In the vacuum before leaving the only significant sound is the signal for departure:

> *Two rings and soon will be the third,*
> *Soon the wave of the farewell handkerchief ...*
> *Who will understand, yet who will forget these*
> *Five minutes before the third bell?*
>
> (M. Tsvetaeva, "Na vokzale" ["At the train station"], 1911; cited in Tsvetaeva, *Sobranie sochinenii v 7 tomakh*)

The train station is not only a place of parting and reunions, but is also a place for a confessional reckoning with the past. The past at a railroad station is annulled, as if in the modernist era the station has become at

---

[48]"And the train stirred ... the locomotive whistle / Forcefully rent the air a third time ... / You saw me off, and did not lower your eyes, / But looked in my eyes sadly and drearily" (Mineeva, *Sbornik*, 6). Cf. the poems entitled "At the Train Station" ["Na vokzale"] by Kriuchkov and Volkov: "The anguish of minutes is broken by the third whistle, / Suddenly your thin profile seems strange. / The train will leave, as everything passes on earth, / And I will remain and not give chase" (Kriuchkov, *Tsvety Ledianye*, 34); and "At the hardened colossus of the train station, / Like birds, weaving a circle, / The frantic sounds of the signal, / Rang out suddenly, summoning" (Volkov, *V pyli chuzhikh dorog*, 96).

[49]In "A heartfelt message" ("Serdechnoe poslanie," 1928): "Midday, sunny, the road, / Pines, a stream, and the train station. / Semaphores, dark blue evening, / The roar of a train and the night ... / At the train station, by the car, / In your quiet city / There is a tender handshake, / *And – separation and anguish*" (Sadof'ev, *Izbrannoe*, 197). Cf. the poem by N. Berendgof from the same year: "*In the train I thought about you till I cried. / I heard the separation louder than the wheels.* / The wheels sang of the same thing, / Though my gaze carried green gold / In a carousel of birches and firs" (Berendgof, *Beg*, 11).

[50]Akhmatova's response to a reading of "Trans-Siberian Express" by Lidiia Chukovskaia (1939): "Trifles ... trifles ... And what a weighty tribute he collected from Pasternak!" (Chukovskaia, *Zapiski*, 1:210). The stanza that seems to have evoked this invective (not to mention other lines that are reminiscent of Pasternak in their rhythm) is as follows: "And, returning home, counting all the breaths of the wheels, / So as not to go crazy, releasing myself to my neighbors on bail, / To remember this face without blood, but without tears, / *This most difficult mask of calm separation*" (Simonov, *Sobranie sochinenii*, 1:67).

FIGURE 2.6 *Group at Train Station. United States, 1929. Photographer: Harris & Ewing. Prints and Photographs Division, Library of Congress.*

once a substitute for religious belief and also a seat of judgment:[51] there, in incense-like smoke and torments that are all but infernal,[52] old debts are paid to fate and new ones are incurred:

---

[51]Cf. Burliuk's "Vokzal" ("Train Station"), 1907: "*Chapel of meetings separation train station /* Quivering hum race of the locomotive / Anxiousness of animated halls / Fiery rose of separation" (D. Burliuk and N. Burliuk, *Stikhotvoreniia*, 130). And in a 1916 poem by Kannegiser: "Fog billowed under the station roof, / Like smoke from a pipe, / And in it, as a shivering crowd, / Stood your slaves. / And there in the sad bustle / No one could remember, / That *soon the station bellringer / Would give the final bell*" (Kannegiser, *Stat'i. Iz posmertnykh stikhov*, 69). Or in the 1921 poem, "Love" by Otsup: "*The bell was rung three times, /* A woman cries on the platform, / Accompanying with her brown eyes" (Otsup, "*Okean vremeni*," 31).

[52]In Eisner's "Razluka" ("Separation"), 1928: "The starlings fly to foreign lands, / Our flowering world spins ... / Stickered suitcases / Are passed by porters into the baggage. // And at stations the dense air / Is drilled by whistles of alarm, / And – like a migratory bird – / The travelers have a frozen gaze. // And we say farewell, we cry, / We cut short our conversations, / And above the tracks the cat's-eye / Semaphore has narrowed now ... // The green flag has been waved – / By *the shaven god* in his scarlet cap ... / And only a piece of writing paper / Now bears the traces of anxiety. // And in a sealed envelope / Through the villages and fields / *Are carried words of love and death,* / And smeared postmarks. // And over them we remember / A spring evening, a dusty garden ... / *And under this wretched earthly Eden / We see a wondrous hell*" (*Volia Rossii*. Prague. 1928. № 9, 62).

Train stations, all of train stations are anticipations,
Here engines, full of suffering,
Burn, exhausted in plain sight,
Pace in the smoke, and draw back.
Perhaps this: here with such anguish
The whole old debt to fate is collected

("Vokzaly, vse vokzaly – ozhidan'ia ...," 1937–40;
Tikhonov, *Sobranie sochinenii,* 1:340)

At stations, as on a train, a different kind of time is activated, and the space is affected by delimited areas: "For some reason they celebrated New Year's Eve in the restaurant of one of the Berlin railroad stations—perhaps because at railroad stations the armament of time is particularly impressive"[53] (*The Gift,* 47). The monumental nature of station clocks reflects the special status of time in that place. In *Ada,* Van Veen displays a doubled concern for time at a train station: "The sound of the rain was lost in a growing rumble of wheels. He glanced at his watch; glanced up at the clock on the wall. He said he was sorry – that was his train" (*Ada,* 170). In a scene from the novel *Despair* (1934), the clock hand is metonymically compared to a predatory beast devouring Time: "The train was due to leave at 10:10. The longer hand of the clock would point like a setter, then pounce on the coveted minute, and forthwith aim at the next. No Ardalion. We stood waiting beside the coach marked 'Milan'" (*Despair,* 135). Nabokov's "chronomachia" involves the image of a clock face in which the hands overlap the numbers, in this case Roman numerals.

As Lidiia Ginzburg observed, the new urban consciousness transformed ancient symbols with its technocentrism, restructuring the theme from inside out—lamentations about that which is past and gone, about the inexorable passage of time, gave way to awe before the future, which was seen as an age of mechanization without humanity (Ginzburg, *O lirike,* 354). Ginzburg illustrated her theory with the example of the railroad motif in the poetry of Annenskii, for whom the locomotive is the counterbalance to the torment of immobility, while the urban world in its most minute manifestation is a part of "the world of pain, beauty, and happiness slipping through powerless hands" (ibid., 358–359): "The faded green flag, / The white bursts of steam, / And the unanswered calls / Of a distant horn. / And the emblem of separation / In a meeting that deceived – / The one-handed conductor / By the clock in anticipation" ("Toska vokzala"/"Anguish of the train station"; Annenskii, *Stikhotvoreniia i tragedii,* 116). Annenskii grinds up his world, presenting a microscopic depiction right down to the flies sticking to the mortar of

---

[53]Cf. in a novel by Thomas Wolfe, *You Can't Go Home Again,* published posthumously in 1940: "The station, as he entered it, was murmurous with *the immense and distant sound of time*" (Wolfe, *A Stone, A Leaf, A Door,* 139).

a station kiosk. In any case, this tendency toward the microscopic was not destined to be heard in the tradition of railroad poetry, which rushed headlong in the opposite direction toward a macrocosmic interpretation of rail technology (in Blok's review of Russian translations of Verhaeren: "the monsters of anguish roar by the schedule"). With the verse of Pasternak, the poetics of urbanism return to the notion of train station time as an enormous flow set in motion by a large explosion (read: the starting point of an individual itinerary) toward the extraterritorial alleyways of the Universe:

> In May, as on the way you read the schedule
> For the Kamyshin branch trains,
> It is grander than holy scripture,
> Though you may read it again from the start.[54]
>
> ("Sestra moia—zhizn' i segodnia v razlive ...," 1922, 1957;
> Pasternak, *Sobranie sochinenii*, 1:654)

The modern city is a point on a map to which "flock the lines / Of infinite railroads" and race "locomotives with mighty pistons" (Shakh, *Gorodskaia vesna*, 20–21).

In addition to the distortion of time, the train station is also characterized by an increase in the force of gravity:

> A minor station flew past, just a platform, a half-opened jewel box, and all grew dark again as if no Berlin existed within miles. At last a topaz light spread out over a thousand tracks and rows of wet railway cars. Slowly, surely, smoothly, *the huge iron cavity of the station drew in the train, which at once grew sluggish.*
>
> (*King, Queen, Knave*, 18)

Nabokov connects the acceleration, real or imagined, of a train approaching Berlin with the psychological state of a passenger, in this case one seemingly more captivated by his own fantasies of the big city than by the fact that the train had entered the "gravitational field" of the capital city. Psychoanalysts have noted the sexual connotations of the image of a train smoothly entering a tunnel or sliding under the canopy of a station (Richards & MacKenzie, *The Railway Station*, 13). In light of the ensuing events involving the protagonist of *King, Queen, Knave*, we cannot rule out that Nabokov intended just this sort of double meaning.

---

[54]On the topographic basis for the Old Testament reference—the Moiseevo (Moses) Station—in Pasternak's "The Steppe," see Timenchik, "Raspisan'e i Pisan'e." Cf. Zamiatin's *We* (1920): "As schoolchildren we all read (perhaps you have, too) that greatest literary monument to have come down to us from ancient days – 'The Railway Guide'" (Zamyatin, *We*, 11–12).

The station, where various types of time and space collide, is a sharp indicator of social classes.[55] During periods of political instability, transportation centers become a focus of rebels and revolutionaries. Ganin recalls standing at Warsaw Station waiting for a suburban train in the year of the revolution. The narrative details signal that there is some disruption in the process of daily life ("While waiting for the bell to ring he started to walk up and down the dirty platform. As he gazed at a broken luggage trolley he was thinking of something different" [*Mary*, 74]). The young Luzhin's attempts to animate the automaton puppet on the platform on the day he finds out that "from Monday on he would be Luzhin" (*Defense*, 15) similarly end in failure: "Finding himself alone on the station platform, Luzhin walked toward the glass case where five little dolls with pendent bare legs awaited the impact of a coin in order to come to life and revolve; but today their expectation was in vain for the machine turned out to be broken and the coin was wasted"[56] (ibid., 20).

As times of rebellion disrupt the social hierarchy, the life of machines is also prone to being undermined. Those who have a schedule and need to adhere to it strictly (a form of regimentation), are likely to become the first victims of chaos. In the description of an incident at a station, the cynical façade of the narrator masks his fear: after a young dandy picks up the cane he dropped on the rails, he rushes to catch "the nightmarishly receding bumpers," and the "sturdy proletariat arm," conforming "to the rules of sentimental fiction (rather than to those of Marxism)," helps him up into the vestibule of the last car (*Speak, Memory*, 243–244). History, all but overturned by the drama, thus discovers that the train and the station dwell in the abode of conservatism. The hierarchical formations built into them from the very start have a margin of error and remain, to a certain extent, inviolable.

---

[55]It is telling that one of the key revolutionary proclamations of Duma chairman Rodzianko on February 28, 1917 was addressed to the railroad workers: "Railway workers! The former authorities which created havoc in all aspects of country life turned out powerless" (cited from *Russian Revolutionary Literature*); cf. the often paraphrased quote from Lenin's *Advice of an Onlooker* (1917), cited in Lenin, *Polnoe Sochineneii*, 34:383): "occupy without fail ... the telephone exchange, the telegraph office, and the rail stations." In belles-lettres, see the scene of the train station uprising in *Doctor Zhivago*.

[56]Nabokov is, as ever, precise in describing even the most marginal details; cf. the reminiscence by his contemporary P. A. Mansurov (1896–1983): "I did *Upmann* [a ballet to the music of Arthur Lourié with set designs by Mansurov] in 1915 as a pen-and-ink drawing for a music box that I had seen at a train station in Pavlovsk near a chocolate stand. It consisted of a windup mechanism and dolls dressed as 18th century ladies and gentlemen as well. This box was activated by a *grivennik*, a 10-kopek silver coin, and the music began to play while the dolls started an elegant dance" (Povelikhina & Kovtun, *Russkaia zhivopisnaia vyveska*, 147).

The Hierarchy of Classes

In the prerevolutionary hierarchy, the railroad fits into a strict semiotic system in which the signifier was the color and the signified was the number of the class determined by the price of the ticket: the color of the train compartments corresponded to the social status of the passengers.[57] In the Russian émigré communities in Paris and Berlin, there was a joke that the reduction in status of former Russians was comparable to moving from the aristocrats' car to that of the plebes.[58]

Class differences are retrospectively the cause for the failure of Ganin's romance with Mary (read: Nabokov's own romance with the prototypical Liusia Shulgina or, in the mirror version, his fiancée Svetlana Zivert[59]); "she always traveled in a yellow one, and now with a second-class ticket she did not want to go inside into a compartment" (*Mary*, 74). But class distinctions also provide the romantic model for relationships in which one participant is in social decline.[60] It would seem to be no accident that the episode in which Ganin meets Mary after a year's absence takes place in the single blue car on the train ("Ganin greeted her awkwardly, there was a clanging of buffers and the railway car moved"; ibid). The unstable space of the vestibule does not allow the characters to get close, and the background noise helps maintain the distance between them, while the circumstances of the revolution soon separate them once and for all. The biographical context is filled out by a journey by rail in *Speak, Memory*: "I do remember < ... > with heartbreaking vividness, a certain evening in the summer of

---

[57]First-class cars were painted blue, second-class cars were yellow, and third-class cars were green. Cf. the familiar lines from Blok: "The cars moved in their usual line, / They shook and creaked along; / The yellow and blue ones were quiet; In the green ones they cried and sang" ("Na zheleznoi doroge" ["On the Railroad"], 1910). In a short story by Leonid Andreev the unpretentious schoolboy Mitia has a face "dull yellow like a second class car" ("Pet'ka na dache" ["Petka at the Dacha"]; Andreev, *Sobranie sochinenii*, 1:145).

[58]Cf. the MAD caricature published in the newspaper, *Poslednie novosti* (*Latest News*) (January 4, 1934): two people are traveling in a sleeping compartment and the inscription below is "– Well, in any case, here we are abroad, and we went to a good school ...; – A school where we brilliantly moved from first to second class" (the Russian contains a pun somewhat lost in translation: the word for class is the same as the word for "grade" in American English or "form" in British English).

[59]Regarding the failed engagement between Nabokov and Zivert due to the difficult financial position of the former, see Boyd, *American Years*, 201–202.

[60]Cf. the 1912 poem, "Oborvanets" ("Ragamuffin"), by Gumilev: "I will set out along the resonant ties, / To think and to follow / In a yellow sky, in a scarlet sky / The unrestrained thread of the rails. // In the sorrowful halls of the stations / I will wander, shivering / Until they chase out the ragamuffin / With the cry of a guard. // And later with a stubborn dream / I will recall for the hundredth time / *The quick glance of a beautiful lady, / Settled in first class*" (Gumilev, *Izbrannoe*, 179).

FIGURE 2.7 *Honoré Daumier. "Mr. Prudhomme: Long live the third-class compartments ...," from "On the train," published in* Le Charivari, *August 30, 1864. Lithograph on newsprint. The Metropolitan Museum of Art.*

1917 < ... >. For a few minutes between two stops, in the vestibule of a rocking and rasping car, we stood next to each other, I in a state of intense embarrassment, of crushing regret" (*Speak, Memory*, 241).

Crisis moments for characters are often resolved in the intensified atmosphere of the railroad. The young Luzhin is thrown into confusion when he is told that he will only be addressed by his family name, i.e., his social status will be elevated through denial of his own name. Luzhin's solitary life begins at a *station*, where he resolves to flee. The suddenness of his flight contrasts starkly with the complete lack of motion on the platform: the automaton is *broken*; the girl *sits* on a bundle; on the other side of the rails is a yellow second-class car *without wheels*, growing into the earth

(*Russian Collected Works*, 2:312).[61] This is Luzhin's first independent act (his second, equal in importance, will be his suicide), and this initial moment of decision corresponds to his "transfer" to another class, thereby creating the necessary condition for his transformation from a sluggish adolescent into a chess genius.

Class, though, could be changed on the move, with someone temporarily taking on a higher social status for an additional fee. This kind of social aspiration was harder to achieve in reality, but in the realm of the train it was available as an exclusive luxury to anyone who could pay, or who would dare to cross over without. The opening pages of *King, Queen, Knave* contain a scene based on the organizing principles of the medieval mystery, setting in motion the spring mechanism of the puppet motif in the novel. Franz's path to the big life begins in a wooden compartment in third class. The author surrounds Franz with monstrous passengers (plush old women, an ugly freak, etc.), prompting an internal crisis that in turn pushes the character toward a symbolic break with the past. Tempted by a taboo thought, Franz crossed "the *unsteady connecting plates*, and < ... > passed into the next car"—to second class. And though "about first-class one could not dream at all—that was for diplomats,[62] generals, and almost unearthly actresses," even second class seems to Franz "something brightly attractive, even slightly *sinful*" (*King, Queen, Knave*, 5).

The declared topic of sin primes the reader to interpret the text in the appropriate register, that of scripture. The process of moving from car to car is described directly a few pages later, retrospectively, as Franz is basking in a sunny compartment:

The transition from the third-class compartment, where a noseless monster reigned < ... > *appeared to him like* the passage from a hideous hell through the purgatory of the corridors and intervestibular clatter into a little abode of bliss. < ... > *He transformed the conductor's click into that of a key unlocking the gates of paradise. So a grease-painted*

---

[61]Cf. the very beginning of Gazdanov's novel, *Polet* (*The Flight*) (1939): a move and a family drama in the life of the young protagonist are doubled by the appearance of most dynamic of possible toys, which his mother mistakenly presumes will soothe the effects of his psychological trauma: "The events of Seriozha's life began on that memorable evening when, for the first time in many months, saw in his room, on the bed where he slept, his mother .... [His mother] told him that he would not be living with her in France rather than with his father in London, and *that she would buy him an electric locomotive and a multitude of various types of cars*" (Gazdanov, *Sobranie sochinenii*, 1:275); for more on Nabokov and Gazdanov, see Leving, "Tainy literaturnykh adresatov".

[62]In the Russian original of the novel it is written: "diplomats wearing traveling caps," which may be an autobiographical detail; cf. the *Vogue* interview (1972): "Wearing gloves and traveling cap, my father sat reading a book in the compartment" (*Strong Opinions*, 203).

gaudy-faced actor in a miracle play passes across a long stage divided into three parts, from the jaws of the devil into pup devil the shelter of angels.
(ibid., 11)

The train is divided into three parts (classes), and if first class is "paradise," then third is "the underworld." In Bakhtin's carnival system the *third-class* car ("like the deck of a ship in an ancient Menippean satire") is a replacement for the square, where people of various origins meet in familiar interactions with each other (Bakhtin, *Problemy Poetiki*, 389). Vasily Ivanovich from the short story, "Cloud, Castle, Lake" (1937), is also brought against his own will into a public spectacle. With a group led by a representative from a pleasure traveling group, he journeys "in an empty car, unmistakably third-class" (*Stories*, 431). In this compartment, the traveling philistine and womanizer Kostia ("A Dashing Fellow") seems more natural. In third class, interactions between men and women are greatly simplified,[63] and its atmosphere of permissiveness permits coarse philandering, clearly demonstrated by Kostia.

Returning to the moment of parting between Ganin and Mary in the vestibule, we see that the intertextual foundation of the scene leaves an impression on the character's emotional state. Ganin's spiritual crisis is neutralized by the railroad journey, and the impending leveling of the social hierarchy in the car is introduced against the backdrop of "distances" and "sunsets"—symbols of epochal change and the destruction of old Russia. Left alone in a completely empty car, Ganin becomes immersed in thought and, "drafty, clattering darkness," observes through the doorway the "smoky sunset <which> amply and sonorously swept past the windows"[64] (*Mary*, 9; cf. the allusion to an entry in Blok's diary from June 16, 1917: "Outside the windows – trees and a *smoky sunset*," to which Nabokov refers in *Speak, Memory*[65] [241]). The collapse of tsarist Russian, coinciding with his own personal drama, evokes "curious thoughts" in Ganin. A hint from the author ("as though this had all happened at some time before"), and the general atmosphere of decay surrounding the character, force us to consider this in the context of Ganin's interest in European philosophy (he reads Nietzsche). Nabokov's talk entitled "On Generalities," delivered in 1926, contained hints at the eschatological predictions of Spengler, a follower of

---

[63]Cf. Tsvetaeva: "At everyone, at everything – an eye with indifference, / of which the end is the origin. / Oh, how natural into third class / From the stuffiness of the ladies' quarters!" ("Poezd zhizni" ["The Train of Life"], 1923; Tsvetaeva, *Stikhotvoreniia i poemy*, 369).

[64]Because of the two rows of windows, a train passenger is able to observe two parallel "ribbons of landscape" at the same time. The sunset would only be visible on one side, which Nabokov accounts for: "Outside the corridor's windows a narrow orange sunset smouldered beneath a black thunderhead. Presently the light went on in the compartment" (*King, Queen, Knave*, 17).

[65]Cf. "the dark smoke of burning peat was mingling with the smoldering wreck of a huge, amber sunset" (*Speak, Memory*, 241).

FIGURE 2.8 On Woman's Train, 1916. Photograph: Bain News Service. George
Grantham Bain Collection, Library of Congress.

Nietzsche who was popular among Russian émigrés ("Doklady Vladimira
Nabokova," 9). It is fitting that Ganin has *strange* thoughts on a train.[66]
In the second and final volume of his *The Decline of the West* (known in
Russian as *Zakat Evropy* ["The Sunset of Europe"]), published in 1922),
Spengler captured the spirit of his European contemporaries: "This is the
outward- and upward-straining life-feeling – true descendant, therefore, of
the Gothic – as expressed in Goethe's Faust monologue when the steam-
engine was yet young. The intoxicated soul wills to fly above space and
Time. An ineffable longing tempts him to indefinable horizons" (Spengler,
The Decline of the West, 504).

In Nabokov's prose of the 1930s appears a character by the name of
Uncle Henry—a passing figure, but not an insignificant one. Henry has
read so much Spengler (though the latter is not directly mentioned) that his

---

[66]Technology and nature, as the German philosopher has it, are in a continuous competitive
dialog, and the first decades of the century most clearly indicate the discord in "in the intellectual
intoxication of the inventions that crowd one upon another." The desire to become separate
from the land and dissolve into infinity led to "the fantastic traffic that crosses the continents
in a few days, that puts itself across oceans in floating cities, that bores through mountains,
rushes about in subterranean labyrinths, uses the steam-engine till its last possibilities have
been exhausted, and then passes on to the gas-engine, and finally raises itself above the roads
and railways and flies in the air" (Spengler, *The Decline of the West*, 503).

predictions have become his own fears:[67] "spoke with horror and revulsion about the *twilight of Europe*, about postwar fatigue, about our practical age, about *the invasion of inanimate machines*," and imagines a kind of "diabolical connection between the fox-trot and skyscrapers on one side and women's fashions and cocktails on the other" (*Glory*, 127). But there is a great distance between the Sirin who wrote *Mary* and the Sirin who wrote *Glory*. The bouts of nostalgia and symbolic sunsets[68] experienced by the Nietzschean Ganin, whose image was practically indistinguishable from the "I" of his creator in the 1920s, are reconfigured to a significant degree in the first half of the 1930s. Nabokov's changing attitudes toward the pathos of Henry and his contemporaries is seen in the position of his updated alter ego in *The Gift*. Godunov-Cherdyntsev shares nothing of the anxieties of Yasha Chernyshevski who, after reading Spengler, "for a whole week < ... > was in a daze" (*The Gift*, 42).

Despite the rigid hierarchical structure of the railroad, a number of incidents in railcars taking place between representatives of different classes in the 1910s point to a gradual reduction in the social gap. In *Ada*, the world of mixed-up times and countries, Van Veen fights a duel with Captain Tapper, whom, judging by a letter to his father, he "happened to step upon in the corridor of a train" (*Ada*, 308). Van also "glove-slapped" the passenger across the face, sending the captain "staggering back into his own luggage" (ibid., 295). The motif of appealing to his father is purposeful: the figure of the Russian captain originates perhaps with the real Russian captain on a train mentioned by Nabokov's father,[69] who is given a new fictional life in this American novel.

The "fume" of Spengler in Russian novels and the victim/aggressor captain are united in that they both originate in print sources: a work of philosophy and a newspaper publication, respectively. In a letter to the editor regarding the new novel, "The Prizmatic Bezel," Sebastian Knight resorts to a railroad metonymy, describing the editor's hint at some "dark secret" in the success of the writer X who "to travel[s] second-class with a third-class ticket"

---

[67]Similarly, Lebedev, a character in Dostoevsky's *The Idiot* (Part 2, chapter 11), states that "a new interpretation of the star called 'wormwood,' which fell upon the water-springs, as described in the Apocalypse < ... > meant the network of railroads spread over the face of Europe at the present time" (translated by Eva Martin).

[68]Cf. the 1913 poem by Komarovskii: "I look in the window of the dining car: / Through the feathers of hats and the gold of epaulettes / Burns a sunset. A wagon descends, / Sheep run in a classical crowd" (Komarovskii, *Stikhotovoreniia*, 66).

[69]To illustrate a judicial precedent in publicity materials, Vladimir Dmitrievich Nabokov chose an incident on a train: "In a railcar an argument took place between a student and a captain on political grounds; the argument ended with the captain hacking the student's head" (Nabokov, V. D., "Printsip zakonnosti," 46). As if following the plot design in his father's piece, Van Veen the "student" encounters the Captain riding "in a rather funerary-looking limousine" (*Ada*, 310).

(*The Real Life of Sebastian Knight*, 46). Clearly Nabokov believes that the
class of the "passenger" as an artist will serve as their ticket to one class or
another in the future history of literature. Alexander Dolinin, developing
this hypothesis, presents an excerpt from a letter to Mark Aldanov dated
January 29, 1938: "You say that *The Gift* is devised to have a long life. If
this is the case, how much more kind it is on my part to take the images of
some of my contemporaries on this journey for free, who otherwise would
have had to stay home" (Dolinin, "Plata za proezd," 15). The quote from
The Real Life of Sebastian Knight above supports the conclusions made by
Dolinin on the basis of Nabokov's statement, which is identical in its sense,
written in the same year he began work on the novel (December 1938).

The impetus for the creation of this image probably came from several
sources: for example a passage from the memoirs of G. Ivanov (see in the
introduction above), and the Il'f and Petrov essay, "The Tram of Literature,"
published in *Literaturnaia gazeta* in 1932 (and cited in Ilya Il'f and Evgenii
Petrov, *Sobranie sochineii v 5 tomakh*, 172–175), which was inspired by
them, and features a group of writers irritated by the passengers on a tram.

The Existential Nature of the Journey by Rail

In the first quarter of the twentieth century, Western modernism affixed onto
the railroad theme the topos of the life journey—the progress of a train
equated with the flow of life.[70] This idea was in circulation even earlier
among Russian poets, who adopted as a kind of calling card Voloshin's
poem "In the Railcar" (1901),[71] which cataloged the poet's impressions
from his long nomadic wanderings outside of Russia:

> Again the cars barely lit,
> Dull spots of shadow,
> The inclined faces
> Of people sleeping.
> Measured, eternal,
> Unending,
> Monotonous
> Sound of the wheels ...
> Like an eternal wandered
> On an endless road

---

[70]"Leaf / Falls / Train / Counts miles / Life / Melts" "Bol'naia osen'" ("Sick fall", 1911; Apolliner, *Esteticheskaia khirurgiia*, 92).
[71]See the introductory article by A. V. Lavrov in Voloshin, *Stikhotvoreniia i poemy*, 14.

Roaming for whole years,
Eternally I strive

(Voloshin, Stikhotvoreniia i poemy, 71–72)

The notion of eternal wandering was expressed in a concentrated form by Kafka in a short story entitled "Im Tunnel" (Kafka, *Sochineniia*, 1:260), aptly translated into Russian as "The Railway Passengers":

> If one looks at us as we are, earthbound, one will see passengers, their train crashed in a long railway tunnel, in a place where the light of the beginning cannot be seen, and the light of the end is so dim, that now and then the eye looks for it and loses it again, so that it is impossible to tell for sure if there is the beginning or the end.[72]

Life as a part of the path between the darkness before birth and that after death is defined in *Speak, Memory* using a familiar formulation: "The cradle rocks above an abyss." Interestingly, the preface to the Russian edition, removed from the later English version, suggests that the entire book is nothing other than the story of a passenger as told to a fellow traveler:

> "Allow me to introduce myself," my fellow traveler said to me without a smile. "My surname is N." The night of the road flew past imperceptibly. "So there it is, sir," he concluded with a sigh. Outside the window of the railcar an unpleasant day smoked, sad copses flashed, the sky shone white above some suburban town, and here or there the windows in the remote houses were either lit or not. ... There's the ring of the roadside bell.

(Other Shores; Russian Collected Works, 5:144)

The cradle/train parallel is equally applicable to the existence "on a kind of steel seesaw" of a waiter in a dining car on a German express train from Nabokov's 1924 short story, "A Matter of Chance," (*Stories*, 51). We see a similar existential *life-on-the-road* situation in this poem by Andrei Bely:

> As an eternal dream
> Space, time, of god
> And life, and life's goal
> A railroad,
> A cold bed.

("Telegrafist" ["Telegraph operator"], 1906–08;
Bely, Sochineniia, 1:95)

---

[72]The story is missing in most of the English-language editions of F. Kafka's short stories. Quoted here is Julga Heiligenbeil's translation.

The monotony of a journey leads to apathy and thoughts about the purposelessness of existence—themes expressed in Russian modernist poetry via the elegiac tone of Verlaine,[73] which were at the heart of programmatic poems by Apukhtin[74] and by Annenskii.[75] The metaphysical level of the journey in time goes back to literary travelogues (e.g., Pushkin's "Cart of Life" and Radishchev's *Journey from Moscow to St. Petersburg*)[76] and is enshrined in the poem, "On the Railroad" (1884) by A. M. Zhemchuzhnikov:

I ride, still I ride … I am lulled …
Scraps of views from both sides;
A crowd of thoughts without end or beginning;
Strange reveries, neither waking nor sleep …

It is hard to utter a word to my neighbor;
The laziness and languor of the anguish of travel …
Days and more days, I ride, still I ride …
The rumble of the car, the rings and the whistles …

I have no more thoughts. Numbed by movement,
I only look and wonder as from every place
And with every moment
Time moves forward and space retreats.[77]

                          (Zhemchuzhnikov, *Stikhotvoreniia*, 130)

---

[73]In Verlaine: "Qu'en dis-tu, voyageur, des pays et des gares? / Du moins as-tu cueilli l'ennui, puisqu'il est mûr, / Toi que voilà fumant de maussades cigares, / Noir, projetant une ombre absurde sur le mur?" (Verlaine, *Oeuvres poétiques completes*, 243); cf. in Gertrude Hall's translation: "What sayst thou, traveller, of all thou saw'st afar? / On every tree hangs boredom, ripening to its fall, / Didst gather it, thou smoking yon thy sad cigar, / Black, casting an incongruous shadow on the wall?" Compare this to the corresponding poems by Rozhdestvenskii, Lutskii, and Simonov: "The air was full of sparking flashes, / Days ran by – freight cars, / Days flew by" (*Serebriannyi vek*, 310); "Beloved ones, close ones … As a tight-knit family / We are going somewhere, to where we are fated, / And the miles as posts flash through the window. / Where is it heading, where is it flying?.. / How terrible to look at the empty spaces! / And mile after mile again races by … / And in memory fear and a dream of the past: / Will I be the last in an empty car?" ("Ia v poezde bystrom. V vagone so mnoi … , 1875–1976; Lutskii, *Sochineniia*, 159). "After traveling much through our land, / *We cherish the railcar, / On a path resembling life* / It extends infinitely" (Simonov, *Sobranie sochinenii*, 1:50).
[74]"As an express train, rushing God knows where, / *Life hurried by … without meaning or purpose*" ("With an express train," early 1870s; Apukhtin, *Stikhotvoreniia*, 198).
[75]"And from below a knock, and from the side a hum, / *And all with no purpose and no name*" ("Three-leaf railcar," 1908; Annenskii, *Stikhotvoreniia i tragedii*, 118).
[76]"You want to know: who am I? What am I? Where am I going?" (Radishchev, *Izbrannye filosofskie proizvedeniia*, 542).
[77]Cf. the late lyric poem by Zenkevich: "This day, like an arrow-train, flashed by / And left in my ears a fading hum … / Night approaches like a long tunnel, / Time – to take a rest and go to bed. / You paid the ticket cost in full / For a dear price – the exhaustion of all your strength" ("Odin den'" ["One Day"]; Zenkevich, *Skazochnaia era*, 320).

This same theme was addressed the popular works of Konstantin Fofanov, a practitioner of the "psychological lyric," in his 1887 poem, "Na poezde" ("On the train"):

> We rush like an arrow, all flies past us.
>   Vanishing without a trace before our eyes,
> But the train keeps aiming forward and knocking,
>   Rattling its iron armor.
>
> (Fofanov, *Stikhotvoreniia i poemy*, 76)

It is typical that Polonskii, while citing this poem in a review recommending that Fofanov be nominated for the Pushkin prize, nevertheless rejected its philosophically oriented epilogue.[78]

The unidirectional nature of the axis of time gives rise to a feeling of determinism (cf. Nina Berberova's short story, "Versts-Ties": "My roads have not been simple; they have for the most part been railroads. It was by rail that my young life rattled, and I shook with them. ... Those transport routes had their own minister – the Lord God"; "Versty-shpaly," 1930; Berberova, *Biiankurskie prazdniki*, 98). Erenburg's poem, "In the Railcar" (1915), establishes a sort of mutual connection: a train inevitably aims towards its final destination, and a human being hurtles towards the final station of existence: death:[79]

> In a compartment a gentleman rocked, nodded, rocking
> To the right and to the left, still a bit more.
> He rocked alone, rootless,
> He rocked from a life lived.
> Dear one, you're also on the road,
> Where should we go tomorrow?
> But I believe the cottony faces,
> The darkness, the bags, the bundles,
> And the dawn, quiet and smoky
> Amid the sun-baked huts,
> Below the white sky, in a race with no goal,

---

[78]The ending of the poem is as follows: "Thus life flies ahead, flies like a locomotive, / Changing dreams and impressions, / And pours, like sparks, the living spell of reveries, / And spreads out the smoke of diversions. // And all races forward, races tirelessly ... / And only the eternal phantom of doubt, / Like the pale moon behind a train, follows / Behind our rapidly flowing life" (Fofanov, *Stikhotvoreniia i poemy*, 77).

[79]Cf.: "The posts run and hum. / The steppe grass whispers: / *"No return, no return!"* (A. Bogdanov, "V puti" ("On the Road" [1909], cited from *Russkaia poeziia Serebrianogo veka*, 410). Also "The light and rustling of the whistle-stop / Will go on for five minutes, / But in the vast, mute expanses / Of night, lifetimes will run by" ("Posle iarkogo vokzala ..." ["After the bright station ..."], 1922; Marshak, *Stikhotvoreniia i poemy*, 177).

Shaking off and once again taking in
Sleep, half-sleep –
Everything languishes, wilts, and rambles
With a single end.[80]

(Erenburg, *Stikhotvoreniia*, 371)

At the same time, however, the train is equated with a means of not only postponing death, but even overcoming its inevitability. Nabokov uses the semantics of time in the railroad, approaching the station, or eternity,[81] at a designated time, to construct an atmosphere almost like something from a fairy-tale; in "Spring in Fialta" he directly refers to this as another world:

Doors were beginning to slam; she [Nina] quickly but piously kissed her friends, climbed into the vestibule, disappeared; and then I saw her through the glass settling herself in her compartment, having suddenly forgotten about us or *passed into another world,* and we all, our hands in our pockets, seemed to be spying upon an utterly unsuspecting life moving in that aquarium dimness.

(*Stories*, 418)

In other words, the train has its own rules of time and space, which are different from those of the mundane world (Nina's pious kiss occurs at the place where earthly power ends, at the junction between two dimensions).[82]

---

[80]Erenburg, *Stikhotvoreniia*, 371. Erenburg here includes an allusion to a poem by Apukhtin with the same title ("In the Railcar," 1858): "*God, where and why will I travel? / Is there simply some goal ahead?*" (Apukhtin, *Stikhotvoreniia*, 95). Years later, in 1948, Erenburg would return to this old motif: "*To live one's whole life in some train, / Deciphering the knocking of the wheels*" (Erenburg, *Stikhotvoreniia*, 586).

[81]Cf. Poplavskii: "A girl boarded a cardboard car, / The world shone to her in flags and years ... / The train stirred. From the balcony into eternity / A wasp flew in pursuit of it" (Poplavskii, *Sochineniia*, 321); the poem "V vagone" ("In the Railcar") by the émigré poet Markova: "The wheels knock. Rapid sparks / Fly out like meteors. / We catch the spark ghosts / With our pensive glances. // In the secure comfort of armchairs / We are fellow travelers on the road. / To greet us the universe / Bears impossible feats of daring. // Without stops; in the early morning we / Fly, metals rattling, / Hurtling into eternity with way stations, / And rails, and ties" (*Chetyrnadtsat'*, 90).

[82]As concerns "Spring in Fialta": "The world is a dual one; death shines through in every episode of life, turning it into an existentially wonderful enigmatic picture. For example, a person says goodbye to those seeing him off, enters the train car and, elegantly framed by the window of the compartment, appears from the platform as if he has moved into another world. Indeed the railroad is not merely a metaphor for the road of life (a somewhat tired metaphor), but is also a rich source of allusions" (Zholkovskii, *Inventsii*, 47).

The internal space of the railcar is also organized in its own unique way relative to the world outside:

> I happened to look out the window. What I saw *was not of my world* ... I saw cows.[83] This was in the quiet of the early evening. Some of them dug their faces into the aromatic green grass, nodding off. Others looked straight at me. I thought *"Why can't I pull the brake handle and burrow my head into the grass?"* I also saw trees. They were thick elms. In the shadows they cast, in the motionless foliage, in its blue hue, there was such calm that *I hastened to shield myself with newspapers, blue and spectral, like the smoke of the train.*
>
> (from the book *Vne peremiriia* (*Outside the Truce*), 1936; Erenburg, *Sobranie sochinenii*, 4:7)[84]

Erenburg's narrator complains about the vanishing possibility of experiencing the fleeting happiness associated with the static nature of the natural world outside the train car (in a variation: the narrator is beckoned by the image of a woman in the framing of nature: "on a bridge / an inside-out seaweed girl / seen randomly by the eye/of a wayward express train / was crying her ribs out" [Kruchenykh, "Lunatism vokzala," 1920; *Poeziia russkogo futurizma*, 233]). But this momentary impulse is blocked and redirected into a third fictional world created by the text of the newspaper (the first two being the train and the scene outside the window). This "emergency brake valve" makes it possible to disconnect the flow and mix the "realities."[85] Krug, the widower from *Bend Sinister* (1946), is distressed after the death of his wife:

> The emergency brake of time. < ... > In the course of our < ... > twelve and three months, years of life together, I ought to have immobilized by

---

[83]Another example of "defamiliarization" through slow-moving cows chewing grass looking at a train and its passengers is seen in the short story, "Detskii rai" ("Childhood Paradise"), by Nizen: "The little paradise was under the rail embankment, dark green and thick at the railway bed itself. ... On one edge there was a birch tree, enormous, leaning, and sad. ... Trains would come and go. ... The little animals did not watch [the people on the platform] because people were all the same and very noisy" (Nizen, *Sadok sudei*, 26).

[84]The naïve mind of the child and the problem of the idiot (in the original Greek meaning simply a private citizen or lay person) is captured by Sasha Chernyi in his 1926 poem, "V poezde" ("On the train"): "Outside the window under the summer sky / A forest and horses flashed by. / In the train car I met / A five-year-old little boy ... // 'What's that?' 'An oak and willows.' / 'What do they do?' 'They rustle and breathe.' / 'And what's that?' 'Those are the grain fields / The flimsy stalks sway.' 'Ah! And what's that?' 'Cows.' 'And why?' / 'So a boy can get up early, / And meet the new day, / Pouring cream from a glass.' // A hundred questions, a hundred answers ... / The wheels densely clicked. / From behind the translucent clouds / The sun suddenly shone sideways" (Chernyi, *Sobranie sochinenii*, 2:266–267).

[85]Cf. the directive from Gumilev: "And in the alley a fence of boards, / A house with three windows and a gray lawn ... / Stop, conductor, / Stop the car right now" ("Zabludivshiisai tramvai" ["The lost tram"], 1921; Gumilev, *Izbrannoe*, 144).

this simple method millions of moments; *paying perhaps terrific fines, but stopping the train. Say, why did you do it? the popeyed conductor might ask.* Because I liked the view. Because I wanted to stop those speeding trees and the path twisting between them. By stepping on its receding tail.

(*Bend Sinister*, 12–13)

This is the pragmatic system that guides the protagonist of "Cloud, Castle, Lake" in his aesthetic choices. Vasiliy Ivanovich is struck by "the anonymity of all the parts of a landscape," by the impossibility of ever finding out where that path leads or the tempting thicket, while he dreams to "*stop the train and go thither, forever*" (*Stories*, 432). In the final analysis, Vasiliy Ivanovich turns out to be the victim of his own initiative, but a number of other Nabokov characters display an enviable resolve in implementing their decisions. Nabokov greatly admired his uncle, Vasilii Ivanovich Rukavishnikov, who has the same name as the character, but is diametrically opposed to him in personality. "Uncle Ruka," disrupting the schedule and the movement of the train (and thereby breaking the predetermined order of thing), had the habit of arranging the emergency brake to be pulled on the approach to the station at Vyra:

He traveled with half-a-dozen enormous trunks, bribed the Nord-Express to make a special stop at our little country station < ... >

(*Speak, Memory*, 69)

Darwin, in *Glory*, also resorts to bribing a conductor. In a Pullman car halfway between Liverpool Street and Cambridge he pulls the conductor aside, hands him a banknote, and triumphantly tugs the brake lever.

The train groaned agonizingly and came to a stop, while Darwin smugly explained to everybody at large that he was born exactly twenty-four years ago. A day later, one of the livelier newspapers had a note about it conspicuously headlined: "YOUNG AUTHOR STOPS TRAIN ON BIRTHDAY."

(*Russian Collected Works*, 3:168/*Glory*, Ch. 23)

The yellow press sees in this event a scandalous act and a bold escapade. However, for Darwin (and Nabokov), such an act, with all its attributes of showmanship, makes no sense without a metaphysical support rod. The birthday is a moment requiring a pause for reflection, and the brake handle in this case confers the right to lodge a protest against the ideological and existential reality in which life is merely a race along a designated route.

The Killing Power of the Train and Engine

The paths traveled by a train and by a person's life to the final station are comparable, and it is no surprise that death is a component in the topos of the railroad. The intersecting theme of "the other world" accompanied the railroad from its first appearance ("The fateful works are ended. ... The dead are buried in the earth"; Nekrasov, "Zheleznaia doroga," *Polnoe sobranie stikhotvorenii v 3 tt*),[86] giving the train all the necessary features to function as a psychopomp.[87] The mass death of forced laborers during the construction of the railroad has become an integral part of the railroad myth in Russian literature and is inextricably entwined with it.

The fatal aura of the locomotive was strengthened by the notion that the railroad as a whole was an unnatural thing,[88] and specifically the idea of serious injuries on the tracks (colloquially called *kostolomki*, "bone-breakers"). In 1900, approximately 1,500 people died on Russian railroads due to accidents, and a third of these were rail service personnel. By 1905 this number had risen to 2,200, and by 1913 it was 3,531 or, in other words, 367 fatalities per thousand kilometers of Russian railroad track (Westwood, *A History of Russian Railways*, 133). We do not have precise data on how many of these deaths were suicides, but there is reason to suspect that the general tendency to an increase in suicides (the number doubled in Russian between 1803 and 1875) was related to the railroad,[89] something that had concomitantly been fixed by Tolstoy as an independent literary topos.

---

[86]In the same poem: "At this moment a deafening whistle / Yawped – a crowd of corpses vanished!"

[87]Cf. the train packed with corpses and hurrying to Elysium in Briusov: "The car sleeps, the gas flickers, / The train races, carries us away. / The distance of fields is endless, / The sorrowful moon above it. // From the south, from the south, to the land of snows / A train of corpses races. The moon looks at us through the window, / But the dead do not care!" ("Spit vagon, mertsaet gaz ...," 1896; Briusov, *Stikhotvoreniia i poemy*, 101).

[88]Vladimir Solov'ev wondered whether "the soulless engine and motionless life" would ever become one, i.e., would harmony between machines and nature ever be achieved. But for the time being: "With the phantom of breathing the irksome engine / Rushes and rumbles with dead thunders, / While the soul of nature with soundless caressing / In motionless splendor over us froze" ("Na poezde utrom" ["On a train in the morning"]; *Russkaia poeziia XX veka*, 6).

[89]Data from A. V. Likhachev (cited from Paperno, *Samoubiistvo*, 88). Specifically, Paperno points out that "suicide is directly connected with the development of civilization." In the early twentieth century, large amounts of literature on suicide were published mainly in two periods: between 1906 and 1914, and then again in the 1920s, and thus the young Nabokov, who was interested in this theme, may have read these works (ibid., 97; also Nesbet, "Suicide as Literary Fact").

The suicidal atmosphere of the railroad remained essentially un-changed in Russian literature from classical realism[90] to symbolism[91] and futurism,[92] but in the eyes of those contemplating suicide the initial exotic air of the railroad abated.[93] There were, of course, exceptions to the rule: the ritual taking of one's own life appeared simultaneously (in 1931) and independently in works by Shershenevich[94] and Poplavskii.[95] These texts describing railroad suicides follow in the footsteps of a well-developed literary tradition of "returning one's ticket" to the creator (cf. Dostoevsky's *The Brothers Karamazov*: "It's not God that I don't accept < ... > only I *most respectfully return Him the ticket*" [Dostoevsky, *The Brothers Karamazov*, 269], which is repeated in Tsvetaeva's "O slezy na glazakh!..." ["O tears in my eyes! ..., 1939] in response to the invasion of Czechoslovakia).[96] Foreseeing how his journey by rail would end, Vasiliy Ivanovich of "Cloud, Castle, Lake" (1937) also tries to "*sell his ticket*" (Pol'skaia, "Voskreshenie korolia Ofiokha"). The motif of the "ticket to the other world" had appeared before this as well in émigré publications, for example, the poem, "Tramvai № 2" ("Tram № 2") by Viacheslav Lebedev, a poet whom Nabokov as a critic found noteworthy.[97]

---

[90]An allusion to *Anna Karenina* is perceptible in Tsvetaeva's "Rel'sy" ("Rails"), 1923: "Deep / The horn like scissors / Cutting the railroad strips. / Spread out the useless dawn / You useless red spot! / Young women are sometimes tempted / Onto those railways" (Tsvetaeva, *Stikhotvoreniia i poemy*, 352).

[91]Blok refuses to specify the psychological motivation for the act: "By love, by mud, or by wheels / She is crushed – all is hurting" ("Na zheleznoi doroge" ["On the Railroad"], 1910; Blok, *Polnoe sobranie sochinenii*, 3:261).

[92]Cf. Maiakovskii: "I lie down / bright, in linen clothes / on a soft bed made of real muck, / and quiet, kissing the knees of rail ties, / the engine wheel will embrace my neck" ("Vladimir Maiakovskii," 1913; Maiakovskii, *Sobranie sochinenii*, 9:7).

[93]Cf. the 1930 poem "Poezd" ("Train") by Andrei Blokh: "In the darkness of night the brakes began to squeal, / Two lights opened up like eyes. / In the silent field the long train stopped / And rested after its long run. // In the mute cars a series of doors slammed. / By the windows the sleepy faces of people / Looked into the dark, half opening the curtains, / And the halls were filled with the wind ... // Suddenly a loud voice pronounced from the ties: / 'Some person was sleeping on the rails, / Whether he sought death or simply was drunk / He was crushed by the rolling train.' // In the cars the noise subsided. 'Suicide!' / The curtains were lowered, faces vanished, / The whistle rang out, and the light gave a nod, / And with a flinch the train began to pull" (*Sovremennyi zapiski*. 1930, Book XLII, 214–215). In a favorable review of Blokh's book *Stikhtvoreniia* in 1927, Nabokov singled out a particular line for praise: "On page 10 I find a wonderful image: 'trains, like rockets in the dark, raced on the bridge'" (*Russian Collected Works*, 2:649).

[94]"On the railroad tracks / Calling to the sound of an oncoming engine, / You lure the careless ones, / To put their head under the rattle of the wheels" (*Poety-imazhinisty*, 127).

[95]"From captivity along the rails / Following their iron sheen, / I will go out into an empty field, / I will find You finally ... / My dead heart, sick heart, I will give back to You forever" ("Polunochnoe svetilo" ["Midnight light"] Poplavskii, *Sochineniia*, 77). Cf. in Kuzmin: "We two souls – one creator, / We two creators – one crown ... / Why is the suitcase locked / And the ticket taken at the station?" ("Forel' razbivaet led" ["The trout breaks the ice"]; Kuzmin, *Sochineniia*, 286–287).

[96]"It's time, it's time, it's time / *To return my ticket to the creator*. / I refuse – to be. / In a Bedlam of unpeople / I refuse – to live" (Tsvetaeva, *Stikhotvoreniia i poemy*, 467).

[97]"And when the tram stops by the park, / After flying into the warm summer evening as into a tunnel, / The conductor hands back to the passengers for free / Their tickets for the road to paradise" (*Volia Rossii*. 1929. № 4, 30).

An *idée fixe* grows out of thoughts of death on the part of Aleksey Lvovich Luzhin in Nabokov's "A Matter of Chance," who regularly imagines "how he would arrange his death." One option is to "get off at night at a certain station, walk around the motionless car and place his head against the buffer's shieldlike end when another car, that was to be coupled on, approached the waiting one. The buffers would clash. Between their meeting ends would be his bowed head. It would burst like a soap bubble" (*Stories*, 56). For the cocaine addict, suicide seems like an escape from the burdensome duty of participating in the daily spectacle played out by reality. The place of the greatest danger from the standpoint of the physical world is, in a metaphysical realm, the border between worlds, where death is perceived otherwise and seems closer: "As he crossed the diaphragm on his way back into the diner, he thought: how simple it would be to die right now!" (ibid., 54). The unstable vestibule between cars draws in the unfortunate man, but in the end he settles his accounts with life in a more traditional manner: "A through train now thundered into the station. Luzhin went to the edge of the platform and hopped down. < ... > At that instant, the locomotive came at him in one hungry bound" (ibid., 59).

The inner conflict of a character may be resolved not by a jump *under* a train, but rather by a jump *from* a train at full throttle. This is the path chosen in the poem, "Nochnaia smert'" ("A death at night") by Nikolai Burliuk, published in the "First Journal of the Russian Futurists":

Out of indifferent leisure
Seized by a chilling whirlwind
I pass the slippery vestibule of the car
With a shaking foot,
And the tree branches passing by,
Raising up their snow-covered faces,
Crash down into the fields of anger,
Like the wings of a wounded bird.

(*Russkii futurizm*, 108)

Tsvetaeva describes a similar situation in first person:

Platform. And rail ties. And a final tuft
In my hand. I let it go. Too late
To hold on. Rail ties. Tired from
So many mouths. I look at the stars.

Through the rainbow of all planets
Lost – has anyone counted them?
I look and see one thing: the end.
It is not worth repenting.

("Poezd zhizni" ["The train of life"], 1923; Tsvetaeva, *Stikhotvoreniia i poemy*, 369–370)

The view of rails and trees on a mound lead Nabokov to the same associations. In his autobiography we read about "the distant meadows opening fanwise, the near trees sweeping up on invisible swings toward the track, a parallel rail line all *at once committing suicide* by anastomosis"[98] (*Speak, Memory*, 144). We can assume that he took the term (an anastomosis, in anatomy, is a junction between two vessels) from his own personal experience from the years between the first English version (1951), the Russian version (1954, which has the quite unobtrusive phrase, "parallel track merges with another") and the second American version of the book (1967). This is not the only example of Nabokov extracting a poetic effect from a specialized term taken from a different discipline: in February 1952 doctors diagnosed him with a "shadow behind the heart," which caused Nabokov to exclaim, "What a wonderful title for an old-fashioned novel!" (Boyd, *American Years*, 216).

Nabokov admired everything about the railroad, and paid close attention to its array of lexical terminology, striving to be as faithful to it as possible in his writing. In search of the right word in English to describe the connecting material between railcars, Nabokov turned to his Anglophone friends, Stevenson and Berkman, who unfortunately were of no help. Véra Nabokov's consultation of references on railroads at Harvard's Widener Library also met with no success. In *Speak, Memory*, Nabokov had to resort to a purely artistic resolution of the problem: there we see "auburn" cars "with their intervestibular connecting curtains as black as bat wings" (*Speak, Memory*, 144). Matters were no simpler with the Russian terminology: in *Other Shores* we read of "black interstitial accordions" (*Russian Collected Works*, 5:236). With a nod to a colleague at the New York Museum of Transportation, Schiff determined that the generally accepted term among specialists for this connecting component is "diaphragm" (Schiff, *Véra*, 135, 400n).

The Train Wreck

Armed with the destructive power and speed of steel machines, European literature of the late nineteenth century was charged with the energy of accident scenes. The first major catastrophe in the history of rail transport occurred in 1841 on the Paris–Versailles line and led to immediate panic

---

[98]Cf.: "Can one really not fall in love with the earth, / That comes out from under the wheels? / Even the willows, like suicides, / Threw themselves to the embankment from their mounds! // The willows did not thus branch out for long / Placing their flesh beneath the wheels. We will return, if we are living, / If the Lord leads us home" (Ivan Elagin, "Rodina! My videlis' tak malo …" ["Homeland! We have seen each other so little …"]; *Literaturnyi sbornik*, 13).

FIGURE 2.9 Train Accident. *United States, 1932. Photographer: Harris & Ewing. Prints and Photographs Division, Library of Congress.*

throughout Europe (Schivelbusch, *The Railway Journey*, 131).[99] In Russia, a significant accident took place on August 11, 1840 when, about 8 kilometers from St. Petersburg, an engine driver went down the wrong track and hit an oncoming train. Both engines were damaged, as were three cars making up each train. Six people died and seventy-eight sustained injuries with varying degrees of severity. Prince Viazemskii responded to the event by composing a poem,[100] and an article entitled "The Wreck of the Tsarskoe Selo Train"

---

[99]Diderot's *Encyclopedia* still defines the word "accident" as a grammatical and philosophical concept, almost a synonym of the word "coincidence." After the incident on the Paris–Versailles rail line, F. Turne's encyclopedia in 1844 devoted a nine-page article to the term "accident."

[100]"Russkie proselki" ("Russian byways"; 1841): "I saw the crash of two locomotives, of two volcanoes / On the fly: head to head they collided, / And they frighteningly grunted and shook – / And fatal was the press of these two hulks. / And there have I painted for you third circle of hell" (Viazemskii, *Stikhotvoreniia*, 274).

(Viazemskii, *Polnoe sobranie*, 2:276–281), lending an overtone of disaster to Russian railroad poetry for a hundred years to come.[101]

In *The Death of Ivan Ilyich*, Tolstoy used a railroad metonym in a clinical description of death:

> Suddenly some force struck him in the chest and side, making it still harder to breathe, and he fell through the hole and there at the bottom was a light. What had happened to him was like the sensation one sometimes experiences *in a railway carriage when one thinks one is going backwards while one is really going forwards and suddenly becomes aware of the real direction.*
>
> (Tolstoy, *The Death of Ivan Ilych*, 151)

Ivan Ilyich's personal drama is symptomatic of a larger spiritual crisis in society that is manifest in urban culture; railway accidents, in the opinion of Nabokov's opponent Georgii Ivanov, are the harbinger of the global collapse of civilization: "A point, an atom, through the soul of which fly millions of volts ... The ocean sinks ships. *Trains fly off onto the embankment.* Everything tears apart, creeps, melts, crumbles to dust – Paris, the street, time ... my love" ("Raspad atoma" ["Decay of the Atom"], 1938; Georgii Ivanov, *Sobranie sochinenii*, 2:25). Nabokov's loyalty to the arsenal of images involving death by railroad, characteristic of both his predecessors and contemporaries, is on display in *Glory* (among the tragic exits that come to the mind of the protagonist, including gunshot, hunting, and grave illness, is also "a railway accident"; *Glory*, 22), and before this in the uncharacteristically long poem, "The Accident" ("Krushenie"; 1925). The battle between two principles, the earthly (the circadian error of technology) and the exalted (divine providence) are presented in eleven lines as two possible reasons for the catastrophe. The structure of the poem is inverted: the synthesis precedes the thesis, the mechanical failure:

> Such a small thing – a flimsy screw,
> and suddenly right under the head
> racing iron, the holding rim
> jumps off the fateful rails.
> And also the antithesis, the will of malevolent angels:

---

[101]E.g. Andrei Bely in *Petersburg*: "The tracks of the railway rush onward! ... / Signals and switches! Embankment! / The soil all weakened by flooding, / The train crashing down from the ties. / The sight of the carriages broken! ... / The sight of unfortunate people!" (Bely, *Petersburg*, 200–201). Cf. also Kochetkov's "Ballad of the wrecked train," which circulated in manuscript copies in the 1930s after an accident involving a Sochi train in 1932 and became widely known due to the popular refrain: "Do not part with loved ones ...": "Shaking in a smoky railcar, / He half cried, half slept, / When the train on a slippery descent / Suddenly twisted with a terrible roll, / When the train on a slippery descent / Tore its wheels from the rails. // An inhuman force, / Maiming all in one press, / An inhuman force, / Threw the earthly from the earth" (*Russkaia poeziia – XX vek*, 273).

... there, howling at the bend,
a host of wheels was hurtling
and two angles pursued
the locomotive to its death.

And the first observed the steam,
laughing, shifted the handle,
shining with feathery fire,
and looked into the flying darkness.

The second, a winged stoker,
Flickered in steel scales,
And with a black shovel
He tirelessly swept the coals.

(*Russian Collected Works*, 1:567–568)

The poem breaks off after offering two possible versions of the wreck, but gives no hints at a resolution. Instead of the customary reduction of the two hypotheses to a common denominator, Nabokov causes a psychological "wreck" in the mind of the reader. The collapse of two approaches, the presence of two different possible explanations of the order of things in the text, is a characteristic doubling device used by Nabokov in his mature prose, and is present here already in his early writing.

The passengers themselves may think of a hypothetical accident as a means of interrupting a journey they did not desire in the first place, a way to delay or accelerate the pace of time. The narrator of "The Passenger" tells his companion of a nighttime journey in an express train sleeping car that brought him together with a strange fellow traveler. The narrator, who turns out to be an anonymous and, judging by his laments, none too successful author (cf. the confessional tale of the failed writer in Chekhov's "The First Class Passenger") suspects his traveling companion of murder, and interprets his crying as a sign of repentance. In this instance the alleged murder takes place outside the narrative, unlike, for example, in Zola's novel, *La Bête Humaine*, where a character named Roubaud is killed right in the railcar compartment. However, like his French predecessor (to prevent the unwanted meeting, Flore, in a fit of jealousy towards Séverine, decides to derail the entire train carrying the lovers), the writer in "The Passenger" understands that "only a railway crash could have cleft our involuntary link" (*Stories*, 185). The fact that the character in the top bunk crying and the one in the lower bunk listening were "sharing the same two-berth compartment, in the same unconcernedly rushing train," the narrator tells us, bound them together as they sped "sideways into night's remoteness at eighty kilometers an hour." In both cases the mind of the creator trumps the fantasies of the characters: Nabokov's weeping passenger turns out not to be a murderer at all, and Flore, the heroine of Zola's novel, after discovering that the accident she caused did not kill her rival, steps into a tunnel in the face of an oncoming train. The genealogy of Nabokov's story also reveals a reference to Pushkin: "and a far stretch of a free novel / I through a magic crystal / still did not make out clearly"; *Eugene Onegin*, 8: L, transl. by V. Nabokov), confirming once again that material for a literary patchwork can come not only from reality, but also from the classics of world literature.

Conductor to Immortality

The industrial trope of endless motion by rail freed modernist authors from the need felt by classical literature to present the life journey of a character to its final destination. If we look closely at texts with railroad themes, we find that sooner or later they develop the motif of the path into the unknown, into a metaphysical black hole. But since the meaning of life almost always remains unknowable, the journey takes on the features of endless movement. Nabokov, far from being an exception, followed this rule:

> And again the monstrous night flooded in,
> And I race, tiny and captive.
> The black road, without a goal, without an ...
> ("V poezde" ["In the Train"], 1921; *Russian Collected Works*, 1:466)

In an attempt to occupy the "black hole," authors invest the train with the features of Charon, making it the ferryman of the technological epoch. Reaching a passenger who is in motion, death opens up a retouched version of the funereal function of the train (a passing character in the short story, "Breaking the News," dies "alone, in a sleeping-car, of heart failure" [*Stories*, 392]). It must be emphasized that funereal, diabolical, or mystery play connotations can enter a text by indirect means, from the superficial resemblance of the locomotive furnace and to the furnace of hell, to more concealed associations, as in the following poem by Bely:

> Time to go home! The fast train
> Screams with its whistle in the fields;
> The windows bubble with light,
> And a momentary sheaf of sparks
> Through the tendrils of smoke
> Struck my forehead with its flashing.[102]
> ("Telegrafist" ["Telegraph operator"], 1906–08;
> Bely, *Sochineniia*, 1:95)

---

[102]See also Iu. Dzhanumov: "And again the cars dragged on, exhausted, / The firemen burned logs like a sacrifice" (*Antologiia poezii russkogo zarubezh'ia*, 1:205).

And also in Bulgakov's 1924 novel, *White Guard*, where the train is the focal point in which the power of hell breaks through the surface as fire:

> Hunched up from the cold and *lit by rapid shafts of light* from the windows, the switchmen watched as the long pullman cars rattled over the junction. Then everything vanished < ... > in the warm, *brilliantly lit* car was the monotonous click of the wheels,[103] Talberg went out into the corridor, opened one of the pale-colored blinds with their transparent letters 'S. – W.R.R.' and stared long into the darkness. *Occasional sparks, snow flickered past*, and in front the locomotive raced on and with a howl that was so sinister, so threatening that even Talberg was unpleasantly affected by it.
>
> (Bulgakov, *White Guard*, 30–31)[104]

The opposition of two types of space, open and closed (the former being overtly hostile and the latter enveloped and compact), as well as the semantic pairings of hot/cold and light/dark in the form of the moving capsule of the railcar, go back to Fet ("Frost and night above the snowy distance / But here it's cozy and warm"; "Na zheleznoi doroge," 1860; Fet, *Stikhotvoreniia i poemy*, 264) and Lev Tolstoy,[105] remaining essentially unchanged through the poetry of the first wave of emigration[106] and of the Soviet period.[107] It was Fet who in the waning

---

[103]Translated as "the monotonous click of the wheels," this same phrase in Bulgakov's Russian original actually refers to passengers' "monotonous muttering"; cf. *King, Queen, Knave*: Franz rides in a trembling train and the "rattle of the wheels has reminded him *dreadful muttering*" (*Russian Collected Works*, 2:303; the English version of Nabokov's novel omits this passage altogether).

[104]During the conversation the lieutenant smokes a cigar that acts as a physical bearer and a personification of fire: "At one o'clock in the morning an armored train like a gray toad pulled out from Track 5, through the dark graveyards of rows of idle, empty freight cars, snorting and picking up speed as it spat hot sparks from its ash-pit and hotted like a wild beast" (Bulgakov, *White Guard*, 30).

[105]From *Anna Karenina*: "then there was the snow, beating against the window on her left, to which it stuck, and the sight of the guard, who passed through the carriage closely wrapped up and covered with snow on one side; also the conversation about the awful snow-storm which was raging outside distracted her attention. And so it went on and on: the same jolting and knocking, the same beating of the snow on the window-pane, the same rapid changes from steaming heat to cold, and back again to heat, the gleam of the same faces through the semi-darkness, and the same voices" (Tolstoy, *Anna Karenina*, 91).

[106]"But the fire-breathing train laughed ... / Eve rapidly descends to the snow" (Poplavskii, *Sochineniia*, 308).

[107]Cf. Aseev: "Over the icy expanses, / Where the frigid star shines, / Fly fire-breathing trains / Like red-hot arrows" ("Poezda" ["Trains"], 1942; Aseev, *Stikhotvoreniia, poemy ...*, 102). Cf. also Sadof'iev: "We light the gloom with the blazing / Of electrical fires, / Along steel tracks we drive / Fire-breathing horses" ("Bratskii klich" ["Call of Brothers"], 1917–18; *Sovetskaia poeziia*, 1:125).

years of the nineteenth century wrote, from his own experience as a
train passenger:

> Through the thicket and ravines
> On a fiery snake we fly.
> It spreads golden sparks
> On the illuminated snows.
> And we dream of other places,
> We dream of other shores.
>
> ("Na zheleznoi doroge" ["On the Railroad"], 1860; Fet,
> *Stikhotvoreniia i poemy*, 265)

The syncretic feeling of curiosity, admiration, and fright created the necessary
foundation to prepare the Russian reader for both the steel colossus on
wheels and the accompanying complex of new railroad mythology.

The Mythology of the Train

The primary means of transport in Russian road mythology (the troika,
tarantass,[108] gypsy cart, and horse and carriage) lost their significance under
pressure from the cultural expansion of rapid transit as early as the nineteenth
century (a symbolic image is noted in passing in *The Gift*, in the chapter on
Chernyshevski: "an engine with a tall smokestack and a top-hatted driver
is overtaking a thoroughbred trotter" [*The Gift*, 200]). This change in
circumstances came not without difficulties as it turned archaic modes of
transportation first into a victim,[109] then into an object of nostalgia.[110]

Pushed out of everyday Russian life by the evolutionary process that led
to the train, the troika gave way to the unambiguously interpreted railroad,
which was identified with Western influence. As G. Piretto observed, at least
in its early existence the train won no admirers or sympathetic observers
whatsoever in Russian culture: "While the troika in and of itself caused no
complaints, the train, on the other hand, caused fear and concern with its
mechanized nature and its foreign origin. Progress and foreign influence
reign all around; the 'smug Teuton' rides on the 'German highway.' ... The
German rushes at full steam, the foreigner is coming" (Piretto, "Dorozhnye

---

[108]A four-wheeled horse-drawn vehicle on a long longitudinal frame for long-distance travel
used in Russia in the first half of the nineteenth century.

[109]In Kuprin's "Iama" ("The Pit"): "steam power killed horse carting" (Kuprin, *Sobranie
sochinenii*, 5:5).

[110]"And now, where are these troikas? / Where is their daring flight? / Where are you, lively
bellringer, / You, the poetry of carts?" ("Pamiati zhivopistsa Orolova" ["In Memory of the
Painter Orolov"], 1837; Viazemskii, *Stikhotvoreniia*, 258).

zhaloby," 92).[111] Naturally, the soulless machine from Europe caused an allergic reaction through to the turn of the century among the "back-to-the-soil" movement, whose gaze was directed at a time when in Russia "even tsars walked on foot."[112] Progressive literary critics were left to deal with the inertia of the masses, who wanted no improvements of any sort:[113]

But alas! Soon
The dead machine
Will draw in even the expanse
Of giant Russia.

Foreigners will scatter
Russian millions,
To place obstacles
To Russian will ...

Our train will not go
As the German one goes:
That one will derail
With youthful force;

It will tear through a hill,
Then pierce a bridge,
Then dashingly aim
At the oncoming train.
    (N. Dobroliubov, "V prusskom vagone" ["In the Prussian Railcar"];
    Leites et al., *Zheleznodorozhnyi transport*, 21–22)

The distance between a German and the devil was, as we know, not far. The theme sketched out by Fet is further developed in Viazemskii's "At Night on a Train between Prague and Vienna" (1853):

---

[111]H. G. Wells in turn noted that the evolution of means of transportation was characteristic of all Western Europe: "The nineteenth century, when it takes its place with the other centuries in the chronological charts of the future, will, if it needs a symbol, almost inevitably have as that symbol a steam engine running upon a railway" (Wells, *Anticipations of the Reaction*, 2).
[112]Cf. "Halfway on his journey Terkin remembered that he had bought a guidebook at the train station. He picked up the pamphlet and tried to immerse himself in the reading of it, to feel within him a Russian man pining in his soul for the old times, when people did not ride on railroads, and not only the 'dregs' – tsars walked on foot or rode solemnly and decorously to pay homage to the relics of the monk, the deliverer of Moscow in her time of calamity" (Borobrykin, *Sochineniia*, 265).
[113]As Pisarev scathingly noted, the masses in Russia "are held to their accustomed order by the force of inertia, not because of some commitment to it; try to change this order and they will immediately embrace the innovation ... *But today's masses ride along awful village roads and is content with them; in several years they will board a train and fall in love with the speed of motion and the comforts of the journey*" (Pisarev, "Bazarov," 240).

And I am swept along in the dark of night
By a serpent not a serpent and a horse not a horse,
A beast monstrously large,
And all steam, and all fire!

(Viazemskii, *Stikhotvoreniia*, 310)

From this point forward, even if any direct reference to the chthonic origins
of the machine is buried deep in the text, incidental signs can convey their
"terrible secret,"[114] as, for example, the spiral emanating from a locomotive
smokestack in a poem by a classmate of one Vladimir Ul'ianov (later known
as Lenin): "The train speeds … *serpentine smoke* / Fades in clouds behind"
(A. Korinfskii, "V vagone" ["In the railcar"], 1892; *Poety 1880–1890-kh
godov*, 425).

This fruitful field with its promise of abundant metaphors was assimilated
in the twentieth century by the symbolists and futurists, but here the myth
of the "journey to the other world" was interpreted as a "rebirth," a door
to "*zaum*'" (the "transrational language" of Khlebnikov), and a means of
attaining the world of one's true essence.[115] It was the avant-garde authors and
their immediate predecessors who revived the themes of the demonic and the
monstrous without which the mythology of the railroad is unimaginable in
recent Russian poetry and prose. In Annenskii the train is likened in an iconic
way to a "bursting dragon" ("Zimnii poezd" ["Winter train"], 1908; Annenskii,
Stikhotvoreniia i tragedii, 118), and in the same year in which Annenskii
published "The Cypress Chest," Khlebnikov's trains become "overgrown" with
scales and the train is transformed into a "snake-rocked palace":

So, winged snake! … It took the form and mien of underground creatures …
Successive instants bent the body of the monster,
Now braiding it in rings, now the body of a horse, standing up like a candle.
The immodest chains of the snake touched the ground …
And the jaws gaped, as if ready to meet a sword.[116]

("Zmei poezda" ["Snake Train"], 1910; Khlebnikov, *Tvoreniia*, 65–66)

---

[114]The malicious underground nature of the volcano metaphor is layered in Pasternak onto
the Christian symbolism of the crucifixion, intertwining with the martyrdom mythology of the
Pompeians and lumpen-proletarians (speaking of the Lodz insurrection in June 1905): "Locomotive
Vesuvius near Lodz. / Nails driven into the air. / Sections of track were baked" ("Muzhiki i
fabrichnye" ["Muzhiks and factory workers"], 1926; Pasternak, *Sobranie sochinenii*, 1:291).

[115]Faryno (*Vvedenie*, 357) writes that the mythological meanings become apparent if we look
more closely at what happens in the work after such a *transition*, after the "stations," "stops,"
and "overnight halts": the trains of Khlebnikov (in "The Tree": And trains rush with the sun
/ To underground dwellings') and Pasternak, "carrying the sun under the ground, repeat the
myth of the sun dying for the night and sailing that same night to the east to be reborn."

[116]When the hallucination begins to wane, the poet's attention is once again focused on the
mundane: "We looked at once and soon / At the sleepers next to us. / Everywhere snoring and
the boredom of conversations." The poem ends with the narrator throwing himself out of the
train at the "fairytale stop."

Khlebnikov's train, a typical representative of the chthonic world with all the corresponding folkloric associations (St. George and his dragon), is later echoed in their younger contemporaries.[117]

The process of assimilating a new cultural formation was accompanied by linguistic inventions (as in those of Sergei Bobrov,[118] the main ideological force behind the "Centrifuge" group), or by a recoding of the myth with a revolutionary flavor, as Briusov noted with satisfaction.[119] By the 1920s the railroad had become a stable archetype, and thus Nabokov's trains originate less in their folkloric ancestry than in the poetic tradition developed by his recent predecessors.[120] Endowed with anti-combustion properties, Nabokov's train is a natural ally of the element of fire:

the train, it seemed, was running up a slope
of steep fiery clouds and along them

---

[117]"And, jumping resoundingly, the car / Plunged buffers into another, / And the jaws of the locomotive / Breathed fire into the fingerless ties" (G. Shengeli, "V peschanykh stepiakh ledianykh ...," ["In the sandy steppes of ice ...," 1925–26]; Shengeli, Inokhodets, 140). "Measured is the hum of the winged wheels, / Resounding the guard whistle / On the gentle slopes pours / Smoke in a wavy plume ... / Full of faith and hope / Rushes the fiery colossus" (I. I. Ionov, "Krasnyi lokomotiv" ["Red Locomotive"], 1919; Proletarskie poety, 386). See also the prose of the émigré writer, A. Eisner: "And five minutes after the black dragon with its fluttering fiery plume whistled and rushed out of the train station and into the night, Elsa, pale and with her eyes opened wide, took me by the hands. 'Darling, we missed the train'" (Roman s Evropoi [Romance with Europe], Volia Rossii. 1929. № 4, 15).

[118]"O, easy rushingness! O rapid flyingness! / Like – the hum of wheels, knock, cry lay down ... / Rushinger, lefter, dearer, livelier, more tender / Than a living snake with a copper voice: – / Wheezing of stars, haranguing of pillars, / And – evenly, wondrously – seemingly, stormily, / And – wearyingly, eatingly, – meagerly, to the blast furnace: Along the bridge flighting – / Graphites ... blackearths ... shales ... / Station. 10 minutes" ("Kislovodskii kur'erskii" ["Kislovodsk Express"], 1915; Poeziia russkogo futurizma, 460).

[119]See A. P. Kraiskii's poem, "Bez ostanovok" ["Without stops"] (1918): "Cutting the black darkness with its blazing breast, / With a rattle, / A whistle, / A hiss / disturbing the silence of the cold fields ... / Behind the weighty tender, like links in a chain, the cars were linked, / Like a flashing snake of shining windows they frighten the cold night" (Proletarskie poety, 402–403). In his essay, "Navstrechu griadushchemu" ["Meeting the Future"], Briusov noted that "Kraiskii achieved a particular expressiveness in depicting the life of machines" (Pechat' i revoliutsiia. 1922. № 7, 65).

[120]See Sviatopolk-Mirskii's poem, "Tvoi golos tikh, litso besstrastno ... " ["Your voice is quiet, your face impassive ... "]: "Spewing pillars of fire and smoke, / The lazy engine crawls into the distance ... / And the black, broken clouds, / Like snakes, like dragons in the heavens, / Arise, silent and powerful, / And creep along, erasing the dust of stars" (Sviatopolk-Mirskii, Stikhotvoreniia).

descending smoothly, soaring again
into crimson fire from golden fire.
> ("Kak chasto, kak chasto ia v poezde skorom ..." ["How often, how
> often in a fast train I ..."], 1923; *Russian Collected Works*, 1:467)

In Nabokov's early comic story "The Dragon" (1924)—about a prehistoric
beast awakening—we see the original mythology of the train (the structure
of the machine resembles the physiology of a monstrous fossil). Some of the
scenes are described as if through the eyes of the dragon: the tunnel is called
a "lair" ("*nora*" in Russian), and the train moving in the opposite direction
is seen as the one that disappeared inside shortly before:

> The first thing he saw upon descending into the valley was a railroad
> train traveling along rocky slopes. The dragon's first reaction was delight,
> since he *mistook the train for a relative* he could play with. Moreover, he
> thought that *beneath that shiny, hard-looking shell there must surely be
> some tender meat.* So he set off in pursuit, his feet slapping with a hollow,
> damp noise, but, just as he was about to gobble up the last car, the train
> sped into a tunnel. The dragon stopped, thrust his head into the black lair
> into which his quarry had vanished, but there was no way he could get
> in there. He dispatched a couple of torrid sneezes into the depths, then
> retracted his head, sat on his haunches, and began waiting—who knows,
> it might come running out again. After waiting some time he shook his
> head and moved on. *At that instant a train did come scurrying out of
> the dark lair, gave a sly flash of window glass, and disappeared behind a
> curve.* The dragon gave a hurt look over his shoulder and, raising his tail
> like a plume, resumed his journey.
>
> (*Stories*, 126)

In the end, however, Nabokov is more attracted to a mythos that is
indistinct and veiled. The promethean pyrotechnics of sparks from the
furnace breed fire outside the compartment, and within they create a
shadow play that "was hard to correlate those halting approaches, that
hooded stealth, with *the headlong rush of the outside night*, which I knew
was rushing by, spark-streaked, illegible" (*Speak, Memory*, 145).[121] In the

---

[121]In *Speak, Memory*: "in the semidarkness of our compartment, I watched *things, and parts of
things, and shadows, and sections of shadows cautiously moving about and getting nowhere.
< ... > Near the door that led to the toilet, a dim garment on a peg < ... > swung rhythmically*"
(*Speak, Memory*, 145). Cf. the opening of Kuprin's 1894 short story, "Na raz"ezde" ("At the
Junction"): "Nets with suitcases, bundles, and hats piled on them, the shapes of passengers who
were either sleeping or shaking evenly and blankly, sitting in their seats, *the stove, the arms of
sofas, the pleats of hanging clothes – all of this was drowned in the long shadows and somehow
strangely and awkwardly mixed up*" (Kuprin, *Sobranie sochinenii*, 1:219).

first half of the 1970s, the era of jet planes and ballistic missiles, Nabokov expressed a fair bit of nostalgia when speaking with interviewer Simona Morini: "Gone the panache of steam, gone the thunder and blaze, gone the romance of the railroad. The popular *train rouge* is merely a souped-up tram. As to the European sleeping-cars, they are drab and vulgar now" (*Strong Opinions*, 203).

The Esoteric Language of Trains

The creation of myths (which "the thunder and blaze," in fact are) is linked from the very start with mystery, and thus signs of esotery are an essential condition for maintaining literary potential, and the railroad is no exception. Even in Nabokov's early works there is a special mysterious language reserved for trains. The rumble of the wheels is, for the careful listener, turned into the "transrational" noise of poetry: "and *the wheels sang liturgy* beneath me, / and I went to sleep on the narrow bench" ("In the Train," 1921). The rhythm of poetic communication governs the movement ("I dreamed of dacha stations, laughter, spring ... and the night was suffocating, / and *the railroad iambs slowed*") and vice versa: the knocking of the wheels governs the poetic meter as well.[122] Soon after this in the 1925 poem, "The Wreck," a description of a compartment at night includes the following familiar trope:

> There sleep, arriving early,
> will lower the leather curtain;
> and keenly in the knocking and crunching
> will seek out the proper tune
>
> (*Russian Collected Works*, 1:567)

As the author stipulates elsewhere, however: "the knocking of train wheels at night is known to encourage aural hallucinations" ("The Passenger"; *Stories*, 184–185).[123] A bit later, poetic meter returns to the representation of motion: the protagonist of *King, Queen, Knave* rides to work every morning on an underground train "to the rhythm of its crude trochee" (*King, Queen,*

---

[122]See also the poem, "V poezde" ("In the train") by Zhozefina Pasternak: "The train stumbles and stops / At the caesurae of stations" (from the collection *Koordinaty* (*Coordinates*), published in Berlin in 1938 under the pseudonym, Anna Nei (Zh. Pasternak, *Koordinaty*, 27).
[123]"The steppes flew and the wind blew, / And space collided / And the locomotive at full steam / Started a conversation with the rails" (S. Kirsanov, "Spor" ["Argument"]; *Zheleznodorozhnik*. 1926. № 3, 56).

Knave, 201; cf. the "rhythmic rumble of the railcars" [Kuprin, *Sobranie sochinenii*, 1:220]). Well before this in 1901 Voloshin offered his own meter for conveying the rhythmic knocking of the wheels:

Thoughts interweave with the weeping of the wind,
Merge with the monotonous noise of the wheels,
And it hopelessly sounds and knocks:
Tí-ta-ta ... ta-tá-ta ... ta-tá-ta ... ta-tá-ta
                    ("In the Railcar"; Voloshin, *Stikhotvoreniia i poemy*, 72)

Five years later, Verkhovskii, with his laconic style and his imperfect rhymes that seem to fall on the wrong juncture, provides a much more effective broken line:

The railcar sleeps.
The wind howls.
I am alone.
Petersburg is near.

FIGURE 2.10 *Fixing the locomotive. 1930s. National Photo Company Collection, Library of Congress.*

Fog again.
Visions again.
I wait betrayals.
I wait for a meeting.

("Struny" ["Strings"]. *Vesy*. 1906. № 12, 14)

There were also attempts to take the soundtrack of imagined railroad language and extract individual meaningful lines appropriate to the lyrical,[124] ideological,[125] or general artistic position of the writer.[126] The importance of semantics could be reduced (sounds begin to resemble a little-understood foreign language),[127] and the meaning is muffled and secondary, yielding pride of place to a musical picture. In the 1914 poem "Zheleznodorozhnye posvistyvaniia" ("Train Whistles"), David Burliuk includes a graphic portion in which the onomatopoetic "r"[128] sound is dominant, and an obscure émigré poet does the same with the Russian letters ч, щ, and x (representing the sounds *ch*, *shch*, and *kh*).[129]

---

[124]In the interpretation of the text subject in a 1923 poem by A. A. Makarov: "The panel like the gray eyes of my beloved; / On the windows the blue of her hair; / The measured rattling of the wheels / Pronounces her name to me ... / I chase to the platform in a heap of smoke, / The engine lights stare" (*Proletarskie poety*, 433).

[125]"And Gek dreamed a strange dream; / As if the whole car had come alive, / As if voices were heard / From wheel to wheel. / The cars race – a long row – / And with the locomotive converse. / (Former) Forward, comrade! The way lies long / Before you in the darkness. / (Latter) Burn brighter, lights, / To the morning dawn itself!" ("Chuk i Gek"; Gaidar, *Sobranie sochinenii*, 3:41).

[126]"Mail train number something or other rushes at full steam from 'Happy Trakh-Tararakh' station to 'Every man for himself!' station. The locomotive whistles, hisses, snorts, and sniffs. ... The cars shake and their *ungreased wheels howl like wolves and screech like owls*. In the sky, on the earth, and in the cars there is darkness. ... '*Something will happen! Something will happen!*' bang out the cars, shaking from old age ... '*Ohoho-hoho-ooo!*' sings the locomotive in response" (Chekhov, "In the Train Car"; *Polnoe sobranie sochinenii i pisem*, 1:115).

[127]"The locomotive drives the wheels, / Flies by like a missile ... / *All that is heard is the cars / Speaking in Japanese*" ("Poezd" ["The Train"]; Utkin, *Izbrannye stikhi*, 90).

[128]"PlatfoRm – a gaRden of flashing lights / Autumn rain scRatches like a broom / The face of a wall of crowding people / [to] Come close to the Road lectern" (Emphasis in the original. *Poeziia russkogo futurizma*, 119).

[129]From the poem, "Dachnye paravozy" ("Dacha locomotives") by B. A. Nartsissov, a member of the circle of Russian poets in Tartu, who later lived in Germany and then the United States: "The train railifies, gnashing: "ZHE, CHE, SHA, SHCHA!" // With a spike, and steam, and bitter smoke, / And a whistle begins this little story: / There by the dacha station of a dry evening / Crept up the two-eyed engine in the darkness. // The tired, warm dacha dwellers climbed out, / Enjoying the coolness, they hurried home, / Like locomotives, the tobacco smokers / Puffed cigarettes in the chill of the night. // And then at noon an express appeared at the crossing, / It rumbled and squealed on its taut brakes, / And its whistle was loud and beastly, / And then it complained: 'zachakh-chakh-chakh-chakh!' // The refreshment bar smelled tasty and fried, / While the lady passengers wafted a rosy scent. / And from the long run, the hot, steamed out / Locomotive suffered in the heat by the platform" (*Antologiia poezii russkogo zarubezh'ia*, 3:167).

It was not only on the level of phonetics that the era of railroads was infused with mysticism. The mystery takes on visible, sometimes palpable, forms when the word is written down: "The lengthy cars painted / Like oak. On the matte wood panel / Above the windows, a *row of pale gold/French words – like a carved out line of verse,* / teasing my anguish with a mysterious call" ("Ekspress" ["The Express"], 1923; *Russian Collected Works*, 1:466). The void where the poetic harmony collapses is filled with incomprehensibility and nonsense, the "language of freight trains," and the malicious connotations associated with trains are reinforced.[130] While in a bookstore contemplating the absurd acronyms in Soviet newspapers, Godunov-Cherdyntsev admits that their terrible connections remind him of "the lettering on freight cars (the banging of their buffers, the clanking, the hunchbacked greaser with a lantern, the piercing melancholy of godforsaken stations, the shudder of Russian rails, infinitely long-distance trains)" (*The Gift*, 158). The figure of the "greaser with a lantern" is symbolically significant. It originates in the railroad scene in *Anna Karenina*, where the fateful stoker appears, a "lean man in a long overcoat," at the same time as "red light blinded the eyes."[131] The black-bearded man also enters into the nightmares of the chess master Luzhin, who, we are told, read Tolstoy's novel;[132] and he crops up in a poem by Annenskii:

These shadows, these
Signs of the locomotive

---

[130]Cf. from Chekhov's "Everyday Adversities": "Up above the ceiling some energetic man, probably a student at the conservatory, was rehearsing a Liszt rhapsody on the piano with such zeal that it seemed as if a *freight train* were passing by on the roof" (Chekhov, *Polnoe sobranie sochinenii i pisem*, 5:144).

[131]See Nabokov's commentary on this motif (*Lectures on Russian Literature*, 233) which has been the subject of dedicated works by contemporary scholars, who note specifically that "the motif of iron in [Tolstoy's] novel serves as a connecting link between two symbolic images: the peasant man (*muzhik*) and the railroad. The latter is a synonym for progress and European civilization beckoning Russian down a path that was, in Tolstoy's opinion, the false one. The blacksmith/muzhik and the 'iron road' [as the railroad is called in Russian] both appear against the background of the ominous image of the *ferreae saeculae* – the 'iron' 19th century" (Sato & Sorokina, "'Malen'kii muzhik …'").

[132]John Burt Foster writes about the intertextual nature of this motif: "[T]his incidental character recalls Anna Karenina's portentous visions of a similar peasant also associated with train travel, whom Nabokov would analyze with loving detail in his lectures on Tolstoy" (Foster, *Nabokov's Art of Memory*, 63). We may also note that this figure bears a facial and typological resemblance to the black-bearded Pugachev in Pushkin's *The Captain's Daughter*. The *muzhik's* beard as a memorable detail from a nightmare has been remarked on a number of times; see, for example, in Tsvetaeva: "even Grinev's declaration of love with Masha *did not for a second replace for me that black beard and black eyes*" (Tsvetaeva, *Sochineniia*, 2:370).

And, made silver
By the pearly moon,
This long, black
Station guard
With an unneeded lantern[133]
On a patterned shadow.

> ("Lunnaia noch' v iskhode zimy" ["Moonlit night at the end of winter"], 1906; Annenskii, *Stikhotvoreniia i tragedii*, 94–95)

The short story "Time and Ebb" speaks to the special nature of the railroad topos in Nabokov: the elderly narrator, who worshiped passenger trains as a child, now tries to recreate in his memory the plum color of the cars, dulled from the mixing of shades from "conquered miles" and the coal dust from workshops and barracks preceding "a city as inevitably as a rule of grammar and a blot precede the acquisition of conventional knowledge" (*Stories*, 584). Like any language with its grammatical code, the network of railroad tracks and lines modifies its lexicon of behavior and the range of accepted deviations from the rules.

In conclusion, the train in a novel is not so much a means of conveyance for the characters, as much as it is a means for transporting references based on the rules of stylistics, grammar, and the game of literature.

Train. Love. Fate

Comparisons between the fates and the switchman and between a parting couple and two trains diverging along different tracks, which may now seem trite, were at one point considered daring metaphors.[134] This theme is played upon in the comic poem, "V al'bom" ("In an album," 1881), read by Nadson at the Tenishev School:[135]

---

[133]From *Anna Karenina*: "She came to her senses for a moment, and knew that the lean *muzhik* in the long nankin coat with a button missing who had come into the compartment was the carriage stoker. < ... > The *muzhik* in the long coat started gnawing at something on the wall < ... > then a blinding red light appeared, and at last everything was hidden by a wall. Anna felt as if she had fallen through the floor" (Tolstoy, *Anna Karenina*, 93).

[134]In the film language of the avant-garde age, an artist expressed this drama using city trams: in Vertov's film, *Man with a Movie Camera* (1929), shots of two trams diverging in different directions are interspersed to emphasize a scene of parting. This is perhaps an urbanized version of the old Russian cliché about parting like two ships in the sea.

[135]See the chapter, "The Tenishev School" (from Mandel'shtam's *The Noise of Time*; Mandel'shtam, *Sobranie sochinenii*, 2:25), and also Nabokov's letter to S. I. Rozov ("Palestinskoe pis'mo Vladimira Nabokova 1937 goda").

FIGURE 2.11 *Two women bathers standing by bushes along a river as a train passes over a bridge spanning the river in Edward Hopper's illustration,* Train and bathers *(1920). Etching. Prints and Photographs Division, Library of Congress.*

> Like two trains (though I hesitate
> To compare you with a locomotive)
> At Liuban' station we came together
> By a happy accident, only to part again.
> And soon I will dart away with helpless anguish,
> I will rush away at full steam.
>
> (Nadson, *Polnoe sobranie stikhotvorenii*, 153)

But, the author promises, "running off into the distance and full of bitter poison," he will never forget the station where "next to me / *A second locomotive puffed in sympathy*." Nadson's metaphor was further developed in an 1894 short story by Kuprin.[136]

---

[136]"*fate sometimes makes fun intentionally.* Example: *two trains stop. They met and they will part ways,* and through the windows two people look at each other and see each other off with their eyes until they are out of sight. And maybe ... these two people ... could have given each other such happiness ... such happiness" ("Na raz"ezde" ["At the Junction"]; Kuprin, *Sobranie sochinenii*, 1:228).

As accommodations were made for the new means of transportation and new everyday reality,[137] its image was used more and more frequently in literature. A quarter century later, the switchman as an instrument of fate would occupy a stable niche in the pantheon of artistic imagery. It gradually crossed over into the realm of comic[138] and so-called "women's" literature,[139] sometimes returning, boomerang-like, its demonic influence from "serious" literature to the interpretation of the switchman in everyday life.[140]

As an instrument of a higher power, the train is a place where meetings (or non-meetings) programmed by the author take place, and yet the passenger is more often than not left unaware of anything having to do with the authorial intention behind his or her fate. In Sebastian Knight's story, "The Back of the Moon," the protagonist, waiting for a train, "helped three miserable travellers in three different ways" (*The Real Life of Sebastian Knight*, 86), but which matters he assists in remains unknown not only to the reader of Nabokov's novel, but also probably to the readers of Knight's

---

[137]From 1866 to 1900, the total length of rail lines in Russia increased from 5,000 km to 53,200 km (Westwood, *A History of Russian Railways*, 59).

[138]In a short story by Sasha Chernyi, a high-school student averts a brewing romantic scandal because "like an experienced switchman, in the very face of a train hurtling towards the wrong track at full steam, he coolly turned the switch" ("Fizika Kraevicha" ["Physics of Kraevich"], 1928; Chernyi, *Sobranie sochinenii*, 4:267).

[139]A writer thus described the reaction of a character whose beloved refuses to marry him: "I was left standing there, stunned, as if my train had stopped at full speed and I had fallen from the top bunk onto my roommate, and then a suitcase had fallen onto us both" (Berberova, *Biiankurskie prazdniki*, 87). Cf. the portrayal of Vaginov's hapless heroine, who trusts in fate: "At the end of the train, alone in a car, sat Ekaterina Ivanovna tearing apart a daisy: he loves me, he loves me not. But who it was that loved or did not, she did not know. Yet she felt that she should be loved and cared for" ("Kozlinaia pesn'"; Vaginov, *Kozlinaia pesn'*, 69). See also the reaction of the lyric persona to a refusal from her beloved: "The platforms became darker and duller; / Your train passed the stations. / I sighed in the captivity of my pillows, / I began to read, at first / By heart, disconnected lines / From letters I had not received ... / And love died hard – / It fought a long time and hurt its wings. / Your train, on the oblivious tracks, / Was lost in the mute fog" (T. Ratgauz, "Veter dolgo metalsia v pole ..." ["The wind swept long in the field ..."], 1934; *Antologiia poezii russkogo zarubezh'ia*, 3:350–351).

[140]A newspaper dramatized the consequences of negligence on the part of a switchman as follows: "Express freight train № 21 suffered a crash 100 versts from Petersburg. As the train approached a switch at almost full speed, the engineer noticed that the entrance switch was pointed in the direction of a track occupied by the oncoming military freight train № 94. There was no switch operator. The engineer in № 21 pulled the brakes and sounded the alarm whistle. The maidservant on the train rushed to the brakes, but at this point it was impossible to stop the train with the handbrakes. Just as the locomotive was passing over the switch, the switchman suddenly appeared, mechanically grabbed the lever, and turned the switch to the other track in an instant. *A deafening clatter and rumble was heard.* ... The switch had been moved between the locomotive and the tender. ... *Ten loaded cars were turned into splinters, and the tracks were bent for 350 feet.* ... The engineer, his assistant, and the chief conductor were injured from the collision. The remaining *conductors escaped with minor injuries and a good deal of fear*" ([B. p.] "Krushenie poezda" ["Train wreck"]. *Rech'*. June 11 (24), 1911. № 157, 4).

story. For his part, Godunov-Cherdyntsev scrolls back through his life like a film, searching for parallels, and comes to the conclusion that perhaps "a woman, for instance, whom one loves since yesterday, appears as a young girl, standing practically next to one in a crowded train" (*The Gift*, 45).[141] The accidental meeting in a train between a pair of lovers and the writer Zegel'krants[142] might have remained one of these unknown "parallels" if not for the fact that it took place in a novel written by an author. The train is a frame in which the dramatis personae are placed. Albinus (Krechmar) recognizes Margot and Axel (Magda and Robert) in the portrait of the pair in the same train compartment: an innocent artistic device leads to tragedy in the end but, as we know from all of world literature, love and death are inextricably connected in the topos of the railroad.[143]

The train has been given various functions in literature, and some of them are diametric opposites. To experience the magical effects of the railroad mythos, one need not be located within a railcar; it is enough to be merely within its gravitational field. We will look at the railroad's function as an instrument of separation. Railroad tracks work as a temporary, physically insuperable barrier for those on either side of a passing train (cf. the cinematographic cliché of using this as a barrier in a chase scene to create a spatial break between the pursuer and the pursued).

The railroad tracks both bring together and separate, dividing space with a movable wall. Aleksandr Blok plays on this in his 1909 poem, "Evening by bright tracks …":

An instant … with monotonous thunder
The black train divided us …
When with a scarcely shaking ring
The rails sang: don't forget,
And the semaphore with a green light
Showed me the free tracks
You were already leaving far away
                    (Blok, *Polnoe sobranie sochinenii v 8 tt.*, 3:180)

---

[141]A similar (perhaps apocryphal) event was related by Nabokov himself. He stated that several times in the early 1920s he had ridden on a Berlin tram with a particular person who had a memorable and hypnotic gaze; Nabokov later saw the same person in photographs and recognized him as Kafka. Boyd, however, believes that Nabokov's story is an anachronism (see Boyd, *American Years*, 202).

[142]The train meeting actually happens only in the Russian original, *Camera Obscura* (*Russian Collected Works*, 3:348)—in the revamped English version it takes place on a bus. The writer also gets to be rechristened in *Laughter in the Dark* assuming the name of Udo Conrad.

[143]As one scholar wrote about Zola's *La Bête humaine*: "Love, represented by the locomotive, is always associated in *La Bête humaine* with the thought of death, and Séverine is at the same time 'instrument d'amour, instrument de mort'" (Matthews, "The Railway …," 58).

The addressee disappears along with the train, and along with the unrealized potential storyline, the psychological intonation of the poem also changes: "An *anxious* whistle and billows of smoke after a turn in the hills."

The railroad and a family conflict form the background for Nabokov's early short story, "A Matter of Chance" (1924). This work has a "scissors" structure. The tense anticipation felt by the reader begins at the point in the story where it becomes clear that a husband and wife who have not seen each other in five years are at opposite ends of the train, and they are now searching for each other without knowing that they are on the same train. The reader is torn by uncertainty: will their reunion succeed? Following the laws of the genre, Fate vacillates between bringing them together and separating them. The author stirs the reader's imagination with a series of successive unrealized possibilities (the wife turns before reaching the dining car where her husband is working, and so on).

In addition to its function of separating people, the train can shield intimate interactions from the external danger of the philistine eye of the general public (Fyodor and Zina "on the other side of the railway bridge" [*The Gift*, 163]). Based on the same principle, Ganin makes a decision in the square near the station that breaks off the course of the narrative: "He waited for the moment when the express from the north slowly rolled across the iron bridge. It passed on and disappeared behind the façade of the station. Then he picked up his suitcases, hailed a taxi and told the driver to go to a different station at the other end of the city" (*Mary*, 114).[144] The appearance of the train leads to a romantic equation that allows no place for a third term in the family of the mathematician Alferov. The final flourish, it seems, originates in a problem posed in an early story by Anton Chekhov, whose literary double (Anton Sergeevich Podtiagin) appears in *Mary*:

> On Wednesday 17 June 1881 at three am, a railroad train was to leave Station A in order to arrive at Station B at 11 pm; but as the train was departing an order was received that the station was to arrive at Station B at 7 pm. *Whose love lasts longer, the man's or the woman's?*
> ("Questions of a Mad Mathematician," 1882; Chekhov, *Polnoe sobranie sochinenii i pisem*, 1:164)

The Boredom of the Road

The leitmotif of boredom on the road was played out in connection with the duration of trips in general, developing unique national features

---

[144]It is significant that the express train carrying Mary comes from the north, while Ganin boards a train going southwest: as if he is fleeing his memories.

FIGURE 2.12 *Train interior with men. 1930s. National Photo Company Collection, Library of Congress.*

in Russian literature (the seeming endlessness of Russian railroads or, another variation, their roughness). And though Pushkin's lamentations in his "Complaints from the Road" (1830) already bear a hint of irony, technological improvements in Russian public transport led to changes in the usual chronotope of Russian literature. "Infinity" was modified from a qualitative characteristic of reality into a trope ("infinitely long-distance trains"; *The Gift*, 158).

Stagecoaches came into use in Russia in the 1820s; these were public carriages that departed according to a set schedule. They covered the distance form Petersburg to Moscow in four to four-and-a-half days. The features of riding in a carriage, britzka, or sleigh (boredom, forced time on the road, limited space for movement) were retained and transferred to the train, as we see in Apukhtin's "In the Railcar" (1858)[145] and in Gertsen's

---

[145]"But the lights are shining dimmer / Behind the glass ... Night is running off, / The heart aches from anguish, / Quietly sleep closes my eyes ... / Sleep, my neighbors!" (Apukhtin, *Stikhotvoreniia*, 95).

"For the Sake of Boredom" (1869),[146] and then later by Blok in a folklore stylization and with a romantic rupture: "Road anguish of iron / Whistled, tearing my heart" ("On the Railroad," 1910).

By the beginning of the twentieth century, however, the tragic and romantic arrangement of the theme gradually gave way to a more pragmatic, everyday approach to the problem.[147] As Mikhail Bezrodnyi observed, if the time in characters' lives had once been divided between conversation, generally a static activity, and movement, which was usually silent, the railcar synchronized movement and conversation (Bezrodnyi, "Rossiia na rel'sakh," 94). The conversations, it must be said, are not entirely empty ("bunkruptcies, expropriations, military emergencies, executions, starvations, cholera, Purishkevich, Azef"; Sholem Aleichem, *Tevye the Dairyman*, 152). Philosophical subtexts are found in the dialogs in Dostoevsky's *Idiot* and Tolstoy's *Kreutzer Sonata*, while the internal and external noise is juxtaposed with the intense mental effort of the character, as in the prose of Boborykin[148] and Vaginov.[149] A metaphysical dialog makes it possible to insert the author's thoughts into the narrative and develop the *fabula* level: "Yes, Life is more talented than we < ... >. The plots life thinks up now and then! How can we compete with that goddess?" ("The Passenger": *Stories*, 183).

Conversations in railcars reflect the general mood of society like litmus paper, and are listened to eagerly by journalists who, as Gordeev notes,

---

[146]"I boarded a car in the most awful frame of mind. To travel when one does not want to is agony ... to sit on a train and know that no one feels like doing this, that no one is paying attention – this is more than human strength can bear. ... Then I pulled out of my pocket a recently purchased copy of the Memorandum and once again looked at those near me. There were four of them – four people in four corners. ... What hideous faces! And yet, on what basis was I expecting Apollo Belvederes in the random influx scraped up by the railroad *chemin faisant*, almost without stopping" (Gertsen, *Povesti i rasskazy*, 421–422).

[147]For example, in Chekhov's *The Seagull*: "So, we are leaving? Back to railway carriages, stations, buffets, chops, conversations with strangers" (Chekhov, *Plays ...*, 121).

[148]In the novel, *Vasilii Terkin* (1892): "Before the train window the public scurried back and forth. ... Terkin sat in the corner and looked out the window. ... The train finally began to move. ... *Never before had he been filled with such an acute feeling of nothingness and the decay of everything on earth.* ... The car rumbled heavily. The train stopped at every station, whistled, smoked, let passengers on and off. Terkin sat in his corner and nothing interested him" (Boborykin, *Sochineniia*, 3:261–264). It cannot be stated with certainty whether there is some sort of unknown factual basis for Nabokov's mention of a meeting with the writer by the protagonist of *Glory* (an old gentleman in an old-fashioned black skullcap in a hallway on the Nord-Express, whom Martin's father identified as "the writer Boborykin" [*Glory*, Ch. 31]), or if this is situated as a reference to resonate with the railroad scenes of Boborykin.

[149]An example of untranslatable onomatopoeic soundplay in Vaginov: "In the last car a philosopher with a bushy mustache was traveling and thinking: '*The world is posed [zadan], not given [dan]; reality is posed [zadana], not given [dana].*' *Chivo chivo*, turned the wheels. *Chivo chivo.. And there's the station*" (Vaginov, *Kozlinaia pesn'*, 69). And before this in Dostoevsky's *Demons*: "I was unable to sort anything out and, I remember, kept muttering to the click-clack of the wheels: 'Vek and Vek and Lev Kambek, / Lev Kambek and Vek and Vek ... ' and devil knows what else, all the way to Moscow" (Dostoevsky, *Demons*, 25).

comment on the decreasing interest in politics and corresponding increase in religious discourse.[150] When he encounters the need to fill the text with banal conversations, Nabokov wastes little time on reproducing it, instead merely sketching the outlines: "Ten minutes later he was deep in conversation with the passenger in the opposite window seat, a neatly dressed old gentleman; *the prefactory theme has sailed by in the guise of a factory chimney*" ("A Dashing Fellow"; *Stories*, 261).

> I was alone in my compartment (as one usually is in a second-class carriage on that sort of train), but then, at the next station, a little man with bushy eyebrows got in < ... > *I do not like chatting in a train*, and at the moment I was particularly disinclined to do so. He followed my gaze. The low sun had set aflame the numerous windows of a large building which turned slowly, demonstrating one huge chimney, then another, as the train clattered by.
>
> (*The Real Life of Sebastian Knight*, 103)

The culture of silence in the train car and the "salvation" found in the scenery moving by outside the windows are, incidentally, a recipe for poetry.

If he needs to kill time, a character can usually employ an additional means to fight boredom: he can immerse himself in reading. As with conversation, reading in a train is governed by a set of conventions:

> [M]eanwhile the white-faced woman dismissed a sickly bouquet of forget-me-nots to the baggage rack, and having produced a magazine from her traveling bag became engrossed in the transparent process of reading: through it comes through our caressive voice, our commonsensical speech.
>
> ("A Dashing Fellow"; *Stories*, 261)

Popular choices among the accepted genres for reading on trains included romance novels and comic literature, as well as the subspecies of "men's" magazines. In this regard, one notices a distinct lowering of the cultural level within the space of the railcar. The range of permissible reading grows in inverse proportion as the socially usable area diminishes: that which is a *faux pas* outside the railroad is within its confines seen as the norm:

---

[150]"Through the train window I see tow-headed village kids pasturing animals by the road, waving their caps to the passing train, racing it, yelling, making some sort of signs. ... I remember: five years ago the same tow-headed children called with their resonant voices when a train was passing: 'Newspaper! Throw a newspaper!' Now I listen: can it really be the same cries? No, it's something else: 'Cigarette! Give me a cigarette! A cigarette! ...' Proof positive that the people have become more sober and calm ... [And] *railcar conversations today show clearly enough that the interest in politics has not so much fallen as it has been topped, to borrow an expression from gardening.*" He then goes on to an upsurge in conversations along religious lines (Iv. Gordeev, "Mel'kom (Dorozhnye vpechatleniia)" ["In Passing (Travel Notes)"]; *Rech'*. July 5 (18), 1911, 1–2).

The seat by the door, opposite Franz, was occupied by a magazine with
the picture of a breathtaking girl.

(*King, Queen, Knave*, 2)

The origin of the magazine presented for public viewing leaves no doubt
as to the situation in which the provincial youth is placed: Franz's parting
gaze through the train window rests on "a news stall hung with seductive
magazine covers – photographs of naked, pearl-gray beauties" (ibid., 1).

Against this background, the absurdity is clear in the protagonist's actions
in "Cloud, Castle, Lake," as he opens up a volume of Tiutchev.[151] The effect of
this gesture is produced by the clear disconnect between the "high-culture"
choice of books and the unwritten rules of acceptable time use on the train.
Dreyer's wife in *King, Queen, Knave* complains of the inappropriateness
of her husband's reading: "An elegant book is all right on a drawing-room
table. *In a railway car, to allay boredom, one can leaf through some trashy
magazine.* But to imbibe and relish poems, if you please, in an expensive
binding" (*King, Queen, Knave*, 10).

However, the conventions of the train do allow for the possibility of
reading "serious" literature, if only in cheap editions published specially
for use on the railroad, as in the popular "Tauchnitz" series mentioned
in "Spring in Fialta": one of the people seeing Nina off "keeping up with
the stealthily gliding car, handed her a magazine and a Tauchnitz (she read
English only when traveling)" (*Stories*, 419). The sale of novels at stations
(adventure novels, detective novels, and so-called "ladies'" novels, all with
highly entertaining content) was, by the time we are dealing with, an honored
century-long tradition. John Dodds states that in 1848 an Englishman
named Smith was the first to be granted exclusive rights to distribute books
and newspapers at special rail station stands, and to lend editions for short-
term use. After only a year the library at Paddington station numbered a
thousand volumes, largely consisting of the works of James Fennimore
Cooper, Henry James, Alexandre Dumas, and Nathaniel Hawthorne. For a
penny one could get a book at the station for reading, take it along on the
train, and then return it upon arrival at one's destination. Responding to
the new fashion, the Routledge publishing house initiated a series called the
"Railway Library" (Dodds, *The Age of Paradox*, 374).

The book read by a passenger on a train offers an alternate universe
to the compartment in which they sit, causing the reading passenger to
temporarily "drop out" of the group forming in the train car. Nabokov

---

[151] The distorted quote from Tiutchev's "Silentium!" (1830) is not so much a jab at Tiutchev's
poem as an accurate simulation of the optical illusions created in reading due to the shaking
of the train. Cf., for example, David Burliuk's "shiftology": "I am sitting in the car ... /
Of a passenger express / Over the trees, gray / From the colors of spring dough" ("Mysli v
vagone amerikanskogo ekspressa" ["Thoughts in a car on an American express train"], 1929;
D. Burliuk and N. Burliuk, *Stikhotvoreniia*, 308).

applies this model to the protagonist of his short story "Lik," who rotates within the émigré orbit, and his colleagues, who do not address him "just as passengers who have established contact among themselves do not address the foreigner absorbed in his book in a corner of the compartment" (*Stories*, 464). This is an exceptional example, since as a rule, passengers on trains tend to keep close and familiar contact, something that is especially apparent between travelers of the opposite sex.[152]

An Erotic Encounter

The random assortment of passengers of both sexes, brought together by fate in an enclosed space for a set period of time, led to genres appropriate for the conditions, from the detective story (Agatha Christie's *Murder on the Orient Express*) to erotic literature.[153] These entered into European poetics in the second half of the nineteenth century[154] and Russian poetics in the early twentieth century,[155] soon rapidly becoming exploited in mass culture, particularly the world of film. In a parody of a film plot (Valentinov's monolog in *The Defense*) Nabokov constructs the rising action of a movie:

> Imagine, dear boy, a young girl, beautiful and passionate, in the compartment of an express train. At one of the stations a young man gets in. From a good family. Night descends on the train. She falls asleep and in her sleep spreads her limbs. A glorious young creature. The young man— you know that type, bursting with sap but absolutely chaste—begins

---

[152]Cf. the 1915 poem, "Vy so mnoi v vagone" ("You and I on the train car") by Tikhon Churilin (*Vesna posle smerti*, 53).

[153]In Kuprin: "And for two days, starting in Petersburg, *the strange whim of fate had made him the inseparable traveling companion and conversation partner of an enchanting woman* whom he liked more and more with each passing hour" ("Na raz"ezde" ["At the Junction"]; Kuprin, *Sobranie sochinenii*, 1:220). And in Proust: "We made haste to find an empty carriage *where I would be able to kiss Albertine all through the journey*. Not having found one, we got into a compartment where was already installed a lady with an enormous, ugly, old face, and a mannish expression, very overdressed, who was reading the *Revue des Deux Mondes*" (Proust, *Sodom and Gomorrah*, 4:257).

[154]E.g. Arthur Rimbaud: "All winter we will wonder in our red wagon / With cushions of blue. / Nice and warm with the nest of creepy kisses / Just for us too" ("Dream in Wintertime" (1870) in Rimbaud, *Complete Works*, 47).

[155]Valerii Briusov: "Two random traveling companions, / In silence, with no lights, / Two random traveling companions, / I became close to her. // The car shook evenly, / And flew along its way, / The car shook evenly, / Rocking us together. // And we felt the influence / Of the rocking and the darkness, / And we felt the influence, / In which we wilted down. // And someone's lips grew near / To other lips in the darkness, / And someone's lips grew near ... / Or were we dreaming this?" ("V vagone" ["In the train car"], 1904–05; Briusov, *Sobranie sochinenii*, 1:417).

literally to lose his head. In a kind of trance he hurls himself upon her.
< ... > He feels her perfume, her lace underwear, her glorious young body.
... She wakes up, throws him off, calls out < ... > the conductor and
some passengers run in. He is tried, he is condemned to penal servitude.
His aged mother comes to the young girl to beg her to save her son. The
drama of the girl. The point is that from the very first moment—there,
in the express—she has fallen in love with him, is seething with passion.

(*The Defense*, 247)

It is rare that visual flirtation crosses over into physical solicitations, however.
In the short story, "A Matter of Chance," a young woman enters a second-
class compartment "with a big painted mouth and a tight black toque that
covered her forehead." She attracts the attention of a gentleman who "peered
at her over his paper" (*Stories*, 53). When everyone goes to the dining car,
the lady "noticed with alarm that the man in the beige suit had waited to get
up"; as they go through, her fellow traveler walks almost close enough to
step on her ("when a jolt threw her off balance < ... > he would pointedly
clear his throat"). The woman, who has recently escaped the USSR, naively
assumes that this is a spy or an informer. A short chase ensues in the hallway
of the sleeping car, and the scene reaches its climax as the woman:

> crossed the joggy connecting plates to the diner, which came after the
> sleeper. And here, suddenly, in the vestibule of the diner, with a kind of
> rough tenderness the man clutched her by the upper arm. She stifled a
> scream and yanked away her arm so violently that she nearly lost her
> footing.
>   The man said in German, with a foreign accent, "My precious!"
>   She felt unbearably hurt. < ... > "God knows what he took me for," she
> reflected, "and all just because I use lipstick."

(ibid., 57)

Of course, the passenger does not in fact take this traveling companion to
be a prostitute, but is merely acting within the allowable limits of semi-
permissibility that are part and parcel of this mutable space.[156] In rejecting
this man with an accent (a feature that, like a minor physical defect, e.g., a
limp, can indicate a connection to supernatural forces), the heroine declines
a sexual initiation into her new world. The scene is made tragicomic by the

---

[156]Shortly before this in 1927 a similar device was used well by Bagritskii in his poem, "Vesna"
("Spring"): "After dipping / In oil to its elbow, / The lever begins / To ooh and ah ... // From
lust the train / Howls with anger: / 'I want it! I want it! / 'I want it! I want it!'" (Bagritskii,
Stikhotvoreniia i poemy, 179–181).

fact that the refusal occurs on a threshold that, if she had crossed it, would have led her to encounter her beloved (in the dining car that she refrains from entering is the husband she has not seen for years). By protecting her dignity, the woman remains faithful to the standards of decency and morality that remain in effect for her, but that no longer have any meaning for her cocaine-addict husband.

The atmosphere between potential romantic partners in a compartment can be one of erotic tension. This is verbalized by a rather vulgar Nabokov character: "Railroad riding, it is proclaimed, disposes one to this kind of thing. Am extremely disposed. After all, say what you will, but the main spring of life is robust romance. Can't concentrate on business unless I take care first of my romantic interests" ("A Dashing Fellow"; *Stories*, 260). The impermissibility (and thus the piquancy) of such situations is in their practical impossibility under the conditions of travel, as we see in the language of gestures in *King, Queen, Knave*: a woman on the train *"automatically pulled at her pleated skirt, automatically noticing* that the awkward young man with the glasses who had appeared in the door corner seemed to be *fascinated by the sheer silk of her legs"* (*King, Queen, Knave*, 7), and in "A Dashing Fellow": "What a good sign—she adjusts every part you look at. < ... > First-rate legs, artificial silk" (*Stories*, 261). We might say that the theme, tossed from the provincial Franz (who trembles in fear of the ladies of the capital cities) to Kostia (with his love for provincial hetaerae), takes on the tone of "railroad romance" clichés that emerged in the interim between *King, Queen, Knave* (1928) and "A Dashing Fellow" (1932). The figure of the railroad voyeur is lushly described in A. Ginger's short story, "An Evening at the Train Station," published and read voraciously in *Chisla* [*Numbers*] (1930), which was hostile to Nabokov:

> Our little town is rather seedy, but the rail station is a junction and is among the bold dots on maps of railroad lines. Each time after I drop off a letter I enter the waiting room in the hope that some transferring *lady passenger will be sitting on the bench, her legs crossed, providing the opportunity for passionate ogling of her calves and part of her thighs*.
>
> (Ginger, *Chisla*, 78)

Fate smiles on the narrator in this instance:

> *A beautiful young woman, almost a lady, sat with her legs crossed. Her light stockings were not wrinkled*, and they had none of the mud spots that regrettably and inappropriately dot women's legs in foul weather. ... She laughed, revealing her large white teeth.
>
> (ibid.)

Only Nabokov's "A Dashing Fellow" shows the courtship in all its phases from flirtation to the heights of intimacy. Kostia, the traveling salesman who peddles fashionable ladies' mirrors, prevails upon his random traveling companion, the poor actress Bergmann:

> You are lonely, and I am lonely. You are free, and I am free. Who, then, can forbid us to spend several pleasant hours in a sheltered love nest?"[157]
> Her silence was enticing. He left his seat and sat next to her. < ... >
> "What is your destination?" she asked. Kostenka told her.
> "And I am returning to—" < ... >
> "All right, I'll accompany you, and tomorrow continue my journey. Though I dare not predict anything, madam, I have all grounds to believe that neither you nor I will regret it."
>
> (*Stories*, 263–264)

The figure of Kostia is created by Nabokov from an array of everyday clichés. And yet there are also authentic literary sources for the story as well, from Chekhov[158] to the satirical Russian journal, *Satyricon*. Averchenko's short story, "Heart under the Scalpel,"[159] begins in the finest tradition of the genre: "A well-built lady entered our compartment at the station, laid a small bag on the sofa, and went back out immediately, probably to say farewell to the friends seeing her off." While she is gone a traveler tells the narrator of his womanizing exploits, which he then attempts on this attractive woman. Compare his treatment of her with the appeals of Nabokov's Kostia:

> *Madame!* Life is so wonderful that one must hurry. Youth will not happen again. One must seize the day! We are young and beautiful – come back with me to my apartment.
>
> (Averchenko, *Britva v kisele*, 208)

---

[157]A similar rhetorical tactic is used on a lady by a passenger in Kuprin's "At the junction": "he began to speak in a hurried whisper. ... *Maybe we will go off in different directions in fifteen minutes and never meet again*, but this will be all right anyway" (Kuprin, *Sobranie sochinenii*, 1:223).

[158]See the railcar compartment intrigue in Chekhov's 1881 short story, "V vagone" ("In the railcar"): "'She's pretty,' whispers the old man talking with me, nodding at the pretty girl. 'Mm-hmm, prrrety. ... Hell, too bad there's no chloroform here! *I'd give her a sniff and then kiss her all over! Everyone would be asleep!*' ... *On my right was a tall noblewoman from the 'needless to say' category*. ... The train stops. Way station" (Chekhov, *Polnoe sobranie sochinenii i pisem*, 1:119).

[159]First published in *Satirikon*. 1912. № 14–15; later in the book *Rasskazy dlia vyzdoravlivaiushchikh* (*Stories for Convalescents*) (Prague, 1917).

Men try various methods of action, including attempts to make an impression by elevating their own social status: "Now all that remained ... was to point up his familiarity with the customs of high society, and then – a kiss on the hand" (Averchenko); "Well, some time later, there was a lucky break, brought me heaps of money. I had four apartment houses in Berlin" (Nabokov). Both men try to conquer their partners through their stomachs. The menu that Sonia Bergmann recites in "A Dashing Fellow" includes: "*Roast beef* < ... > White bread. Butter. Our celebrated cheese. Coffee. A pint of cognac. Goodness me, can't you wait a little? Let me go, it's indecent" (*Stories*, 266). "Heart under a Scalpel" has similar fare: "Perhaps you would like something to eat – grouse, ham, chops – I'll run and get them at the first station" (Averchenko, *Britva v kisele*, 212). The lady passenger in Averchenko's story, unlike Kostia's companion, refuses everything and ends up jumping out of the compartment.

The novel, *King, Queen, Knave*, begins with future lovers meeting on a train. Nabokov introduces railway symbolism at significant points in the narrative: places that require a development of the plot. The train serves not only as a physical means of conveyance for the passengers in the fictional space-time, but also a tool for expressing the idea of movement as a whole, as in the familiar juxtaposition of the static and dynamic characteristics that, according to Goncharov, make up the Russian soul.[160] Franz lays Martha's coat on the bed, and this act is duplicated by a comparison in his subconscious ("this was like a train passenger marking the seat he is about to occupy"; *King, Queen, Knave*, 95). The foreshadowing of the compartment bunk is no coincidence, as the ensuing love scene is resolved through road metonymy:

> Presently the bed stirred into motion. It glided off on its journey creaking discreetly as does a sleeping car when the express pulls out of a dreamy station. "You, you, you," uttered Martha, < ... > following with moist eyes the shadows of angels waving their handkerchiefs on the ceiling, which was moving away faster and faster.[161]
>
> (ibid., 97)

The act of sex, packaged in phrases such as "the bed stirred into motion" and "the bed returned to Berlin from Eden," is presented as a chain of nouns (cork, tie, mirror) linked like railcars in the train of a sentence and set in motion by a random jolt of kinetic energy. The grammar of love makes

---

[160]"Why do people race to build railroads and steamships everywhere when the ideal of life is to sit in one's place?" (Goncharov, *Oblomov*, 174).

[161]Emma Bovary's bed (on which she is unfaithful to her husband) is compared with a canoe. For more allusions to Flaubert's novel in *King, Queen, Knave*, see Couterier, "Nabokov and Flaubert," 405–411.

words submit to its syntax (despite the paucity of terminology for sex in the Russian literary tradition, Nabokov's inclusion of silence here is entirely deliberate); in this syntax inanimate things form pairs with action verbs:

> A blue-tinted cork, which had been recently removed from a small ink bottle when a fountain pen had to be refilled, hesitated for an instant, then *rolled* in a semi-circle to the edge of the oilcloth-covered table, hesitated again, and *jumped off*. With the help of the lashing rain the wind *tried to open* the window but failed. In the rickety wardrobe a blue black-spotted tie *slithered off* its twig like a snake. A paperback novelette on the chest-of-drawers left open at Chapter Five *skipped* several pages. Suddenly the looking glass made *a signal warning gleam*. It reflected a bluish armpit and a lovely bare arm. The arm stretched and fell back lifeless.
>
> (*King, Queen, Knave*, 97–98)

The "lifeless" hand as a detail of the stopped train intensifies the effect of the end of an intimate encounter.

Violence and the Railroad

The events associated with the Revolution destroyed ethical and aesthetic conventions of behavior and confused the roles and hierarchical positions of train passengers. Class boundaries were erased at best and, in some cases, the members of classes switched places on the social ladder. The literary plot of the "*paysan* on a train" is generally based on an innocent victim (often lowered from a former status, e.g., a representative of the dethroned aristocracy) who is subjected to aggression (often sexual) from individuals identified with the lower classes, but who have now climbed to a higher social rung.

Isaak Babel's 1923 short story, "Salt," from his *Red Cavalry* collection, was written in first person in the form of a letter to the editor of an unidentified publication. Babel' skillfully imitates the style of a semiliterate "soldier of the revolution," a fighter in the second platoon of Nikita Balmashev's cavalry. On the plot level the story is a description of an incident at the provincial railroad station at Fastov. Though Babel' does not write about it directly, the soldiers, as M. Iampol'skii has shown, rape the women who are in the station (Zholkovskii & Iampol'skii, *Babel'/Babel*, 287–288). The narrative centers on the unsuccessful attempt of one of the female passengers with an infant to avoid the fate of the other women on the train. In response to a request to let her have a seat on the train, the soldiers yell: "Let her in ... Once we're done with her, she won't be wanting that husband of hers no more!" (Babel, *Isaac Babel's Selected Writings*, 139). The author of the

FIGURE 2.13 *Illustration by artist Bernhard Gillam showing a man hoping to cause the oncoming train labeled "N.Y. City Reforms" to derail. Cover illustration from* Puck, *vol. 17, no. 427 (13 May 1885).*

epistle tries to reason with his comrades, but soon, suspecting something is amiss, he discovers the trick: the woman is holding a bag of salt, not a child. Owing to the vigilance of the red soldier, the woman's deception is caught. As a punishment she is thrown out onto the embankment at full speed.

Here is how Babel' describes the station, the actions of the citizens, and the reaction of members of the "authorities":

It was a quiet, glorious night seven days ago when our well-deserved Red Cavalry transport train, loaded with fighters, stopped at that station. We were all burning to promote the Common Cause and were heading to Berdichev. Only, we notice that our train isn't moving in any way at all, our Gavrilka is not beginning to roll, and the fighters begin mistrusting and asking each other: "Why are we stopping here?" And truly, the stop turned out to be mighty for the Common Cause, because the peddlers, those evil fiends among whom there was a countless force of the female species, were all behaving very impertinently with the railroad authorities. Recklessly they grabbed the handrails, those evil fiends, they scampered over the steel roofs, frolicked, made trouble, clutching in each hand sacks of contraband salt, up to five *pood* in a sack. But the triumph of the capitalist peddlers did not last long. The initiative showed by the fighters who jumped out of the train made it possible for the struggling railroad authorities to emit sighs from their breasts. Only the female species with their bags of salt stayed around.

(Babel, *Isaac Babel's Selected Writings*, 138–139)

The reader's inclination is to explain the perceived lacuna in meaning as a stylistic dissonance caused by the confused speech of a lower-class narrator. The primary intrigue (the trick played by the passenger, who pays for her deceit with the asymmetrical vengeance taken by the soldier) is entirely clear, it is the details not apprehended that answer the general tone of the short story collective. Meanwhile, one can construct the picture of what happened based on the literary context in which Babel's work is situated.

There is a possible inspiration and source for Babel's "Salt" in a scene from the eleventh chapter (part 1) of the novella *Salon Car* (*Salon-vagon*) by Andrei Sobol' (1887–1926). This work was finished in Odessa in 1920–21 and published in 1923 (see analysis of it in Shersher, "Poetika otchaianiia," 483–499). "Salt" was published in an Odessa newspaper in late 1923.

This chapter begins by setting the scene: "In Fastov a train was delayed for half a day," and Sobol' then goes on to describe how

about thirty foot soldiers with a full allotment of ammunition silently, with only rare breaks of conversation among them, detached the locomotive and without further ado beat the engineer and forced him to turn back towards Znamenka, gathering a couple dozen heated cars overfilled with people, whence a mustachioed man in a yellow chapan, with the help of two henchmen with laceless shoes on their bare feet, but with angled sheepskin hats, tossed out all the Jews.

(Sobol', *Oblomki*, 90)

The main argument from this point is over the seats in the remaining cars.

Babel' makes no attempt to hide the subtext of his short story, and this demonstrativeness demands explanation. We may note the identical geography in the two works: as with Sobol's, Babel's train is also going in the direction of the Jewish town of *Berdichev*,[162] but it stops in the town

---

[162]In Jewish folklore and literature, as well as in the Russian anti-Semitic traditions of the nineteenth and twentieth centuries, Berdichev became a symbolic model for the Jewish city. In the middle of the 1920s, Jews made up 56 percent of its population.

of *Fastov*, where the main action takes place. This fairytale place, Babel'
hints, has already been written of in literature: "you ... have not overlooked
the far-flung station of Fastov, lying afar beyond the mountains grand, in a
distant province of a distant land, where many a jug of homebrewed beer we
drank with merriment and cheer. About this aforementioned station, there
is *much you can write about* " (Babel, *Isaac Babel's Selected Writings*, 138).
The Jewish theme seems not to be present at all in Babel's story—until the
disgraced woman utters a phrase with no apparent external impetus:

> "As it is I've lost my salt, so I'm not afraid of calling things by their
> real name! Don't give me that about saving Russia – all you care about
> is saving those Yids, Lenin and Trotsky!" "Right now our topic of
> conversation is not the Yids, you evil citizen!"
>
> (Babel, *Isaac Babel's Selected Writings*, 140)

It would seem that Babel' intentionally leaves the beating and ousting of
the Jews from the train in Fastov out of his narrative, with the assumption
that using this particular geographical location serves as a reference to his
source in Sobol's work. In addition, the very title of the story and its "salty"
connections call to mind associations with the "sacrificial salt," strongly
associated in Russian culture with Rozanov's striking passage on Jews as the
salt of the human race: "All waters of the earth must be salted. The whole
world must be infused with the taste of us. ... Salt must be salt; released into
water, or as a seasoning for food, it gives the water more than a diamond
would if let go into the water" (Rozanov, *Bibleiskaia poeziia*, 16). Turning
to the pogrom scene on the railway in Sobol's work, we see the following:

> "Berdichev people, come out. We don't need Berdichev people."
>   Into the puddles flew pillows, bundles, parcels, disappearing right
> there, and then returning to the same cars, but to new owners. A fat
> old Jew clung to the edge of the car[163] and hung over the rails; his pants
> were lifted up above his deep galoshes, revealing his checkered colored
> undergarments. His reddened derby fell to the ground and his gray hair
> whipped around in the wind. Grabbing his legs, one of the passersby
> pulled him down. Two Jewish women wallowed about near the switch
> and, crying, got their skirts tangled up, while one of them had a wig
> slipping down on the back of her head. A nearby woman in a dressy wrap
> skirt smacked her thighs and screeched with delight. Sparse snowflakes
> fell and melted before hitting the black earth, mingled with the cries of
> stumbling children and the moans of blindly rushing women.

---

[163]Cf. in Babel': "they grabbed the handrails, those evil fiends" (Babel, *Isaac Babel's Selected
Writings*, 139).

"The engine whistled; as a parting shot the yellow chapan knocked a Jewish woman with bagels into the puddle, and the bagels spread out like a fan. Snapping them up, the soldiers splashed to the cars; in one of them they were singing the Marseillaise. The train began to move.

"'Let's renounce the old world,' the voices moving into the distance concluded; the old Jew went to get his hat."

(Sobol', *Oblomki*, 91)

Both writers give a sympathetic portrayal of the traditional anti-Semitic bacchanalia, with the Cossacks (cf. Gogol's *Taras Bul'ba*) replaced by the red army soldiers (who are still addressed in a markedly Gogolian way: "Let me in, my dear Cossacks"; Babel, *Isaac Babel's Selected Writings*, 139), while the fictional interests of the national liberation movement become the seemingly spontaneous revolutionary struggle, making the world safe for sexual anarchy. The problem with men, in this case a Jew, is that unlike women they are in no way attractive to the aggressor and are therefore completely vulnerable to being liquidated as a mere obstacle ("those evil fiends among whom there was a countless force of the female species"; ibid.). A man cannot bargain his way out of dying, even by symbolically renouncing physical purity. There can be little doubt about the fate of the female passengers from Berdichev whom Balmashev points out, nor about their Jewish origins: "Turn back to those two girls crying right now like they were hurt last night."

Babel's Jewish complex seemingly forces the pogrom scene out of the main body of the narrative; his innovation is that, with regard to this micro-episode from another text, the author creates (knowingly, it would seem) an autonomous satellite work that reconstructs the point of view of one of the participants in the conflict, and with a minor shift in the plot and the inserted story of the salt.

The clockwork of the "Jew on a train" plot, which was wound up in the nineteenth-century Russian classics, is set in motion with enviable consistency in a new, more democratic location for modern urban culture: the train station. In Chekhov's "In the Train Car," the engineer's assistants "run around the malfunctioning locomotive, knocking, yelling. ... The stationmaster stands nearby in a red cap and tells his assistant jokes from jolly Jewish life." The Christmas eve night spent in a train car by the narrator of Leskov's "Journey with a Nihilist" ends with an incident at the station containing the "nihilist" (who turns out to be a public prosecutor) and a Jewish victim: "Then at the very moment a Jew burst into the office with a desperate wail and shouted that that was his basket, and the dress in it was one he was delivering to a lady in high society < ... > 'But what about your ticket?' the Jew was asked. 'Well, about the ticket' – he answered. 'I didn't know where to get a ticket.' ... The Jew was ordered held" (Leskov, *Satirical stories*, 102–103). The symbolic patriotic substitution of the ticketless Jew

with a young Cossack in the railroad train at the beginning of the First
World War was described by Evgenii Shvarts:

> [Ober] unlocked the door with his key and pulled some teenager in a white
> shirt and loose Cossack pants in onto the platform. And immediately
> after this he attacked me: "a man is hanging at the edge of death and
> you're there yelling." After this, crimson and with cheeks trembling, he
> started to check tickets. After finding out that I had none, he instructed
> the dapper conductor to leave me at the next station, which the latter
> did with no small pleasure. ... The train moved off into the distance. The
> conductor looked at me with a grin from the last platform.
>
>   (Shvarts, "*Ia budu pisatelem* ...," 500)

Approximately a year after the publication of Babel's story, Marina Tsvetaeva
came out with a semiautobiographical prose work, printed in *Sovremennye
zapiski* (Paris. 1924. № 21) called "Free Passage" ("Vol'nyi proezd"), in
which she describes her travels with the military provisions unit (*prodotriad*)
during the Civil War. The Red Army soldiers remove everyone from the
train, but a few passengers manage to sneak back on. Among these is the
female narrator, identified in the text as "M. I.," and a Jewish family, which
Tsvetaeva describes using the classic anti-Semitic template: "a Jew with a
gold ingot around his neck" and his wife, a "little (a spider!) extremely dark
Jewish woman who 'adored' things made of gold and fabric made of silk"
(Tsvetaeva, *Sobranie sochinenii*, 4:430). The random passengers, as with the
characters in Babel's "Salt," are united by a common goal: to take items
from the rich village—fatback (*salo*), wheat, sugar, salt—to exchange for city
goods (ibid., 427). During a scandal scene at the requisition point at Usman'
station, M. I., in the presence of the Jewish passengers and the soldiers,
recalls that Kannegiser, the murderer of Uritskii, and Kaplan, the would-be
assassin of Lenin, also belonged to this dubious nation ("Old woman, not
understanding: 'Who did the Yids kill?' Me: 'Uritskii, head of the Petersburg
secret police.' Old woman: 'Oooh. What, was he also a Yid?'"; ibid., 437).
When the Jew Lavit tries to stifle the clearly anti-Semitic conversation, the
soldiers rise up in defense of the Russians ("Kuznetsov: 'You, comrade, keep
it down. I am a member of the Communist Party myself, and the fact that I
said yid, well, it's a habit of mine!'"; ibid., 438).

Meanwhile, Tsvetaeva's station scene, in comparison with those of Sobol'
and Babel', is turned inside out: the narrator herself, rather than the Jews,
is presented as the victim suffering on behalf of the truth; she is the one
accused of "counterrevolution" and "judaeophobia" (ibid., 444) and forced
to leave the station with a basket weighing 70 pounds. Despite the throng
of humanity, M. I. manages to squeeze into a heated car whose contents
are a hyperbolized image of a single generalized body engaging in sinuous
movements in a common erotic rhythm:

I stand, barely swaying with the cramped, collective human breathing: back and forth, like a wave. My breast, my side, shoulder, knee adhering, I breathe in harmony. And from this extreme bodily cohesion there is a complete sensation of losing my own body. I am that which is moving. The body, in a stupor – is a thing. The car is a forced stupor.

> (Tsvetaeva, *Sobranie sochinenii*, 4:450)

The grotesque Rabelaisian/Bakhtinian concept of the collective body here elides with the description of "mixed train No. 57" in Pil'niak's novel, *The Naked Year* (*Golyi god*)[164]:

People; human legs, arms, heads, bellies, backs, and human droppings; people as thick in lice as the wagons are in people. People herded here, maintained their right to travel by force of their fists, because out there, in the famine districts, at every station, scores of famine refugees have rushed the train, struggling over heads and backs and necks and legs over other people inside – and these struck out, and those struck out, tearing off and throwing down those already aboard, the scrimmage going on till the train started and bore off those that happened at the moment to be stuck on.

> (Pilnyak, *The Naked Year*, 233–234)

Tsvetaeva's "Free Passage" contains clear parallels with Pil'niak's novel, e.g., in the peddling of chintz in a peasant hut:

"Merchant woman, how much for a yard?" "I don't sell for money ...." "*Then how much millet* for the chintz?" "*Your item, your price.*" "I already said, twenty pounds."

> (Tsvetaeva, *Sobranie sochinenii*, 4:432–433);

Cf.: "*Your goods are our money,*" the fellow is ready with his words. "We want flour." "We know that. *Flour here costs sixty-two the pood.*"

> (Pilnyak, *The Naked Year*, 245)

---

[164]From 1921 to 1923, Pil'niak's *Golyi god* was published in monograph form four times (in 1921 and 1922 by the Grzhebin Publishing House, Prague, Moscow, and Berlin).

Pil'niak's railway scene fits into a general typological structure that we might provisionally call the "incident at a station," with the familiar motif of a woman paying for her passage with her body.[165]

The mixing of the moral humiliation/physical abuse motifs in combination with the stark plot detail of throwing people from a train allows us to form a hypothesis that the situation was transferred in a reductionist form into the prose of another émigré author known for several texts involving the banditry of soldiers during the Civil War in which such stories recur. Nabokov's 1932 novel, *Glory*, is suffused with the spiritual illness of the fourteen-year-old Irina Zilanova.[166] This illness began during the Revolution when the girl and her mother found themselves in a railcar "crammed with all sorts of riffraff":

[D]uring the long journey *two rowdies, ignoring the protests of some of their pals, palpated, pinched, and tickled the child, saying monstrous obscenities to her.* Mrs. Pavlov, wearing the smile of helpless horror, and doing her best to protect her, kept repeating, "Never mind, Irochka, never mind—oh please leave the child alone, you should be ashamed of yourselves—never mind, Irochka—" then, on the next train, nearer to Moscow, with similar cries and mutterings, she again cradled her daughter's head when *other roughs, deserters or the like, ejected her corpulent husband*[167] *by squeezing him through the window with the train going full speed.* Yes, he was very fat, and he laughed hysterically, having got stuck halfway through, but finally, with a unanimous heave-ho they

---

[165]Cf.: "Yesterday at a small station a peasant woman had wanted to get in. A soldier was standing at the door. 'Darling,' the woman said, 'for the love o' Jesus, darling, let me in. There's no room anywhere, you see, darling.' 'No room, Auntie! Don't you try. There ain't no room at all!' said the soldier. 'For the love o' Jesus Christ our ... ' '*How'll you pay m' back?*' '*That'll be all right.*' '*Are y' on f'r ... ?*' '*That'll be all right ... we'll settle that ....*' 'Right-ho! Come along, get under that there bunk. There's our coats. Eh, Semyon, let the wench in'" (Pilnyak, *The Naked Year*, 235–236). As the plot develops the scale of the violence grows: a few pages in we read that the soldiers at the Mar Junction station stop the train and demand the taking of "about a score of the best looking" for the night ("*Now the lasses as is still whole 'd better not go*"; ibid., 250); when the women return, the train departs from the station in the sunset.

[166]Nabokov stated that from all the proletarian literature that had been written in the quarter century after the revolution he could select a maximum of a dozen worthwhile authors, of which the third in the list was Isaak Babel' (the recipient in fact goes on to list only seven). See the letter to Edmund Wilson dated January 3, 1944 (Nabokov, *The Nabokov–Wilson Letters*, 122). Regarding Nabokov's opinions of Tsvetaeva and Pil'niak, see Stark, "Nabokov – Tsvetaeva," 150–156; Nabokov, *Selected Letters*, 430–431; and Nabokov, *The Nabokov–Wilson Letters*, 177. At the end of the 1920s Nabokov called Tsvetaeva's prose "vague and absurd" (Review in *Volia Rossii*. 1929, Book 2).

[167]Cf. the "fat, old Jew" in Sobol', *Oblomki*.

succeeded, he disappeared from sight, and there only remained the blind snow driving past the empty window.[168]

(*Glory*, 150)

We must also not forget Nabokov's own personal experience: his 1917 trip to Crimea began, according to the author, in an atmosphere of comfort: "with the heat still humming and the lamps intact in the < ... > first-class sleeper, and a passably famous singer < ... > stood in the corridor, tapping upon the pane," but somewhere "after Moscow all comfort came to an end. < ... > the train, including our sleeping car, was invaded by more or less Bolshevized *soldiers who were returning to their homes from the front*" (*Speak, Memory*, 242–243). Nabokov and his brother decided to lock themselves in the compartment and not allow anyone in, much to the dismay of the soldiers occupying the train. The young men are not subjected to sexual obstruction, as in Babel's "Salt" or the scene from *Glory*, but the conditions of the carnivalesque atmosphere the aggressors drive them to forced bodily contact by flooding them with excrement: "Several soldiers traveling on the roof of the car added to the sport by trying to use, not unsuccessfully, the ventilator of our room as a toilet" (ibid., 243). The underbelly of railroad mythology is exposed in a secondary way in *Lolita*, where in combination with the elegant railroad metaphor the image of fleeting youth, in the form of ripped toilet paper, literalizes the expression "a life shat away" (in Russian *prosrannaia zhizn'*):

The days of my youth, as I look back on them, seem to fly away from me in a flurry of pale repetitive scraps like those morning snow storms of used tissue paper that a train passenger sees whirling in the wake of the observation car.

(*Lolita*, 17)

The Poetics of Description

Descriptions of nighttime compartments and the views of stations from inside them are found across Nabokov's work. The invariable appearance of a moth flying around a light gives these scenes a particular sense of the sacred and invites the reader's interpretation. Sebastian Knight inherited from his

---

[168]Cf. the "blind snow" in Sobol': "Sparse snowflakes fell ... with the moans of blindly rushing women" (Sobol', *Oblomki*, 91).

mother a "strange, almost romantic, passion" for sleeping cars and European express trains, a passion that was translated into his impressionistic prose:

> [T]he soft crackle of polished panels in the blue-shaded night, the long sad sigh of brakes at dimly surmised stations, the upward slide of an embossed leather blind disclosing a platform, a man wheeling luggage, *the milky globe of a lamp with a pale moth whirling around it*; the clank of an invisible hammer testing wheels.
>
> (*The Real Life of Sebastian Knight*, 9)

Compare this with a parallel description in *Glory*:

> [Martyn] raised the leathern curtain—for this he had to undo a button, after which the curtain slid smoothly up. < ... > he could not tear himself away from the window, beyond which the oblique hillsides of night rushed past. < ... > Soon the train braked and stopped in darkness. < ... > A little later the train began to move, but then stopped for good, emitting a long, softly sibilant sigh of relief, and simultaneously pale stripes of light passed slowly across the dark compartment. < ... > *Several midges and one large moth circled around a gas lantern*; shadowy people shuffled along the platform conversing about unknown things as they went; then there was a jangle of buffers and the train glided off.
>
> (*Glory*, 21)

The episode figures twice in *Speak, Memory*, although with minor changes:

> It was marvelously exciting to move to the foot of one's bed, < ... > to undo cautiously the catch of the window shade, which could be made to slide only halfway up, impeded as it was by the edge of the upper berth. Like moons around Jupiter, *pale moths revolved about a lone lamp*.
>
> (*Speak, Memory*, 145–146)

The memoirist's recollection is the last refuge of vanishing realia whose sweetness (coffee and cream) is magnified in direct proportion to the significance of the established poetic hierarchy, which in this case traces all the way back to Pushkin's *The Bronze Horseman* ("hard-ringing hoofbeats" ["*tiazhelo-zvonkoe skakan'e*"]; *Polnoe sobranie*, 4:396), but also tangentially encompasses the bestsellers of Soviet children's literature.[169] Samuil Marshak, more or less a contemporary of Nabokov, recalled how as a seven-year-old boy he experienced a fit of railroad

---

[169]A similar scene with mountains and light outside the window, observed by a child from within a train car, is found in the canonical Soviet literary work "Chuk i Gek" ["Chuk and Gek"]: "Gek woke up at night to have a drink. *The ceiling light was off, but everything around Gek was illuminated by a blue light*" (Gaidar, *Sobranie sochinenii*, 3:39).

joy.[170] The description of the details on the journey and the emotional state of the young passenger echo those of Nabokov:

> All is joyous and new to me –
> The bitter-smelling fumes,
> The long noise of the whistle at night
> And the lantern of the patrolman.
>
> To a land far away and unfamiliar
> My whole family goes.
> For three days, instead of a house
> We have just a single bench ...
>
> Before me in the window frame
> The nearby forest rushes back.
> But the faraway forest, together with us
> Makes its way ahead.
>
> Like children's toys,
> The village huts,
> Flashed by on the fly,
> Along with a horse cart on a bridge.
>
> And there's the little station house,
> A thick net of wires,
> And the countless railcars
> Of trains flying past.
>
> I fall asleep at a late hour,
> And, rocking me to sleep,
> The train rushes,
> Spreading red sparks.
>
> I listen closely to the whistle,
> To the resonant singing of the wheels,
> Grateful to the engineer
> For driving our locomotive.
>
> (Marshak, *Stikhotvoreniia i poemy*, 70–73)

---

[170]The first English version of his autobiography, *Conclusive Evidence,* was published in 1951, while Marshak's poem was published in 1950 (*Pioner.* № 1, 29), and later appeared in collections of his poems about childhood *Memories of Childhood* and *Beginning of the Century,* as well as in a piece of autobiographical prose written about 1930, wherein Marshak described the long moves with his family when he was a child. The first known evidence of Nabokov's familiarity with Marshak's works is from 1937 (a pun on his name, "Koshmarshak" ["Nightmareshak"] in a private letter to an addressee in Paris [Letter to Irina Guadanini, Private Collection]).

The poem ends with a declaration that "a few years have passed since then" and now the author is ceding his place by the window to the next generation. The reminiscences of a number of memoirists from this generation are close in tone to Marshak and Nabokov: in a diary entry from 1951 Shvarts confesses that he

> passionately loved train cars, locomotives, steamships, everything associated with traveling. Scarcely had I boarded the train, sat on the little table by the window, scarcely had the wheels started knocking, and I was in ecstasy. ... I remember the enormous halls in hub stations (there were few direct trains then, and I learned the word "transfer" at a very young age); I remember the well-appointed tables, holiday feasts, they seemed to me .... I am carried for a moment into an enormous room, I hear the locomotive whistles behind the high arched windows, and I feel joy – we are on the way.
>
> (Shvarts, *Memuary*, 44–45)

Paustovskii in his 1956 autobiographical novel, *Nachalo nevedomogo veka* (*Beginning of an Unknown Century*), writes:

> From childhood I have had a marked passion for railroads. Perhaps this is because my father was a railroad man. ... Everything associated with the railroad is to this day steeped in the poetry of travels, even the smell of the coal smoke from locomotive furnaces.
>
> (Paustovskii, *Sobranie sochinenii*, 4:593–594)

Among the various manifestations of the railroad myth in Nabokov, instances where only signals and signs, rather than the train itself, are described also warrant attention: "From the silent, snow-blanketed platform of the little station of Siverski on the Warsaw line < ... >, I was watching a distant silvery grove as it changed to lead under the evening sky and *waiting for it to emit the dull-violet smoke of the train* that would take me back to St. Petersburg" (*Speak, Memory*, 211). Compare this with the panoramic recollection in the opening pages of *The Defense*, presented through the eyes of a "a man in gaiters," who is also waiting on the platform for a Petersburg dacha train: "looking at the distant fringe of the forest, whence in a few minutes would appear the train's harbinger – a puff of white smoke" (*Defense*, 20). Details representing the movement of a train (its speed and rhythm) while the locomotive remains out of sight can be found in numerous visual representations from the time and in early Soviet texts,[171] but the original conception for this device seems to come from Marcel Proust:

---

[171]For example, in Il'f and Petrov: "The smoke was coming out. Locomotive puffed up the snow-white side whiskers of smoke" (Il'f & Petrov, *The Twelve Chairs*, 145). And in émigré poets: "*Blue smoke, like a veil, from the locomotive smokestack*" (from the poem "Na vokzale, gde zhdali, pykhtia, parovozy ..." ["At the station, where the engines waited, puffing ..."] by Yuri Odarchenko; *Antologiia poezii russkogo zarubezh'ia*, 3:45).

The little train was not yet there, but you could see the slow, lazy plume of smoke that it had left behind along the way, and which now, *reduced to its own resources as a not very mobile cloud, was slowly climbing the green slopes of the Criquetot cliffs*. At last, the little tram, which it had preceded only to then take a vertical direction, *arrived in its turn, slowly*.

(Proust, *Sodom and Gomorrah*, 4:255–256)

Personification and Animation

The railroad topos has inspired unusual modes of artistic expression. Assigning trains animalian traits is a particularly widespread device, not so much in the overall appearance of the engine as the "anatomy" of separate parts as in the "behavior" of the machine.[172] Because the pulling power of the train as a close competitor and replacement for the horse,[173] it was this animal with which the train was most actively and most often compared at the turn of the century (for example, Robert Louis Stevenson's "The Iron Steed," where a locomotive/horse standing in a "pen" tells of a nighttime train journey[174]). Attributing animal traits necessarily distorted notions of the machine and its resting place: "Under the arches of colossal landing platforms *the torsos of snub-nosed locomotives sweated*" (*Okhrannaia gramota* [*Safe Conduct*]; Pasternak, *Sobranie sochinenii*, 4:168); "depot workers *were herding a locomotive into its stall*. The train's joints creaked as the breaks were suddenly applied. < … > The train came to a halt by an asphalt platform" (Il'f & Petrov, *The Twelve Chairs*, 145).[175]

---

[172]"An iron lightning – a coil of sheep armor! / I craned my neck after the running sheep" (Livshits, "Nochnoi vokzal" ["Train Station at Night"]; Livshits, *Polutoroglazyi strelets*, 56). "And the tension of bestial veins / The hissing of steam / The flight of distant sparks / The receding fumes" (D. Burliuk, "Zimnii poezd" ["Train in Winter"], 1914; D. Burliuk and N. Burliuk, *Stikhotvoreniia*, 177).

[173]"Let hazy tears fall from the sky / onto the iron breast – / today they fixed the paw / of the sick engine at the depot. / The whistle fiercely pierces / The low-hanging clouds. / Today the driver will torture / The bubbling boilers. / The locked-in fire makes noise, / The iron flute sings, / Today the iron horse / Will tear off of the taut rails" ("Rel'sy" ["The Rails"]; Svetlov, *Stikhotvoreniia i poemy*, 44).

[174]It is noteworthy that this poem was published in an English anthology for lovers of railroad literature, *The Railway-Lover's Companion* (531), while a Soviet anthology included a translation of Heinrich Heine's "The Steed and the Ass" (Leites et al., *Zheleznodorozhnyi transport*, 12–13). Many major European writers at various times composed works on the railroad theme, including Rupert Brook, Thomas Hardy, Rudyard Kipling, Gilbert Chesterton, T. S. Eliot, W. H. Auden, Stephen Spender, and others.

[175]Cf. the same metaphor of "creaking joints" in Narbut's poem, "The Railroad": "Father locomotive! / Your joints are creaking, / Cisterns are felling their hocks, / Trains formed into cadres / You thin out at night with your hand" (Narbut, *Stikhotvoreniia*, 325).

Animalian characteristics are also attributed to a locomotive in a 1923 poem by Nabokov ("Ekspress" ["The Express"]):

All is a
Concentrated rush, all is blessed
Tension, all is thirst, all is movement,
An enormous, living engine shakes,
And steam beats hotly in its iron veins,
And in the blackness drops of oil pour
From its monstrous shining wheels.

(Russian Collected Works, 1:467)

Nabokov uses the same technique in his short prose: "The locomotive, *working rapidly with its elbows,* hurried through a pine forest, then—with relief—among fields"[176] ("Cloud, Castle, Lake"; *Stories*, 431). And later, self-quoting,[177] in the early story, "Perfection": "on curves the semicircles of the front cars would become visible, with the heads of passengers who leaned on the lowered frames. Then the train, its bell ringing, *its elbows working ever so rapidly*, straightened out again to enter a beech forest" ("Perfection"; *Stories*, 342).

The basic principles of their motion make the locomotive and the horse comparable: a piston stroke (=joints) is accompanied by the iron clanging of "shining" wheels (=hooves):

"The train's motion seemed smoother and more relaxed, as if it had become accustomed to the rapid pace."

(Glory, 22)

"Puffing in the groin of the locomotive, / Overflowing, bubbling in its stomach, / While, *suffocating* from neurosis, / It sweated a glycerin blast."

(Narbut, Stikhotvoreniia, 324)

"Its pale jaws stuck in a snowdrift, / *The rumps of fallen engines show black*"

(Spektorskii, 1925–31; Pasternak, Sobranie sochinenii, 1:330)

---

[176]Cf. Iosif Utkin's poem, "Poezd" ("The Train"): "The engine pulls the cars, / Releasing steam over the embankment, / And *twists its long elbows*, / By the wheels of iron" (Utkin, *Izbrannye stikhi*, 90).

[177]There is an interesting textological anachronism here: the metaphor was originally used in the short story, "Cloud, Castle, Lake," with a manuscript date of June 25–26, 1937. The phrase is absent in the newspaper publication of "Perfection" (*Poslednie novosti.* June 3, 1932), but was inserted in the book publication in 1938.

"Wake up, arise, / At dawn I give a rusty neigh, / Heat and flame, / Drive away pain and rust. / *Pour me some oil, / Iron sides*"
(N. G. Poletaev, "Pesnia razbitogo parovoza" ["Song of a wrecked engine"], 1923; *Proletarskie poety*, 343)[178]

Between stations, trains yell and behave like wild beasts:

"*the heartrending wails* of locomotives in the dark of night."
(*Glory*, 24)

"The garden smells of linden trees, / And somewhere *a train, flying past, raises a scream.*"
(Erenburg, *Stikhotvoreniia*, 293)

"The arrival of a fire-breathing mountain, / Borne with thunder by a *sweating* locomotive."
(Pasternak, *Sobranie sochinenii*, 1:319)

"The armored train, its buffers clanging, *jumped back and with a screech rushed* to the station."
(Ivanov, Vsevolod. *Izbrannye proizvedeniia*, 63)

And trains sigh endlessly in various different ways:

"The train stopped with a clang of bumpers, and a *long, sibilant sigh* of brakes" ("A Matter of Chance"; *Stories*, 52); "The car stopped *with a prolonged sigh of relief.*"
(*Stories*, 57)

"The station was willed with a motley crowd ... / ... And a whistle rang out, smoke shot up along the road... / And *breathing heavily, as if tired from the road,* / The iron locomotive stopped before them."
(Apukhtin, *Stikhotvoreniia*, 197)

---

[178]Like human remains, the skeletons of wrecked trains are buried in specially designed places: "All around are cars, scrap, / All around the skeletons / Of old engines" (M. Iurin, "Na vagonnom kladbishche" ["At the Train Graveyard"], 1926; *Komsomol'skie poety*, 368).

"The engine *sighed deeply*. The speed slowed, the train shook, then stopped."

(Don-Aminado, *Poezd na tret'em puti*, 81)

"The good-hearted, stout locomotive, *with a sigh of relief*, dragged six cars of Japanese soldiers to the platform."

(Ivanov, Vsevolod. *Izbrannye proizvedeniia*, 15)

More rarely, the locomotive is given physiological attributes,[179] personality traits,[180] or aspects of human anatomy,[181] usually female, as in Andrei

FIGURE 2.14 *Train rounding a curve. Dry plate negative, between 1910 and 1920. Detroit Publishing Company photograph collection, Library of Congress.*

---

[179]In M. Garasimov's 1919 poem, "O parovoze" ("On a Locomotive"): "A wise forehead / Wrinkled by fumes, / Dark curls of smoke climbed out. / The driving rods – disjointed arms, / Helpless on the resonant / Rusty belly of the shell. Fallen joints – the bushings – / Pitifully nuzzled / To the bare tendons / Of copper pipes" (*Proletarskie poety*, 220).

[180]"This train, *stealing like a thief*, / These creeping stumps ... / It whimpered like a dog under the semaphore, / It was afraid to light the lights" (I. Elagin, "Zvezdy" ("Stars"); *Na zapade*, 322).

[181]In captions for photographs of a snowplow locomotive on the front page of the journal, *Veshch'* (edited by El' Lisitskii and Ilia Erenburg): "Depicting an engine is the same thing as painting a nude"; "The engine is a lesson in clarity and economy" (*Veshch'*. Berlin. 1922. № 3).

Platonov (the only Russian writer of his generation who actually worked on trains). As A. Toporkov shows in his unjustly forgotten 1928 popular science book, full of subtle observations and well-argued conclusions, *Tekhnicheskii byt i sovremennoe iskusstvo* (*Everyday technology and contemporary art*), it is in no way a coincidence that people who work with machines end up personifying them:

> "The engineer who loves his locomotive calls her 'Masha'; for this the machine is a living creature with whom he is prepared to share his joys and sorrows. This personification is, on the one hand, a remnant of primitive animism, but on the other hand it is an entirely natural requirement. Working with a machine, a man merges with its rhythm in his breathing, his heartbeat, and his blood, and only in this way does the work become as productive as it can be. ... Here, in these feelings, in this love, in this psychology of the technician, the professional, is the *key to understanding the machine as a work of art*. Here is the initiation of new beauty, here is the birth of a new aesthetic form."
>
> (Toporkov, *Tekhnicheskii byt*, 212)

Translating this allegory into the language of universal categories, the scholar reformulates the most important tenet of Dadaism, constructivism, and abstract art: any object has aesthetic value, and everything depends on an individual's attitude towards the object.

Clichés: Russians and the Railroad

In the Russian collective consciousness at the turn of the twentieth century, the story of the railroad was built on a foundation of tragedy comparable to the construction of St. Petersburg. Nekrasov's poem, "Zheleznaia doroga" ("The Railroad") (1864), reflects popular folklore: "A right little road: narrow mounds, / Columns, rails, bridges. / *And by the sides all Russian bones*" (Nekrasov, *Polnoe sobranie*, 2:160). The blood poured into the earth forges the connection between Russians and the road, and turns it into an element of the national mythos, something that would change its cast with the historical conditions,[182] but would nevertheless remain fundamentally the same.

---

[182]Nekrasov's poetics of suffering gave rise to the literary archetype of the "new man"—the absence of fathers in proletarian literature of the 1910s is presented as an education and a positive experience; cf. "Rails" (1913) from the industrial poetry cycle, *The Machine*, by A. K. Gastev: "Heavy, strong rails everywhere went, laid down, ran through, and banded around the earth. ... But then comes an eternally growing worker-creator, conceived in battle, born in fire, taken from under the hammer, nourished by a machine and nurtured by the factory whistle" (*Proletarskie poety*, 154).

Writing on Tolstoy in 1963, the Soviet literary critic Viktor Shklovskii provided a precise definition of the slight discomfort felt by his contemporaries when reading Tolstoy's *Alphabet*: "life is really quite simple and very little happens there. … New things mentioned are the railroad and electricity" (Shklovskii, *Lev Tolstoy*, 319). In the entry, "Strength from Speed" (subtitle: "A True Story"), Tolstoy describes a horse cart which gets stuck at a railroad crossing when it loses a back wheel. The engineer of a fast approaching train assesses the situation and decides not to slow down: "The man had run away from the cart and the engine threw the cart and horse off the road like a matchstick, but the horse didn't get shaken, she ran on" (Tolstoy, *Polnoe sobranie sochinenii*, 22:106). As Shklovskii explains, the story is intended as a parable against cowardice and dawdling. However, what seems far more important for Tolstoy is the collision of the patriarchal village ways of the Russian countryside and the locomotive that tears into this idyllic world and crushes everything in its path. The rational principle of Tolstoy's story supports Shklovskii's interpretation, but the emotional side of the conflict between the old and the new, the familiar and the alien, takes precedence over reason.

One of the most important attributes of the railroad is the "alien/ native" (*chuzhoe/rodnoe*) parameter. This makes itself most apparent at the intersection of worlds: at borders and at train stations. When Luzhin's mother returns to Russia, the sole thing that sticks in her memory from Europe is "that sparse un-Russian lilac in the station garden those tulip-shaped lamps in the sleeping car of the Nord Express" (*Defense*, 74). At the age of five, Nabokov was taken abroad for an entire year, at the end of which he, "as a six-year-old, had the first real occasion to experience the wood-smoke ecstasy of returning to one's homeland" (*Other Shores*; *Russian Collected Works*, 5:152). The smoke in question is not merely a concealed citation from Griboedov's comedic play,[183] but also a specific realistic detail: returning to within the borders of the Russian Empire, the locomotive furnaces switched to birch wood from coal. Crossing the border by rail also had a mechanical significance due to the lack of international standard rail gauges. As his memory untangles the route of "the then great and glamorous Nord-Express" from Petersburg to Paris,[184] which traveled twice a week before the revolution, Nabokov demonstrates some knowledge of

---

[183]The fascinating genealogy of the quote, "And the smoke of our homeland is sweet and pleasant," is traced by N. S. and M. G. Akushin from Homer and Ovid to Derzhavin and Viazemskii (Ashukin, *Krylatye slova*, 136–137). Homer's "*Patriae suae et fumus est duleis*" was used as early as 1801 in an epigraph to I. Glushkov's guidebook, *Hand Guide for Use on the Road Between the Capitals of Imperial Russia* (cited in Piksanov, *Griboedov*, 36).

[184]The advertising brochure for this route is reprinted in Zimmer, *Nabokovs Berlin*, 34. The trip from St. Petersburg to Berlin through Verzhbolovo took thirty-two to thirty-three hours.

the topic: "at the Russo-German frontier (Verzhbolovo-Eydtkuhnen), where the ample and lazy Russian sixty-and-a-half-inch gauge was replaced by the fifty-six-and-a-half-inch standard of Europe" (*Strong Opinions*, 202).[185] A half century before this, dry material comes to life in one of Nabokov's Russian novels, where the train is moving in the other direction: "The Nord-Express, *russified at Verzhbolovo*, retained the brown facings of its cars, but now became more sedate, wide-flanked, thoroughly heated, and, instead of gathering full speed right away, took a long time to gain momentum after a stop" (*Glory*, 24). The name of the border station (Verzhbolovo) has a special place as a toponym in Russian poetry, being both a geographical crossing point and culturally marked location in Russian poetry, as Rozanov described.[186] These properties are played on in a macaronic poem published in the popular art and literature journal, *Solntse Rossii* (*Sun of Russia*), in 1913,[187] entitled "*Shirokobokost'*" ("Wide-sidedness"). The lordliness of the Russian locomotive is rhymed with the breadth of the Russian soul, embodying it, and being interpreted as a typically Russian phenomenon, equal in its significance to the symbols of the home.[188] This is in contrast to the West, which, with its short distances between stations, "with its uninterrupted human dwellings and workplaces outside the windows, keeping nature from thinking its eternal thoughts" (Stepun, *Sbyvsheesia i nesbyvsheesia*, 174), does not know the romance of the Russian railroad.

---

[185]More accurately, the Russian gauge was 60 inches (5 feet) and the European gauge was 4 feet 8.5 inches. The common impression that the difference was intentionally maintained for strategic purposes is a widespread misconception. The width of the gauge in Russia varied during the early years of the railroad, from the common European standard to as much as 6 feet (as in nineteenth-century Great Britain). As was seen in the First World War in Poland, it is much easier to narrow the gauge than to widen it.

[186]"For the second time I cross a short little bridge cast across the wide ditch carved out between Deutschland and Russia, and have the same impression ... inhale deeply: that is Verzhbolovo ... at seven in the morning the passengers drink 'Russian coffee' for the final time. This 'worn smell' of unwashed linens, sweaty, suffocating, unpleasant, followed me the whole time" ("Pogranichnye zapakhi" ["Border Smells"]. *Russkoe slovo*. July 2, 1910. Cited in Rozanov, "*Inaia zemlia, inoe nebo ...*," 447).

[187]"Along the well-appointed express / The public decorously scurries; / Traveling along with us is / Baroness Elsa Butter-von-der-Brod. / Five are really quite mysterious / Three are businessmen in the elite, / So we find it impossible / Not to respect our random companions ... / Now Verzhbolovo has vanished, / Our native gendarme gone by, / And forward we rush again / Past the kirks and the barracks. / Firmly sewn 'bahnhofs' / Fly past us, / And the possibility of accidents / All of a sudden became less" (V. Golikov, "V Germanii (Iz putevogo al'boma)" ["In Germany (From a travel album)"]. *Solntse Rossii*. May 1913 (173). № 22, 15).

[188]"Recalling my travels around Russia, I remember first and foremost that the railcars were entirely different from those in Western Europe, both in terms of the knocking rhythm of the wheels and the prevailing mood therein. < ... > *if every home is merely a station, then why can't a railcar too be a real home?*" (Stepun, *Sbyvsheesia i nesbyvsheesia*, 165).

On the Road and Longing for Russia

As we have seen, the image of the Motherland in railroad lyrics by Russian poets signified a cultural expanse, broadening the sphere of influence of railroad poetics and creating a system of emotional connections between the lyric subject and the cultural space. The growth of national themes in the general literary topos—a phenomenon seemingly limited to Russian poetry—was matched by the increasing value of the railroad as an artery that connected to the homeland. Andrei Bely poem, "From the Train Window" (1908), on blood ties with the motherland even includes a game with the paronyms *rosa* (dew) and *Rossiia* (Russia):

> The train laments. In the distances of the homeland
> Stretches a telegraph network.
> Dewy fields fly by.
> I fly into the fields: to die ...
> Mother Russia! My songs are for you,
> O mute, stern mother!
>
> (Bely, *Sochineniia*, 1:92)

Cf. Solov'eva's 1909 poem, "On the Road," no less full of pathos:

> "Faster, faster!" the wheels insist.
> The forests race, the fields fly,
> A stream runs blue by the embankment.
> Hello, dear native land!
>
> (*Poety 1880–1890-kh godov*, 371)

Twenty years after Solov'eva, the émigré poet Eisner used the *"polia-zemlia"* ("fields-earth") rhyme to close the band of alienation that divides the foreign land and the homeland, which can be crossed painlessly only in the capsule of a train car:

> And from the train window, early in the morning,
> Looking at the receding fields,
> I will say through the waves of soft fog:
> Goodbye, alien and boring land![189]

Russian poets in exile, both in the post-October wave in Europe beginning in 1917,[190] and in the society that developed around the Second World War

---

[189]"Vozvrashchenie" ("The Return"; 1926). Cited from *Volia Rossii*. Prague. 1928. № 1, 37.
[190]Cf. the 1927 poem, "Rossiia" ("Russia") by M. Forshteter: "And they reach to the cursed stations / where an iron row of trains awaits, / where with a strange and muffled voice / the locomotive sirens wail" (*Antologiia poezii russkogo zarubezh'ia*, 1:416).

in the United States,[191] used an essentially ready-made nostalgic railroad topos. A boarding house full of Russian expatriates in *Mary* is placed in the immediate vicinity of a railroad junction (the trains "passing through that cheerless house in which lived seven Russian lost shades"; *Mary*, 22) with a view of "the fan of the railway tracks"—a motif fairly widespread, if not downright banal,[192] in émigré literature. The location near the station stimulates and catalyzes Ganin's nostalgia for Russia: "the longing for yet another strange land, grew especially strong in spring. His window looked out onto the railway tracks, so that the chance of getting away never ceased to entice him" (ibid., 9).

In addition to the rails and the ties, the outward appearance of the train itself can also evoke the longing of migrants. At a Berlin train station the erstwhile aristocrat Ukhtomskaia observes "lugubrious, iron-colored German carriages" of a train: "The varnished brown teak of one sleeping car bore under the center window a sign with the inscription BERLIN–PARIS; that international car, as well as the teak-lined diner < ... > were alone reminiscent of the severely elegant prewar Nord-Express" ("A Matter of Chance"; *Stories*, 52). As an old woman she associates her hopes of returning home with a train whose nostalgic transport function in literature remained unchanged from the classic establishment of the "little homeland" theme in Chekhov's *The Cherry Orchard*. Chekhov composes the paradigmatic recognition of a familiar landscape through the windows of a moving train in the figure of Ranevskaia returning from Paris: "God knows, I love my country, I love it dearly. *I couldn't see anything from the train*, I was crying so much" (Chekhov, *Five Plays*, 248).[193]

The dichotomy of space in the émigré consciousness is overcome by connecting two systems—the Soviet and the prerevolutionary—via the railroad. The protagonist of Nabokov's short story, "The Visit to the Museum" (1939), surreally finds himself in a frightening, gray version of Soviet reality with painted railcars, undergoing a cycle of tests. The rite of return to the old/new world is expressed as movement around a room devoted to the history of steam engines at a provincial museum. As he loses

---

[191]Cf. the choice of the editor of the New York anthology, "Segodnia russkoi poezii" ("Today's Russian Poetry"), Vorontsovksii: "Through the dim glass of the railcar / I look at dim Russia / And in my bare heart / I find the whole of Russian dimness" (R. Ivnev; From "Solntse v grobe" ["Sun in a Grave"]; *Segodnia russkoi poezii*, 1924, 17).

[192]In the prose of V. S. Ianovskii, which evoked Nabokov's criticism: "Outside my window is a square of wasteland – a clearing where freight cars and passenger cars floated; at the nearby station unseen engines are maneuvering: there whistles, still following me from childhood, pierce my heart again and again" ("Portativnoe bessmertie" ["Portable immortality"]; *Novyi zhurnal*. 1943. № 6, 133).

[193]The railroad that brings the exiled woman back to her homeland is also destructive at the same time: the new owner of the cherry orchard is banking on the fact that the estate is close to the rails, which he believes ensures that it will be commercially successful to divide it into dacha plots to rent out.

his guide, the main character finds an inch from him "the lofty wheels of a sweaty locomotive" and in his solitude tries long and hard "to find the way back among models of railroad stations" (*Stories*, 283). Through the image of the museum/station in this short story, presenting the museum as a writ of protection offering "safe conduct" for the recent past in post-revolutionary consciousness, the mature Nabokov seems to be polemicizing with the prose of Boris Pasternak. The "lofty wheels of a sweaty locomotive" in Nabokov's story originate here in Pasternak:

> Pawed by the station lights, beer in clean beakers shone clear. Along the stone platforms empty luggage barrows disappeared smoothly. ... Under the arches of gigantic passenger-bridges sweated the torsos of flat-snouted locomotives. It looked as if they had been borne to such a height by the play of their low wheels which had unexpectedly died down in full action.
> (Pasternak, *Safe Conduct*, 43)

The antithesis in "The Visit to the Museum" is reinforced by a mirror-image contrast in geography[194] (the train carrying Pasternak is going to Berlin, while Nabokov's character is going to Leningrad). In the scene where the protagonist gets lost in the darkness ("until I finally saw a red light[195] and walked out onto a platform that *clanged* under me"), Nabokov's ellipsis may, in the overarching railroad text of Russian literature that we have constructed, indicate a silence that presumes an appeal to tradition. In his chapter devoted to trains, Pasternak describes the changes in platforms like the shuffling of a deck of texts:[196] "Clanging familiar names as on naked steel, the journey took them one by one *from read descriptions*, as from dusty scabbards, prepared by the historians" (Pasternak, *Safe Conduct*, 43).

It was not only Russians in emigration who fondly recalled prewar and preRevolution aesthetics. Il'f and Petrov, for whom Nabokov had a liking, touched on the superficial nature of Bolshevik transformations in a cautious critique of the regime. As the target of their parody they choose a Soviet express train and make no effort to conceal their nostalgia for the models used in Russia before the Revolution: "Someone told someone that somewhere on earth there are blue express trains famous for their speed,

---

[194]On the poetics of railroad toponyms, cf. Don-Aminado: "*The names of stations and whistle-stops had their own inexplicable poetry about them*, a sort of special rhythm, a mystery of primordial magic and great enchantment" (Don-Aminado, *Poezd na tret'em puti*, 15).

[195]Cf. the name of the fictional Soviet journal that Nabokov connects with the railroad tracks leading into the USSR: "between *The Star* and *The Red Lamp* (trembling in railway smoke)" (*The Gift*, 158).

[196]The first part of *Okhrannaia gramota* (published in English as *Safe Conduct*) was published in *Zvezda* (1929. № 8), while the second and third parts were published in *Krasnaia nov'* (1931. № 4). The first publication of the entire work was in Leningrad in 1931.

comfort, and brilliance." And so the Kiev–Moscow line gets an express train on which all the cars, including the baggage car, are duly painted in a bright blue, but beyond that the resemblance ends. The Soviet comic writers continue, noting that:

> First of all it is not an express: it makes 800 kilometers in 20 hours. And its lounge cars are outfitted worse than the same cars in ordinary trains. *And its dining car is filthy and the food is no good. However, there are enormous pots with tedious flowers on the tables in the compartments, and the windows have rigid ribbed curtains. They would probably have brought in some palm trees had there been room.*
> (Il'f & Petrov, "U samovara" ["By the Samovar"]
Pravda. September 23, 1934. № 263)

In conclusion, the authors write that "it's easier to render a person senseless with underworld songs meant for a foxtrot than *to achieve genuine sparkling cleanliness at a station and true comfort in the train.*" The reader in exile would have immediately recognized in the rail station crowd the metaphor of Soviet society in the heat of competitiveness and five-year plans. But even the conscientious Soviet reader must have asked a seditious question: will this locomotive, rushing forward, decorated with posters and flowers, turn out upon closer inspection to be an outdated car hitched to the end of the train of history?

Nabokov and Tsvetaeva: Synoptic Chart of a Dialog

The topic of "alien but hopelessly native" Soviet Russia was continued in a striking intertextual dialog between Nabokov and Marina Tsvetaeva in the 1920s and 1930s. In *The Gift*, Nabokov has his character Godunov-Cherdyntsev fantasize about returning to Russia:

> Perhaps one day, on foreign-made soles < ... > I shall again come out of that station < ... >. The day will probably be on the grayish side. < ... > *but still* [I will] *make out something* < ... > *if only because my eyes are, in the long run, made of the same stuff as the grayness, the clarity, the dampness of those sites.*
> (*The Gift*, 30)

The foggy aura of the railroad mythos, along with its semantics of crossing over and its capability of deforming time, is here clustered into a vision on the level of a weather forecast. The phonetic game is reminiscent of another attempt to reconstruct Russia in Tsvetaeva's poem, "Rassvet na rel'sakh" ("Dawn on the Rails"), written October 12, 1922:

Iz syrosti i shpal	From dampness and rail ties
Rossiiu vosstanavlivaiu ...	I am restoring Russia ...
Iz syrosti i svai,	From dampness and poles,
Iz syrosti i serosti.	From dampness and grayness.
Pokamest den' ne vstal	Before the day breaks
I ne vmeshivalsia strelochnik ...	And the switchman intervenes ...
Iz syrosti i shpal,	From dampness and rail ties,
Iz syrosti – i sirosti	From dampness – and orphanedness

Fyodor Dviniatin suggests that Tsvetaeva's poem served as a source for the later reverberation in *The Gift* (Dviniatin, "Nabokov i futuristicheskaia traditsiia," 137). However, a passage from Nabokov's early poetry indicates that the opposite might be the case: more than a year before Tsvetaeva's poem, the newspaper *Rul'* (July 10, 1921) published Nabokov's "On the Train" with the following stanza:

Light on the curtains, like a phantom, passed by.
Heeding the shaking and friction
Of the quieting wheels, I lowered the frame:
It smelt of dampness and lilac (*syrost' i siren'*)
                              (*Russian Collected Works*, 1:465)

By the time of their first meeting three years later in Prague on January 24, 1924, Nabokov and Tsvetaeva had had the opportunity to scrutinize each other in print in émigré publications. The seemingly conscious allusion in Tsvetaeva's text and her interest in the promising young poet (younger by nine years), culminated in a "strange lyrical stroll" (*Other Shores*; *Russian Collected Works*, 5:317) involving the two poets in the Czech capital.

It should be noted that, in addition to the common motif of the return to Russia by rail, Tsvetaeva's poem includes the word *sirost'*, while Nabokov's poem was published under the name *Sirin*. Afterwards, the thematic scope of the words is expanded by Nabokov, who in the late 1920s develops Tsvetaeva's *syrost'-serost'-sirost'* triad as a euphemistic code for the *SSSR* (Russian for the USSR). In his 1927 article, "Iubilei" ("The Anniversary"), written ten years after the October coup, Nabokov offers his own etymology for the Bolshevik abbreviation: "At this time when they are celebrating the gray, SSR anniversary ['*seryi, esesernyi iubilei*'], we are celebrating ten years of hatred, faithfulness, and freedom" (*Russian Collected Works*, 2:647).

Using the word *siren'* ("lilac") in Russian poetry to stand for the landscape of the homeland and nostalgia for Russia became a trend as early as the mid-nineteenth century (see Belousov, "Akklimatizaciia sireni"), and this tradition was carried on by Sirin.[197] In the poem *"Siren'"* (*Rul'*, May 13, 1928), Nabokov prepares the lexical grouping that was later developed in *The Gift*: "The night ... quivered with lilac, gray [*drognula siren'iu, seroi*] ... my night, hazy and light" (*Russian Collected Works*, 2:549–550).

Thus behind a sentence about the weather in *The Gift* stands an intricate network of motifs growing out of a give-and-take with Tsvetaeva, a fragment of poetic two-part harmony, which, by the end of the 1930s, had receded into the past, such that Nabokov in his mature prose could pay tribute to it.

The Beckoning Distance

Gogol's concept of *the distance* went through a number of versions over a century of Russian literature. As the troika was forced out by more modern means of transportation, "distance" was rolled up, changing from a spatial quality to a virtual abstraction. In parallel, the purely national connotations are supplemented by universalist ones: the view from the moving window in any given place in emigration, by (un)focusing one's gaze, becomes something larger than a piece of the native landscape:

> How often, how often, in a fast train
> I have sat and wondered at the floating expanses,
> And clung to the glass with my forehead growing cold!..
> ... And the distance of fields
> Blissfully turned in a light-blue delirium.
> ("Kak chasto, kak chasto ia v poezde skorom ...")
> ["How often, how often in a fast train I ..."], 1923;
> *Russian Collected Works*, 1:467)

The ghostly "distance" becomes synonymous with a sort of "sixth sense,"[198] and this dualism combines two opposing categories: light (the sky/fog/haze) and darkness (the abyss/chasm). The sources of the former can be traced

---

[197]In "To Prince S. M. Kachurin" (1947), regarding an imagined return to his homeland: "I imagine chirping ... / and a station, and slanting rain / visible in the dark, and then / The lash of lilacs at the station" (*Russian Collected Works*, 5:430).

[198]"Ah, this sixth sense, / The sense of the rails, wheels, space, / That which Russians have taken / To calling the 'beckoning distance'" (Don-Aminado, *Poezd na tret'em puti*, 120). After first formulating it in "Golubye poezda" ("Light-blue Trains") in 1927, years later Don-Aminado (Shpolianskii) repeated this definition in the 1954 poem "Poezd na tret'em puti" (Train on the Third Rail): "The sixth sense, which only the district had, was *the sense of the railroad*" (ibid., 15).

to nature, and of the latter to the human subconscious. It is no accident that Nabokov's characters begin to daydream, falling into delirium when traveling:

> and in the black depths a ruby flashed,
> behind it a strip of amber, and a hum
> flew up to the station, a mighty iron hum,
> from the abyss of abysses, from the heart of a moonlit night.
>
> ("Ekspress" ["The Express"], 1923;
> *Russian Collected Works*, 1:466)

Projected into the deep subconscious, dreams open up a view into the "abyss of abysses" within. The railroad takes the sleeping Krug (from *Bend Sinister*) away to his schoolyard, which is easily recognized as a location in Petersburg, and specifically the yard of the former Tenishchev Academy at 33 Mokhovaia, with an entryway that survives to this day. The "tunnel of sorts" that leads to the schoolyard turns into a railway tunnel in Krug's mind, and then takes on the properties of a dark pipe connecting the past and the future, with their different frames of reference:[199]

> Now he found himself running (by night, ugly? Yah, by night, folks) down something that looked like a railway track through a long damp tunnel (the dream stage management having used the first set available for rendering 'tunnel', *without bothering to remove either the rails or the ruby lamps* that glowed at intervals along the rocky black sweating walls). < ... > *he reached the diner.*
>
> (*Bend Sinister*, 66)

Scholars generally have little trouble finding in Nabokov's prose scenes written over the permanent ink of his biography. One example of this sort of palimpsest is the railroad dream passed on to Martin Edelweiss by the author. It is well known that Nabokov suffered from chronic insomnia his whole life, but as a child he successfully applied the following stratagem: "I would put myself to sleep by the simple act of identifying myself with the engine driver"; "the carefree passengers were enjoying the ride" he was giving them, while he, "goggled and begrimed," peered out of the engine cab (*Speak, Memory*, 145). Based on the recipe from Nabokov's memoirs, Martin, lying in bed, imagines "the long, brown, diaphragm-joined cars"

---

[199]On the movement of a train passenger as a relativistic narrative device, see Grishakova, *The Models of Space*, 85–86.

of an express train that he is driving. The experience of the trip leads to something approaching a spiritual catharsis for the child:[200]

[H]is mind would gradually catch the rhythm, grow blissfully serene, be cleansed, as it were, and, sleek and oiled, slip into oblivion.

(*Glory*, 108)

Nabokov himself also had some experience of transcendental connections with the mythology of the rails in his day-to-day life as a young man in Petersburg. As he tells of his morning strolls with his governess past the model of a sleeping car on Nevskii Prospekt, he elevates his childhood whim to the level of a religious ritual: "I *always* stopped and *worshipped it*" (*Other Shores*; *Russian Collected Works*, 5:234).[201]

To possess such a portable model, to hold casually right in my hands the sleeping car which was taking us abroad each fall, would be almost tantamount to being it all at once – an engine-driver, and a passenger, and colored lights, and a station flying by with its immobile figures, and polished silky rails, and the tunnel in the mountains.[202]

Simpson, the main character from the short story "La Veneziana," has from childhood been subject to "auditory hallucination," and the latest manifestation of this takes him to a quiet forest at evening. The mental disorder, which we might call "Simpson's symptom," seems to parody Chekhov's manifesto from the monolog of Nina Zarechnaia from *The Seagull*, with an adjustment made to substitute futurist realia for that of the decadent era: the "geese, spiders, and silent fishes" are replaced by wheels, rails, and urban asphalt. Simpson begins to believe he is hearing:

[T]*he entire, enormous world traversing space with a melodious whistle*, the bustle of distant cities, < ... > the singing of telegraph wires above the deserts. < ... > He could hear the chugging of a train, even though the tracks might have been dozens of miles away; then the clanging and screeching of wheels and—as his recondite hearing grew ever more

---

[200]A. Dolinin interprets the life journey of Edelweiss as the conflict between two types of travels: the trip by train and the pilgrimage on foot, which concludes with him offering himself as a sacrifice to a romantic idea (Dolinin, "Istinnaia zhizn' pisatelia Sirina;" *Russian Collected Works*, 3:23).

[201]Cf. in "Time and Ebb": "I am also old enough to remember *the coach trains: as a babe I worshipped them*; as a boy I turned away to improved editions of speed. With their haggard windows and dim lights they still lumber sometimes through my dreams" (*Stories*, 584).

[202]This passage is found only in *Other Shores* (*Russian Collected Works*, 5:234) and it is missing from the *Speak, Memory*. Transl. from the Russian by Y. Leving.

acute—*the passengers' voices, their coughs and laughter, the rustling of their newspapers, and, finally, plunging totally into his acoustic mirage, he clearly distinguished their heartbeat, and the rolling crescendo of that beat, that drone, that clangor*, deafened Simpson.

(*Stories*, 97)

The further abstraction of the notion of *distance*, becoming an "auditory mirage" in the mind of a character, leads to it being substituted for in the urban landscape by the street view, the labyrinth of alleyways, the flashing of walls with giant advertisements. The two main cities in the European period of Nabokov's life, Petersburg and Berlin, represent different ways of organizing the urban space. The difference between Western metropolises and Russian ones is that in the former the network of rail tracks grew together with the municipal landscape and is understood as an organic part of the city (Luzhin's drawing of a train on a bridge over a chasm combines a viaduct and the yard of a house, presumably the same one that swallows up the character on the final page of the novel). Martin is familiar with the phenomenon of neutralizing the Russian "distance": in the evening as he approaches the German capital and looks out at the illuminated streets from the train car, he "relived his childhood impression of Berlin, whose fortunate inhabitants could enjoy daily, if they wished, the sight of trains with fabulous destinations, *gliding across a black bridge over a humdrum thoroughfare*; in this respect *Berlin differed from St. Petersburg, where railroad operations were concealed like a secret rite*" (*Glory*, 133).

Nabokov describes the layering of the romance of the railroad and urban aesthetics in all its phases in *Speak, Memory*:

When on such journeys as these, the train changed its pace to a dignified amble and all but grazed housefronts and shop signs, as we passed through some big German town, I used to feel a twofold excitement, which terminal stations could not provide. I saw *a city, with its toylike trams, linden trees and brick walls, enter the compartment*, hobnob with the mirrors, and fill to the brim the windows on the corridor side. This informal contact between train and city was one part of the thrill. The other was putting myself in the place of some passer-by who, I imagined, was moved as I would be moved myself to see the long, romantic, auburn cars, with < ... > their metal lettering copper-bright in the low sun, unhurriedly negotiate an iron bridge across an everyday thoroughfare and then turn, with all windows suddenly ablaze, around a last block of houses.

(*Speak, Memory*, 143–144)

Before Nabokov, the view of an enchanted boy from a train window was described by Andreev in his short story, "Pet'ka na dache" ("Petka at the

Dacha"), using the same effect of the objects outside the window seeming to be "toys":

> To the right of the tracks stretched a bumpy plane, dark green from the constant dampness, at the edge of which were strewn little gray houses that looked like toys, while on a tall green hill, at the bottom of which shone a strip of silver, there was a toy church just like them. When with a sonorous metallic clang, heard unexpectedly, the train raced up to the bridge and seemingly hung in the air over the reflective smoothness of the river, Pet'ka went so far as to shake from the fright and unexpectedness, and he stepped back from the window, only to return to it right away, afraid to miss the slightest detail of the voyage.
>
> (Andreev, *Sobranie sochinenii*, 1:144)

Nabokov's voyeurism is constructed differently: the observer "fishes out" and establishes the sequence in the development of the theme presented by the train window. The city is the most saturated and shortest part of the journey, and so it is more difficult to notice a consistent pattern. Another matter entirely is the pastoral landscape, always included in the system of railroad motifs from the later nineteenth century, of which an inalienable component is the telegraph pole.[203]

Telegraph Poles

> Here is how the telegraph is made: electricity is sent along a wire, and this wire is wrapped around an iron cylinder. Above the cylinder a little iron hammer is suspended. ... And in this way a person at one station can bang the hammer at another station. And there are agreed-upon meanings for these knocks.
> —Lev Tolstoy, *Russkie knigi dlia chteniia* [*Russian Books for Reading*]

In early cinematography, the windows of a train evoked associations with the frame of a screen, within which the scenery moved in ways that paralleled devices from rapid shooting to the incidental composition of shots. The moving images viewed through the window of a train had a special power to stimulate the creative mind: a tunnel that suddenly appears that breaks the monotony of the scenery, or a stop at an unfamiliar way-station that could contain a secret plot. A character from Nabokov's "Cloud, Castle, Lake" looks out of the window at some children waiting on a station

---

[203]The first electric telegraph was installed in Russia in 1856 (Westwood, *A History of Russian Railways*, 25).

FIGURE 2.15 *Telegraph poles. Photographer: Paul Strand. Illustration appeared in* Camera Work, *no. 48 (October 1916).*

platform and "[tries] with all his might to single out at least one remarkable destiny—in the form of a violin or a crown, a propeller or a lyre" ("Cloud, Castle, Lake"; *Stories*, 432). The fleeting speed of such visions, and the *incompleteness* of the act of watching force the reader/passenger to finish drawing the picture in his mind: the rapid disappearance of the omens by which one might calculate the future of a musical virtuoso is compensated for by the drama of eternal loss.[204] But the creator of a film can augment plot tension using additional means, from sound effects to the composition of a shot. Associations with the cinematic experience are also evoked by the notion of the passenger as observer, as a *spy* watching the intimate moments of a stranger—"Beyond the glass was a magical world, magical because *I was looking in on it unexpectedly and against the rules, without the slightest possibility of participating in it*" (*Other Shores*; *Russian Collected Works*, 5:238)—a vantage point paralleled by the telegraph poles that line the track: "Telegraph poles – / The spies of fate!"[205]

Nabokov focuses on these poles, and particularly the telegraph wires, which function as a constant in the window scenery: "[they] were doing their best to slant up, to ascend skywards, despite the lightning blows dealt them by one telegraph pole after another; but just as all six, in a triumphant swoop of pathetic elation, were about to reach the top of the window, *a particularly vicious blow would bring them down, as low as they had ever been, and they would have to start all over again*" (*Speak, Memory*, 143). The energy of this beating is converted into a meaningful stroke: "a telegraph pole, black against the sunset, flew past, *interrupting the smooth ascent of the wires*. They dropped as a flag drops when the wind stops blowing. Then furtively they began rising again" ("A Matter of Chance": *Stories*, 54); "*the telegraph poles, cutting short the wires' upward sweep*" (*Glory*, 60). The appearance of the poles affects the rhythmic organization of a lyric poem:

And past the broad roaring windows
twined and melted curl after curl
of flying smoke, and pole after pole
skipped past, breaking the flow
of the soaring threads.
    ("Kak chasto, kak chasto ia v poezde skorom ..." ["How often, how
    often in a fast train I ..."], 1923; *Russian Collected Works*, 1:467)

The sweep of the wires and the regular interval of the poles they are connected to sets a rhythm in which a poet might see musical notation. The musical stave is evoked both by the stretching wires and by the combination of ties and rails that makes up the railroad tracks.[206] Nabokov is not interested in the notes on these staves, but in what they might produce, comparing the poles and their wires to the bridges and strings of a violin—"The telegraph

---

[204]Cf.: "And so the station flies and flickers / And is lost (forever, forever!)" (V. Narbut, "Zheleznaia doroga" ["The Railroad"], 1922; Narbut, *Stikhotvoreniia*, 184).

[205]Cf. I. Elagin: "Telegraph poles – / The spies of fate!" (*Literaturnyi sbornik*, 14).

[206]"In some sort of musical staff / Lounging like bedsheets – / The railroad strip, / The cutting blue of the rails!" (Tsvetaeva, "Rel'sy" ["The Rails"], 1923; Tsvetaeva, *Stikhotvoreniia i poemy*, 351).

poles, like violin bridges, flew past with spasms of guttural music" (*The Enchanter*, 68); "*The columns fly past in the ecstasy of the sunset / and black strings soar on wings*" ("How often, how often in a fast train," 1923; *Russian Collected Works*, 2:467). In the 1924 story, "A Matter of Chance," the motif transforms into a harp: "Five distinct harp strings swooped desperately upward alongside the windows" (*Stories*, 54) (the number of strings varies; cf. in *Speak, Memory*: "six thin black wires"; *Speak, Memory*, 143).

Earlier on in the story, the telegraph poles in Nabokov's description take on an ethereal quality—"between the airy walls of a spacious fire-bright evening" and "through the corridor window beyond the glass compartment door the even row of telegraph wires could be seen swooping upward" (*Stories*, 54)—which echoes Nabokov's depiction in a poem from 1920:

> The porcelain bells of uniform poles
> by the roadway, and six
> buzzing strings. Message after message slips –
> the hum of countless anxious voices ...
> And you, on the pale strip of road,
> you, sun-baked, barefoot pilgrim,
> slow your pace and freeze with the wind,
> heeding the singing floating by.
>
> (*Russian Collected Works*, 1:531)

Here the anxious voices dictating messages are heard only in the imagination, but in certain cases the reader can puzzle out the key to the coded dispatch. As Shklovskii put it, telegraph poles are like gossips, and the telegram in process is "saturated with rumors."[207] Here the voltage of the telegraph takes on an emotional aspect:

> And along the whole plane of the night
> the telegraph beats like a heart,
> and people rush on the handcar
> raising torches in the dark.
>
> ("Krushenie" ["The Wreck"], 1925;
> *Russian Collected Works*, 1:567)

A transmitter can even be equated with a super-sensitive addressee (as in Tsvetaeva's cycle "Provoda" ["The Wires"][208]), or the wires might switch

---

[207]Shklovskii, *Gamburgskii schet*, 240. On the impact of telegraph wires in poetry in the first quarter of the twentieth century, see the chapter entitled "Elegizm telegrafnoi volny" ("Elegy and the telegraph wave") in Viacheslav Ivanov's book on Pasternak (*Izbrannye trudy*, 1:125–130).

[208]"The lyrical wires / Of my high tension hum. / Telegraph pole! Is there a shorter way / To choose? While there is still a sky – / The immutable transmitter of feelings, / Palpable message from the mouth" (Tsvetaeva, *Stikhotvoreniia i poemy*, 327).

places with the nerves of a poet.[209] The apotheosis of the dialog between the wanderer and the telegraph conductor is the prophecy of Russia recognizing its prodigal son: "*One after another the telegraph poles will hum at my approach.* < ... > I think that as I walk I shall utter something like a moan, in tune with the poles" (*The Gift*, 30). The vibration of the poles coincides with the psychological mechanism of the exile, who discerns a wave of response in "the hum of countless anxious voices."

The affinity between the rhythms of verse and of the telegraph, and the use of one in a meta-description of the other, have been noted before (see Khazan, "Iz nabliudenii"). Poetry, unlike a telegraph operator, is fundamentally concerned with breaking down the barriers of generations, languages, and cultural codes. The role of the author as someone who breaks down feelings of solitude and social isolation is transferred to communication technology, as in Georgii Ivanov's contemporary reworking of Lermontov's conversation among the stars in the night sky:

> Quietly I walk in a dead garden
> And hear in Morse code
> Star clicking to star.
>
> ("Posmertnyi dnevnik" ["Posthumous Diary"], 1958;
> Georgii Ivanov, *Sobranie sochinenii*, 1:568)

The poet, creator of new information signals and updater of old ones, defines fate as the relentless march of telegraph poles, and thereby connects his own works to the communications networks of culture.

The View from the Train Window

By the beginning of the twentieth century, the view from a train window had become an elegiac template. Typical examples can be seen in "V vagone" ("In the Railcar") by Korinfskii (1892) and "V doroge" ("On the road") by Solov'eva (1909):

> The twists of silver streams
> Flash everywhere before me,
> Bristled crests of bushes

---

[209]"The bared, strung-out nerves / Of chilled telegraph poles!" ("Chto oni noiut tomitel'nym stonom ..." ["Why do they howl with a torturous groan ..."]; Zenkevich, *Skazochnaia era*, 170).

Float like a green wave ...
The train rushes ... Overtaking it,
A pale swarm of reveries flies

(*Poety 1880–1890-kh godov*, 425)

I look out of the train. Outside the window
A fleece of smoky clouds stretched,
And behind the pale, curling fleece
Golden wine poured.

(ibid., 371)

Nabokov's landscapes did not conform to traditional notions of poetic representation. For example, the Soviet critic Mikhail Osorgin reproached Nabokov for the fact that in his works "*nature may flash in a train window or a frame at a resort, but it never appears in an unkempt form. The author has no need for nature in such a form; it does not inspire him*" (*Pro et contra*, vol. 1, 240). Nabokov's nonconformist interpretation of his environment bothered his contemporaries. Although he was not formally allied with the futurists, whose aim was to deliver a "slap in the face of public taste," he nevertheless had his characters focus on things that would have provoked a feeling of distaste in a reader reared on the Russian classics. The "author's representative" in "Cloud, Castle, Lake" focuses on "the configuration of some entirely insignificant objects from his train window – *a smear on the platform, a cherry stone, a cigarette butt*"[210] (*Stories*, 432); the main character in "A Dashing Fellow," looking out the window of a train starting to move, waits while "the background will show through [a lady on the platform] – *a refuse bin, a poster, a bench*" (ibid., 260); and the protagonist of *King, Queen, Knave* bids farewell with a glance at the stretching platform, carrying off "on an unknown journey *cigarette butts, used tickets, flecks of sunlight and spittle*" (*King, Queen, Knave*, 1).

The insignificant shares its space with the shocking, and pathos is generated by the juxtaposition of objects, the contrast between their meaninglessness and the mystical programming of their "particular interrelation." These patterns that the character "see[s] with such deathless precision" ("Cloud, Castle, Lake"; *Stories*, 432) are unique and never to be repeated.[211]

---

[210]Cf. the first catch-line in Erenburg's novella, *Summer 1925*: "The main thing is the cigarette butt, the fat cigarette butt, lying on the pavement near the 'FA' bus station" (Erenburg, *Sobranie sochinenii*, 2:357).

[211]A somewhat similar mini-drama plays out in the mind of a passenger in Shefner's "Dorozhnaia elegiia" ("Road Elegy"; 1940), who is in a train passing the familiar haunts of his childhood and at a certain point feels tempted to jump out of the train (Shefner, *Sobranie sochinenii*, 1:46).

What do Nabokov's characters actually see and, more importantly, how do they see through the frame of the train window? Let us take the following example from *King, Queen, Knave*:

> A wall of beech trees was flickering by the window in a speckled sequence of sun and shade. < ... > now it was no longer a fence-like forest glancing by but vast meadows majestically gliding past, and, in the distance, parallel to the tracks, flowed a highway, along which sped lickety-split a lilliputian automobile.
>
> (*King, Queen, Knave*, 5–6)

This passage is constructed on the classic parameters of Nabokov's prose, from alliteration ("lickety-split a lilliputian" ["*ulepetyval liliputovyi*" in Russian; *Russian Collected Works*, 2:134]) to a perspective that has objects moving in the same direction at different speeds. The speed of the car is clearly greater than that of the train, while both are presented against the background of a smoothly shifting landscape.[212] Nabokov, of course, has a privileged perspective as the creator of this scene—only he has access to all its information, of the panorama, the details it contains and all that cannot be seen. As Bakhtin states, the author "not only sees and knows everything that each character and all the characters together know, but even more than that" (Bakhtin, *Raboty 1920-kh godov*, 96). Essentially, an author knows and sees what is inaccessible to his characters. In opposition to this authorial focus, the following passage offers a pastoral view from a train shown through the eyes of a character:

> He was left alone with his gray sandwich in the now spacious compartment. He munched and gazed out of the window. A green bank was rising there diagonally until it suffused the window to the top. Then, resolving an iron chord, a bridge banged overhead and instantly the green slope vanished and open country unfurled fields, willows, a golden birch tree, a winding brook, beds of cabbage. Franz finished his sandwich, fidgeted cozily, and closed his eyes.
>
> (*King, Queen, Knave*, 12–13)

The marked earthiness of the rural landscape and the cyclical structure of the description, with the excerpt being framed by the alimentary and bodily component, correlate with the limited worldview of the provincial traveler. A comparison of these two passages reveals the different interpretations

---

[212]Cf. what Nabokov calls "optical amalgamations": "the car < ... > being recklessly sheathed, lurching waiters and all, in the landscape, while the landscape itself went through a complex system of motion" (*Speak, Memory*, 144).

of the scenery by a fictional character (with his divided and punctuated impressions) and by the implied author, who is capable of uninterrupted thought and can overcome compartmentalized representation ("no longer a fence-like forest"). The continuum of vision on the part of the creator is juxtaposed by the discreteness of emotions felt by the neurotic Franz, who is shocked upon entering a tunnel: "A short tunnel deafened him with its resounding darkness," and then "it was light again but the conductor had vanished"—the momentarily lost picture is compensated for by light.

The absence of the visual image therefore not only undermines the full value of the traveler's experience, but can also lead a sensitive person to depression. Nabokov takes this further in constructing all the nuances of a blind person's experience on a train. The blind Krechmar in *Camera Obscura* (Albinus in the English version, *Laughter in the Dark*), on a train to Zurich, "felt his gorge rise with nausea, because he could not harmonize the clatter and rocking of the carriage with any forward motion, *no matter how hard he tried to imagine the landscape which, surely, was speeding past*" (*Laughter in the Dark*, 249–250).

In contrast to Krechmar's/Albinus's blindness is the type of voluntary blindness we see in Zilanov (*Glory*). He always travels "light, with three clean handkerchiefs in his briefcase, and would sit in the railway carriage *completely blind to picturesque spots* (which the fast train traversed in its trusting efforts to please), immersed in a brochure and making occasional notes in the margin" (*Glory*, 77). The irony Nabokov generates here (including by the dual meaning of the word "*polia*" [*polia*, meaning both "fields" and "margins" in Russian]) confirms that the view out of the window acts as a necessary component in the full experience of a journey: the moving scenery is a constant subject of the romance of the railroad.

Nabokov is interested in the virtual reality of images, the architecture of sentences and the rhythmic arrangement of prose in general, precision in word choice, and the richness of metaphors. But what means does Nabokov use to achieve the effect of movement and evoke a sense of velocity?

It was morning in the corridor, the sun had just risen, the fresh, blue shadow of the train ran over the grass, over the shrubs, swept sinuously up the slopes, rippled across the trunks of flickering birches—and an oblong pondlet shone dazzlingly in the middle of a field, then narrowed, dwindled to a silvery slit, and with a rapid clatter a cottage scuttled by, the tail of a road whisked under a crossing gate—and once more the numberless birches dizzied one with their flickering, sun-flecked palisade.[213]

("The Passenger"; *Stories*, 185–186)

---

[213]Cf.: "Outside the window the pine trees / Execute a wild circle dance. / The distances are unbearable in their brightness, / The sun is a burning coal" ("V vagone" ["In the Railcar"], 1920; Briusov, *Sobranie sochinenii*, 3:415).

We can identify six basic narrative properties that might be called the "load-bearing structures" not only in this excerpt, but in the poetics of movement in general:

- An accumulation of action verbs: *to run, to sweep, to scuttle, to whisk.*
- Discrete visual perception expressed by verbs (*to ripple, to flicker*) and adjectives (*flickering*).
- The cinematic device of breaking down the shot, in this case showing each successive still image from different perspective distances: a) *oblong pondlet* ("oblong" only from the point of view of someone moving in the train) → b) *narrowed* → c) *dwindled to a silvery slit.*
- Conveying acceleration by transferring the characteristics of speed and noise to an object being observed (*with a rapid clatter a cottage scuttled by*).
- Filling the text with words describing the reaction of the main character ("he got dizzy"; this phrase is present only in the Russian original—"zakruzhilas' golova").
- Finally, moderate lengthening of sentences to grammatically mimic the elongation of the track.[214]

Here is another excerpt from the same work:

The birches suddenly dispersed, half a dozen small houses poured down a hill, some of them, in their haste, barely missing being run over by the train; then a huge purple-red factory strode by flashing its windowpanes; somebody's chocolate hailed us from a ten-yard poster; another factory followed with its bright glass and chimneys; in short, there happened what usually happens when one is nearing a city.

(ibid., 186)

Verbs of motion attributed to inanimate objects (small houses *poured down*, factory *strode by*) create an effect of metonymic freshness, while the repetition of items in one line (*factory* < ... > flashing its *windowpanes* < ... > another

---

[214]In Pasternak's poem, "Kosykh kartin ..." ("Oblique Pictures ..."), the movement of a train is shown from the point of a moving object: a car tearing down a highway (on the description from the observer's shifting position, see Boris Uspenskii, *Semiotika iskusstva*, 86–88). Uspenskii notes that movement can be conveyed not only as an aggregate of separate scenes presented from their position in space (like the combination of still shots on a roll of film), but also by another method: as a single scene captured from a moving position (associated with the deformation of objects caused by this movement).

factory < ... > with its bright *glass*[215]) is calculated to bombard the eye, to overfill and weary the reader in his role as spectator. The maximum repetition of lexemes in the minimum amount of textual space creates the required rhythm of movement, even if it is at the expense of including tautologies and puns, as in *Ada*, where "the length of the journey varied according to Van's predormient mood, when < ... > he imagined the landscapes unfolding all along his comfortable, too comfortable, fauteuil. < ... > the room moved as slowly as fifteen miles per hour but across desertorum or agricultural drearies it attained seventy, ninety-seven, night-nine, one hund, red dog—" (*Ada*, 346).[216]

The sentence from "The Passenger" quoted above about the anthropomorphic advertisement is worthy of separate analysis as an example of the semantic complexity in Nabokov's phrasing: "somebody's chocolate hailed us from a ten-yard poster." "Chocolate hailed"[217] may refer to a placard caption (an oblique version of advertising exhortations such as "Eat at Joe's" or "Drink Van Houten's Cacao!"), the image of the languid beauty with a chocolate bar in her hand for potential customers, or a combination of the caption and the illustration of the advertised product. All possible versions are compressed cryptically in the word Russian verb *okliknut'*, which is chosen quite deliberately. *Okliknut'* (as opposed to other possibilities such as *pozvat'* [call], *kriknut'* [cry], or *obratit'sia* [address]) means *to cause to turn around*, the same turn of the head that a traveler makes when distracted for a moment by something out of the window.

The origins of this mode of perception and the means of effectively conveying it in a literary text can be found in Nabokov's poetry. As we see in the three stanzas below, with italics indicating the stylistic devices Nabokov uses to achieve the effect of movement, the poem serves as a medium in which to test them out before converting them to prose. In the 1918 almanac, *Dva puti* (*Two Paths*), published with A. Balashov, another pupil from the Tenishev Academy, Nabokov reproduces the moving picture outside a train window, but without including the most essential words (train, locomotive, engine, etc.):

The fields and swamps *float by.*
Speckled trunks run out,

---

[215]In the English translation this effect has been captured not as well as in the Russian original, which repeats the word "glass" ("*steklami ... stekla*") twice.

[216]A move towards complete absurdity and lack of sense is brought about by a character falling asleep, as we seen in the pun in the original English: "the room moved as slowly as fifteen miles per hour but across desertorum or agricultural drearies it attained seventy, ninety-seven, night-nine, one hund, red dog"; Cf. another attempt by a Nabokov character to fall asleep, also conveyed with a metaphor of motion: "I thumbed a mental ride with a very remote automobile but it dropped me before I had a chance to doze off" ("The Vane Sisters"; *Stories*, 630).

[217]Cf. a different means of metonymic transfer in "a notice in longhand (runny ink, blue runaway dog)" (*The Gift*, 12).

Then *walk away*. Wisps of smoke,
Circling, chase each other down.
    A bridge *rumbles.* The *flashing* of poles
    Cuts the triple wire.
    Suddenly the muffled muttering
    Of the rails turns into gnashing.
A crossing gate. *Like a thread the road is cut.*
The pines *shrink into* the ravine.
The long whistle resounds,
And faster and faster the knocking of the wheels.
    And now, up *floats* the platform
                (*Russian Collected Works*, 1:437–438)

The same strategy is used in the 1925 poem, "Vesna" ("Spring"), where the locomotive, initially visible, dissolves into the birch forest, leaving only a trail of smoke behind it as a reminder of its existence:

The locomotive *rushed* to the dacha.
In a light and timid crowd
the trunks run up to the embankment:
smoke *filtered through* as a white wave
in the *variegated* April birches.
    (*Russian Collected Works*, 1:565; cf. the short story "Perfection": "the
        fleeting, speckled world of automobile racers"; *Stories*, 340)

The literary techniques honed by Nabokov in his Russian period retain their relevance in his English works. In *The Real Life of Sebastian Knight*, the gaze of the protagonist through the train window encompasses a road that "drew out and *glided for a minute along the train, and just before it turned away a man on a bicycle wobbled among snow and slush and puddles. Where was he going? Who was he? Nobody will ever know*" (*The Real Life of Sebastian Knight*, 165); while Pnin "*repaired to the vestibule of the car so as to wait there for the confused greenery* skimming by to be *cancelled* and replaced by the definite station he had in mind" (*Pnin*, 17).

The Underground

The subway, merely by virtue of its location, beckoned twentieth-century writers to mythologize it, providing a ready formula of the "iron labyrinth"[218] inherited from antiquity in the story of Theseus and the Minotaur. Taken as

---

[218]See Bobrick, *Labyrinths of Iron.*

FIGURE 2.16 *Berlin's new subway, 1920. A new crosstown subway designed to relieve the downtown congestion after the manner of subway building in New York. Heavy steel girders form the foundation for the street, the subway being directly under it. Glass negative. American National Red Cross photograph collection, Library of Congress.*

the literal spawn of hell, combining the earth's surface with its forbidden underside, the underground validated the most deep-seated fears in European culture.[219] The underground—a subterranean vault—takes away a person's last hope at contact with the divine, cutting off the connection to the world of open space under the sky, which remains under the control of the Creator:

O Lord, from the depths of the metro
I will not appeal to you about myself ...
There above the tunnel is the dance of worlds,

---

[219]Above the wheels turn, the cabs sweep through, / The trains fly, focusing their efforts / Towards the stations, – miles and miles / Stretching a fiery thread of a golden pediment. / The rails crawl, branching, under the earth, / Along the tunnels, the craters, / To appear once again and, flashing of steel, rush past / In a cloud of steam and smoke (E. Verhaeren, "La Ville"; Russian translation in Voloshin, *Stikhotvoreniia i poemy*, 469).

But the elegant complexity of the heavenly machine
Is clouded by the rebellious pain
Of your wingless creation

(Chernyi, *Sobranie sochinenii*, 2:293)

The rich industrial mythopoetics of the underground ("The underground snake crawls, / It crawls and carries people" (Tsvetaeva, 1935; *Antologiia poezii russkogo zarubezh'ia*, 1:372]), in its pagan diversity, evokes associations with pre-Christian times. Nabokov projects these onto contemporary reality:

In front of the temple of Isis stood magical urns. They supplied believers with the blessings of the goddess in the form of a few drops of holy water. All one had to do was drop a five-drachma coin into the slot on the urn, *as is now done when a lady at a metro station wishes to purchase a box of almonds.*

(*Zvezda*, 21)

The underground space is equated with a temple that people must surrender a symbolic payment/sacrifice to enter.

The entrance to the metro also, however, offers the prospect of sanctuary, as described by the narrator of Nabokov's "The Fight": "The last time I was there, the evening, as I remember it, was muggy and pregnant with the promise of an electrical storm. Then the wind began gusting violently and *people in the square ran for the subway stairs; in the ashen dark outside, the wind tore at their clothes as in the painting* The Destruction of Pompeii" (*Stories*, 144). Nabokov's inclusion of his alter ego in the windstorm scene is based on a similar device used by Briullov when he placed a self-portrait among the crowd at Pompeii (on Nabokov and painting in general, see Leving, "Uzor vechnosti," 237–255; De Vries & Johnson, *Nabokov and the Art of Painting*; Shapiro, *The Sublime Artist's Studio*); in the perspective of meaning, Pompeii should symbolize for Nabokov the immortality of art. The mythological underground with its concealed infrastructure operating in high-speed mode functions as a dense system of time in a compressed space (antiquity and modernity are combined), and access to this world is gained through the *tube*.

The Gift, with its complicated narrative structure, contains yet another multidimensional model bringing in new intertexts. In the novel's third chapter, Godunov-Cherdyntsev gives private English lessons to a young woman. Nabokov describes in great detail the protagonist's inner struggle with the temptation to take advantage of his position of closeness with this accessible and beautiful woman. After a lesson where Godunov-Cherdyntsev, as he has been doing for three months, reads Stevenson with his attractive pupil, he sets off for a book store. One of the most saturated intertextual episodes in the novel (due to the abundance of real and fictional texts referenced in a small space) begins with a panorama of the city:

> Crossing Wittenberg Square where, as in a color film, roses were quivering in the breeze around an antique flight of stairs which led down to an underground station, he walked toward the Russian bookshop: between lessons there was a chink of spare time.
>
> *(The Gift, 154)*

The Berlin metro at Wittenbergplatz made an earlier appearance in émigré prose of the 1930s in a novel by R. Batalin.[220] In the paragraph before the passage quoted above, Nabokov writes of the renunciation that occurs in Fyodor's soul: "their reading of Stevenson would never be interrupted by a Dantean pause, [he] knew that if such a break should take place he would not experience a thing, except a devastating chill." This decision, and the station mentioned in the sweeping sentence from the quote above, are connected with the plot and the composition: the "Dantean pause" echoes the "chink of spare time"[221] between two lessons, but the two breaks differ in intonation: darkening (a dip in morale) vs. illumination (reading as enlightenment).

As he crosses the square towards the bookshop, Fyodor registers "the vagabond *phantom* of a Russian boulevard"; "*pale ghosts* of innumerable foreigners"; and Koncheev reading a newspaper "with a marvelous angelic smile" (*The Gift*, 155–156). It is later explained that he was reading a damning review of his own book, which seemed to Fyodor to be a "séance for the summoning of a spirit." An injection of "spirits" develops the tangentially included, by virtue of the mention of the underground, other world, as when Khodasevich compares passengers exiting the metro to "shadows of Hades."[222]

Godunov-Cherdyntsev is carried away to book heaven, as Dante on his underground trip through hell with Vergil—both journeys are associated with the crystalline, i.e., multidimensional, structure of the poetic text,

---

[220]"We descend along broad stairs under the long, dark, underground vault. The stone slabs hum under our paces. From the depths a velvet rumble approaches in black waves. Suddenly it grows around us. We rush to and fro, *as if expecting a god*. We are pushed into the glazed sparking. Rocking, we are carried away into the distance. We fly into a black abyss and rush forward, holding onto leather straps, and rumbling deep underground" (R. G. Batalin. *Petersburg am Wittenberplatz*. Detmold, 1931, 92. Cited from Shlegel', "Vospriiatie goroda," 112).

[221]The "Dantean pause" refers to the scene in which Paolo and Francesca, sitting together on the book, first kiss (*Inferno*, Canto V).

[222]"Where it smells of black carbolic acid / And the reeking earth ... / And there, from the deep half-dark / An old man, stooped but tall ... / Walks on a broad staircase, / Like a shadow of Hades – into the white light, / The Berlin day, the shining oblivion" ("Pod zemlei" ["Under the ground"], 1923; Khodasevich, *Sobranie sochinenii*, 1:264).

as decoded by Mandel'shtam, who proposed that the poetic fabric of the *Inferno*[223] be read as an "etched landscape of hell."[224] The proprietor turns out not to be in the store, but instead there is "a rather accidental young lady reading a Russian translation of Kellerman's *The Tunnel*" (ibid., 155). It is important that the first book that Godunov-Cherdyntsev notices in the shop is a novel from 1913 by Bernhard Kellermann, which was a Soviet bestseller in translation in the 1920s. This futuristic utopia shows humanity conquering of the bowels of the earth; in the novel an ingenious inventor and a billionaire team up to construct a tunnel under the Atlantic Ocean through which a train can reach America from Europe at 295 km/h, faster than a German dirigible. In the book's third part the work on digging the tunnel is described as a grandiose Dantean hell, and the visual texture of half-naked people fleeing from wind, dust and heat once again recalls Pompeii:

> The place where the boring machines worked, the head of the drift, was known among the Tunnel men as "Hell." The din was here so awful that in spite of plugged ears almost all the workers became more or less deaf. Allan's borers, as they cut their way into the working face of the rock, set up a shrill ringing sound, and the rock cried out like a thousand children in their death agony, laughed like an army of madmen, raved like a hospital of fever-stricken wretches, and at last roared as with the thunder of a great waterfall. < ... > Huge reflectors flung out their dazzling cones of light, now gleaming white, now blood red, athwart the chaos of sweat-streaming knots of men, isolated figures, tumbling blocks of stone, that themselves looked in the obscurity like falling men, and the dust rose whirling like thick clouds of steam in the reflected rays. And in the forefront of this chaos of struggling men and falling rock there quivered and crept ever onwards a grey dust-covered mass, like a monster of primeval ages – Allan's great boring machine! < ... > Driven by an energy that might compare with that of two express locomotives it crept forwards, and while a brilliant light shot out from its jaws as it worked

---

[223]Cf. in "Razgovor o Dante" ("Conversation about Dante"): "No one yet has approached Dante with a geologist's hammer, to puzzle out the crystalline structure of his ore, to learn about its impregnation deposits, its haziness, its eye spots, to evaluate it as a rock crystal subject to the most varied occurrences" (Mandel'shtam, *Sobranie sochinenii*, 2:234). Mandel'shtam's shadow is sensed in the book shop in the citation from Koncheev's "Days of ripening vines!" from the article by the critic Linyov, also examined there by Fyodor (*The Gift*, 158) (noted in Maslov, "Poet Koncheev," 179).

[224]The construction of the Moscow metro is reflected in Mandel'shtam's "Lamarck" (1932). The archaeological and biological symbolism of movement on an escalator to the depths of the social underworld is examined in the industrial context of the times in Freidin, *A Coat of Many Colors*, 224–227.

with the lips, feelers and antennas of its variously armed mouth, it gripped the face of the rock. < ... > Groups of men, with pale faces and a crust of dirt on their lips, pressed around the grid and the trucks, rushing, turning, shovelling and shouting, and the fierce light of the electric projectors beat down with merciless, blinding force upon them, while the blast of air from the ventilating shaft blew over them like a hurricane.

The struggle around the boring machine was like a murderous battle, and every day there was a toll of wounded and often of deaths.

(Kellerman, *The Tunnel*, 117–119)

Though he bypasses the underground movement of the metro, Fyodor nevertheless ends up in a kind of hell, one of bad taste rather than of mythological proportions: the Berlin bookshop is filled with philistine Soviet publications.

Like a mediator between two worlds, the poet on the surface is constantly remembering the presence of another foundation. The feeling among émigrés of the ground shifting beneath their feet is reinforced by the absence of a home base in an alien city:

> And under the earth rush trains,
> Swaying the pavement with an invisible tremor.
> The leaves of trees, cool and light,
> Wave in a diffuse hello.
> O, my life is asphalt and clouds,
> The shaking of the sidewalk and bright wind!
>
> (Nikolai El'iashov, "Fehrbelliner Platz," *Roshcha*)

It is in this underground world that social leveling is taken to its extreme. In the subway car, as in "a glass box / A hundred different souls / Were randomly packed into a pile ... / Exiting and entering"—from the 1930 poem, "V metro" ("On the Metro"), by Nabokov's old friend Sasha Chernyi, who also lived in Berlin:

> As if fate from the horn of being
> Is spreading with a sweeping hand
> Fragments of words, smiles, sparks in eyes
> And the funny games of children.
> A black man and a Frenchman, an old woman and a boy,
> An artist with a folder and a businessman with a notebook ...
> Fused together in a noisy flow for five minutes,
> We fly into space as if in a nucleus.
> Only politeness, a studied mask,
> Connects us through our common indifference.
>
> (Chernyi, *Sobranie sochinenii*, 2:292)

The absence of scenery in the window and the sense of eternal night do not bode well. Shortly before the death of the daughter of the main character in *Camera Obscura/Laughter in the Dark*, Irma, she awaits the *"rumble of the electric train which emerged from underground very near the house.* But it did not come. Perhaps it was too late, and the trains had *stopped running"* (*Laughter in the Dark*, 158). Nabokov's passengers suffer in panic during their time in the underground chthonic burrow: "[Franz] plunged into the depths of the subway and < ... > waited impatiently for the coaly clattering blackness to be replaced at last by paradises of luxury and sin that kept eluding him" (*King, Queen, Knave*, 58). Movement in the underground almost always concludes at a dead end, as the city street on the surface breaks off into the metro tunnel with its entrance decorated in a pseudo-classical style: "The street abutted on a stone portico with a white U on blue glass, a subway station" (ibid., 100).

In her affair with Franz, Martha carefully covers her tracks, taking a convoluted route to the room rented out by her lover. She refuses the services of her chauffeur and takes pleasure in the combinatorial calculus of the means of transportation available to city's residents—the subway:

> she had to resort to other means of transportation, of the most varied kind, *including even the subway, which brought one very conveniently from any part of the city* (and a roundabout route was essential < ... >) to a certain street corner < ... >. She casually mentioned to Dreyer that she loved taking a bus or a tram whenever she had a chance because it was a shame not to take advantage of the cheap, exhilaratingly cheap, methods of transportation put at one's disposal by a generous city. He said he was a generous citizen who preferred a taxi or a private car.
>
> (ibid., 132)

The preferences of characters reflect the essential nature of their personalities: the covetous Martha feels far more comfortable in the dark labyrinth of the underground than the naïve and good-natured Dreyer. Franz is forced to live a double life, remaining outwardly loyal to his uncle while satisfying his lover/aunt, and is likened to an automaton, whose descent into and movement through the labyrinths of the metro becomes one of the most important elements of his robotic existence. In the morning he would *"walk to the subway station,* get on a non-smoking car, *read the same old advertisement ditty overhead, and to the rhythm of its crude trochee reach his destination"* (ibid., 200–201).

Nabokov constructs the motion of his characters based on the rhythms and appearances of works of art, be they rhymed slogans ("advertisement ditty"), great works of the Renaissance (Dante), or paintings. As he does this, he uses the mode of transportation that best meets his artistic objective; transportation reflects the psychological state of the character, and its movement governs the composition and dynamics of the text.

* * *

The Russian railroad enjoyed unparalleled success, revolutionizing daily life and inspiring writers to make full use of it, to even canonize it, as the émigré writer Fyodor Stepun explains:

> Anna Karenina's romance with Vronskii begins and ends on a train. It is to the accompaniment of knocking wheels that Pozdnyshev, in *The Kreutzer Sonata*, tells a group of complete strangers the story of how he murdered his wife, and we have the sense that nowhere else but in a train would it be possible for him to make this confession with such sincerity. Katiusha Maslova [in Tolstoy's *Resurrection*] knocks with a frozen finger on the brightly lit window of a first-class car and, her eyes fixed on Nekhliudov, almost falls as she runs along the platform. "Smoke, smoke, smoke" – the mournful thoughts of Turgenev's Litvinov unfurl in a train. As he accompanies the wife of his friend and bids her farewell on the train, the modest protagonist in one of Chekhov's most touching stories suddenly comes to understand that he has loved only her his entire life, and that all is finished for him as she departs. In Bunin's "Lika" the theme of sacred and star-crossed love and of the creative nomadism of the soul is still more deeply and mysteriously connected with the theme of that same railroad anguish sung by Aleksandr Blok.
>
> (Stepun, *Sbyvsheesia i nesbyvsheesia*, 173–174)

It is no accident that Stepun places *Anna Karenina* at the very source of the railroad topos in Russian prose—the significance of the novel's ending has only increased over time in the Russian cultural consciousness. Among the viewers of early film screenings at the Petersburg cinema "Akvarium" was the 72-year-old Vladimir Stasov. The temperamental critic wrote to his brother on May 30, 1896:

> What ecstasy was I given on Monday by a *moving photograph* [italics in the original—Y.L.], the latest ingenious innovation of Edison … How an entire railroad train suddenly flies from the distance, across the picture, flies and then gets ever bigger and seems just a second away from running over you and crushing you, just as in *Anna Karenina* – it's simply beyond words; and how the people look, and bustle about, agitated, some disembarking, dragging their luggage, someone boarding in the same place, to the next station, everyone hurrying, moving, looking around, looking for something or someone – a real living crowd!
>
> (Shifman, "V. V. Stasov o kinematografii," 127–128)

Moving the lyrical writings of Stepun the memoirist and Stasov the critic back into the realm of theory, it bears repeating that the appearance of the train in literature is always predicated on a specific impetus, from a character's task of crossing the dangerous space of the station with the possibility of an (un)desired meeting, to deliverance from persecution or a death that may or may not be an accident. Initially identified with Western influence, the train gradually took on typical nationalistic features in Russian railroad lyrics, merging with pre-existing topos in culture. The technical innovation of the train was no longer seen as an attack by soulless European machines on Russia's independent identity.[225] The ideologist and central figure behind the Slavophile movement, the poet and philosopher Aleksei Khomiakov (1804–60) saw in his own father an example of the base influence of superficial Europeanism. Khomiakov himself designed steam engines, and one of his inventions, the "Moskowka," was honored at the 1851 London industrial exhibition.[226] In the same year, Iakov Polonskii wrote a poem (in pulsing anapests) singing the praises of the newly completed railway branch connecting Petersburg and Moscow:

The iron steed races, races!
Iron clashes on iron,
Steam billows, smoke rises;
The iron steed races, races,
Caught, landed, and rushing ...
The forest rushes to meet it.
Bridges rumble across beams,
And steam clings to the bushes;
The iron steed races, races,
And the signal posts flash, flash.

(Polonskii, *Stikhotvoreniia i poemy*, 197)

The railroad, with its situational variability, was primarily viewed in literature as a powerful topological generator.[227] Over time the railroad

---

[225]Just a month after the signing of the 1842 order to build the first major line from Moscow to Petersburg, the Slavophile journal *Moskvitianin* published an ode to the future railroad. The poem's author, Professor Stepan Shevyrev, argued in bombastic verse that the railroad on Russian land was a godly endeavor: "By the thoughts of the strong sovereign – / By the will of God himself / Be done, great labor, / Triumph of the light of knowledge! // Lie down, mountains! Arise, chasms! / Submit to us, o earth! / And ride, iron road, / From the Neva to the Kremlin" (*Moskvitianin*. 1842. № 3. Pt. II, 7). For comments on this ode, see Chukovskii, *Sobranie sochinenii*, 4:374–375.

[226]A detailed description and drawing of this machine are included in the third volume of Khomiakov's complete collected works (Moscow, 1914).

[227]A detailed treatment of the role of the railroad in nineteenth-century Russian literature is presented in Baehr, "The Machine in Chekhov's Garden," 99–121 and Baehr, "The Troika and the Train," 85–106.

developed its own set of plots, with poetry and prose offering a meta-language for describing and decoding them. In Russia the locomotive became a hero of the age, a visible embodiment and symbol of the technological remaking of the earth, representing the raw principle of movement: rods, flywheels, pistons, and giant wheels brought out to the surface (Shteiner, *Avangard i postroenie*, 157).

We have hardly begun to cover the topos of *poems composed on a train* (a separate category, akin to "poems composed during a bout of insomnia"). The distinguishing characteristic of texts written on trains (often dated and marked with the author's location: "On a Train") is that, despite the seeming autonomy relative to the principal topic of the railroad with its set of intersecting motifs, the features or psychological atmosphere of the place where the poem is written inevitably affect the semantic picture and the syntactic texture of the work, producing corresponding imagery, rhythm, and even stanzaic pattern. Most worthy of mention are Akhmatova's poem, "Ne byvat' tebe v zhivykh" ("Not for you to be among the living," composed on a railcar vestibule); the diary entries of Blok and of Rozanov from "Uedinennoe" ("Solitary"); and Briusov's "Mladshim" ("To the younger ones," 1902). Briusov was not generally known as an improvisational poet, but as Pertsov recalled "in this instance the immediacy of inspiration won out over the accustomed rationalism and completely took control of the poet—on this dark night, accompanied by the knocking sound of the train, before the spectacle of the winter landscape with its uniform flickering of fir trees" (Pertsov, *Literaturnye vospominaniia*, 321).

Nabokov, whose works can be read together as a single "railroad symphony," was, like his predecessors, interested in the mobile space between the profane and the sacred, between the everyday practical significance of the railroad and the mythology of the road,[228] representing a broad spectrum of motifs, from the fatal locomotive to the problems of class and social hierarchies, all of which were expressed in sharp relief during the early years of the railroad. However, Nabokov's main achievement, to borrow a metaphor, is that his texts always have an internal engine—a "living heart" ("Biology"; *Russian Collected Works*, 1:549), and the reader consistently feels that the locomotion of the plot is moving in a trajectory strictly controlled by him.

---

[228]For example: "Only when the train jerked and began to move did his brain start working again, and in this instant he was possessed by the feeling that comes in dreams when, *speeding along in a train from nowhere to nowhere*, you suddenly realize that you are traveling clad only in your underpants. < ... > He was sitting with his face turned toward the window, listening *to the wheels beating out the rhythm Abattoir ... abattoir ... abattoir*" ("An Affair of Honor"; *Stories*, 215).

3

The Automobile in the Works of Nabokov: The Semantics of Driving and the Metaliterary Process

Auto vs. Train

Initially, it was the train, not the automobile, that represented the New Era: it was productive, fast, faceless, isolated, and indifferent to individual human regimens and needs. After the First World War, however, the railroad was pushed out by the automobile and its role in developed countries was diminished. The car, in contrast to the railroad, did not inspire artists to great architectural feats, but it brought a feeling of mobility to people's lives, strengthened the social division between the new owners of cars and the users of traditional public transportation (Richards & MacKenzie, *The Railway Station*, 16–17), and affected the perception of distances and spatial points of reference within the landscape.[1]

Riding in an automobile was retrospectively more reminiscent of travel in a coach: unhurried, accessible to a select few, close to nature, more individualized and intimate. Trains on approach routes to large cities usually passed through industrial areas and slums. The automobile driver could discover a new city via the impressive central thoroughfare or, on the contrary, could avoid the city altogether and proceed past picturesque

---

[1] "Time has been reared up / By the automobile, / The world measured / In miles, not versts" (M. Pasynok, "O letchike s barabanom" ["On a pilot with a drum"]; *Let. Aviastikhi*, 41; a *verst* is an archaic Russian unit of length approximately equal to a kilometer).

FIGURE 3.1 *Automobile travel in the tsarist era. This photograph is from an album produced by the artistic studio of the* Obrazovanie *(Education) association in Moscow that documents the construction of the western portion of the Amur line of the Trans-Siberian Railroad in 1908–13. Russian State Library.*

pastoral landscapes.[2] Instead of being restricted to a designated schedule or at the mercy of a conductor, the driver could stop and then continue traveling at any point along the way. While rail passengers sat helplessly and waited if their departure was delayed, automobile drivers, united at least by a tacit code among the select few in the early days of motoring, tried to help each other on bad roads or at confusing intersections.

The car and the motel became their own brand of alternative to the train and the hotel and, consequently, to the lifestyle represented by the latter (Belasco in Lewis & Goldstein, 109). The mass production of cars was marked by the transition of a number of manufacturers to the use of interchangeable parts and a tendency towards automation of the chain of production.[3] The

---

[2]As Norman Moline, an American specialist on urbanism, put it: "the railroad, for the most part, merely gave rise to a system of through-line routes, 'a kind of skeletal articulation between the national units or between the highly centralized focal points within the nation,' which left modes of local transportation in rural areas largely unchanged ... . The automobile, however, because of its greater flexibility and availability for private ownership revolutionized the pattern of local relations throughout the country" (Moline, *Mobility and the Small Town*, 5). The quote inside the quote belongs to Mueller, "The Automobile: A Sociological Study," 42.

[3]In 1902 Olds produced about 2,500 low-production cars (4,000 in 1903 and 5,000 in 1904), while Ford exceeded 10,000 by the year 1909 (Lilli, *Liudi, mashiny i istoriia* [*Men, Machines, and History*], 194–195).

Russia of Nabokov's youth attentively followed the progress in this area. "The automobile business is now growing with a kind of rapidity that the railroad in no way enjoyed in its own time," noted one columnist for the newspaper *Rech'*.[4] Based on data from late October 1925, the Ford Model T was produced from the conveyor belt at a rate of one every ten seconds, and the price of the car itself fell from $850.00 in 1921 to $350.00 in 1925 (Laird in Lewis & Goldstein, 249).

As Warren Belasco, who expounded the dichotomy between car culture and railroad culture, explains, it had become clear by the early twentieth century that train travel was too monotonous and dull, while the automobile appeared as a move towards recovering a lost individualism, the discovery of new perspectives, and a challenge to the conservative tastes and monopolizing institutions of urban industrial civilization (Belasco in Lewis & Goldstein, 111). In literature, the opposition between a growing love of automobiles and the long-established railroad was expressed by Marcel Proust, who compared entering a city by train and by car, the former likened to some inscrutable magic, and the latter either to a visit behind a theater stage or to revealing the mechanism of a circus trick (Proust, *In Search of Lost Time*, 1352).

The rise of automobile transport increased road injuries by a factor of hundreds, though, becoming a constant fatal risk for both motorists and pedestrians.[5] High-speed roads had by the mid-1930s briefly eclipsed wars as the main locus of violence in the world,[6] and European modernist literature could not help but remark upon the lethal potential of the automobile.

The Ride to School

For the Nabokovs, the mark of their social status was not a coat of arms, but rather the collection of automobiles that they owned. Amongst his explanations as to why he stood out at the Tenishev Academy, is Nabokov's description of the irritation provoked by the fact that "a liveried chauffeur" brought him "to and from school in an automobile and not < ... > by

---

[4]"In Germany this past year more than 6000 automobiles were made for a total of 70,000,000 marks. ... In the US 12 years ago the number was 3000 automobiles for the entire country. According to the count for 1912, there were 652,461. There are no fewer than 200 companies engaged in this sector there, and production for the past year has been established at approximately 30,000" (*Ezhzegodnik gazety* Rech' *na 1913 g.* St. Petersburg: Izdatel'stvo gazety Rech', 488).

[5]Automobiles account for 92 percent of accidents involving all modes of transportation (motorcycles, trains, watercraft, and aircraft), and 98 percent of injuries resulting from accidents (Buel, *Dead End*, 41).

[6]In 1931 alone, accidents on roads in Great Britain (where there were two million cars in operation) resulted in 6,700 casualties (Pettifer & Turner, *Automania*, 219, 233).

FIGURE 3.2 *Vladimir and Véra Nabokov, and Dorothy Leuthold (Dasha), VN's student who drove the Nabokovs from New York to the American West, 1941, with Leuthold's 1941 Pontiac ("Pon'ka").*

streetcar or horsecab as the other boys, good old democrats, did" (*Speak, Memory*, 185–186). Nabokov, however, admits that to begin the day with a ride in a new car was to begin the day well.

In his memoirs, Nabokov meticulously reconstructs the route from his house to the school on Mokhovaia Street. Topographical memory connects the personal experience of the erstwhile inhabitant of Petersburg to the sweeping literary tradition and poetics of the Petersburg text. The central transportation artery of nineteenth-century Russian literature, Nevskii Prospekt, begins to carry the mechanical demon, the automobile. The reader sees not only overtaking on the road, but the breaking of a myth in the process of literary evolution:

> Our house was No 47 in Morskaya Street. Then came Prince Oginski's (No. 45), then the Italian Embassy (No. 43), then the German Embassy (No. 41), and then the vast Maria Square < ... >. Upon reaching Nevski Avenue, *one followed it for a long stretch, during which it was a pleasure to overtake with no effort some cloaked guardsman in his high sleigh drawn by a pair of black stallions snorting and speeding along* under the bright blue netting.
>
> (*Speak, Memory*, 184–185)

The pedantic listing of the house numbers leads us to take a closer look at the "biographies" of the houses themselves, among which № 45 bears the most literary significance. As Malikova noted, this house never belonged to Oginskii ("it is not clear why Nabokov refers to this as 'Oginskii's house,' when the Oginskii family had № 20 Karavannaia" [*Russian Collected Works 5*: 705]). It seems as if the name was chosen not out of confusion (Nabokov tried scrupulously to verify all the details for his autobiography), but because of its phonetic resemblance to the surname "Onegin" from Pushkin's novel in verse. This hypothesis is supported by the literary history of the house—from 1776 to 1780 the house belonged to A. I. Musin-Pushkin, the discoverer of the national epic, *The Lay of Igor's Campaign*, who bought the house from Prince S. S. Gagarin (Broitman & Krasnova, *Bol'shaia Morskaia*, 172). In 1792, the plot was bought for 20,000 rubles by the merchant Karl Amburger, whose son A. K. Amburger, a civil servant in the foreign affairs collegium, was a second at the duel between Griboedov and Iakubovich in Tbilisi. Nabokov might not have known all these details, but there is a mention of Griboedov's duel a few pages later and another instance of traveling in the same direction.[7]

The ride through the labyrinthine space, with its turns, gateways, descents into tunnels, and crossing of watery boundaries (intersections with rivers and canals), and roadside phantoms in the form of stone animals on building facades, concludes at the destination: a new and alien world *outside the home*:

A street on the left side with a lovely name – Karavannaya (the Street of Caravans) – took one past an unforgettable toyshop. Next came the Cinizelli Circus *with its rounded, stone horse heads growing out of its cream-colored walls.*

Finally, after crossing the ice-bound canal[8] one drove up to the gates of Tenishev School on Mohovaya Street (The Street of Mosses). *After jumping over the gate I ran through the passage tunnel and crossed the wide courtyard to the school doors.*

(*Russian Collected Works*, 5:264/*Speak, Memory*, 185)

The passage of an adolescent into the life of a society has a ceremonial basis—the dedication of a young person in the adult world upon reaching

---

[7]The difference between the two trips is that in this case the tempo is artificially drawn out and the means of transportation is archaized: "As the sleigh in which I was hunched over moved in fits and starts along Nevskii ... I thought about the weighty black Browning ... *Griboedov showed his bloody arm to Iakubovich. Pushkin's pistol fell barrel down into the snow. ... The forty-year-old Onegin takes aim at curly-headed Sobinov ... my drowsy horse carriage turned onto Morskaia and crawled along*" (*Russian Collected Works*, 5:269–270).

[8]Nabokov's mistake: this should refer to the Fontanka river (a branch of the Neva), not a canal.

sexual maturity (initiation, *rites de passage, Reifezeremonien*). Propp, comparing the fairy-tale with the corresponding social institutions, emphasized the close connection between initiation rites and conceptions of death (Propp, *Morfologiia*, 148). The city block on Mokhovaia, to which the writer's memory reaches out, looks as if it is surrounded by an impenetrable forest from folklore (including a possible play on words with *"mokh"*—moss), in which a tormented farewell to childhood takes place (cf. the description of the schoolyard in *Bend Sinister*: "It was difficult to go on dribbling through the tangle of rickety scaffolding < ... > and when he reached < ... > the threshold of the goal, because the goal was a door";[9] *Bend Sinister*, 63). The automobile, easily overcoming the obstacles of the urban forest, performs the folkloric role of the horse.[10]

The mature Nabokov was indifferent to luxurious means of transportation, and it irritated him when others displayed an undue interest in them. In 1948, he, among other things, notes to his sister that he received a "rather stupid letter" from their brother Kirill, wanting "to find out which are the best American automobiles" (Nabokov, *Perepiska s sestroi*, 52). On the other hand, as a child born at the turn of the century, Nabokov knew from experience that owning a car conferred a particular social status.[11] The parents of the object of the ten-year-old Nabokov's first love, a French girl named Collette, came from Paris to Biarritz in a private blue and yellow limousine, which Nabokov remarks was "a fashionable adventure in those days" (*Speak, Memory*, 150). The future writer was impressed by this bourgeois gesture and remembered the car's entourage his whole life, as he remembered the appearance and driving style of the chauffeurs who drove his family's cars in Petersburg: "Pirogov, the second chauffeur, was a very short, pudgy fellow < ... > with a russet complexion < ... >. He frankly preferred to drive the hardy convertible Opel < ... > and would do so at sixty miles per hour (to realize how dashing that was in 1912, one should take into account the present inflation of speed)" (ibid., 182–183). If, Nabokov wrote, a delay on the road forced him "to apply the brakes (which he did by suddenly distending himself in a peculiar springy manner), or when I bothered him by trying to communicate with him through the squeaky and not very efficient speaking tube, the back of his thick neck seen through the

---

[9]Cf. the description of Aeneas' descent into Hades in the sixth book of *The Aeneid*: "There was a vast cave deep in the gaping, jagged rock, / shielded well by a dusky lake and shadowed grove" (Virgil, *The Aeneid*, 190).

[10]"The horse flies 'higher than the still forest' ... the forest of fairy tales, on the one hand, reflects the memory of the forest as a place where rites took place, and on the other hand the entrance to the kingdom of the dead" (Propp, *Morfologiia*, 152).

[11]Even in the developed US in 1904, with an average income of $600 per year, an automobile for traveling cost $7,000 (Pettifer & Turner, *Automania*, 14), to say nothing of the Russian Empire, where only the extremely well-off could afford a car.

glass partition would turn crimson" (ibid., 182–183 [from *Drugie berega*: "*I would squeeze the squeaky, pale gray bulb wrapped in pale gray fabric and mesh, which connected to him via a pale gray cord*"; *Russian Collected Works*, 5:262–263]).

Just as the author communicates to his driver, by a magic thread, the automobiles of his childhood become a link between autobiography and his creative fiction. Childhood car trips are for Nabokov associated with Russia, and the ease of the road is compared with the difficulty of exile: "Smoothly undulating, the milky-white road flowed on, the open cover of the car rattled as the wheels bounced over bumps and holes—and the feeling of speed, the feeling of spring < ... > suddenly fused into a delicious joy which made it possible to forget that *this light-hearted road was the way leading out of Russia*" (*Mary*, 100).

Russian roads are characterized by potholes, and Russian drivers are inert and physically ill-equipped for an elegant Western cabriolet. When the old seemingly stable world fell apart with the Revolution, the automobile was also broken down into parts that were then carefully concealed, like hidden treasure in a novel by Robert Louis Stevenson:

> When in the second year of World War One Pirogov was mobilized, he was replaced by dark, white-eyed [in *Other Shores*: "a *clumsy, bow-legged*" – a physical defect borrowed from a pirate/hoarder of other people's treasures (*Russian Collected Works*, 5:263)—Y.L.] Tsiganov, a former racing ace, who < ... > had had several ribs broken in a bad smash in Belgium. Later, sometime in 1917 < ... > Tsiganov decided – notwithstanding my father's energetic protests – to save the powerful Wolseley car from possible confiscation by dismantling it and *distributing its parts over hiding places known only to him.*
>
> (*Speak, Memory*, 183)

History was on the side of the racing car driver, who here played the archetypal role of the sly servant with a scrupulous master. Decades later, Nabokov determines that his mission was to use the pen and his powers of memory to put these details of his childhood back into a unified whole.

The Nabokovs' American Cars

Nabokov, who went through dozens of cars over the course of his life, was one of the first prose writers in the history of Russian literature to grow up in a family that owned automobiles. As Brian Boyd writes, "Nabokov himself never learned to drive a car, but he had always loved the poetry of motion – bicycles, trains, imagined flight" (Boyd, *Russian Years*, 428).

The lack of their own car in the Nabokovs' first few years in the USA had a significant effect on their personal plans, from the impossibility of planning individual summer vacations to being forced to travel to work in his colleagues' cars. Motivated by the desire for entomological expeditions and enjoying the security of a stable university salary, Nabokov decided to buy his first car in 1948. His choice was an eight-year-old Plymouth four-door sedan. It quickly became clear that this old sedan was literally falling apart, and in 1949 the Nabokovs traded it in for a black 1946 Oldsmobile (Boyd, *American Years*, 140). The experience was not without incident from the start. As they left on June 22, 1949 for a trip out west, Véra entered the middle lane of a three-lane highway near Canandaigua, N.Y., and almost hit an oncoming truck. A student of Nabokov's who was accompanying them, Richard Buxbaum, had to take the wheel from that point.

In 1951, Nabokov wrote to his sister, mentioning their search for another car and sharing with her his reservations: "We are still looking for a used car, which can be bought here for 800 francs (about 200 dollars), but we greatly fear that there will be a huge mass of associated expenses. On the other hand, we would so love to go everywhere, and the trains here are prohibitively expensive" (Nabokov, *Perepiska s sestroi*, 70–71). The search for a "healthier car" (Boyd, *American Years*, 261) became urgent again during preparations for the summer butterfly hunt in 1954. As Boyd writes, "[w]ary of any kind of machine and averse to all kinds of purchase, he would consult friends at wearisome length before committing himself" (ibid.). This time Nabokov settled on a "frog-green" Buick, a car in which he and Vera in the spring and summer of 1956 "made about 16 and a half thousand kilometers < ... > and caught wondrous butterflies in Utah, Arizona, and Montana" (Nabokov, *Perepiska s sestroi*, 86).

Satisfied with this car, the Nabokovs three years later decided on another Buick, a black one that was not sold until the end of a summer trip in 1959 to Arizona and the mountains of California: they decided to return to New York from there by train (Nabokov, *Perepiska s sestroi*, 96). In an interview with *Sports Illustrated* (published on September 14, 1959), Robert H. Boyle told of a few days from the writer's summer butterfly hunt. One morning began as follows:

Mrs. Nabokov smiled indulgently and followed him down the porch steps to their car, a black 1956 Buick, where she got behind the wheel. Nabokov, who does not drive, did not want to go fast, and to be sure that his wife did not exceed forty miles an hour a warning klaxon was attached to the speedometer. But just as he moves clocks forward a half-hour, his wife moves the klaxon up to sixty. "I always put it a little higher so he doesn't know," she said as he listened intently. "Now I'll put it at forty."

FIGURES 3.3 AND 3.4 *Vladimir Nabokov and Dmitri at a tennis court in front of the family's 1950 Buick Special. Ithaca, N.Y., 1951.*

The car would not start. "The car is nervous," Nabokov said. "The car?" asked Vera. "The car," said Vladimir. At last it started. Mrs. Nabokov drove onto Highway 89A and headed to a butterfly hunting ground several miles north. The klaxon went off, and Mrs. Nabokov slowed down. A motorcyclist whizzed by in the opposite direction, and Nabokov shuddered discreetly.

(*Nabokov's Butterflies*, 528–537; Boyd, *American Years*, 384)

In the spring of 1960, the Nabokovs settled in Los Angeles, where Nabokov worked on the screenplay for *Lolita* with Stanley Kubrick. To travel on the high-speed California freeways, a Chevrolet Impala was rented for six months (Boyd, *American Years*, 406). Later in Europe, the Nabokovs once again avoided having to think about buying a car by renting a modest Peugeot (ibid., 419). Another Peugeot purchased later was sold in the fall of 1964, the reason being that the pain in Véra's wrists was getting worse and she had "stopped enjoying fighting ice and snow" on the roads (ibid., 488). A year later, in the spring of 1965, the Nabokovs bought a Lancia Flavia.

In an interview with *Vogue* in 1972, Nabokov (insisting that he was preserving the order in which they were bought) listed the cars in which he and his wife traveled west every year for decades for his butterfly hunts: "Plymouth, Oldsmobile, Buick, Buick Special, Impala," a tongue-twister of foreign brand names that only Shklovskii could match in the world of Russian literature.[12] In an earlier interview for *Time* (1969), Nabokov gave a rough estimate of the mileage covered during his entomological travels: "Between 1949 and 1959 [Véra] has driven me more than 150,000 miles all over North America – mainly on butterfly-hunting trips" (*Strong Opinions*, 125). The resoundingly antisocial declaration (150,000 miles on butterflies – and not even one interesting personal encounter worth mentioning) echoes the hymn to car culture in Victor Shklovskii's novel, *Zoo, or Letters Not about Love*, which ends on a note designed to produce a shocking effect: "All of this is more interesting to me than the fate of Russian émigrés." As Robert Roper puts it, "like real Americans," the Nabokovs denominated "periods by the cars owned: first the Oldsmobile and then the '54 Buick, and meanwhile Dmitri has been living his own car-inflected history, driving what Véra called a 'Ford-Keyser' (actually a '31 Model A Ford, dark blue) and later a '38 Buick 13, which took him to the Tetons" (Roper, *Nabokov in America*, 237).

The poetics of automobile names certainly had a magical meaning for Nabokov, who cleverly invented nonexistent automobile makes for his

---

[12]"Hispano-Suiza? Not a good car. An honest, noble car with a reliable drive, on which the driver sits sideways, flaunting his powerlessness, is a Mercedes Benz, a Fiat, a Delaunay-Belleville, a Packard, a Renault, a Delage, and the very expensive but serious Rolls Royce, which has an extraordinarily flexible ride" (Shklovskii, *Gamburgskii schet*, 75).

characters. The name of an automobile (or the absence of one) in part reflects the personality of its owner. Pnin, for example, gets around in an unpresentable sedan, a "poor man's car" (*Pnin*, 145). Van Veen, though he drives to the duel with Tapper in a cheap semi-racer, Nabokov gives the vehicle a mysterious name: "Paradox" (*Ada*, 310). Nabokov's invented "Icarus" ("Ikar" in Russian) make of cars figures in both his Russian and his American prose. It seems to stem from a composite image of the many ornamental figures that graced automobile grills in the 1910s and 1920s, of which the best known were the so-called Rolls-Royce "Silver Lady" (a half-naked winged girl commissioned by the company in 1911 from the famous sculptor Charles Sykes[13]); the gilded, winged devil figure on Leon Bollée automobiles (1912); the flying stork on Hispano-Suiza hoods; and the classical archer on Pierce Arrow limousines. Based on tracks in the form of a double T, the police in *Despair* first establish the brand of the tire, and then, with the help of witnesses, the owner of the blue two-seater "Icarus" convertible—"small model, wire wheels," left on the crime site—thanks to the "bright and pleasant fellows at the garage in [Hermann's] street who added information concerning horsepower and cylinders, and gave not only the car's police number, but the factory engine and chassis numbers too" (*Despair*, 190). A car with the same name and color appeared earlier in *King, Queen, Knave*: "It gleamed with its new coat of black paint, the chrome of its headlight rims, the blazon-like emblem that crested the radiator grill: a silver boy with azure wings" (*King, Queen, Knave*, 76).

In the English version of "Spring in Fialta," Nina perishes in a yellow Icarus, and in the Russian version of *Lolita*, Humbert's blue car is given a name that is lacking in the English original, and of course that name is "Ikar" (Icarus). An anagram of the name appears in the Russian name "Amil'kar," in whose back seat the "lady with a lapdog" sleeps in *Transparent Things* (1972). In the novel, *Look at the Harlequins* (*LATH* 1974), a character receives "a bonus in the form of an Icarus phaeton" (*LATH*, 21). This combination of model and name intertwines the fates of two mythological characters, Icarus and Phaethon: the former died when the wax in the wings his father, Daedalus, made for him melted as he flew too close to the sun; the latter (the son of Helios, the sun, and the nymph Clymene) was turned to ash by the heat of his father's chariot. Van and Ada twice return from picnics in a "Victoria" phaeton (chapters 13 and 39 in *Ada*). It should be noted that "Victoria" was the real name of a car manufactured by Benz in 1890, the first car in the world with a speed selector that prevented it, unlike other models of the time, from rolling backwards at the bottom of a hill (Evans, *The Motor Car*, 12).

---

[13]As Sykes stated, his goal was to create the image of a woman that has "road travel as her supreme delight and has alighted on the prow of a Rolls-Royce car to travel in the freshness of air and the musical sound of her fluttering draperies" (Pettifer & Turner, *Automania*, 17).

Driving Experience

In early 1935, Véra Nabokov began work as a translator at the Berlin engineering company Ruthspeicher, which designed heavy machinery. There she dealt with all the company's correspondence in English. Because of her evident ability in the field of technical translation, Véra received a small raise, and, inspired by her surroundings, decided to invent a mechanism for parallel parking. An extra moveable wheel was attached to the car's chassis with a button which lowered it to the ground, enabling the car to roll perfectly into a space. Véra Nabokov attempted to patent her invention and submitted it to Packard. The marvel is not that she took the initiative of doing so, writes her biographer Stacy Schiff, "but that she designed the parking system when she had not yet learned to drive" (*Véra*, 74). After four

FIGURE 3.5 *Véra Nabokov next to Dmitri's Bizzarini GT, Montreux, 1969.*

months of work, however, Véra, along with all the other Jewish workers at the company, was fired under pressure from the Nazi regime.

Véra's experience as a translator was soon needed for the fictional biography of the narrator in *The Real Life of Sebastian Knight*, who enrolled in a "'be-an-author' course," "buoyantly advertised in an English magazine," and whose prior literary experience, by his own admission, amounted to "two chance English translations required by a motor-firm" (*The Real Life of Sebastian Knight*, 29). Nabokov inserts this detail to set off the flexible, mystical prose of Sebastian Knight and the mechanistic, soulless writing of his brother, which grows in expressiveness as the plot develops, merging with the powerful referential layers of the late writer's works, ultimately overtaking them in terms of quality.

The automobile operator's manual is on the lowest rung of the hierarchy of printed documents: a piece of paper, a text devoid of any artistic value. V., the novel's narrator, is not even its author, but merely a mediator. He is the connecting thread between languages, and this is only the first stage in the process of bringing to light the "real life" of Knight, which will culminate in mediation between the languages of this world and the world beyond.

Unfamiliar with Nabokov's early works, a journalist for *Time* noted in 1969 that some of his "funniest remarks" in recent novels "have concerned driving and the problems of the road (including the image of the author groping with time as with contents of a glove compartment)" (*Strong*

FIGURE 3.6 *Véra Nabokov with Dmitri's 1977 Ferrari 308 GTB, 1978.*

Opinions, 125). The interviewer asked Nabokov whether he could drive a car and whether he liked doing so. In response he shared the story of his first and last solo drive: in the summer of 1915, he discovered that their chauffeur had left the family convertible "throbbing all alone" directly in front of the garage, which was a part of the huge stable: "next moment I had driven the thing, with a sickly series of bumps, into the nearest ditch." Another attempt at driving that met with no greater success, as Nabokov told it, occurred thirty-five years later, "somewhere in the States, when my wife[14] let me take the wheel for a few seconds and I narrowly missed crashing into the only car standing at the far side of a spacious parking lot" (ibid., 125). This autobiographical moment receives an ironic treatment in the novel, *Look at the Harlequins,* when the narrator confesses that if his wife "did occasionally allow me to take the wheel, it was only in a spirit of fun":[15]

> With what sobs I now remembered the time when I managed to hit the postman's bicycle which had been left leaning against a pink wall at the entrance of Carnavaux, and how my Iris doubled up in beautiful mirth as the thing slithered off in front of us!
>
> (*LATH,* 155)

Yet the lack of practice had no discernible influence on the effect produced by works written by a man who had no driver's license. While Véra Nabokov was perfecting her parking, her husband was working on elastic phrases in *Despair:* "The asphalted surface of the yard was somewhat higher than that of the street so that upon entering the narrow inclined tunnel connecting the yard with the street, my car, held back by its brakes, lightly and noiselessly dipped" (*Despair,* 155).

---

[14]The effects of the automobile on women's emancipation in the twentieth century, the sense of mobility and social independence, is a topic of discussion in a number of feminist works; cf. the most concise argument in the book by Scharff, who states: "The wealthy women, accustomed to deferring to men of their own social standing, might have had mixed feelings about asserting control in a masculine arena. ... The automobile was not only a symbol and a source of independent mobility, but also a badge of status, a tool of leisure, and a very expensive material possession" (Scharff, *Taking the Wheel,* 69).

[15]Cf. Barabtarlo's observation regarding the driving style of women in Nabokov's prose: "Nabokov's male heroes seldom drive, and cars in his novels are usually manned by women. Albinus of *Laughter in the Dark,* a 'Krechmarish driver,' loses his sight in a horrible accident < ... >; Krug of *Bend Sinister* is a 'non-driver'; Dreyer of *King, Queen, Knave* drives badly; John Shade of *Pale Fire* always sits beside his wife who drives him everywhere; even Humbert H. < ... > is an erratic motorist (he never drove when Charlotte was alive). In *Pnin,* Joan Clements is always at the wheel, with Laurence occupying the passenger seat" (Barabtarlo, *Phantom of Fact,* 192–193).

The Model

In the spring of 1927 an émigré journal reported that a large exhibition of mechanical toys had opened in London, where "all the achievements of modern technology were reflected in miniature." As the correspondent stated, "the beautifully executed model cars, planes, and submarines bring delight not only to children, but to adults as well" (*Illiustrirovannaia Rossiia*. March 12, 1927. № 11, 4). The newspaper photograph depicted George V and Queen Mary visiting the exhibition, along with a boy sitting in a miniature model automobile.

In emigration, the Nabokovs tried to do everything possible so that their son would feel no worse off than the boy in the shadow of the royal couple in this photograph.[16] A photograph has survived from the European period showing the Nabokovs standing next to Dmitri, who also sits in a toy car. A picture taken in the summer of 1942 at the Karpovich farm (the professor's Vermont estate would later serve as a model for Cook's farm in *Pnin*) shows the author pushing Dmitri in a "Trojan Flyer" toy car (Boyd, *American Years*, 274–275). Several apocryphal stories are now in circulation with regard to how the young Dmitri acquired his cars (some of them apparently told by him). According to Brian Boyd, some rich friends/patrons of the Nabokov family gave Dmitri a silver pedal-driven Mercedes, a racing model four feet in length, when the boy turned two (ibid., 498). Schiff states that the little car is a pedaled Rolls Royce bought with money lent by a certain Russian taxi-driving poet (Schiff, *Véra*, 75; this may refer to Korvin-Piotrovskii, a friend of Nabokov's), while Dmitri himself recalled that it was a Renault. As far as toy cars were concerned, by the end of the 1930s Dmitri had accumulated more than one hundred (*Russian Collected Works*, 5:329).

The Nabokovs' financial position improved greatly in the United States. In August 1950, Dmitri was already driving the family car (Nabokov, *Perepiska s sestroi*, 62), then three years later "drove a third car into the ground" and was preparing to buy a used airplane.[17] The success of *Lolita* allowed Nabokov once again to possess the extravagances of the rich, which had changed little since the late nineteenth century. In 1964, to help Dmitri get to his singing lessons, his parents helped him buy a limited-edition Alfa Romeo

---

[16]Most people in emigration could not, of course, afford a real car. A typical caricature by MAD (M. A. Drizo, 1887–1953) appeared in the émigré press: two people are standing in front of a models of a Rolls Royce Grand Luxe, a Packard, and an Hispano-Suiza. The heading reads: "Russians at an automobile show." The caption to the drawing is: "'My wife ripped me to shreds because of my love for cars.' 'Did you buy one?' 'No, I paid 10 francs for a ticket!'" (*Poslednie novosti*. October 7, 1930. Quoted in *Satira i iumor v russkoi emigratsii*, 23).

[17]Cf.: "In the summer he ... was beating a path in Oregon, wielding a giant truck. ... In his car he makes 1000 miles (1600 km) a day – it's unbelievable! – driving sometimes 20 or 30 hours straight" (Nabokov, *Perepiska s sestroi*, 76).

FIGURE 3.7 *Dmitri Nabokov and his first car, a Mercedes Benz. Berlin, 1937.*

FIGURE 3.8 *Dmitri Nabokov in his racecar, Alfa Romeo GTZ. Monza, Italy, 1964.*

GTZ racing model, which was ideally suited to their son's height. Nabokov displayed his complete ignorance about the practical aspects of this matter to Petr Ustynov, his neighbor at the Montreux Palace and a great fan of auto racing: "Was I overcharged? <...> What is a sports car? Is it a car with a very particular kind of engine?" (Boyd, *American Years*, 481).

Dmitri became a racing driver and although he left the sport after an accident at a professional competition, his passion for cars remained. A number of times after listing the automobiles he currently or had owned in the past, Dmitri would take his interviewer to the garage. On the occasion of the 100th anniversary of Vladimir Nabokov's birth, and in connection with the release of Adrian Lyne's screen version of *Lolita* (1999), the Russian press published a series of interviews with the writer's son. One of these was with Igor Svinarenko for the magazine *Avtopilot*. The excerpts below from this conversation with Dmitri echo his father's passion for the automobile and the art of their design, along with a fascination for archetypal notions of speed, but also for Dmitri in particular, the appeal and flamboyance of owning expensive models, and especially their potential for attracting the opposite sex:

The Ferrari is a little dusty. Nabokov takes a handkerchief out of his pocket and wipes the windshield. I can't believe that this tall, large man can fit in this snuffbox! Then, as if on a dare, he slowly climbs in, folding and pressing himself. It's difficult, of course, <....> But for racing you have to get used to it. And if I'm just going to the store I have a Grand Cherokee. The ideal car! I'm big, it's big. And then it's impossible, for example, to drive a Ferrari in Italy. It would be stolen instantly.

So why did you pick a Ferrari specifically? It's not snobbery, not a way of proving something to anyone.

I've had more than fifty cars, including highly collectible ones: an MG, Alfa, an Iso Rivolta. There is a certain Italian instinct that Michelangelo and da Vinci once had in painting and sculpture. And that is now carried on in the shape of cars and in the fashion for them. It's an area where everyone is behind and copying Italy ...

So what you're trying to say is that if Michelangelo were alive he would be designing Ferraris? I wouldn't rule it out. The Ferrari is the paradigmatic Italian form ...

How many cars do you have at this point? Now? Let me think. I have two Ferraris left after I sold one recently. One Jeep, one 1989 Subaru Turismo, that's a spare for guests. That's what I have here in Europe. So that's four. Then my big truck in America, and two Vipers there too. I guess I only have seven cars now ... Well, or eight, I don't remember. I'll soon have a new Ferrari. I ordered it and I'm just waiting ...

Nabokov also likes to race boats, of which he has several, with 750 horsepower engines. But what gets him excited is piloting a helicopter.

Some might think that Nabokov flies helicopters in circles over airports, or uses them to get from point A to point B. But no! (D. N.) I like to use the helicopter to check the snow if I'm getting ready to go skiing. I send two servants to stop traffic, send a fax to the gendarmes (they asked me to), and the helicopter lands right on the highway. But do you know how much this costs? 50 francs a minute! *he says modestly and diplomatically …*

Well, you probably race your Ferraris here! It seems like you must break the law every five minutes? The only law I break is the speed limit. And I only do that on the highway. You don't race cars in the city! And statistics show that accidents don't happen because of speeding. They happen because of drinking, drugs, and lack of experience. So I'm all for safe driving, because I've seen a lot of pain. Here in Switzerland you have to drive slow because a lot of roads are narrow. I always use my turn signal on mountain roads – someone who's not used to things here might jump out all of a sudden.

Do they catch you a lot? And how much do they fine you? They do. I pay 100–200 dollars. Why 200 dollars? I was driving in one of my Vipers from Palm Beach to Atlanta to put the car on a Swiss Air plane to come here. I was afraid I'd be late and I was doing 97 miles an hour in a 65 mile per hour zone. I had all my equipment with me – radar detector, laser detector, and the most expensive thing – a machine where you push the button for a particular state and it shows all the police bands and beeps when the police turn on a radio anywhere within three miles of you. I also have polarized glass over my license plate, so the number isn't visible at the angle (20 degrees) that the automatic police cameras use to photograph it. I got upset: "Listen, I have all this equipment, how did you catch me?!" It turned out they were following me in an airplane and didn't turn on the radio so I wouldn't hear it. Once on a bridge between Palm Beach (an island) and West Palm Beach (the mainland) the police caught me when I made a rare schoolboy mistake. I was chasing down a Camaro on the bridge. The speed limit was 35 and I was doing 105.

Did you pass him? He saw the police car before I did and he slowed down. He waved his hand off to the side and then I saw it too. And they stopped me. The officer was an attractive blonde. And she said: if you promise to take me for a ride in your car, then I'll … Let you go! No, I'll fine you not for the actual speed, but only for "driving for a speed not appropriate for the conditions," which would be 30 dollars. Instead of 200.

So did you do it? Not that time, but she later started riding a motorcycle and I met her at a parking lot. Then I did. Very nice.

And did you ever meet her again after that? No, but it may yet happen. I generally prefer brunettes, to tell the truth. But the funniest thing was in Switzerland. The police here like what they call *banalissee* cars, without any markings. They're old and dirty. I was hurrying from Montreux to Laussane and I passed one of these unmarked police cars in a tunnel.

FIGURE 3.9 *Dmitri Nabokov and Viper GT2 at Moroso, 1998.*

I was going 197 and the limit in the tunnel was 100. When we came out of the tunnel they put on their hats and turned on their lights ... They stopped me and took me to the *gendarmerie*. I could see that they were looking at my car excitedly ... with such envy! And there I was in court. The judge was a fan of my father's books, knew that I raced cars and was not going to stop, and fined me only 700 francs.[18]

Using the example of his own family's cars in various generations, Nabokov the author once noted the change in technical parameters of modern automobiles that affected the concepts of time and distance:

[H]e [the family chauffeur] vastly preferred the red Opel Torpedo with leather seats that we used in the country to the expensive city car we had;[19] he was driving us in it along the Warsaw highway, *he opened the muffler and drove at a speed of 70 km per hour, which at that time seemed intoxicating*, and how the wind roared, how the dust in the light rain and the dark green of the fields smelt. *And now my son, a Harvard student,*

---

[18]Cited from a republication in *Magazine* (a weekly digest supplement to the Israeli newspaper *Vesti*). January 4–10, 1999, 37.
[19]A photograph of a red 1911 Opel Torpedo identical to the one that the Nabokov family owned is reprinted in the illustrated biography in Grayson, *Vladimir Nabokov*, 42.

*incautiously covers the same distance in half an hour, easily driving from
Boston to Alberta, California, or Mexico.*

(*Russian Collected Works*, 5:263)

The poetics of speed and the intoxicating feelings of control over a moving
car were inherited by Dmitri Nabokov from his father, but Vladimir Nabokov
never carried his ambitions for overcoming space beyond steering cars in his
fiction or, what is more interesting to us, steering his texts like a car.

Car Controls (a Novel on Wheels)

The idea of an artistic text as a sort of elegant mechanical model is
characteristic of romantic literature with its Hoffmannesque interest in
the inner workings of things and in mimetic toys. A hint at the hidden
mechanism in Gogol's "Diary of a Madman" slips out when the narrator,
looking at the house of the director's daughter where the symptoms of his
madness will soon first appear, exclaims: "What a machine!" Then after
receiving the letters he hopes that "all the springs" within the secrets will
be revealed to him (Gogol, *Sobranie khudozhestvennykh proizvedenii*,
3:239, 247). In contrast, the Russian translator of Constant's *Adolphe*
remarks on the careful concealment of the compositional architecture from
the reader as a virtue, stating that "the author does not resort to dramatic
springs" and in his drama "one sees neither an engineer or a decorator"
(Viazemskii, "Predislovie k perevodu," 124). The mechanism of the plot is
bared in Balzac, who said of the relationships between the characters in one
of his novels that they "amounted only to superficial connections, to the
movement of wheels with no lubrication" (*Pere Goriot*; Balzac, *Sobranie
sochinenii*, 2:285).

On the first page of *Despair*, and again later in *The Gift*, a passage
imitating the slight confusion of the author before beginning a long narrative
(the technique, common since ancient times, of the narrator "apologizing"
for being a bit tongue-tied) includes the exceptionally significant appearance
of a motorized vehicle in the shape of a bus:

It may look as though I do not know how to start. Funny sight, the
elderly gentleman who < ... > eventually overtakes [the last bus] but is
afraid to board in motion and so, with a sheepish smile, drops back,
still going at a trot. Is it that I dare not make the leap? It roars, gathers
speed, will presently vanish irrevocably around the corner, the bus, the
motorbus, the mighty montibus of my tale. Rather bulky imagery, this.
I am still running.

(*Despair*, 3–4)

FIGURE 3.10 *Men fixing tire. Glass negative, between c. 1920 and c. 1925. George Grantham Bain Collection, Library of Congress.*

After another fifteen pages or so, once the book is moving in its well-traveled ruts, the game with the metaphor of a novel on wheels, which Hermann is managing to drive, continues: "writing with me has become an easier matter: my tale has gained impetus. I have now boarded that bus (mentioned at the beginning), and, what is more, I have a comfortable window seat. And thus, too, I used to drive to my office, before I acquired the car" (ibid., 32). Moreover, the main character, who presents the narrative, begins to develop a taste for his new status as a writer, as we see in the following phrase with a possibly ambiguous sense: "Yes, I was quite taken by my new toy" (ibid., 32). The protagonist of another Nabokov work, this one with an autodiegetic narrative structure, also steers his novel. Humbert, agitated as he drives his car, at some point begins to believe that if he and

Lolita do not reach a hotel at that very moment he will "lose all control over the Haze jalopy with its ineffectual wipers and whimsical brakes" (*Lolita*, 107). It is emblematic that when translating *Lolita* from English to Russian the author makes use of a road metaphor, complaining in a letter to Grinberg that "reverse translation from asphalt to ice is awful."[20] The subtext for this reductionist metaphor for the literary craft is a quote from Viazemskii's 1829 poem, "Stantsiia" ("The Station"), famous for being included by Pushkin in his notes to *Eugene Onegin* (XLVII):

> Russian travel is unconstrained
> Only in two cases: when
> When our MacAdam and MacEve –
> Winter, shaking with anger, executes
> A devastating attack,
> Binds the way with icy iron
> And powders it with early snow
>
> (Viazemskii, *Stikhotvoreniia*, 172)

(Macadam was the name for roads covered with broken gravel, based on the name of its Scottish inventor, John McAdam; the memory of the "biblical" genesis of asphalt was passed on and culturally transferred to its diabolically boiling tar).

Not long before Nabokov, Evgenii Zamiatin resorted to a meta-description of the artistic text through the metaphor of steering in his article "Behind the Scenes" ("*Zakulisy*"), offering a profound analysis of the mechanics of writing:

> It once happened to me that I keenly felt as if I had lost one arm – that my third arm was missing. This was in England, when I first drove an automobile in place of the driver: I had to simultaneously control the wheel, move the gear shift, and operate the accelerator, and blow the horn. *I experienced something similar long ago when I was beginning to write: it seemed entirely unthinkable to simultaneously control the movement of the plot, the feelings of the people, their dialogs, the instrumentation, the images, and the rhythm.*[21] I later discovered that two hands were completely sufficient for driving a car. This happened when I could do most of the complicated movements unconsciously, as a reflex. *This sensation with driving sooner or later transfers to the writing table as well.*
>
> (Zamiatin, *Litsa*, 271)

---

[20]In Yangirov, "Druzia, babochki i monstry ...," 539–540. Per another statement of Nabokov's: "everything related to technology, fashion, sports, the natural sciences, and the unnatural passions – in Russian become clumsy, prolix, and often repulsive in terms of style and rhythm" (Nabokov, "Postscript to the Russian Edition of *Lolita*," 190–191).

[21]Cf. Andrei Bely *Petersburg*: "And consciousness, dividing from the body, like the handle of a gearshift lever began to hover around the organism" (Bely, *Sochineniia*, 2:24).

The English word "automobile" led to one in a series of mini-dramas in the correspondence between Nabokov and Edmund Wilson when the former was confronted with his shortcomings in understanding English poetic meter.[22] It all began when Wilson read Nabokov's poem, "The Room," published in the *New Yorker* on May 13, 1950 and containing the following stanza:

> Whenever some automobile
> subliminally slits the night
> the walls and ceiling would reveal
> a wheeling skeleton of light.[23]

Bypassing all of the other topics in the letter, the wounded Nabokov begins his response directly with the "automobile" problem and devotes three-quarters of his letter, including examples from the classics of English poetry (and from Pushkin!), to arguing that the word can be used in mixed iambic-trochaic lines, concluding with irritation: "Once [and] for all you should tell yourself that in these questions of prosody – no matter the language involved – you are wrong and I am right, always" (Nabokov, *The Nabokov–Wilson Letters*, 248). In his epistolary fit, Nabokov was very likely forgetting that twenty-five years earlier in the literary circles of Berlin he had spoken out on the "linguistic aspects" of converting words for the automobile into Russian culture: "in his so-called English stories Pil'niak ostentatiously calls the autobus a 'bess!' though the English name should be 'bus' with one 's,' and calls the automobile a 'carr,' though one 'r' is sufficient" (cited in "Neskol'ko slov ob ubozhestve sovetskoi …," 7–23).[24]

"Crossroads of Life": The Symbolism of Driving

A pivotal point for understanding the automobile archetype in Nabokov's works is the explanation of the conception of an unwritten novel—a riddle that has not yet received adequate attention from scholars (it is mentioned but not commented on by Boyd).

---

[22]"I liked very much your New Yorker poem – but it involves a false accent on automobile – *auto'mobile* – which evidently betrays your mistaken ideas about English metrics" (Nabokov, *The Nabokov–Wilson Letters*, 247).

[23]Perhaps an echo of V. Briusov's poem, "When I am sitting lonely in a dark room …" (*Stikhotvoreniia i poemy*, 133) employing similar imagery of shadows.

[24]In his commentary on this publication, Dolinin specifies the passage from Pil'niak's story that so piqued Nabokov in this essay: "the street … was so swirling with taxis, buses (*bessami*), and cars (*karrami*)" (Pil'niak, *Angliiskie rasskazy*, 7).

Nabokov left very few literary plans unrealized. The "automobile novel," at first glance, seems to be among these. The sole source, based on which we can conjecture on the composition of the book, is an excerpt from a letter by Nabokov to his wife on April 16, 1932, sent from Prague to Berlin:

> Imagine this. A person prepares for an automobile examination on the city's geography. The first part will talk of the preparations for this and conversations linked with it, and also, of course, his family and his human surroundings, with a misty detailedness. Then an unnoticed transition to the second. *Off he goes, finds himself at the examination, but not at all an automobile one but – how shall I put this – an examination of earthly existence. He has died and they are asking him about the streets and crossroads of his life.* All this without a shade of mysticism. In this exam he tells all he remembers of … the brightest and most solid parts of his whole life. And those examining him are people long dead, for instance, the coachman who made a toboggan for him in childhood, an old high-school teacher, some distant relatives he had only heard about in life.
>
> (quoted in Boyd, *Russian Years*, 378)

The metaphysical route is dictated not by the topography of the area, but by the logic of fate.

FIGURE 3.11 *Famous Sequoia tree in California. Véra Nabokov, Dmitri Nabokov, and family friends, Bertrand and Lisbet Thompson with their Studebaker, 1940s.*

It is remarkable that as early as the mid-1930s the automobile paradigm was compelling enough for Nabokov that he was for a time captivated with the idea of devoting an entire work to the symbolism of driving. We can only guess that shapes and plot lines would have developed in the final form (early fragments may yet be found in manuscripts from the period between *Camera Obscura* [*Laughter in the Dark*] and *Despair*), but the most plausible suggestion is that the theme dissolved into a number of elements and the remaining motifs ricocheted into Nabokov's prose over the ensuing decades, becoming most perceptible in novels such as *Lolita* and *Pnin*.

It is in *Pnin* that we can trace the reverse transfer of the automobile metaphor from the realm of literature back into "real life." Before appearing at Cook's farm, Pnin, the owner of a "pale blue, egg-shaped two-door sedan" fails his first driving test.[25] Pnin (like his creator) finds pleasure not in real driving, but in imaginary driving. Pnin begins to understand this only after two months of driving lessons at the Waindell driving school. The hapless professor derives his knowledge of the art of driving from the entry for "automobile" in the *Encyclopedia Americana*, with its images of transmissions, carburetors, brake shoes, and a portrait of a participant in the Glidden tour (an American circumnavigation of the world by car in 1905),[26] and from his studying "with deep enjoyment" of the forty-page Driver's Manual "issued by the State Governor in collaboration with another expert" (*Pnin*, 112–113). When the ailing Pnin is lying on the hospital with nothing else to do, "wiggling his toes and shifting phantom gears," "then and only then was the dual nature of his initial inklings transcended" (ibid).

The draft materials for this novel contain a fragment meant for inclusion between chapters 4 and 5. This excerpt describes the hospitalized Pnin engaged in his independent study of "a 1935 manual of automobilism" that he found in the hospital library and practiced "by manipulating the levers of his cot" (quoted in Barabtarlo, *Phantom of Fact*, 190). (When he composed this scene in early August 1955, Nabokov was himself in hospital, although

---

[25]Pnin "started an argument with the examiner in an ill-timed effort to prove that nothing could be more humiliating to a rational creature than being required to encourage the development of a base conditional reflex by stopping at a red light when there was not an earthly soul around, heeled or wheeled" (*Pnin*, 113). Vadim from *Look at the Harlequins!* becomes "legally and physically fit" for the road only after two failures of the exam, while "learning to drive that 'Caracal' (as [he] fondly called < ... > new white coupe) had its comic as well as dramatic side" (*LATH*, 155).

[26]In his commentary on this passage, Barabtarlo indicates that early editions of the *Encyclopedia Americana* (vol. 2) did in fact include this picture: "The sentence in the text is culled from the legend under the picture which says 'Member of an early Glidden Tour stuck in the mud of a country road. Paved surfaces came much later.' The boxy vehicle ... has cardboard in place of a windshield, saying, ironically, 'AAA Official Glidden Tour Pathfinder.' Pnin the pathfinder will soon be lost in the 'maze of forest roads' on his way to The Pines" (Barabtarlo, *Phantom of Fact*, 193).

his library book was Hemingway's *The Old Man and the Sea*.[27]) In the final, printed, version of the text, Pnin's enlightenment is preceded by an agonizing time of "actual lessons with a harsh instructor who cramped his style" and who "issued unnecessary directives in yelps of technical slang, tried to wrestle the wheel from him at corners, and kept irritating a calm, intelligent pupil with expressions of vulgar detraction" (*Pnin*, 113). The comic effect here comes from the fact that the situation is presented from the point of view of the suffering party, the one being examined. The problem, Nabokov concludes, was that Pnin "had been totally unable to combine perceptually the car he was driving in his mind and the car he was driving on the road."

Worlds Unknown to Each Other

The most enigmatic work in Nabokov's late Russian period, the prose fragment, "Solus Rex" (1940), begins by describing the life of the king of an island nation.[28] After a few pages of uninterrupted folkloric stylization, a meta-descriptive frame is unexpectedly added to the narrative:

> Such, incidentally, were the thoughts that occurred to the no longer independent artist Dmitri Nikolaevich Sineusov, and evening had come, and in vertically arranged ruby letters *glowed the word* RENAULT [in the Russian original of the story the neon sign reads: GARAGE].
> ("Solus Rex"; *Russian Collected Works*, 5:89/*Stories*, 526)

Given the vague structure of the unfinished work, we will refrain from interpreting the character of the artist and simply note what obviously follows from the passage in question: the opening pages of the novel contain an accretion of the fictional world's attributes that mirrors a cosmogony—in literature, particularly romantic literature, this is a topos which in this case is reinforced by clear Old Testament intonation (Genesis 1:3–5). The burning letters should call to mind the fiery inscription on the palace wall of the Babylonian King Balthazar.[29] And yet what is important here is not the content of the text, but the encoding: the Babylonian wise men were unable to make sense of the words which, according to the prophet Daniel, were a prophecy of the coming destruction of Babylon (Daniel, Ch. 5). The poet Voloshin prophesies the downfall of modern civilization in a similar way:

> The whistling, rumbling, clanging, and moving
> Have drowned out living human speech,

---

[27]Boyd, *American Years*, 270; Barabtarlo, *Phantom of Fact*, 190; Nabokov, *Strong Opinions*, 84–85.
[28]For more on the genesis of the unfinished novel, see Dolinin, "Tri zametki," 215–224.
[29]An old man named "Menetekelfares" appears in *King, Queen, Knave* (*Russian Collected Works*, 2:187).

They have made prayer unthinkable,
And conversation, and contemplation; they have turned
The king of the universe into a greaser of wheels."
(Voloshin, Stikhotvoreniia i poemy, 320)

Nabokov begins playing with the prophetic illumination of the electrical advertisement as early as his first novel, Mary:

> Occasionally, braying like a stag, a motorcar would dash by or something would happen which no one walking in a city ever notices: a star, faster than thought and with less sound than a tear, would fall. Gaudier, gayer than the stars were the letters of fire which poured out one after another above a black roof, paraded in single file and vanished all at once in the darkness
> "Can—it—be—possible," said the letters in a discreet neon whisper, then the night would sweep them away at a single velvet stroke. Again they would start to creep across the sky: "Can—it—."
>
> (Mary, 26)

The mystical inscriptions (mystical if only because they are burning) in the poetic mind are closely connected with the mystery of the cosmos,[30] entering into a dialog with the most keen observers, though, to be sure, the conversation does not make it possible to guess "what it really is that flickers up there in the dark above the houses—the luminous name of a product or the glow of human thought; a sign, a summons; a question hurled into the sky and suddenly getting a jewel-bright, enraptured answer."[31] Despite the suspicion that at this late hour "at that late hour down those wide streets passed worlds utterly alien to each other" (ibid.), their position relative to each other remains a code for the character, and it is impossible to choose the hermeneutic key ("a wholly isolated world, each a totality of marvels and evil"; ibid.). One approach to a solution might be an étude by Nabokov's friend in emigration, Ivan Lukash, List'ia (Leaves), written before the two writers met. In the sketch that opens the eponymous collection, printed at a Constantinople publishing house by Russian literati stranded in the city,

---

[30]Cf. Vladimir Maiakovskii's "Ia" ("I"), 1913: "Behind the crew noisily stretches a motley-striped crowd of constellations. / Crowned by a garage" (Maiakovskii, Sobranie sochinenii, 1:76). And also in Bagritskii's "Mozhaisk shosse" ("Mozhaisk Highway"; 1931): "And calling like an orator, / At forty horsepower, / The radiator enters, like an equal, / into a constellation of lights. / Behind the glass: orbits, chords, / And, bending in, grizzled and gray, / Lopsided, crooked-faced, / The driver presses lightning" (Bagritskii, Stikhotvoreniia i poemy, 227).

[31]In the late nineteenth century, the story of electricity and its "divine origin," no less dramatic in its own way than the Prometheus myth, was spun as a miraculous means of transforming reality. Even at the final class in a lecture series on the phenomenon of electricity, representatives of the Edison company in Boston in 1887 conducted a séance (Marvin, When Old Technologies were New, 56–58).

FIGURE 3.12 *Véra, Dmitri, Vladimir Nabokov, and Vladimir Sikorskii (the son of the writer's sister Elena). The car is a Triumph TR3-A. San Remo, December 1959.*

Russian exiles are compared to fallen autumn leaves swept to the pavements of foreign lands. As would be repeated later in Nabokov, the lyrical persona looks at the urban landscape through which the face of his lost city emerges:

> The placards are like a fire, like searchlights. Fiery and ridiculous. Roaring with each letter. I remember at home, at Petersburg, *a whole wall had the fiery letters "Triangle Tires,"* and below that "Ara Pills." ... They were there. We had all that. We know all that – the red trams, the soft shining of the automobiles, and the chocolate, and the stonemasons, and the placards. ... I walk as if asleep. We had all of this, and now it's all foreign. This life is not ours with its placards and automobiles. ... And in the evening when I sit down in the corner on a bench by the dark steamship window *where the stars and the lights of the shore float, I will outline my cherished monogram on the dingy glass.*
>
> (Lukash, *List'ia*, 4)

In the beginning of creation there was the WORD; in Nabokov's opinion this was a written word. The *garage* as a workshop space, returning to the quotation from "Solus Rex" at the beginning of this chapter, is seemingly a metonymic designation for the workshop of the demiurge/writer;[32] the inscription on it in some sense ought to read: "Professionals Only."[33] This idea has a purely formalist platform with its reference to the "madeness" (*sdelannost'*) of literature.

Metaphysics of the Garage

As Lidiia Ginzburg recalled in her memoirs, Tynianov once stated that Shklovskii wished to study literary works as if they were automobiles that could be taken apart and put back together (Ginzburg, *O starom i novom*, 309). Shklovskii himself compared a person writing a "great thing" (*bol'shaia veshch'*) with a driver of a 300 horsepower car, which itself seems to control the author (Shklovskii, *Gamburgskii schet*, 33),[34] but this brash metaphor evoked the ire of proletarian writers, who objected to the Formalists' "peelings of gimmickry."[35] In *The Gift*, where Fyodor Godunov-Cherdyntsev dreams of writing "a good, thick old-fashioned novel" (*The Gift*, 11), the literary undersurface of the car mythos unfolds into a visual image presenting the central axis of the entire novel:

> Behind the brightly painted pumps a radio was singing in a gas station, while above its pavilion vertical yellow letters stood against the light blue of the sky—the name of a car firm—and on the second letter, on the "E" (a pity that it was not on the first, on the "B"—would have made an

---

[32]This interpretation seems less arbitrary if we remember that, for example, shortly before Nabokov the technique was used by B. Bozhnev (whom Nabokov esteemed quite highly: see *Rul'*. May 23, 1928) in his 1936 poem, "Silentium sociologicum": "The days of the weakest push have come, / The days of the strongest collapse have come, / *And from an automobile horn / You will fall in a wall of singing. / Your pen in numbed fingers / Drowns out the wrists of existence*" (Bozhnev, *Bor'ba za nesushchestvovan'e*, 132).

[33]In the Roman alphabet the word (written the same in English, French, and German) invites a number of readings, of which the most likely seems, in my opinion, to be the temporal idea of the "age," evoking the notion of a boundary; the visual component is important as well, with the internal mirrored rhyme of ga-ag.

[34]Cf. his thoughts on the "upshift plot," inspired by the transmission of a car, and his general mechanistic approach to literature: "Plot devices are lying over by my door, like copper springs from a burnt sofa. They're crushed and not worth repairing" (Shklovskii, *Gamburgskii schet*, 122).

[35]In the preface to a collection of poems by young Communist Youth League poets called *Razbeg* (*Take-off*; Leningrad: Priboi, 1928), Il'ia Sadof'ev polemicizes with Shklovskii without naming him: "Even a fully Soviet person, one of the leading Formalists, assiduously promotes a confused *theory of the turning wheel in literature*. < ... > *But what we need is for all four wheels of the new proletarian literature to turn. We need the automobile not to be sitting there surrounded by gapers; we need it to be moving towards socialist reconstruction of the world*" (10–11).

FIGURE 3.13 *Assembly. Detroit Publishing Co., 1923. Dry plate negative possibly made for Ford Motor Company.*

alphabetic vignette) sat a live blackbird, with a yellow—for economy's sake—beak, singing louder than the radio.

(ibid., 162)

The company name revealed to Fyodor but, like the company name on the furniture truck at the beginning of the novel, not yet given to the reader to make out, is Daimler-Benz (on inscriptions as palimpsests in the novel and the literary genealogy of this device, see Leving, *Keys to* The Gift, 282; 348).[36] From a letter by Nabokov to Shakhovskaia dated to early March 1936, we can deduce that the novel was initially going to be titled *Yes* (*Da*, instead of *Dar*, *The Gift*)[37]; this automobile passage that

---

[36]The name, composed of two surnames, appeared in approximately 1924 with the merger of the Daimler and Benz companies, founded respectively by Gottlieb Daimler (1834–1900) and Karl Benz (1844–1929), who never met in their lives (Evans, *The Motor Car*, 10).

[37]"I fear that my next novel (whose title has been extended by a letter: not *Da* [Yes], but *Dar* (*The Gift*), having turned the initial assertion into something blossoming, pagan, even priapic) will disappoint you" (The Papers of Vladimir Nabokov. Library of Congress. Manuscript Division. Box 16, No. 19, cited in Dolinin, "Tri zametki," 703–704). "Da" is the first syllable of the company name "Daimler" (*Russian Collected Works*, 4:694, notes by Aleksandr Dolinin).

was retained in the novel functions in its own way as the hero's manifesto in his modern European odyssey à la Joyce ("Yes" is the final word in his *Ulysses*).[38]

The structural features of Nabokov's prose include the extreme textualization of space in the fictional world, which has at least two dimensions; everyday objects that seem mundane at first glance soon betray their attachment to the world of books. The type of bird sitting on the letter, through an ornithological cue, returns the character and the reader to the semiosphere surrounding them both, and returns the spatial world of the novel to its typeset frame (delimited by the book page).[39] An example of the above, based on materials from 1926—the year chosen by Nabokov as the starting point for *The Gift*—may be provided by the illustrations of N. F. Lapshin (1888–1942) for Mandel'shtam's children's book. The two-page illustration for the poem, "Avtomobilishche," depicts a car with the word "AVTOGARAZH" ("AUTO GARAGE") in big letters on its cab (a similar car also graces the cover: see Mandel'shtam, *Shary* [*Balls*]):

What else must I, the big car, be sure not to forget?
They cleaned me, washed me, filled me with gasoline.
I feel like carrying bags. I feel like puffing some more.
My tires are fat – I'm the elephant of cars.
I don't need to hurry –
I've gathered strength.
I've gathered strength –
I'm the big car.
And I'm driving an armful of young pioneers.

(Mandel'shtam, *Shary*, 6–7)

Upon closer inspection, this seemingly simple poem reveals connections to Mandel'shtam's cycle from the summer of 1931 on the poet's right to the literary craft. The "childish" rhetoric (permitting the assumption of innocence) primes the declarative canvas that will later be important for

---

[38] In 1933–34, Nabokov was earnestly preparing to translate *Ulysses* into Russian and even tried to conduct negotiations with the author through Paul Leon (see letters from Nabokov to Joyce, November 9, 1933 and to Paul Leon, November 29, 1933 and January 6, 1934. James Joyce-Paul Leon Papers. National Library of Ireland). On the parallels between the *Da/Yes* of *The Gift* and the final words spoken by Molly Bloom "and yes I said yes I will Yes," see Boyd, "The Expected Stress," 27–28.

[39] Cf. the vignette at the end of "*The Enchanter*": "for all was over, and it was imperative, by any stratagem, by any spasm, to get rid of the no-longer-needed, already-looked-at, idiotic world, *on whose final page stood a lonely streetlamp with a shaded-out cat at its base*" (*The Enchanter*, 94).

Mandel'shtam at the crossroads between artistic silence and awareness of
the rapidly growing cost of speaking out in poetry against the background
of a general devaluation of the word. The probing of the topic also
begins with the naïve poetics of childhood verses borrowing motifs from
"Avtomobilishche."[40] Taking up the baton, Nabokov selects peripheral
materials, anti-aesthetic to any other author, and turns them into a sample
of high lyricism.[41] Godunov-Cherdyntsev walks along a rainy Berlin street
on his way to meet Chernyshevski to talk about the promised review of his
book of poetry and catches the objects that come into his field of vision with
the detail of an X-ray photograph:

> He decided he could already set off for the Chernyshevskis' so as to be
> there towards nine, Rhine, fine, cline. As happens with drunks, something
> preserved him when he crossed streets in this state. *Illuminated by a
> street-lamp's humid ray, a car stood at the curb with its motor running:
> every single drop on its hood was trembling.* Who could have written it?
> (*The Gift*, 35)

The idling motor, animated by Nabokov between two sentences about two
types of literary creation, poetry and criticism, is a projection of Fyodor's
animated state of creative process (a paragraph before this he is playing with
variations of rhymes for "noticed" and "remotest"). The poet's consciousness
turns on the axis of meaning in this evening: around the imaginary review,
which is constructed over twenty pages of the densest of text, before Fyodor
actually crosses the Chernyshevski's threshold.

An example of the transformation of base, clearly "unliterary" material into
an artistic text is the unnamed character who momentarily appears in *Lolita*
for the sole purpose of wiping the glass of Humbert's car (*Lolita*, 130) and, at
the same time, reminding him of a classic Russian work.[42] The less noticeable a
semantic node is in Nabokov, the greater are the chances that it might branch
out on several levels, including word-creation, syntax, and intertext.

---

[40]The image of the five-year-old car-animal full of optimistic, irrepressible energy is in contrast
to the 1931 model poet, bruised but confident in his voice: "It used to be that I, a bit younger, /
would go out / In a taped up rubber jacket [cf. *my tires are fat*] / Into the broad branchingness
of boulevards." Starting off as an advocate for time ("It's not to blame for its own racing"),
Mandel'shtam, "also a contemporary," protects himself from attack as well: "Look how my
coat ripples on me, / How I can step and speak!"; "It's a long way still between me and the
patriarch"; Mandel'shtam, *Sobranie sochinenii*, 1:177–178 (cf. "I feel like puffing some more").
[41]Cf.: "An automobile advertisement, brightly beckoning in a wild, picturesque gorge from an
absolutely inaccessible spot on an alpine cliff thrilled him to tears" (*Glory*, 127).
[42]Among the things that delighted Nabokov about Gogol's *Dead Souls* was the use of "an
entirely new literary device" related to the carriage image.

The garage mystery in *Mary* (a novel where the metaphor of book-as-house is taken to an extreme)[43] serves as a conduit to the character's past:

[T]he sun tangled with the wheels of motorcars. Near the beer-hall there was a *garage* and from the *gaping gloom of its entrance* came a tender whiff of carbide. And that chance exhalation helped Ganin to remember more vividly yet the rainy Russian late August and early September, the torrent of happiness, which the specters of his Berlin life kept interrupting.

(*Mary*, 66–67)

The gaping orifice of the entrance functions as a black hole of memory in which space and time collapse and are converted. The visual blackness of the typeface letters on the white surface of the page is in and of itself a *semantic fissure*, a way into the artistic dimension established by the author of the text.

The meta-descriptive key to the metaphysics of the garage is found in *Lolita*. After visiting the grown-up Lolita, Humbert falls into a state of prostration, which is duplicated by the behavior of his car.[44] The repairman helps him extract his car from the mud, and the drunken H. H. makes it to the nearest town and looks at the advertising signs lighting up the night. One of the signs is a cryptogram devised by the omniscient author (V. V. Nabokov), notifying the reader that the novel's denouement is close at hand, and more precisely that the outcome will be lethal in a metaliterary sense (after dispensing with three central characters: the murder of Quilty, the fall of H. H., and the death of Mrs. Richard F. Schiller in childbirth, the author bids farewell): "On the other side of street a garage said in its sleep 'they've killed the author' ['*Avtora ubili*' (in actuality: 'automobiles' ['*Avtomobili*'])."[45]

---

[43]In the final scene the workers, Sirin's extras, are *binding* red tiles reminiscent of *large books* into the roof (*Russian Collected Works*, 2:126). On the symbolism in this episode, see Toker, *Nabokov: The Mystery of Literary Structures*, 46 and Nakata, "Angels on the Planks," 25–26. See also the book-embryo metaphor on the opening pages of *The Gift*, as Fyodor sees through the window of his newly rented apartment a house "half enclosed in scaffolding," which presages the future uncompleted biography and the already started novel (*Russian Collected Works*, 4:195).

[44]"the short-cut in question got worse and worse, bumpier and bumpier, muddier and muddier, and when I attempted to turn back after some ten miles of purblind, tortuous and tortoise-slow progress, my old and weak Melmoth got stuck in deep clay. All was dark and muggy, and hopeless. My headlights hung over a broad ditch full of water. The surrounding country, if any, was a black wilderness. I sought to extricate myself but my rear wheels only whined in slosh and anguish" (*Lolita*, 281).

[45]Translated back from Russian; Nabokov occasionally amended his Russian translation of *Lolita* in such a way as to adapt certain wordplay. Quoted from *Lolita* in *Amerikanskoe sobranaie*, 2:345.

The "murder" of the author appears only in the 1967 Russian version of the novel,[46] but this was still a year before the publication of Barthes's famous article, "*La mort de l'auteur*" (in the journal, *Manteia*. 1968. № 5), providing a theoretical foundation for the term, "death of the author," and introducing it into popular scholarly circulation. Barthes articulates what would seem to be important principles for Nabokov as a prose writer, particularly the assertion that the text does not represent merely a linear chain of words expressing a single "teleological" meaning, or, as the French philosopher writes, a "message" from an Author-God; it is rather a multidimensional space in which various types of writing combine and come into contact, with none of them being original material. The text is woven together out of citations that refer back to thousands of preexisting cultural sources (Barthes, *Mythologies*, 388).

The Route Through the Text

The foregoing analysis leads us directly to the notion of a vehicle's movement through textualized space as seen in *Lolita*. The roads that, like rays, diverge across "the crazy quilt of forty-eight states" (*Lolita*, 152) are absorbed by Humbert like the lines of a novel. And they are eventually reincarnated in the confession of the White-Widowed Male (or, if you like, in a book by Nabokov called *Lolita*), as the road led in a similar way to the written confession of *Despair*'s Hermann Karlovich. The literary quality of Humbert's narrative time and again shines through his descriptions of landscape, as in the incident where Gogol's calligraphomaniac Akakii Akakievich notices "that he is not in the middle of a line, but rather in the middle of a street" (Gogol, *Sobranie khudozhestvennykh proizvedenii*, 3:180):

> [T]he road shimmered ahead, with a remote car changing its shape mirage-like in the surface glare, and seeming to hang for a moment, *old-fashionedly square and high*, in the hot haze. < ... > then the mysterious outlines of *table-like* hills, and then red bluffs *ink-blotted* with junipers, and then a mountain range, dun grading into blue, and blue into dream, and the desert would meet us with a steady gale, dust, gray thorn bushes, and hideous bits of tissue paper.
>
> (*Lolita*, 140–141)

---

[46]The "pun" in the English original is: "On the other side of the street a garage said in its sleep – genuflexion lubricity; and corrected itself to Gulflex Lubrication" (*Lolita*, 282). Unfortunately Alfred Appel provides no commentary on this passage, limiting himself to the obvious: "lasciviousness and lewdness" (ibid., 443).

FIGURE 3.14 *Cover of the Soviet magazine* Motor, *No. 2, 1929.*

What we have here is nothing other than a descriptive discourse on the creation of a novel, dotted with mentions of sitting at a desk, of an agonized soiling of paper, etc. The metatext, as Iu. Levin states, actualizes the situation of the text's creation and gives rise to a multitude of narrative forms, reducing reality and memory (actual or imagined), historical time and directly lived time, to a common denominator (Levin, *Izbrannye trudy*, 298). In addition to the "unconscious" references the text points to a code of thematically related works, including Gogol's "Overcoat," as we have indicated; the mirage in the iridescent shining of the road in this case might be Il'f and Petrov's *Odnoetazhnaia Amerika* (*One-story America*):

> A trip through America by car resembles a journey across an ocean, monotonous and magnificent. ... Any time you look out the car window there is always a wondrously smooth road with gas stations, tourist lodges, and billboards along the roadsides. ... Before speaking about the Eastern United States – which is mountains, or desert, or forest – we must state the most important thing: *this is a land of automobiles and electricity.*
>
> (Il'f & Petrov, *Sobranie sochinenii*, 4:107)[47]

The authors of *One-story America*, along with Nabokov, were among the first Russian writers to conclude that an understanding of American society was rooted more in the anthropology of car culture than in political ideas.[48]

Less obviously in *Lolita* and more clearly in *The Gift*, the automobile (in the form of the furniture truck) represents a multidimensional and stereoscopic literary instantiation. The bookshop that Godunov-Cherdyntsev enters is, by definition, a hyper-textualized world. The Berlin shop window contains, among the abundance of "zigzags, cogs and numerals of Soviet cover designs" (*The Gift*, 155) on which the character's gaze falls, a handbook entitled "What a Driver Should Know" (ibid.). The literary stylization of the title clearly carries on the tone of Nabokov's own article from 1931, "What Must Everyone Know?" and it is not out of the question that such a document was in fact published.[49] The work of Vladimir Maiakovskii as a connecting link in this case might also be the target of parody: Nabokov's namesake was the author of the attention-getting 1926 guidebook, "How Is Poetry Made?" ("*Kak delat' stikhi?*") for the laboring masses, which agitated the émigré press.

---

[47]Cf.: "American psychology loves that which is strong, sudden, and big. Like an automobile engine, American life moves in bursts" (Zenzinov, *Zheleznyi skrezhet*, 53). And also on "10 l.s" ["10 hp"] by Erenburg (1929): "The automobile moves nervously. It jumps like a kangaroo. It stops, then suddenly lurches forward. It fills the streets with a repulsive stench. It is louder than a spring thunderstorm" (Erenburg, *Sobranie sochinenii*, 7:13).

[48]Cf.: "The grandiose spontaneous spectacle of car traffic ... . Drive a thousand miles through America and you will know more about it than all the institutes of sociology or general works of political science research" (Bodriiar, *Amerika*, 123–125).

[49]Some typical titles of instructional brochures issued in the USSR at the time: "What Teachers Need To Know about the Ministry of Education's Pedagogical Press" (Moscow, 1929); R. I. Dovgard, "What Locomotive Repair Technicians Should Read at the Depot" (Moscow, 1952), and "What Locomotive Drivers and Assistants Should Read" (Moscow, 1954).

The instruction book or object-guide inside a book represents the same sort of descriptive apparatus that activates the reader's memory and conveys the coded information with which we "open up" a text. It has long been remarked that Nabokov's texts are structured in such a way as to instruct the attentive reader: for example, the accumulation of Shakespeare allusions in *Lolita* should in the end hint at the kabbalah-like digits on the license plate recalled by Humbert (WS 1564 and SH 1616), which in fact encode the initials and dates of the greatest of English playwrights.[50]

The Automobile in the Landscape

The apogee of the gradual metamorphosis of the car and its transformation into a new class of fauna came when its inner workings began to be identified with human or animal organs (heart = motor,[51] headlights = eyes, etc.).[52] In Otsup's 1919 poem, "Automobile," streets and people are seen as if through car headlights:

> The heart, in working order, knocks,
> The pounding of the valves is even,
> All keys for the race from above:
> The heart knocks all by itself! ...
>
> How many heavy like elephants,
> Light and quick like a dugout canoe,
> How they can call and howl,
> How many quick legs they have.
>
> The headlights burn, the skeleton knocks,
> Springy exhaust puffs,
> Just a lingering pungent trace,
> Just a momentary row of columns.
>
> (Otsup, *"Okean vremeni,"* 39)

---

[50]William Shakespeare (1564–1616). For commentary on these literary allusions, see Proffer, *Kliuchi*, 42–43. Also Samuel Schuman, *Nabokov's Shakespeare* (2014).

[51]"The hum of an unseen engine, / Beyond the turn a heart is beating" (Kuzmin, *Sochineniia*, 301); "The draggle-tailed car with a sputtering heart" (Shklovskii, *Gamburgskii schet*, 142).

[52]Valentin Gorianskii: "the dull snouts of automobiles / Suddenly on guard, full of meaning" ("Neobychnaia istoriia (Orfei na Nevskom)," 1916; *Peterburg v russkoi poezii*, 266).

The diversity of animals into which the car is transformed is enormous and includes mammals,[53] fish,[54] and insects.[55]

The automobile in Nabokov's works is adapted to the landscape and seen as a part of it; their union is so harmonious that it almost reaches the level of high art, as in the car in the painting entitled "Seen Through a Windshield," by Cynthia in "The Vane Sisters,"[56] or the level of poetic subject matter, as in *Glory*, where Pushkin and the automobile are combined in a single semantic stroke. The audio-visual palette embodies for the character the wonderful fullness of being, which combines sounds (*susurrous sound*) and vision (*warm tints*): "The taxi sped with a susurrous sound; he admired the Tiergarten crowding around him, the lovely warm tints of its autumn foliage: 'O dismal period, visual enchantment—'" (*Glory*, 185). The parallel ideas of the foundations at the base of urbanist poetics are developed in a theoretical work from 1923 by Malevich. The excerpt cited below is from a long (almost two-page) passage devoted to the car in his treatise on things' and objects' "conditional and illusory reflection on the record of our consciousness":

> If the automobile as an objective thing exists only as a conditional thing, then yes, it exists objectively. For me personally, the automobile does not exist, for what is an automobile? This question itself can shake its objective foundation, and I will find supporters, and my point might become conditionally objective. From my point of view, the automobile is a system of a number of technical elements from our everyday life of interactions, or the automobile is the construction of power connections that caused a series of linkages, *created a system expressing a particular speed of movement in a pure, objectless form*, later applied to a set of practical needs of the masses. *This*

---

[53]"Do you hear the cries of the automobile?" (Maiakovskii, *Sobranie sochinenii*, 1:299).

[54]"And towards columns and cafes, / And motors, steel sharks" ("Benzinnaia liubov' (Iz putevogo al'boma)," 1925; Chernyi, *Sobranie sochinenii*, 2:224).

[55]"*a heavy car, buzzing like a giant bumblebee,* passed an endless stream of automobiles returning to Paris" (*Avantiurnyi roman*, 1930; Teffi, *Smeshnoe v pechal'nom*, 268).

[56]Correcting a mistake made by the "great artists of the past," Nabokov imitates a painted canvas – glass "a windshield partly covered with rime, with a brilliant trickle (from an imaginary car roof) across its transparent part and, through it all, the sapphire flame of the sky and a green-and-white fir tree" ("The Vane Sisters"; *Stories*, 624). In the short story "Perfection" the protagonist fantasizes about "*the fleeting, speckled world of automobile racers, < ... > about the pleasures of very rich people amid very picturesque-natural surroundings*" (*Stories*, 340).

is a whole series of elements that created the phenomenon on the model of all phenomena in the world of plants and other organisms, with the sole difference that the automobile is a planned mechanical <phenomenon>, while the other is organic. *An objective point of view on an automobile can only be the same as that on any plant in nature;* a birch tree has an objective existence for everyone, but the birch tree does not in fact exist: we do not know how the phenomena of the plant world are classified. The birch is one of the phenomena of the plant world that has an infinite connection by its elements with the entirety of the world of plants.

("On the Subjective and the Objective in Art and in General"; Malevich, *Chernyi kvadrat*, 213–214)

FIGURE 3.15 *Dmitri Nabokov and his 1957 MG-A. New York, c. 1959.*

Sentimentalist prose inherited an interest in the metropolis from the classical period, and revised it to include fields, forests, nymphs, etc. (Vaiskopf, *Siuzhet Gogolia*, 405). Nabokov's approach to the shape of the landscape synthesizes established prose tendencies and stimulates the creation of a new urbanist canon. Take the following comparison of three excerpts from Nabokov's work during various periods, each of which presents a car as part of the fauna among the motionless flora of the scenery:

"The road was brightly sunlit and had many turns; a wall of rock with thorny bushes blooming in its cracks rose on the right, while on the left there was a precipice and a valley where water in crescents of foam ran down over ledges; then came dark conifers clustering in close ranks now on one side, now on the other; mountains loomed all around, imperceptibly changing position; they were greenish with streaks of snow; grayer ones looked out from behind their shoulders, and far beyond there were giants of an opaque violet whiteness, and these never moved, and the sky above them seemed faded in comparison with the bright-blue patches between the tops of the black firs under which the car passed." (*Glory*, 42–43)

"Their car was standing close to the parapet, a stout stone wall a foot high, behind which a ravine, overgrown with brambles, sloped steeply down. Far below could be heard the swish and rumble of a rapid stream. On the left-hand side rose a reddish rocky slope with pine trees on its summit. The sun was scorching. A little way ahead a man with black spectacles was sitting on the edge of the road breaking stones. < ... > The bends became more and more frequent. On one side soared the steep cliff; on the other was the ravine. The sun stabbed his eyes. The pointer of the speedometer trembled and rose." (*Camera Obscura*, in *Russian Collected Works*, 3:363/*Laughter in the Dark*, 235)

"Pnin had now been in that maze of forest roads for about an hour and had come to the conclusion that 'bear north,' and in fact the word 'north' itself, meant nothing to him. < ... > and since he had little experience in manoeuvring on rutty narrow roads, with ditches and even ravines gaping on either side, his various indecisions and gropings took those bizarre visual forms that an observer on the lookout tower might have followed with a compassionate eye; but there was no living creature in that forlorn and listless upper region except for an ant who had his own troubles." (*Pnin*, 114–115)

In all three extracts the scenes are presented from the point of view of the implied author and structures based on principles close in spirit to those posited by Eisenstein in his 1929 article, "Za Kadrom" ("Beyond the Shot," published in English as "The Cinematorgaphic Principle and the Ideogram"). Eisenstein illustrates his cinematic theories using the aggregated category of pictograms *huei-i*: the combination of these two very simple characters is seen not as a sum, but as the product of magnitude of another dimension. According to Eisenstein, this is the same as montage technique, whereby unambiguous and semantically neutral "representational shots" are combined into "meaningful contexts and series" (Eisenstein in Braudy and Cohen, *Film Theory*, 15). In its condensed form, it is the starting point for "intellectual cinema," which seeks out the greatest possible economy in the visual presentation of abstract concepts. From among the many examples of close-ups and montage effects in Nabokov's prose, let us take the following description of the motion of Pnin's car in parallel to the motion of an *ant* who "after hours of inept perseverance, somehow reached the upper platform and the balustrade (his *autostrada*) and was getting all bothered and baffled much in the same way as that preposterous toy car progressing below" (*Pnin*, 115). This passage contains a hitherto unnoticed allusion to Akhmatova's 1910 poem "Zharko veet veter dushnyi …" ("Hot blows the stifling wind …"):

> The dry smell of the everlastings
> In a braid swept back.
> On the trunk of a gnarled fir tree
> *A highway of ants.*
>
> (Akhmatova, *Stikhotvoreniia i poemy*, 34)

In *Pnin*, Nabokov stages an experiment that "dissolves" the automobile into the environment: Pnin's stepson, Victor Wind, makes "the scenery penetrate the automobile." The technique used for this is as follows:

> A polished black sedan was a good subject, especially if parked at the intersection of a tree-bordered street and one of those heavyish spring skies whose bloated grey clouds and amoeba-shaped blotches of blue seem more physical than the reticent elms and evasive pavement. *Now break the body of the car into separate curves and panels; then put it together in terms of reflections.* These will be different for each part: the top will display inverted trees with blurred branches growing like roots into a washily photographed sky, with a whalelike building swimming by – an architectural afterthought; one side of the hood will be coated with a band of rich celestial cobalt; a most delicate pattern of black twigs will be mirrored in the outside surface of the rear window; and a remarkable

desert view, a distended horizon, with a remote house here and alone tree there, will stretch along the bumper.

(*Pnin*, 97)

The way the reflections on the car are broken up and reconstituted embodies Nabokov's "star" metaphor for constructing an urban hypertext that reflects and refracts,[57] among other things, the works of his contemporaries. For example, certain thematic and lexical parallels are discernible between Gorodetskii's 1918 narrative poem, *Shofer Vlado* (*Vlado the Chauffeur*), about an automobile accident in the mountains, and Sirin's sonnet, "An Automobile in the Mountains," published in *Rul'* on April 20, 1924. Presented below are the main parallels, identified separately (here we are pointing out not a quoted "intertext" as traditionally understood, but rather a message shared by the passages based on the similarity of their cultural codes and formulas and their common rhythmic texture):

1. Gorodetskii: "Like a whirlwind chased by a devil, / *Thundering*, whistling, throwing up dust, / The automobile *flew* headlong … / Along the bends of the road, / *Flying* like a bird amidst the heavens, / He drove his weighty Mercedes … / And now above him he hears, / As if in *the blue heights*, / The automobile *roars with its horn* … / *Into a gorge the thunder* rumbled … / And, o wondrous *dream*! / Wings suddenly grow from the blood."

Nabokov: "Like a *dream*, the road *flies*, and like the rib / The moon rises over the *mountain* top. / With my black racing car / I compare – the *thunder* tearing itself free!"

2. Gorodetskii: "Now *silver*, now bright, / There in the abyss foamed the river. / Autumn shone. And the forests / Were tormented by the crimson leaf-flying. / The trees bent exhausted, / *Their foliage crept as carpets*."

Nabokov: "hear *as the debris under the frenzied tire* / emanates as weeping *silver*."

3. Gorodetskii: "Acceleration / Mad. *Hands like steel* / *Grabbed the wheel*. The wind strevvams, / *And the brake pedal moans*. / *The slope* winds like a snake / And pulls downward."

Nabokov: "*Squeezing the sloped* and flexible *wheel*, / where am I flying? By an alpine shanty / I see a vision of a homeland hearth; // and on the

---

[57]Cf. in *Lolita*: "The reflection of the afternoon sun, a dazzling white diamond with innumerable iridescent spikes quivered on *the round back of a parked car*" (*Lolita*, 43–44).

way back, *pressing the cone / with my sole* and shifting the side lever / in an arc, I move."

In the polygenetic picture of the world, nature itself infuses the car, forming an eco-mechanical environment in conjunction with it. A deus ex machina, like Aphrodite from the foam, the car is born out of the elemental forest reflected on its shining metal surface ("A car materialized behind the foliage"; *The Enchanter*, 78). The reader sometimes gets the impression that Nabokov's car is slipping out of control, but the author need only call out the reanimated objects of the earth and everything is put back in its place: "A station wagon popped out of the leafy shade of the avenue, dragging some of it on its roof before the shadows snapped, and swung by at an idiotic pace, the sweatshirted driver roof-holding with his left hand" (*Lolita*, 69). The sweatshirted ("half-naked" in the Russian version) driver is yet another representative of the organic world and perhaps a gentle nod in the direction of the popular 1950s films about Tarzan with all their accompanying horse-transport symbolism and its deep roots in ancient mythology.

The rhythmic changing of the status of nature brings into relief the psychological machinations of the driver and the poetics of motion, as we see in the following example from *Lolita*:

[A] lovely, lonely, supercilious grove < ... > started to echo greenly the rush of our car, a red and ferny road on our right turned its head before slanting into the woodland, and I suggested we might perhaps –
"Drive on," my Lo cried shrilly.
"Righto < ... >".

(*Lolita*, 129)

The punctuation break (a dash) takes the place of the driver's intention in the dialog. The omitted sentence, remaining unspoken but replaced by a partial gesture (the unfinished turn of the wheel in the direction of the road) should have sounded like an invitation to retire into the thicket. What is noteworthy here is the discrepancy between the two authorial manifestations: the aching Humbert suppressing the desires of the flesh (H1) and Humbert the author of the narrative (H2). H2 uses grammatical means to convey the reaction of H1 to the landscape: what "turned its head" is of course not the path, but, for a fraction of a second, H1. (There is a peripheral game here with the visual image of the vagina: a beckoning path lined with ferns in Humbert's obsessed mind).[58] Lolita intercepts his gaze and preempts the instinctive drive.

---

[58]In the literary tradition, the garden and the forest are *locus amoenus*, compared with the locations most amenable for solitude and carnal love, and the places themselves then metonymically take on the functions of the female body (cf.: "the imagination associates the

Another means of conveying the dynamics of car travel through language is found in *Despair*, where the texture of the locale influences the narrator's speech,[59] which is supposedly distorted by riding on a bumpy road:

I turned the steering wheel, with the car slowly moving. *Ick. And once again: ick. (We left the road for the field.)* Under the tires thin snow and dead grass crackled. The car bounced on humps of ground, we bounced too. He spoke the while:

"I'll manage this car without any trouble *(bump). Lord, what a ride I'll take (bump). Never fear (bump-bump)* I won't do it any harm!"

(*Despair*, 165)

Vehicular Mimicry

The bionic approach was not unusual in the early automobile industry, as we see in the terminology used by a Russian observer writing that to the eye "the automobile is divided into new independent types: the normal car, the electric, the aerodynamic (with a propeller) and, finally, the motor sleigh."[60] In *The Gift*, Nabokov reveals the physiological genealogy of Godunov-Cherdyntsev's cabriolet:

[A]n open motorcar, crimson both inside and out, awaited us: the idea of speed had already given a slant to the steering wheel (sea-cliff trees will understand what I mean), *while its general appearance still retained—out of a false sense of propriety, I suppose—a servile link with the shape of a victoria; but if this was indeed an attempt at mimicry* then it was totally

---

body with particular, well-defined places, such as garden, cave, island, valley, or forest bower. Limitation and enclosure are more comforting than the mystery and possible danger of limitless spaciousness, and such places easily become associated with ease, beauty, and the pleasure of love"; Lutwack, *The Role of Place in Literature*, 95).

[59]The experiments of David Burliuk's American period date to approximately the same time: in his poem "Automobile" (1930) the flickering of houses is conveyed by the lengthening of the word and then by the internal alternation of letters providing an anagram of a familiar biblical city: "Eternal self-propulsion / I am not alive ... Domas / They run past Sodom intently / They whistle" (D. Burliuk and N. Burliuk, *Stikhotvoreniia*, 244–245).

[60]And later as a utopia of eco-culture: "[Military] maneuvers each year are accompanied by newer and newer evolutions of the automobile. ... Freight trucks every year find newer and newer uses: they water the streets, carry away the dirt, carry construction materials and large stones, but they are especially indispensable for the army when shipping its heavy and complex baggage" (cited in *Ezhegodnik gazety* Rech' *na 1913*, St. Petersburg, 488.

FIGURE 3.16 *Horace Allen Gasoline Station, San Jose, C.A., 1933. This structure is an excellent example of the so-called "domestic style" that characterized gasoline station design in the late 1920s and early 1930s. With its massive brick chimney, steep shingled roof, and full-arched multi-paned windows, the station closely resembled the English Cottage style house. Historic American Buildings Survey Collection, Library of Congress.*

destroyed by the roar of the motor with the muffler bypass opened, a roar so ferocious that long before we came in sight a peasant on a hay wagon coming the other way would jump off and try to hood his horse with a sack—after which he and his cart would often end up in the ditch or even in the field.

(The Gift, 30)

According to Nabokov's phylogeny, the car has undergone a metamorphosis from animal to carriage and from carriage to automobile,[61] in accordance with the stages of technological progress, each of which leaves the stamp of

---

[61]In *Bend Sinister*: "That puritanical leather < ... > was the very last remnant of a phylogenetic link between the modem highly differentiated Pullman idea and a bench in the primitive stage coach: *from oats to oil*" (*Bend Sinister*, 113).

its previous incarnation.[62] As with almost every other aspect of his art, the origins of Nabokov's ideas on mimicry can be traced back to the world of his childhood. For example, the archive of the Tenishev School has preserved documents from the 1908–09 school year on the purchase of visual aids for biology classes, including the school's insect collection and materials regarding mimicry.[63] From that time Nabokov gives us a description of the two family cars:

> I would ascertain which of our two cars, the Benz or the Wolseley, was there to take me to school. The first, a gray landaulet < ... >. Its lines had seemed positively dynamic in comparison with those of the insipid, noseless and noiseless, electric coupé that had preceded it; but, in its turn, *it acquired an old-fashioned, top-heavy look, with a sadly shrunken bonnet, as soon as the comparatively long, black English limousine came to share its garage.*
>
> (*Speak, Memory*, 182)

The dimensions of the car with aristocratic blood in its pipes instead of gasoline (which, according to Nabokov, smelled like tea in 1910 [*Speak, Memory*, 130]) are conveyed stylistically: four modifiers (new, long, black, English) express the length of the limousine.

The theme of bloodlines, projected onto the Benz, is reinforced by the historical genes that connect the story of the Nabokov family with legendary events of imperial proportions. Kerenskii asked to borrow the Nabokovs' car to escape from the Winter Palace, but "father explained that the car was weak and old and hardly fit for historical flights, unlike the marvelous carriage of his progenitor that had been lent to Louis for his escape to Varennes" (*Russian Collected Works*, 5:262). The source for this semi-apocryphal story can be found in the memoirs of Nabokov's father, "Archive of the Russian Revolution," published in 1921 where the motivation for the refusal is given almost word-for-word: "the old Benz landaulet was suitable only 'for trips in the city, weak and battered, absolutely unfit for the proposed purpose'" (*Russian Collected Works*, 5:704, commentary).

After meeting a former classmate, K. Nellis (the apparent prototype for the protagonist of "The Doorbell," 1927), in Berlin in 1928, Nabokov was struck by his selective memory:

---

[62]On the origins of Nabokov's theory of mimicry, see Boyd, *American Years*, 219.

[63]Among the titles listed: "Harmful Animals, Imitative Mimicry and Protective Coloration; the Metamorphosis of the Dragonfly Through Five Phases, Presented in Large Format; The Metamorphosis of the Silkworm from Seven Objects; The Metamorphosis of the Cabbage Butterfly," and so on (St. Petersburg State Historical Archive, f. 176, op. 1, d. 31, sheet 202).

"The main thing and seemingly the only thing he remembered was that 'we were the only two in the class who had cars.' And he said it as if this were something that bound us tightly together forever! As we bade farewell he noted somewhat wistfully that no matter how many such meetings there were, no-one from among his former comrades ever called him again later. The 'automobile' frightened me to such an extent that I fully confirmed his trepidation."

("Palestinskoe pis'mo Vladimira Nabokova 1937 goda," 20)

Nabokov unwittingly reproduces almost verbatim the intonation of the diary entry by Chukovskii on the day his father was killed: "The first word on everyone's lips when remembering Nabokov was, yes, this was a lord. We on the editorial board of *Rech'* were always struck by the fact that he arrived in a car, that he had a chef, that he had a box at the opera, and so on" (Chukovskii, *Dnevnik*, 1:205).

Sex in a Car

The automobile, as with any vehicle, from a boat to an airplane, creates an intimacy in the interior space that can lead to involuntary closeness between those inside them. Reaching back to the common French literary motif of sex in a carriage,[64] amorous fashion forces itself on Russia from outside: while touring Petersburg, the Italian Marinetti confronted Russian men over their indecision in interacting with women ("After discovering that you like a woman you dig deep in your soul for three years to think about whether you love her or not, and then waver for another three years deciding whether or not to tell her"); he then shared his own urbanist prescription: "It's entirely different with us: *If we like a woman, we sit her down in a car, lower our pants and in ten minutes get what would have taken you years.*"[65]

But love poetry quickly caught on to the new prospects (in the 1910s there was even a popular record called "Flirting in a Motor Car"[66]), shifting from the old-fashioned carriage to the car: "In vain the automobile

---

[64]One of the earliest instances of this might be the scene with Jean-Jacques and Madame de Larnage in chapter 6 of book one of Rousseau's *Confessions*; in Maupassant's *Bel Ami*, Clotilde first gives herself to Du Roy in a carriage.

[65]Cited in a retelling by Livshits, who makes no effort to conceal his embarrassment: "What could be compared to this hundred-horsepower phallic pathos?" (Livshits, *Polutoroglazyi strelets*, 491–493).

[66]The "automobile" as a theme also figured into popular sketch comedies and the music stage. In the summer of 1911 in Petersburg, there was a benefit for the actor B. S. Ol'sh-ii entitled *Car № 99* (see *Rech'*. Aug. 4 (17), 1911, 1).

FIGURE 3.17 *Two ladies in a convertible automobile.* Automobility, *1906. Campbell, Metzger & Jacobson. Popular and applied graphic art print filing series, Library of Congress.*

winds the gray strands of the road on gray rustling tires. You and I are firmly tied and bound by anguish" (Shklovskii, 1915; *Poeziia russkogo futurizma*, 325).

> In a lightly jostling car
> His lips occasionally closed my eyes.
> "For love, for love this rustling of carrying wings"
> He said in a quickly flying whisper.
>
> (Otsup, *"Okean vremeni,"* 41)

The relationships of the passengers inside the small cab, electrified by each other's presence, are infused with an erotic charge from the very start. Severianin, whose praises were sung by the critic Chukovskii[67] for his introduction of industrial tropes into poetry, stylizes a summer flirtation to the accompaniment of a film plot in his "July Midday" ("Iul'skii polden'"), in which the shots of a silent film are imbued with color and sound.[68]

In pointing out the sexism in ads for cars, which, like beautiful women, confer the connotations of luxury on their "owners," Tim O'Sullivan notes that in the "magical system" of advertising, people do not merely like, want, or buy objects; they also imbue them with a hidden symbolic value, identifying "things" with signs of social well-being, difference, style, and power, and projecting an image corresponding to the owners' own ideas of themselves to the general public (O'Sullivan, "Transports of Difference and Delight," 289).[69]

It would seem that Nabokov anticipated the opinions of present-day psychoanalysts who believe that car manufacturers, knowingly or unknowingly, include erotic elements in the design of their cars, influenced by their sexualization in the adverts they themselves commission. Seemingly teasing Freudians, Nabokov flatly puns on the word "bumper" in *Lolita*,[70] while Humbert, accusing Lolita of betraying him, notices in the parking lot of the motel "a red hood protrud[ing] in somewhat cod-piece fashion" (*Lolita*, 195). Proffer remarks that this "red phallic protuberance" symbolically wounds Humbert's self-confidence and manly dignity (Proffer, *Kliuchi*, 42). The psychologists Joyce Brothers and Herbert Hoffman state that the automobile for many men represents an extension of themselves, as a powerful symbol of masculinity and sexual maturity: "In their minds there is a link between horsepower and sexual prowess. They may also equate driving with sexual function which leads to the assumption that the bigger the car the better" (Lewis, "Sex and the Automobile," 127). Cars

---

[67]While generally treating futurism and the work of Severianin in particular with some negativity: "with what crazy musicality in the poem 'Violet Trance' *does the author express the hurricane flight of the madly roaring automobile*" (Chukovskii, *Futuristy*, 7).

[68]The final stanza of the poem descends into hints of indecency, stirring the reader's imagination: "The channel with a rustling like lighting beneath the wheels, / And the emboldened chauffeur got drunk on the wine of ecstasy" (*Poeziia russkogo futurizma*, 334–335).

[69]An appendix to the article reproduces images from automobile advertising in periodicals from 1907 through the 1960s. Much of the illustrations and statistical material is also taken from the book by Schmidt on European automobile advertising (Schmidt, *Automobil-Werbung*).

[70]Proffer calls this "phallic infiltration": "a hairy bumper" or "Harry bump her" (Proffer, *Kliuchi*, 34).

with extended and rounded forms are interpreted as phallic symbols, and the radiator grill between the headlights is identified with female genitalia (ibid.).[71] And some researchers have concluded that the hidden sexual fantasies of men[72] can be revealed by which type of car they prefer.[73]

The most important difference between the automobile cab and the train compartment is in the marked delineation between public and private transportation (sometimes reinforced by curtains in the side or rear windows, creating an additional visual barrier). The car belongs to a particular owner (leaving aside, for now, the liminal position of the taxi cab), while the space of the train belongs to everyone at the same time, including current and future passengers. Lewis hypothesizes that the car has become something more than just a mode of transportation: "they were a destination as well, for they provided a setting for sexual relations including intercourse" (Lewis, "Sex and the Automobile," 123–124).[74]

In *Mary*, the act of love between Ganin and Liudmila in the taxi becomes, strangely enough, the "end point" of their romance: "That music had stopped at the moment one night when on the jolting floor of a dark taxi, he had possessed Lyudmila, and at once it had all become utterly banal—the woman straightening her hat that had slipped down onto the back of her neck, the lights flickering past the window, the driver's back towering like a black mountain behind the glass partition" (*Mary*, 19).

Nabokov pits incompatible amplitudes against each other (on the physical level: vertical friction with the horizontal movement on the plane of the road; on the mental level: Liudmila's growing love with Ganin's waning passion), with the result that the two-fold dynamic gives rise to motion in motion, a "new altar of passion" to quote Briusov: not the bed, but its absence; not stasis, but a headlong flight in a space of flickering lights. The quoted passage was jarring for Edmund Wilson, who shared his impressions

---

[71]Cf. in Shershenevich: "You somehow intently threw yourself under / The pneumatic breasts of the car" ("Vy vchera mne vstavili lunu v petlitsu ..." ["Yesterday you put the moon in my buttonhole ..."]; Shershenevich, *Listy imazhinista*, 100).

[72]According to Dr. Hoffman, men who think about "jazzy sports cars" fantasize about sexually aggressive women; men who like "luxury cars" dream of romantic encounters in exotic locales; if the driver wants a powerful Jeep, it means that he likes "healthy women with well-developed bodies and physical endurance"; and a customized two-door car reveals a hidden desire to live the life of a playboy (Lewis, "Sex and the Automobile," 127–128).

[73]In the classification of these American researchers, Severianin would belong to the second category of motorist, while Mandel'shtam evokes a floral scent in a poem about a loving/ sporting match: "All motors and horns – / *And the lilac smelt of gasoline*" ("Tennis," 1913; Mandel'shtam, *Sobranie sochinenii*, 1:90).

[74]In the early years of the automobile industry open-bodied models predominated, but while in 1919 they comprised 80 percent of the market, by the end of the 1920s 90 percent of cars had the driver and passenger concealed from passersby (Lewis, "Sex and the Automobile," 131).

as a reader with Nabokov: "But do I understand that Ganin and Ludmila are supposed to have had their first *étreinte* on the *floor* of a taxicab? I don't think you can have had any actual experience of this kind or you would know that it is not done that way" (Wilson–Nabokov, January 19, 1945; Nabokov, *The Nabokov–Wilson Letters*, 147. Italics in the original).

Two days later Nabokov composed his response:

My dear Bunny,
     It could be done and in fact was done, in Berlin taxi-cabs, models 1920. I remember having interviewed numerous Russian taxi-drivers, fine White Russians all of them, and they all said yes, that was the correct way. I am afraid I am quite ignorant of the American technique. A man called Piotrovsky, a poet *à ses heures*, told me that one night his fare happened to be a well-known film star and her escort; wishing to be exquisitely polite (exiled nobleman, etc.), he briskly opened the door when they arrived at their destination, and the pair *in copula* shot out heads first and dialed past him, like a "double backed" dragon he said (he had read *Othello*).
                    (Nabokov–Wilson, January 20, 1945; ibid., 147–148)

Such situations were in fact common in private and commercial automotive transport in the 1920s: erotic trysts such as that described by Nabokov took place both in Russia and in the émigré community. Nabokov also adds that *Mary*, written twenty-one years earlier, was his "first experience in prose" (ibid., 148). But years later in his sixteenth novel, despite the fact that the design of American cars since the 1920s had far outstripped European ones in terms of suitability for love-making,[75] Nabokov reproduces the scene almost exactly. In *Ada*, Cordula de Prey drives without stopping, at 100 kilometers per hour, to pick up Van at the hospital. They flee the health resort by car. Sitting next to her, Van does not hear anything she tells him because he "was at the moment much more anxious to enjoy Cordula as soon as humanly and humanely possible, as soon as satanically and viatically feasible" (*Ada*, 320). The middle-aged chauffeur, driving the "a smart, pale-gray four-door sedan"

---

[75] "Henry Ford allegedly designed the Model T seat so short to discourage the use of this car as a place in which to engage in sexual intercourse. But determined couples found ways to thwart Ford's intentions, and the auto makers came to facilitate lovemaking in cars with such innovations as heaters, air conditioning, and the tilt steering wheel. The 1925 Jewett introduced the fold-down bed, and the bed conversion option on Nash cars after 1937 became popular as 'the young man's model'" ("Courtship and Mating," Flink, *The Automobile Age*, 160).

FIGURE 3.18 *Edith and Irene Mayer, daughters of Louis Mayer, head of the Metro Goldwyn Mayer Corp., posing next to the automobiles and wearing fur-trimmed coats. National Photo Company Collection, Library of Congress.*

(ibid., 318), is sent by the lovers to have a cup of coffee. Van, impatient, asks Cordula to drive him to "some secluded spot":

> As soon as they reached a suitable area he transferred Cordula to his lap and had her very comfortably, with such howls of enjoyment that she felt touched and flattered.

(ibid., 321)

Nabokov's scoundrels and ruffians are far better drivers than his less fortunate characters. Hermann's driving in *Despair* and that of Gorn/Rex in *Camera Obscura/Laughter in the Dark* is beyond comparison with the clumsy driving of Pnin and Krechmar/Albinus.

As a youth he had never taken his bicycle to pieces, nor, indeed, could do anything with it save ride it; and when he punctured a tire, he pushed the disabled machine—squelching like an old galosh—to the nearest repair shop. < ... > During the War he had distinguished himself by an amazing incapacity to do anything whatever with his hands. In view of all this it is less surprising that he was a very bad driver than that he could drive at all.

(*Laughter in the Dark*, 232–233)

And neither Pnin nor Krechmar/Albinus can boast of their amorous prowess, while the skilful lover Gorn/Rex finds satisfaction even while driving:

Roads bordered with apple trees, and then roads with plum trees, were lapped up by the front tires—endlessly. The weather was fine, and toward night the steel cells of the radiator were crammed with dead bees, and dragon-flies, and meadow-browns. Rex drove wonderfully, reclining lazily on the very low seat and manipulating the steering wheel with a tender and almost dreamy touch.

(ibid., 201)[76]

The erogenous zones of the car and the gestures of the driver (cf. the tactile game in "A Nursery Story"[77]) are unambiguously combined with the *Garden of Eden* theme (the apple tree) along the highway, while the dead bees in the radiator can be associated, on the one hand, with the barrenness of Magda/Margot and the creative impotence of Gorn/Rex and, on the other, with the death of Krechmar/Albinus's daughter: in chapter 32, his

---

[76]Cf. the scene in which Humbert leaves the doctor in an excellent mood and "steering < ... > wife's car with one finger," rolls homeward: "the sun shone < ... > my ignition key was reflected in the windshield" (*Lolita*, 89). Van Veen recognizes the arrival of his father by the "rich purr" of his motorcar, and when they meet says that the new car "sounds wonderful" (*Ada*, 237); Dreyer adores his car and the "gentle purr" of its motor (*King, Queen, Knave*, 77).

[77]Control over the style and the insertion of images that stir the imagination allow the author to tease the reader with transparent hints in the scene of Erwin's visit to the amusement park when he is observing four girls in jerseys and shorts with "their bare legs working at full tilt" ("A Nursery Tale"; *Stories*, 169). The plural in this striking shape is no accident, since the passage is describing group sex.

wife Anneliza/Elisabeth recalls a trip to a cemetery, "bees settling on her flowers." (In "Spring in Fialta," honey reinforces the leitmotifs of forbidden love and death in a car accident.) The bee motif reproduces the famous erotic figuring of the taking of Moscow by Napoleon in *War and Peace*, which is described as a metaphorical rape of the Russian capital, which the Frenchman before entering her sees as a "large and beautiful body" and afterwards as a "*hive without a queen*," in which there was "no more life ... the work of the honeycomb ... not in the same form of virginity in which it was before ... the bees withered, meek, languid." The leitmotif appears in an even more refined form in the "Song of Solomon": "Thy lips, O my spouse, drop as the honeycomb" (4:11); "My beloved put in his hand by the hole of the door, And my heart was moved for him. I rose up to open to my beloved; And my hands droppeth with myrrh, And my fingers with liquid myrrh, Upon the handles of the bolt" (5:4–5).

Krechmar/Albinus is ignorant not only of the inner workings of soulless cars, but also of the lives of people close to him. Gorn/Rex, despite the seeming deftness in his relations with Magda/Margot, is in essence no less of an unfortunate, and the little beast in the rear window, which once praised the creator of "animated sketches" (*Russian Collected Works*, 3:254) now serves as a reminder of his dried-up creative spring and his former successes: "In the back-window hung a plush monkey, gazing toward the North from which they were speeding away" (*Laughter in the Dark*, 201). The scenery running in reverse in a car window is a stylization in shots pasted into material produced in a studio (the characters sit in the cab and nature flashes by in the window, a device practiced for ages in cinematography). The automotive concerns of cartoon characters were also a frequent motif in Hollywood animation from the late 1920s.[78] In 1931, when Nabokov was beginning *Camera Obscura/Laughter in the Dark*, Disney's *Traffic Troubles* first appeared on the screen, with Mickey Mouse driving an out-of-control taxi with all the resulting comic situations that ensued.[79]

---

[78]On this topic, see Wells's *Automania: Animated Automobiles 1950–1968*, which states that "As early as 1927, Walt Disney had produced *Alice's Auto Race*, a part-live action cartoon, and *The Mechanical Cow* ... crucial in the understanding of the increasing impact of mechanism itself upon previously simple, normally rural agendas in cartoons. ... Mickey and his friends become embroiled in a brave new world best epitomized by the developing role of the motor car and the concordant expansion of the city and urban society" (Paul Wells, *The Motor Car and Popular Culture*, 85). On the depiction of the car in American film, see Smith, "A Runaway Match ... ," 179–192, and Hey, "Cars and Films ...," 193–205, both in *The Automobile and American Culture* (Lewis & Goldstein, *The Automobile and American Culture*).

[79]One example of early humorous literature centered around a car trip is Fitzgerald's novella written after a trip with his wife Zelda in a car bought after their wedding in the spring of 1920 (published in 1924 in the magazine, *Motor*). The story is reprinted with commentary and background materials, including automobile advertising from the 1920s and 1930s, in Fitzgerald, *The Cruise of the Rolling Junk*.

An Incident on the Street

The paradigm of the street accident underwent a gradual evolution across the course of nineteenth- and early-twentieth-century Russian literature, with bodily harm being inflicted by carts, coaches, carriages, horse-drawn cabs, and finally cars. Characters hit by horses, cabs, and carriages range from Akakii Akakievich in Gogol's "Overcoat" (1842) and Chekhov's postman in "The Post" (1887) to Professor Korobkin in Bely's *Moscow* (1926–31) and Ostap Bender in *The Twelve Chairs* (1928). Injuries to characters under the wheels of cars began to occur after the urban landscape had adapted to the new technology, which introduced the corresponding mechanical terminology to the public consciousness, such that it became an active part of the cultural lexicon of the age.

In poetry, journeys by car were surrounded by an aura of catastrophe. The automobile was generally associated with an unbridled, elemental force with mythological potency, as we see in poems by, for example, Briusov[80]

FIGURE 3.19 *Automobile accident recreation with miniature cars, between 1915 and 1923. Harris & Ewing photograph collection, Library of Congress.*

---

[80]"Trams toss blue lightning, / Cars – a sheaf of fire" ("Vechernii priliv" ["Evening Tide"], 1906; Briusov, *Stikhotvoreniia i poemy*, 309).

or Khodasevich.[81] The car brought death, and often in very public circumstances:

> I keep waiting for someone to be crushed
> By a manic automobile,
> A poor onlooker will bloody
> The dry pavement dust.
>
> And that will start in motion:
> Stirring, eversion, and trouble,
> A star will fall to earth,
> And the waters will become bitter.

("From the window" ["Iz okna"];
Khodasevich, *Sobranie sochinenii*, 1:209)

A quarter century later, the topos of the crowd ogling an unfortunate event, the spectacle of the car accident, operates in Pasternak's 1956 poem, "At the Hospital" ("V bol'nitse"), which has a metonymic description of an accident, layered onto the author's own experience of being hospitalized (taken on a stretcher with a heart attack) shortly before the poem was written:

> They stood as if before a shop window,
> Almost damming the sidewalk.
> They pushed the stretcher in the van,
> The paramedic jumped in the cab.
>
> And the ambulance, passing by
> The pavements, the alleys, the gapers,
> And the nighttime confusion of streets,
> Plunged its lights into the dark.
>
> The police, the streets, the faces
> Flashed in the beam of the headlights.
> The nurse rocked back and forth
> With a vial of ammonia.

---

[81]"He casts off black lacquer, / Glass edges shining, / In the dusk of night he stretches out / Two white angel wings ... / And all that merely falls / Under the black sheaf of his rays, / Disappears without a trace / From my fragile memory" ("Avtomobil'," 1921; Khodasevich, *Sobranie sochinenii*, 1:225).

The aftermath of an accident on the Kurfürstendamm, which Fyodor Godunov-Cherdyntsev witnesses, features ready-made melodramatic clichés, such as the discarded blood-stained handkerchief:

> [A] small car with a heavily damaged wing, broken windows and a bloody handkerchief on the running board; a half-a-dozen people still loafed around, gaping at it.
>
> (*The Gift*, 151)

Another accident on a Berlin street occurs in *King, Queen, Knave*. Nabokov depicts this scene of chaos using broken grammatical connections, which in the original Russian is simply a catalog of nouns (cf. Khodasevich and Pasternak: "Stirring, eversion, and trouble" and "The pavements, the alleys, the gapers"):

> While this motorized frenzy was in progress, Martha and her husband had assumed all imaginable positions, and had finally found themselves on the floor. < ... > The shock, the search for the beads of her necklace, *the crowd of gawkers, the vulgar aspect of the smashed car, the foul-mouthed truck driver, the arrogant policeman.*[82]
>
> (*King, Queen, Knave*, 50)

From Frankenstein to Golem, the scenario in which the monstrous machine takes control of its creator, has become a common plot device in modern European literature. It has led to antagonism between spiritual civilization and the trans-urban era of technology,[83] between which the soul of the artist races.[84]

In the fictional mode, the accident topos is reconfigured such that the potential for catastrophe can extend beyond the purely didactic or have a greater consequence than mere emotional shock. Whether literary or cinematic, the street accident becomes a moving plot element: using the confusion on the road, the author distracts his character's attention from something that must be temporarily concealed from him; it serves as a retardant, slowing the pace of the narrative, or it sets up an obstacle for the character. In films

---

[82]Cf. Khodasevich's "manic automobile."

[83]Cf. Herman Hesse's *Steppenwolf* (1927): "Cars, some of them armored, were run through the streets chasing the pedestrians. They ran them down and either left them mangled on the ground or crushed them to death against the walls of the houses. I saw at once that it was the long-prepared, long-awaited and long-feared war between men and machines, now at last broken out. On all sides lay dead and decomposing bodies, on all sides, too, smashed and distorted and half-burned cars. Airplanes circled above the frightful confusion" (Hesse, *Steppenwolf*, 180).

[84]"Why, slave-soul / Do you not fly to freedom, / To the tempestuous waves of the ocean, / To the noisy wide streets of cities, / To the spread of an airplane, / To the Rumbling of trains" ("Snova savany nadeli ... ," 1921; Sologub, *Stikhotvoreniia*, 434–435).

shot between 1900 and 1920, approximately five hundred of them used an automobile to implement a particular theme, often developed along familiar lines.[85] Some typical obstacles that likely date back to the factography of early cinema appear in Nabokov's detective novel parody, *The Prismatic Bezel*. In the novel written by Sebastian Knight "owing to a combination of mishaps (*his car runs over an old woman* and then he takes the wrong train)" (*The Real Life of Sebastian Knight*, 77), the detective takes a very long time to appear at the scene of the crime. The satirical element in chase scenes from ostentatious detective films was also made use of by Mandel'shtam.[86]

Forewarnings

As happened initially with the train, poets (particularly the early symbolists steeped in the tradition of classic Russian nineteenth-century lyric poetry) tried, albeit briefly, to capture the aura of mystical awe surrounding the appearance of the automobile on city streets. In a poem entitled "Motor cars, like birds, flash," written by K. M. Fofanov (a poet who worked until the last days of his life, but was almost forgotten by his contemporaries), a phantom car beckons passengers to execution:

> Proud with a lightning-shining flight,
> Bombastic in its brilliance,
> A life alien to bittern concerns,
> They scatter like smoke.
>
> And one wants to shout, where are you going?
> In pursuit of mad passions,
> In pursuit of mad amusement
> Or to your scaffold of shame?
> (Fofanov, *Stikhotvoreniia i poemy*, 248–250)

---

[85]Cf.: "Perhaps the most persuasive and frequent cinematic image relating to the car in early films is that which Julian Smith calls the 'happy incident'" ... that "lead almost invariably to happy outcomes: rich motorists stranded in the country fall in love with beautiful farm girls, villains are punished in last-minutes crashes ... inconvenient spouses die so that love can triumph" (Pettifer & Turner, *Automania*, 250); see also the accident involving Martha's husband in *King, Queen, Knave* where, per Nabokov's habit of contravening the reader's expectations, the victim survives to the chagrin of the lovers. Cars become an exceptionally effective "moralizing device" and part of a narrative system.

[86]"In a road dress, with a travel bag / In a car or and on a train, / She is only afraid of a chase, / Tormented by a dry mirage" ("Kinematograf," 1913; Mandel'shtam, *Sobranie sochinenii*, 1:89–90).

King, Queen, Knave mixes mad passions and mad amusement: shortly before the car accident in which the family chauffeur dies, Martha reads that "a car had overturned killing its occupant, the famous actor Hess, on his way to his sick wife's bedside" (*King, Queen, Knave*, 115). Martha does not connect this report with the accident that her husband was fortunate to survive, and the reader must retrospectively figure out that the role of the "sick wife" will ultimately be played by Martha herself.

The introductory portion of a narrative using transportation metaphors often reflects a brewing instability, stirs a feeling of discomfort, and presages coming changes in the plot structure of the book or pivotal moments in the fates of characters. When Krechmar/Albinus is caught cheating on his wife, resulting in her panicked flight from the house, he observes as his brother-in-law and the maid "hastily packed the trunk *as though they were in a hurry to catch a train*" (*Laughter in the Dark*, 87). A line repeated twice in the Russian version of that scene is meant as a signal: "This is a catastrophe" (in English translation: "This is a tragedy"). The utterance refers, of course, to the downfall of the family, but at the same time by the internal logic of the novel, the automobile catastrophe that Krechmar/Albinus later gets into does in fact begin with the crisis in his personal life and the destruction of his accustomed family structure. It is telling that at the end of the packing scene Nabokov inserts: "A motor lorry drove past; the window panes rattled slightly" (ibid., 88).

The appearance of an unwieldy truck in Nabokov's fiction generally indicates impending drama: it is a sign of tragedy and a harbinger of difficulty. *The Enchanter* is resolved by an accident: the protagonist perishes under the wheels of a truck. As Barabtarlo argues, there is a logical connection between three particular scenes: the crossing of the railroad bridge, the protagonist's car ride with his stepdaughter, and the car crash, with each scene being dominated by the action of kinetic force. Either the observed object (the train) is moving, or the observing object is moving, or a motionless observer sees two moving objects (cars) collide. What seem at first glance to be insignificant circumstances, Barabtarlo concludes, take on new meaning when we consider that "the character's life is cut short by a monstrous impact, or perhaps more accurately a discharge, of kinetic energy" (Barabtarlo, "Prizrak," 197–204).

Here, specifically, is how the theme of the hulking truck[87] develops over the final eight pages of the story: "the roar and throb of two, three, four trucks taking advantage of the deserted night-time street to descend with appalling

---

[87]We hear an echo of this phobia in *Lolita*: "At night, tall trucks studded with colored lights, like dreadful giant Christmas trees, loomed in the darkness and thundered by the belated little sedan" (*Lolita*, 140). The giant trucks seem to come from Il'f and Petrov's *One-Story America*: "Kemp stood right by the side of the road. Cars rushed by with the noise of wind. Frenzied traveling salesmen raced, and truck giants rumbled heavily. The beams of their headlights were constantly coming through along the wall" (Il'f & Petrov, *Sobranie sochinenii*, 4:194).

speed from behind a bend that concealed a whining, straining, grinding upgrade" (*The Enchanter*, 80); "A rumbling approached and receded beyond the window" (ibid., 82); "With the roar of cannon fire a truck ascended from the bottom of the night" (ibid., 87); "Yet another truck hurtled past, howling and filling the room with a tremor" (ibid., 90); "a grinding whine came from behind the hump of the street … illuminating the descent with two ovals of yellowish light, about to hurtle downward < … > that's it, drag me under, tear at my frailty – I'm traveling flattened, on my smacked-down face – hey, you're spinning me, don't rip me to pieces" (ibid., 94–95).

The reader of "Details of a Sunset" (1924; original Russian title, "The Catastrophe") is told that the protagonist, Mark Standfuss, works at a fabric store not merely as a salesman: he is "salesclerk, a demigod" (*Stories*, 79). The true meaning in this case is expressed at the symbolic level rather than the figurative level: in ancient mythology demigods are given special connections to the natural elements; in this case the element in question is fire. Here we will point out a few semantic moments that are important for analyzing the accident scene, without looking in detail at the rich but straightforward (by comparison with the later prose) motif of fire. A precondition for incident is seen in the very names of the characters. Mark's fiancée's name is a concentration of light (Klara = Latin *Clarus*), while his name is an anagram of the Russian word for darkness (*mrak*).[88] The theme of fire is meted out gradually, beginning with the introductory sentence in the story, describing the last tram departing into the darkness of the streets, above which on the wires "a spark of Bengal light, crackling and quivering, sped into the distance like a blue star" (ibid.). Then, marking the location: "In the middle of a square stood a *black wigwam*: the tram tracks were being repaired" (ibid., 142). The ethnic and folkloric element balances the mythological in the European topos. The stereotypical items in Nabokov are brought about by the pagan demonism of the unfaithful bride. Klara is a witch, and her fiery powers are fed by erotic energy, which illuminates her body.[89] The increasing fiery bacchanalia captivating the protagonist[90] eventually burns right through him:

> Mark < … > reached the front end of the car. He grasped the iron handrails with both hands, leaned forward, calculated his jump. Down

---

[88]Nabokov emphasizes that the choice was not random: "You're all dirty, and your new pants too" ("Details of a Sunset"; *Stories*, 80).

[89]Klara's occult nature is meant to be "outed" by the sentence, "*The russet tufts of her armpits showed through the sunlit openings of her short sleeves.*" ("Details of a Sunset"; *Stories*, 84). Cf. Nabokov's poem "Lilith": "flashing / a ruddy armpit" (*Russian Collected Works*, 5:437). A work by Frazer, published a year before the Russian version of "Details of a Sunset" presents numerous examples of connections between the evil powers of witches and their hair.

[90]The character's mother is also associated with the Promethean principle. Mrs. Standfuss meets her son in the alley carrying *a kerosene lamp in her hand*, with the *haze* of her hair from under her cap (cf. his *climbing up* to the landing – with the *tram* vestibule from which Mark jumps *down* under the bus [*Stories*, 83]).

below, the asphalt streamed past, smooth and *glistening*. Mark jumped. There was a *burn* of friction against his soles, and his legs started running by themselves, his feet stamping with involuntary resonance. Several odd things occurred simultaneously: < ... > the conductor emitted a furious shout; the *shiny* asphalt swept upward like the seat of a swing; a roaring mass hit Mark from behind. He felt as if *a thick thunderbolt had gone through him* from head to toe, and then nothing.

(ibid., 83)

The scene of the accident is constructed on the principle of illumination, and at its foundation is a gesture with symbolic roots in the sacred motif of the chosen: the "thick thunderbolt"[91] symbolizes the finger of God which points to the individual (in this case Mark) to be called to the next world (on the mechanization of Death in the story, see Ronen & Ronen, "'Diabolically Evocative'," 373–374).

The configuration of the cargo truck and the cab of an automobile is reminiscent of a tomb (and could potentially end up as such).[92] The news of her mother's death is given to Lolita in the confines of a moving car,[93] and is prepared for by flashes of several small accidents. As Humbert prepares to tell Lolita, the car passes the body of a squashed squirrel, then almost runs over "some little animal or other that was crossing the road with tail erect" (*Lolita*, 130).

The Car Accident

Nabokov's novels can be classified based on the preferred method of locomotion chosen by the author, or based on which of these take on the role of a concentrating force. *Mary* and *Glory* are "railroad" prose; *Despair*, *Camera Obscura/Laughter in the Dark*, and *Lolita* are "car" novels, while *King, Queen, Knave* synthesizes the two urban themes. The first detailed treatment of the car motif in Nabokov's Russian period was in *Camera Obscura/Laughter in the Dark*, where the author also first met with the need to give a developed description of a car accident. The trip, the gradual preparation of the characters and the reader for the impending accident,

---

[91]This is preceded by a "prophecy": "An arrow of bright copper struck the lacquered shoe of a fop jumping out of a car" (ibid., 82). We may note that the second part of the character's surname is Fuss (German for *foot*. Cf. the arrow of Paris that strikes the heel of Achilles), provoking a series of little events: several times over the course of a few pages Mark "accidentally" missteps or twists his ankle.

[92]Cf. the illustration in the German magazine, *Jugend* (1903) in which a skeleton symbolizing death visits a grave on wheels, reproduced in Pettifer & Turner, *Automania*, 225.

[93]Humbert instinctively narrows the spatial boundaries of any possible reaction: "Get in. < ... > Get in and slam the door. < ... > your mother is dead" (*Lolita*, 130).

FIGURE 3.20 *"Don't blame the motorist for all the automobile accidents in city streets. Look at some of the things he is up against," by artist Will Crawford. The illustration shows an automobile driver trying to negotiate workmen in the roadway, children playing ball in the street and darting in front of automobiles, absentminded pedestrians stepping off the curb, and people exiting streetcars into oncoming traffic (New York, N.Y.: Keppler & Schwarzmann, Puck Building, January 29, 1913).*

and the description of the events and consequences, are given four pages by Nabokov, combining as if in a screenplay,[94] a camera reportage technique and close-up shots quickly shifting to wide-angle shots. The scene develops several lines in parallel, including the passengers and the witnesses to the accident (on the ground and from the air), and these lines are gradually narrowed by the ring of motifs and plot points around the event. At the crucial point in the narrative, the once powerful critic Krechmar/Albinus is transformed into a helpless and defenseless invalid.

It is worth considering the narrative techniques with which Nabokov achieves the impact of this scene. At the end of chapter 30, a minute before Gorn/Rex finds out that his secret affair with Magda/Margot has been discovered and that she has been taken away, he notes in amazement

---

[94]See in Stuart, *Nabokov: The Dimensions of Parody*, 87–113; Barbara Wyllie gives a detailed description of the cinematic aspect of this scene in *Nabokov at the Movies*, chapter 3; and Julian Connolly also discusses cinematics in his chapter on *Laughter in the Dark* in *The Garland Companion to Nabokov*.

"beyond the magnolias, in the road near the garage < ... > Albinus' car. The car swerved awkwardly and disappeared" (*Laughter in the Dark*, 230). We have already been informed that Krechmar/Albinus is an inept driver ("a very bad driver"); here the perceptive gaze of Gorn/Rex again reminds us of this. Albinus's poor driving skills are exacerbated by his depressed psychological state. On the narrow streets of the provincial town, which are packed with pedestrians, Krechmar/Albinus "had to sound his horn, pull up with a jerk and turn clumsily," ibid., 233). However, even after the car makes it out onto the intercity highway, signals of the impending accident are scattered about the text:

< ... > "And please do keep to the right. If you can't drive, we had better take a train or hire a chauffeur at the nearest garage." He put on the brake violently because a motor coach had appeared in the distance. "What are you doing, Albert? Keep to the right, that's all you've got to do." The motor coach, filled with tourists, thundered past. Albinus started off again.
(ibid., 233–234)

The end of the chapter brings the first distinct pulsation of the accident:

A sharp bend was approaching and Albinus proposed to take it with special dexterity. High above the road an old woman who was gathering herbs saw to the right of the cliff this little blue car speed toward the bend, behind the corner of which, dashing from the opposite side, toward an unknown meeting, two cyclists crouched over their handlebars.
(ibid.)

The chapter breaks off at this point. After holding the structural (and, according to Tynianov, semantically loaded) pause, the narrator continues: "The old woman gathering herbs on the hillside saw the car and the two cyclists approaching the sharp bend from opposite directions" (ibid., 237). The threefold focus on the old woman—she also closes chapter 32: "The old woman was gathering herbs on the rocky slope. For a whole year at least she would be telling people how she had seen ... what she had seen" (*Laughter in the Dark*, 237)—slows the discourse, encloses the action, and, as in a Mobius strip, directs its internal motion in interconnecting, repeating circles. The relaying of the central event—the accident—takes place through several levels of "shooting." This woman foraging for herbs watches the situation develop from an earthly elevation, while a pilot watches from the troposphere.[95]

---

[95]*Laughter in the Dark*, 237. A simultaneous cross-section of different levels of movement by vehicle in the heart of Petersburg/Leningrad was also attempted by Vaginov in his 1929 novel, *Svistonov's Works and Days* (*Trudy i dni Svistonova*; Vaginov, *Kozlinaia pesn'*, 268), which bears a certain conceptual similarity to Nabokov's *The Gift* (a novel about how a novel is composed).

The details of the accident are reconstructed in the next chapter (33), in which the injured driver calls up in his memory "a picture that was, in its gaudy intensity, like a colored photograph on glass: the curve of the glossy blue road, the green and red cliff to the left, the white parapet to the right and in front of him the approaching cyclists" (ibid., 240). The moment of the accident, as in the finale of *The Enchanter*, is conveyed with what now might seem to some readers a rather antiquated metaphor of the torn film of life: "a grinding whine came from behind the hump of the street ... illuminating the descent with two ovals of yellowish light < ... > this instantaneous cinema of dismemberment < ... > and *the film of life had burst*" (*The Enchanter*, 94–95). Cf.: "*A sharp jerk of the steering wheel* < ... > *and up the car dashed, mounting a pile of stones on the right, and in the next fraction of that second, a telegraph post loomed in front of the windscreen.* Margot's outstretched arm had flown across the picture—and the next moment the magic lantern went out" (*Laughter in the Dark*, 240).

Critical reaction indicates that the accident scene was felt by readers to be a strong point in the novel. Despite many reviewers' comparisons of the novel to a flat screenplay, this scene nevertheless drew a lot of attention. Nikolai Andreev was amazed at how the "calm, stable world changes its appearance as if under the pitiless rays of a searchlight: it is awakened, the usual perspective is distorted, and now there will be an accident" (*Volia Rossii*. July 1932. № 4/6; *Klassik bez retushi*, 102). Iu. Terapiano wrote with annoyance in *Chisla* in June 1934: "the automobile accident and the consequences associated with it for the characters in *Camera Obscura*, depicted so brilliantly, are brought about by nothing more than the whims of the author" (ibid., 112).

In *King, Queen, Knave*, Dreyer's "unfortunate" Icarus gets into two accidents. The first time, in trying to overtake a truck, it "hit a wooden railing where the tram tracks were being repaired, and swerving sharply had collided with the side of the truck; the Icarus had spun around and crashed into a pole" (*King, Queen, Knave*, 50). The second time, it plows into a tram at full speed. In the collision with a three and a seven (the significance of these tram numbers derives from Pushkin's story, "The Queen of Spades," about game, fate, and madness), the king, Dreyer, the owner of the car, gets away with just a bruise, but his driver is less fortunate, cracking his skull and his ribcage (ibid., 131). The accident, about which the impressionable Franz reads in the events section of the newspaper, is described by him in morbid detail:

[A]ll that jagged glass hitting you in the face, that crunch of metal and bones, and blood, and blackness. I don't know why but I picture such things so clearly. Makes me want to vomit.

(ibid., 133)

The Dreyers decide to sell the car without repairing it, for which Martha has her own compelling reasons: when visiting her lover she prefers not to use the services of a chauffeur whom "she would have to bribe < … > to be silent about her real destination" (ibid., 131).

Death of the Hero

In 1936 the Nabokovs were living in Berlin, in a neighborhood full of garages and machine shops. Nabokov, who, in the words of his biographer, "had always loved the poetry of motion … was grateful" (Boyd, *Russian Years*, 428). Every morning from 9:00 a.m. to 12:45 p.m., weather permitting, Nabokov went out for a walk with young Dmitri. The elder Nabokov curiously watched as his son skillfully drove on the sidewalk in his pedal-driven car and was instinctively drawn to the tram depot, the miniature bridge over the rail crossing, and the trucks parked alongside (ibid.). Nabokov attentively watches this swarming of life and is captivated by the rhythm of the big city,[96] at the same time as his personal physical and metaphysical fears, as with Franz in *King, Queen, Knave*, find expression in his prose.[97]

As we see in the manuscripts for a continuation of *The Gift* (dated to the late 1930s), a part tentatively entitled "Final Chapter" includes Zina Mertz being killed by a car:

> I went out with Zina, said goodbye to her at the corner (she was going to see her parents), stopped in for cigarettes (Russian drivers play with dice supplied by the tavern at the counter), returned home, saw the back of a tenant going out into the street, and found a note by the phone: the police just called (on some street), and asked me to come immediately; I remembered a fight in the street (with a drunken author) last week and set off immediately. There on the leather couch, wrapped in a sheet (where did they get a sheet?) lay Zina, dead. *In these ten minutes she*

---

[96]Shlegel' presumes that Nabokov "despises and hates" the Berlin of taverns, coach drivers, and Grunewald beaches (Shlegel', "Vospriiatie goroda," 116), but this position is called into question by an album compiled by another German, richly illustrated with photographs of Berlin locales that appear in Nabokov's works from 1928–37 (Zimmer, *Nabokovs Berlin*).

[97]A family friend, the critic Aikhenval'd, was killed by a tram on the Kurfürstendamm in Berlin on December 15, 1928 as he walked home from a literary soiree organized by the Nabokovs (Boyd, *Russian Years*, 287–288). N. N. Kolomeitsev, the husband of Nina Dmitrievna Kolomeitseva (Nabokov's aunt), was in a car accident when returning home from his own wife's funeral in 1944 (see Nabokov, *Perepiska s sestroi*, 25). Ivanov's peripheral vision in the story "Perfection" "was narrowed by the glasses, he was afraid of a sudden automobile" ("Perfection"; *Stories*, 345).

had managed to step down from the bus right under an automobile. A woman I hardly knew was also there, who had happened to be on the same bus. Now she was in the vulgar role of consoler. I parted ways with her at the corner. I walked, sat in the squares. (*Falter collapsed*) ... Early in the morning I left to go to the south. She is no longer, I want to know nothing, no burial, there is no one to bury, she is no longer.[98]

It is worth remembering that this is an extract of a future text, its quintessence. It is not out of the question that the clear epistemological aura of the manuscript would in the final version have been wiped away.[99] In any event, the appearance of the taxi drivers before the impending car accident could hardly be accidental,[100] and the theme of the afterlife introduced by the ominous game of dice is somewhat prophetic.[101]

There is a thematic connection between the excerpt from the continuation of *The Gift* and the unfinished novel, *Solus Rex* (see Dolinin, "Tri zametki," 218). Both characters (Godunov-Cherdyntsev and the artist Sineusov) have their wives die; both are unable to compose themselves after this tragic loss; both find salvation in the creative drive; and in the end they both attempt to seek some secret of existence from Falter. Is it a coincidence that Sineusov, attempting to engage in spiritual contact with his late wife, has recourse to a mysterious "Garage," while after the line about the death of Fyodor's wife after being hit by a car we see the phrase "Falter collapsed"? The very fact that a completed car originates in a jumble of parts, essentially from nothing, makes it relatable to the occult. In a talk from 1928, Nabokov stated that "Man is God's likeness; a thing is man's likeness" (Nabokov, *Think, Write, Speak*, 72). The same work presents arguments in defense of

---

[98]The Nabokov Papers, Library of Congress, Washington, D.C.

[99]The spatial and temporal symbolism of movement ("*soiti ... pod avtomobil'*," literally "to descend under an automobile" resembles the expression "*soiti v Tartar,*" "to descend to Tartarus") is seen in reverse semantic perspective in the published text of *The Gift*: "straight out of the orangery paradise he [Fyodor] transferred to a Berlin tram" (*Russian Collected Works*, 4:264).

[100]The experience imprinted by Russian taxi drivers themselves leads to a picture of the mores and social topography, the array of civilizational forms and their degradation; for the attentive emigrant taxi driver the car becomes a probe, or a time machine with which he can sense the forward movement of time (Shlegel', "Vospriiatie goroda," 115, 116). One out of five taxi drivers in Paris was a Russian immigrant, and these included authors such as Gaito Gazdanov. The lover of Humbert's Valechka is a Paris taxi driver, whom H. H. calls "White Russian ex-colonel," "the taxi-colonel" (*Lolita*, 28–29).

[101]The image of driver/oracles is accompanied by smoking (Fyodor stops in for cigarettes), visions, and auditory hallucinations; the ritual/symbolic meaning of dice (*kosti*, "bones," in Russian) to a certain extent also assumes a belief in future resurrection, as the skeleton of the deceased in ancient times was kept from harm.

the age of technology, though Nabokov seems to overvalue the abilities of his average contemporaries in the final sentence:

> I find it unpleasant to hear people talk about machines: oh, our mechanical age; oh, robots; oh, this and that. Machines and tools have served us all. ... We interpret a number of parts as complexity, but the parts in and of themselves are simple, and they are assembled, in the final analysis, in a simple way. When a man looks at a locomotive, his creation seems unbelievably clever, because his imagination separates the object from the mind that devised it. The mind is clever and complicated, the resourcefulness of humanity is amazing, but the creation itself is of course simple. The joy of machines is that any intelligent and capable person can create one.
>
> (ibid.)

A garage can be a shelter for cars assembled from parts, and the car itself in its ideal form approaches the Cartesian model of the world, as it is imagined, for example, by the narrator of *Pale Fire* at his time of ruin:

> I imagine, that during that period the Shades, or at least John Shade, experienced a sensation of odd instability *as if parts of the everyday, smoothly running world had got unscrewed, and you became aware that one of your tires was rolling beside you, or that your steering wheel had come off.*
>
> (*Pale Fire*, 166)

The moving and driving mechanism reflects a world based on the wheels and gears of causation,[102] cleverly concealed from the eyes of the crowd.[103]

---

[102]The mechanistic nature of the world is defined in *The Gift* as follows: "the ghostly wheels of the city day revolved through the interior bottomless scarlet" (*The Gift*, 61). For more on this see the chapter entitled "City Life and Machinery" in Berdjis, *Imagery in Vladimir Nabokov's Last Russian Novel*, 83–86.

[103]As Roland Barthes wrote on this subject, "cars today are almost the exact equivalent of the great Gothic cathedrals: I mean the supreme creation of an era, conceived with passion by unknown artists, and consumed in image if not in usage by a whole population which appropriates them as a purely magical object. < ... > It is well known that smoothness is always an attribute of perfection because its opposite reveals a technical and typically human operation of assembling: Christ's robe was seamless, just as the airships of science-fiction are made of unbroken metal. < ... > There are in the *D.S.* [a new model of Citroën 'D.S.-19'—Y.L.] the beginnings of a new phenomenology of assembling, as if one progressed from a world where elements are welded to a world where they are juxtaposed and hold together by sole virtue of their wondrous shape, which of course is meant to prepare one for the idea of a more benign Nature" (*Léttre nouvelle*. December 1955. № 33. English transl.; Barthes, *Mythologies*, 88–89).

In the talk Nabokov gave at the Berlin literary society in 1928, this principle manifests itself openly:

> We have christened the parts of things, weapons, machines, with words we use for different parts of our bodies, making these diminutives as if we were talking to our children. "Toothlet, eyelet, earlet, hairlet, noselet, footlet, back, handle, head." *It is as though I am surrounded by little monsters, and it seems to me that the little teeth of the clock are gnawing away at time,* that the "ear" of a needle stuck into the curtain is eavesdropping on me, that the teapot spout, with a little droplet poised on its tip, is about to sneeze like a man with a cold. But with larger objects, in houses, *trains, automobiles, factories, the human element sometimes becomes startingly unpleasant.*
>
> (Nabokov, *Think, Write, Speak*, 72)

The spectral universe composed of parts from dreams and reality, like the "puzzles" of Nabokov's childhood, could be disassembled and collapsed[104] into wondrous mosaics. The overarching hermeneutic task of the reader (and the character) is to try to get oriented within the text, to correctly identify the "the agent of fate" within "the intricacies of the pattern" (*Lolita*, 95–96). In *Lolita*, the role of this emissary of fate is played by the driver of the car that delivers Humbert from the nymphet's mother.

The accident scene in *Lolita* was pivotal to the development of the motif of movement in Nabokov's fiction. The protagonist is notified of the incident by phone, but while in the continuation of *The Gift* the information network is clogged (the spoken message goes over a number of obstacles: phone→note→false recollection of a fight), in *Lolita* there is a direct notification initially interpreted as someone's bad joke: "Mrs. Humbert, sir, has been run over and you'd better come quick" (ibid., 90). The author provides a detailed inventory and topography of the street, of the roles and trajectories of the participants in the accident:

> I rushed out. The far side of our steep little street presented a peculiar sight. A big *black glossy Packard had climbed Miss Opposite's sloping lawn at an angle from the sidewalk (where a tartan laprobe had dropped in a heap), and stood there, shining in the sun, its doors open like wings, its front wheels deep in evergreen shrubbery.* To the anatomical right of this car, on the trim turn of the lawn-slope, an old gentleman with a white mustache < ... > lay supine < ... > the laprobe on the sidewalk < ... > concealed the mangled remains of Charlotte Humbert who had

---

[104]"Falter" may relate back to German *falten*, to collapse or fold.

been knocked down and dragged several feet by the Beale car as she was hurrying across the street to drop three letters in the mailbox.

(ibid., 91)

The shock of the witnesses to the scene is conveyed by Nabokov the stylist through verbal expressiveness, distorting and transforming the use of narrative language, mixing the relationship of the subjective (authorial) and objective ("others," from the character and narrator) with repetitions and accumulations of nouns, each of which in the overall picture strives for equal weight (or, by analogy with a film shot, for equal sharpness of focus in a suddenly dissolved composition where the foreground and background are on equal footing). The defamiliarization of the narrator is emphasized by the grammatical shift of the narrative to a tableau[105] in which Humbert begins to talk about himself in the third person: "The widower, a man of exceptional self-control, neither wept nor raved. He < ... > opened his mouth only to impart such information or issue such directions as were strictly necessary in connection with the identification, examination and disposal of a dead woman, *the top of her head a porridge of bone, brains, bronze hair and blood*" (ibid., 92).[106] While reviewers may not have found Charlotte's death entirely convincing,[107] it does unfold, fan-like, the principal themes of the novel. Nabokov does everything necessary to make the car a integral part of the game of "precise fate, that synchronizing phantom" (ibid., 96), which when set in motion deploys the hurrying housewife, the slippery sidewalk, the dog, the steep descent, and the "baboon at its wheel." The topos of the automobile accident therefore becomes Nabokov's version of the will of fate. Ultimately, though, it could be argued that this form of narrative euthanasia is nothing more than a banal method of easily doing away with a character.

The Furniture Truck

The opening of *The Gift* depicts "a moving van, very long and very yellow, hitched to a tractor that was also yellow, with hypertrophied rear wheels and a shamelessly exposed anatomy" (*The Gift*, 11).[108] The Russian word

---

[105]Cf.: "decrepit lady [Miss Opposite] herself *may be* imagined screeching" (*Lolita*, 91).

[106]The markedly naturalistic description of the victim reaches back to a long tradition in Russian literature, represented by Leskov and Tolstoy, among others. For more on this, see Wyllie, *Nabokov at the Movies*.

[107]"The death of Charlotte Haze, knocked down by a car as she rushes to post letters ... cannot realistically be regarded as much more than a device for moving the narrative logically on to its next stage. ... Charlotte *must* now be removed from the scene to allow Humbert access to Lolita, and so the car that hits her is more a convenience than a metaphor" (Allan, *Madness, Death and Disease*, 59).

[108]For a close reading of the opening of *The Gift*, see Leving, *Keys to* The Gift, 346–351.

used for the yellow van is *furgon*, a word originally referring to a horse-drawn wagon, making it a centaur composed of a horse and a car. This image on the opening page of *The Gift* fulfills not only the metaliterary function of imitating a draft, with all the concomitant awkward repetitions, clumsy alliteration, and plodding, seemingly unpolished stylistic structure, but also introduces the theme of the literary process itself, representing essentially the unconcealed anatomy of the creative text (note in the Russian original: "in my suitcase there are more manuscripts than shirts"). In this regard it is symbolically significant that the theme of the manuscript appears here through a double allusion to Pushkin: in the metaphor, "The van's forehead bore a star-shaped ventilator,"[109] and in the epigram, visible through the metamorphosis of the van into a horse, which contains an allusion to another well-known literary process.[110] In addition to the nod towards various manifestations of the literary craft, corresponding to the theme of the birth of a work before the eyes of the reader, Nabokov also establishes the presence of cultural memory crystallized by intertextuality. This marks the first page of *The Gift* with a seemingly insignificant detail (though one in keeping with Nabokov's tastes): the means of transportation.

In 1926 Sasha Chernyi published a story entitled "Zheltyi furgon" ("The Yellow Van") in *Illiustrirovannaia Rossiia*.[111] The plot is very simple: the five-year-old daughter of Russian émigrés gets lost in Paris and the only thing she can remember as an indication of her residence is a large yellow van parked by her hotel in the morning. The story's main focus is on Russian émigrés and their attempts to fit into the patterns of an alien city.

In both Chernyi and Nabokov the yellow van is moving furniture. The name of the moving company in *The Gift* runs along the side of the van "in yard-high blue letters, each of which (including a square dot) was shaded laterally with black paint" (*The Gift*, 3). It is worth noting the motif, important for Nabokov, of letters that appear and vanish ("in somewhat the same way as the jumbled letters find their places in a film commercial"; ibid., 5), which is also present in Chernyi's story. When the French policeman asks the girl her last name, the following conversation ensues: "'Shcherbachenko.' 'What?' 'Shcher-ba-chen-ko.' 'What's the first letter?' 'Shcha' [Russian Щ]. 'Hmm … *There's no such letter in the French alphabet*'" (Chernyi, *Sobranie sochinenii*, 5:373). The letter Щ doesn't exist in the French alphabet to the same extent that the inscription on Nabokov's van also doesn't exist (the same sound requires four letters to reproduce in

---

[109]"And on his forehead burns a star" ("Skazka o tsare Saltane" ["The Tale of Tsar Saltan"]; Pushkin, *Polnoe sobranie*, 4:456).

[110]In the foreword to his translation of *Eugene Onegin* into English: "Pushkin has likened translators to horses changed at the posthouses of civilization. The greatest reward I can think of is that students may use my work as a pony" (Nabokov, *Eugene Onegin*, vol. 1, x).

[111]*Illiustrirovannaia Rossiia* [*Russia Illustrated*]. № 26. (Chernyi, *Sobranie sochinenii*, 5:372–374). For more, see Leving, *Keys to* The Gift, 350–351.

Latin characters, *shch*, while the name of the moving company is for now not visible only to the reader, although Fyodor, a character in the novel, can see it just fine). The game with letters taken to the level of pathos is no accident. The "hypertrophic" method of literary borrowing, with the van moving from Paris to Berlin or, we might say, from one capital of the Russian emigration to another, itself becomes an "attempt to climb into the next dimension," and an entirely conscientious attempt at that. The publication of Sasha Chernyi's story (1926) coincided with the start of Nabokov's work on *The Gift*, which sheds additional light on the Max Lux furniture van that stopped briefly on April 1 of that year in the western part of Berlin. In thematic terms the van plays the role of an ornament from émigré life: it is a detail both of everyday life and of transience: "The van had gone" (*The Gift*, 34); "the big yellow van for moving furniture ... had already left" (Chernyi, *Sobranie sochinenii*, 5:373).

The van drives off, but what remains in its place is a set of palpably literary tracks (Leving "Six Notes to *The Gift*," 36–37). If we look closely at the place "where its tractor had recently stood": "there remained next to the sidewalk a rainbow of oil, with the purple predominant and a plumelike twist. Asphalt's parakeet" (*The Gift*, 34).

The "migratory birds" of Russian literature did not land on the Berlin asphalt immediately, but rather made several stops first, as in the 1922 narrative poem *Aleksandra Pavlovna* by Vladimir Narbut:

> *Orange, iridescent feathers*
> And the trembling eyes of women –
> *Peacock oil!*
>
> (Narbut, *Stikhotvoreniia*, 176)

And then on to *The Egyptian Stamp* (1925–28) by Osip Mandel'shtam: "Thousands of eyes looked into the oily, *iridescent water, shining with all the tones of kerosene from mother-of-pearl dishwater and peacock tail*" (Mandel'shtam, *Sobranie sochinenii*, 2:71), and Shengeli's poem, "Oily Rainbows and Peacocks" (1933):

> Oily rainbows and peacock
> Runoffs of spectra are receding:
> Dull poisons are crawling in aniline,
> And Vrubel' is dying forever.
>
> (Shengeli, *Inokhodets*, 178)

Nabokov's van ends up traveling from Berlin to Paris. In *The Real Life of Sebastian Knight*, the narrator and Knight with his girlfriend witness a near accident near the Arc de Triomphe: "The groan of a motor-lorry in the act of avoiding a furniture van *sent the birds wheeling across the sky*" (*The Real*

Life of Sebastian Knight, 62–63). The van is concealed from the reader's vision, but its episodic appearance, evoking "groans," takes on added significant in context. When crossing the Avenue Kléber, Claire "nearly got knocked down by a bicycle"; the pigeons, in the words of Sebastian, smell of "iris and rubber"; finally the narrator sets off for the metro station. All of these details taken together create the conditions for a dramatic conflict, in the theatrical sense rather than the everyday sense. The metatextual level of the narration confirms that the text is permeated by literariness—when the pearl-gray pigeons fluttered from the Arc de Triomphe, "it seemed as if bits of the carved entablature were turned into flaky life" (ibid., 63), and then several years later the writer's brother recognizes the very same scene in Knight's new book.

All instances where the furniture van appears in Nabokov's fiction have to do with a typological variation of the Flying Dutchman, a self-driving animated machine[112] without the slightest hint of a driver. We see this, for example, in the behavior of the truck in *Lolita*: "a truck with a mattress from Philadelphia was *confidently* rolling down to an empty house" (*Lolita*, 97). Sometimes a tragedy can be detonated even by a passively parked *furgon* such as the one in a strange accident involving the architect David van Veen in the spring of 1869 in *Ada*. The driver is fortunate to have "escaped uninjured when the motorcar he was driving from Cannes to Calais blew a front tire on a frost-glazed road and tore into a parked furniture van; his daughter sitting beside him was instantly killed by a suitcase sailing into her from behind and breaking her neck" (*Ada*, 347). In this instance Nabokov remains true to a mythological system that he had created in the early 1920s. In the early story, "Details of a Sunset" (1924), the reader has little difficulty recognizing in the story's system of imagery a small stock of symbolic objects. The warning omen of the accident is the appearance of furniture vans that are twice compared with enormous coffins ("Details of a Sunset"; *Stories*, 80, 83). The reader expects to see "dusty mountains of sumptuous furniture" (ibid., 80), but inside there is only a three-legged wicker chair. The decrepit exhibition piece in the tomblike van functions something like a jack-in-the-box and phonetically reduces the vitality of full, plush furniture.

* * *

The car eclipsed the railroad in Western culture's search for maximal mobility, and literature supported the idea of the private automobile as its own alternative to the mores and lifestyles offered by the "iron 19th century" (Blok, *Polnoe sobranie sochinenii*, 3:304). Even in the authoritative opinion of Émile Zola, who sang the praises of the railroad, the future still belonged to the more compact automobile.

---

[112]Cf. the etymological origin, Greek *autos* (self) + Latin *mobilis* (moving).

Zola has gray hair, but he is far younger than his era. Breathing through his asthma, he endeavored to look into the new century. ... The trip from Paris to Versailles [1898] was for him not a heroic picnic: it was an exploration in the 20th century and, laughing, he said to the [Automobile Club] chairman: " ... Distances are shrinking, which means the automobile is the new conduit of civilization and peace."

(Erenburg, *Sobranie sochinenii,* 7:14)

The dawn of car transportation increased, rather than decreased, the number of fatal excursions among passengers resulting from accidents on the road, moving the risk of injury from primarily the open space outside the cities to directly within the urban space. European modernist literature wasted no time in using this lethal role of the car, overlaying the maiming capabilities of the automobile onto the previously established paradigm of the road accident. In general terms, we might argue that the introduction of transportation metaphors into narratives reflects a growing instability on the level of the plot, creating a sense of discomfort, presaging impending changes in the plot or composition, or, more narrowly speaking, signaling pivotal moments in the fates of characters in a literary work.

In this part I have examined the means of representing the car in literary texts and the interactions of the automobile with its environment, including not only the drivers and passengers, but also passersby and the city streets themselves. The structural-morphological system formed in a work of literature along with the image of the (self-)moving car includes motifs already familiar to modernist literature by analogy with the railroad topos: amorous adventures,[113] the symbolism of the car as an instrument of the will of fate, an aid in mnemonic techniques for recollection,[114] or a successor to the fairy-tale steed taking heroes through a hostile space; the types of mimicry the car adopts relative to the urban landscape and against the background of nature; problems in the relationship between cars and their diminutive copies (models); the borrowing or transportation principles and motifs in various urban plots; and the evolution of individual formal elements within these plots, as well as all of these narrative categories in combination.

This part of the book devoted special attention to analyzing the intertextual thematic strata connected with stock images that inhabit and migrate within literary works. In Nabokov's fiction, the words and thoughts of others are

---

[113]"We didn't finish our tea. / We left the tarts. / In the light Opel, / To the beach, to the beach! // The sand shines white in the blue, / In the gossamer water. / Smash the guitars! / The world is ours, the world is ours. // The siren furiously / Calls in fright / At the pure space / Of millions of miles ... // Ruts and furrows / Not on the road. // Through the air we will / Furrow a corridor" (Tret'iakov, *Zheleznaia pauza,* 6).

[114]"Memory rushes like a car, / Along the heights of bygone years" (B. Sarvanskii, "Most" ["The Bridge"]; *Zheleznodorozhnik.* 1926. № 10, 61.

often combined into a complex amalgam of texts within a text, and the genesis of these borrowings can be quite random. A model for making a montage of several (in this case exclusively poetic) subtexts can be seen in the following excerpt from the first paragraph of "Ultima Thule," subtly remarked on by F. Dviniatin: "Remember the time we lunched at the hotel < ... > near the luxuriant, many-terraced Italian border, where the asphalt is infinitely exalted by the wisteria, and the air smells of rubber and paradise?" (*Stories*, 500). The mixing of the industrial and the natural, touching on the olfactory, leads the researcher of the text to a possible intertextual basis in the echoing verses of Akhmatova ("The smell of gasoline and lilacs"; Akhmatova, *Stikhotvoreniia i poemy*, 56) and Mandel'shtam ("And the lilacs smell of gasoline"; Mandel'shtam, *Sobranie sochinenii*, 1:90). In this case, corresponding to the duality of the sources in terms of tastes, the citation is bifurcated in Nabokov: the gasoline of Akhmatova and Mandel'shtam corresponds, on the one hand, to the asphalt, and on the other hand to the rubber.[115] Similarly, the lilacs are reflected by the wisteria (a lilac-colored flowering tree) and paradise. The synthesis of gasoline, asphalt, and rubber has a parallel in Don-Aminado, whose poem "Goroda i gody" ("Cities and Years") contains the same triad in an urban context:

> In terrifying stone New York
> It smells of chewed rubber,
> Asphalt evaporation,
> And the breathing of gasoline.

(Pro et contra, vol. 2, 294)

The connotations of hell in automobile symbolism coexist quite peacefully with the connotations of paradise. Moreover, the artificial heaven is directly connected with the biblical cosmogony in terms of the occult cultural dimensions ascribed to the car. The space in which the car is born from a chaos of parts is a place of collective co-creation where the magical atmosphere of assiduous creative work finds support and the boldest plans of humanity are incarnated. On the other hand, this is reduced to an automatic process and reduces the usefulness of the creative principle seen in the individual craftsman. This is a problem dealt with by Nabokov in his conception of the 1928 novel, *King, Queen, Knave* where, as Dolinin puts it, "the theme of humanoid automatons and humans resembling automatons"[116] plays a leading role. The miraculous aura that, for the

---

[115]The former in semantic terms, with the "road/transport" connection, and the latter in phonetic terms: *rezina* (rubber) and *benzin* (gasoline) in Russian contain obvious phonetic parallels (Dviniatin, "Piat' peizazhei," 293–294).

[116]Cf. his foreword to the publication of manuscript materials from the 1920s: *Zvezda*. 1999. № 4, 10.

uninitiated, surrounds the assembly of complicated machines accompanies the poetic significance given to the garage, which in Nabokov takes on the semantic value of an artisanal space, a factory/laboratory, or, in the words of Nabokov's friend V. M. Zenzinov, an "anatomical theater" where "a whole is assembled out of disparate inanimate parts":

> The assembled motor is moved on a chain to another building. Here there is the same fever of work, but it is also an organized fever. Two endless wide belts stretch a yard high as two parallel strips through the entire long building. On one belt the chassis (frame) is built and on the other the body. The work is performed on the move. Ceaselessly, relentlessly, the frame moves forward – step by step it grows, holes are drilled in it, and bolts are affixed. The body grows next to it – first a skeleton, then the skin is attached ... at the same time someone's hands *pour gasoline (like the blood in an organism)*, the motor is started and begins to operate, possessed – now it will not stop operating until the automobile has left the facility. *This is the moment of excitement: you feel as if you are present at a birth; a hitherto inanimate machine has come to life.* The wheels are bolted on, the radiator is installed, and a wheel appears. ... Some workers sitting on something like a tall sled on little wheels swarm below like gnomes, drilling something, screwing something, moving their legs and pushing their sleds-on-wheels further and further after the now completed car
>
> ...
>
> *Moving from one shop to another, I could not escape the impression that I was in something between an anatomical theater and a clinic.* In places the smells were even like something from a clinic or a hospital. ... Even during the day a deadening blue color shines in long pipes, making the faces of the workers look like those of corpses.
>
> (Zenzinov, *Zheleznyi skrezhet*, 65–68)

The familiar image of the cauldron in which a creator/demiurge mixes human flesh and the parts of future cars appears a year later in Erenburg's "10 hp" ("On 7 September a worker's finger was torn off. On the 10th a woman lost three fingers, a worker lost a hand, and another woman lost three fingers. On the 11th, two fingers under a press, and a hand was taken by a band saw. On the 26th one finger under a press. On 5 October two fingers" [Erenburg, *Sobranie sochinenii*, 7:38]; "American presses shred workers. 10-horsepower cars crush helpless pedestrians. The machine cannot be reconciled ... with feelings"[117]; ibid., 44). In the preparation

---

[117]Cf. the description of Ford's factory: "However, from here I see directly / The racing flight of the cradle of cars / From an easy chain of screws and frames / To the warm rustling of the first tires. // From all the ceilings the owner hung / Cars, and their path, like drudgery, is yellow, / And there is no person growing up happy, / And there is a person of levers and bolts" ("America," 1923–29; Tikhonov, *Sobranie sochinenii*, 1:153).

room there is an ideal order, and work is raised to a phenomenal level of automation:

> The chassis move through the long workshop. Wheels meet them at a crossing. The wheels rush to the chassis. A person takes the wheel and puts it on. One wheel. Another puts on another wheel. *The role of the human being is simple and solemn*: he puts on the left rear wheel. Always left, always rear … . He never looks to his left. *He is no longer a person.* He is just a wheel, the left rear wheel. And the belt keeps moving on.
>
> (ibid., 21)

The modern workshop does not merely create a mechanism; it creates a homunculus, and texts act as a metaphor for man-made monsters. The author creates a model, but with the significant difference that this is a unique creation rather than the product of a conveyor belt or mass production. But the main "Craftsman/Creator" parallel is preserved (cf. the poetics of the automobile industry: "Mr. Citroen expanded his business but had to narrow himself. *He discovered that high level of self-restraint that Goethe attributed to true creators*").[118] And it is further transferred to the paradigm of vital existence, as we see in the example of the unfinished sketch by Nabokov in the early 1930s for his "automobile" novel, and the passing of the test for driving the metaphysical roads of "earthly existence."

---

[118]The parallel with Goethe is likely borrowed from a 1925 article by Marina Tsvetaeva, with the standard title "A Hero of Labor," about the work of Briusov: "Regardless of whether it was a *city, office, or workshop*, if it wasn't exhausted by him [Briusov] then it took on his features. Listening closely to Goethe's unsilenced words 'In der Beschränkung zeigt sich erst der Meister' – words aimed at overcoming immeasurability … it must be said that in this regard Briusov had nothing to overcome: he was born restrained" (Tsvetaeva, *Sobranie sochinenii*, 4:13).

4

Symbolism of the Airplane: Breakthrough to Another Dimension

The Airplane Schematic

Poetic consciousness has always been attracted to transcendent states promising spiritual nirvana. It will suffice to cite as evidence Tiutchev's poem, "Fontan" ("The Fountain"), written at a time when humanity could only dream of mechanical flight, and the refraction of Tiutchev's transcendental tradition in the poetry of the absurdist Oberiu ("Society for Real Art") group.[1] We have already noted the paradoxical affinity between symbolist aesthetics and the art of the avant-garde, between the concept of a "shift" in the theories of Kruchenykh and Malevich and symbolist poetry's desire "to fly to other worlds," and in their treatment of space and reverse perspective (Bowlt, "Here and There," 65–66). The manifestations of the *fin de siècle* period in European and Russian modernist art and literature, the attempt to cross over to the other side of the material façade of civilization, overlapped with the mechanical breakthrough into another, vertical, dimension. Chekhov's *The Seagull* (1896), Maeterlinck's *The Blue Bird* (1908), Bely's "The Silver Dove," Blok's poetry about floating on air, Vrubel's *Flight of Faust and Mephistopheles* (1896), Bakst's *Terror Antiquus* (1906), *Aviator* paintings by Kliun (1912) and Morgunov (1912–13), Goncharova's *Airplane Above a Train* (1913), Malevich's *Aviator* (1914) and *Flying Airplane* (1915), and Tatlin's experiments with the "Letatlin" non-motorized flyer (1923–29) all use the language of contemporary

---

[1]E.g.: "lying in complete silence / on a heavenly height" ("Happy Man Franz," 1929 or 1930; Vvedenskii, *Polnoe sobranie*, 1:99).

FIGURE 4.1 *Russian aviator Mikhail Efimov (1881–1919) seated on airplane, c. 1910. George Grantham Bain Collection, Library of Congress.*

art to transfer the accumulated cultural attraction of movement from the earth into a new space. The passage of time provided flights of fancy with a corresponding tangible object. In the twentieth century humanity was carried to the "sacred height" by a technological revolution, and the exploits of aviation inevitably began finding reflections in art and in artistic styles, including even the figure of the poet. Gershtein recalled an occurrence at a health resort where the public asked Mandel'shtam to recite his poetry. In response, the poet acerbically addressed a man in a pilot's uniform:

> "And if I ask you to take off flying right now, how would you feel about that?" Everyone was stunned. Then he began vexedly explaining that poetry exists not for entertainment, that writing and even reading poetry were for him the same sort of work as driving an airplane was for his interlocutor.
>
> (Gershtein, *Memuary*, 5)

Aviation's rapid conquest of cultural space, combined with the heroic, romantic, and sometimes tragic aura that surrounded the pioneering aviators, took poetry by storm, inspiring artistic interpretation. In a letter to his mother in 1911, Blok expressed the spectator's amazement at these pioneers' literal flights of fancy: "everyone watched as someone whose name seems to have been Blériot, made circles over Petersburg at a height that he seems not to have seen before" (Blok, *Pis'ma A. Bloka k ego rodnym*, 2:221).

In his final book about Russian culture, Dmitri Likhachev wrote that a literary work is surrounded by so-called "crossties." In other words, it is located in an environment where the artistic and the ideological coalesce, and in which literary tradition and cultural heritage are also influential. To provide a visual depiction of this schematic Likhachev made a drawing resembling an airplane with wings and a tail (Likhachev, *Russkaia kul'tura*, 258–259). Likhachev studies these confluences in a largely typological way, and includes not only works of literature, but also other arts and styles. He examines these deep connections in sociological terms, while "the horizontal 'tail' stretching from the 'airplane schematic' is the study of traditions and influences" (Likhachev, *Russkaia kul'tura*, 259). Faced with the question of what holds this airplane design in the "air," Likhachev presents the primitive common misconception that the plane's wings are "supported" on top of the air, while in actual fact they are "sucked into the sky" by the void created above the wings. Literature also, in Likhachev's opinion, is "sucked into the sky" by its striving to influence the world around it, to correct that world, to look into the future and inculcate principles of kindness ("heavenly" principles) in human life.

Likhachev's model, when projected onto the structure and function of literary texts, from a methodological standpoint reflects the process by which the "aviation theme" was assimilated into Russian literature. Studying the body of texts related to the notion of flight, systematizing aviation motifs and images (Ingold, *Literatur und Aviatik*), calculating the frequency of poetic word use, etc. all point to the presence of a multilayered architecture of subtexts and vectors (*width*, *depth*, and *height*, to use Likhachev's terms) in the thematic and historical cross-section of Russian poetry. Applied to itself, Likhachev's system begins to operate on the principle of immanence.

Nabokov's work is inscribed into the multilayered and self-writing "airplane schematic," like the skywriting in an ad campaign that evokes reverent awe: "When, at an amazing height in the blue sky above the city, a mosquito-sized airplane emitted fluffy, milk-white letters a hundred times as big as it, repeating in divine dimensions the flourish of a firm's name, Martin was filled with a sense of *marvel and awe*" (*Glory*, 127). Cf.: "Mr. Citroen must sign the azure sky. He orders airplanes. Lindbergh's modest comrades must now write Mr. Citroen's name in smoke" (Erenburg, *Sobranie sochinenii*, 7:36).

Flight in the Russian Periodical
Press in the 1910s

We can get an idea of the public reception of aviation in the early twentieth century through memoirs, private correspondence, and the periodical press. This last provides a particularly valuable insight because it documents the cultural interpretation of the phenomenon by the reading public, which was many thousands strong, but of whom only hundreds had actually been able to see demonstration flights with their own eyes.

The All-Russian Air Club was founded in Petersburg in 1908. Beginning in the spring of 1909, members of the club started experimenting with flying machines on the Gatchina military field, and in July of that year the First Russian Flight Society and the Aerotechnics Society opened the first Russian airplane factory in Petersburg.

In the 1910s, in an era of rapid development for the aviation industry, there were two airfields in Petersburg: one at the former military training ground at Gatchina and the other, Komendantskii, hastily erected near the Kolomiazhskii hippodrome in the fall of 1910. The first International Aviation Week at the hippodrome, planned to take place April 25 to May 2, 1910, was welcomed by the main Petersburg newspapers with announcements of the participants in competitions, drawings of the latest systems of flying machines, and photographs of famous aviators. "Until recently we only knew two means of mechanized movement," wrote an amazed observer in the newspaper *Rech'* (*Speech*), referring to railroad and steamships. "But now we have no fewer than eight: 1) *ground transportation*: steam, electrical engines, and automobiles; 2) *water transportation*: steamships, motorboats, and hydroplanes; and 3) *air transportation*: the airplane and the dirigible" (*Ezhegodnik gazety* Rech' *na 1913*, 488). The airplane, a kind of "sky car,"[2] was taken to be yet another phase in the natural development of existing ways of movement.

An attempt to reconstruct the theme of "Russian Poetry and Aviation" based on the comparatively small amount of newspaper material from the 1910s was undertaken with regard to Aleksandr Blok, who had witnessed the flights of early aviators near Petersburg.[3] In a letter to his mother, Blok made a comment that would be quoted many times in future years, that "in human flights, even unsuccessful ones, there is something ancient and fated for humanity, and thus something grand" (letter dated April 24, 1910;

---

[2]"Citizens of Petersburg before the spring of 1910 had not seen actual airplane flights. Now they could be certain that airplanes were not toys and that *they could be used to move through the air just as automobiles were used to travel on the ground*" (*Novoe vremia*. January 1, 1911).
[3]See Chursina, "Blok i aviatsiia," and also E. Zheltova on the poetry of Marina Tsvetaeva (Zheltova, "Ob otnoshenii ...").

FIGURE 4.2 *Cover of a magazine,* Global Panorama, *published in Petrograd (formerly St. Petersburg), showing a British spy hydroplane. August 29, 1914.*

Blok, *Pis'ma A. Bloka k ego rodnym*, 2:75). Blok was present among the public at the Komendantskii airfield where V. F. Smit's plane crashed on May 14, 1911. A correspondent reported on the last seconds of the pilot's life: "from a terrifying height the machine begins to descend, properly at first, but then – a turn, the plane lurches forward, goes vertical, and like an arrow falls down across from the bleachers ... Helplessness among the enormous crowd of viewers, and useless assistance by a doctor" (*Rech'*. May 15, 1911. № 131, 4). Smit sustained a skull fracture and died several minutes after the fall. The accident inspired Blok to complete work on his poem "The Aviator," which he had begun as a rough draft the year before (Chursina, "Blok i aviatsiia," 223).

The Third International Aviation Week in Petersburg opened on May 14, 1913 and its major innovation, as Chursina states, was flights beyond the bounds of the airfield itself. Airplanes flew past over Novaia Derevnia, Kolomiagi, and Kamennoostrovskii Avenue. On May 16, newspaper reports announced that the dirigible "Lebed'" ("Swan"), piloted by Captain Nizhevskii and carrying five passengers, completed a flight over the center of Petersburg" (ibid., 225). However, as early as October 5, 1910, a budding Russian aviator named Sredinskii took off from the Komendantskii airfield in a Farman biplane, and managed to fly for four hours and thirty minutes despite howling winds. A journalist reported that he "immediately ascended to a height of 150 meters, then flew in the direction of the city and was immediately out of sight. When he had made it to St. Isaac's Cathedral he made two large circles over the church at a height of 200 meters, then set out to return but, lost in the air, accidently took a course for Shlisselburg" ("Polet A. N. Sredinskogo nad Peterburgom," *Vozdukhoplavanie, nauka, i sport*. October 10, 1910. № 1). The curious conclusion of this unauthorized flight over Petersburg seems to have been the punishment of the "brave aviator," who, "rumor has it, will be held responsible" (ibid.).[4]

Russian journalism played a major role in fostering the growing interest in aviation throughout society, and it was no accident that in *Rech'* (which, in 1910, had regular weekly columns for "Flight" and "Sport") Kornei Chukovskii took his literary contemporaries to task using the example of these avid newsmen: "Aviation has been met in Russia uncordially and without enthusiasm. I am speaking of Russian literature. This literature has seemingly not found the words to sing hymns and hosannas to the Zeppelin. Journalists, it is true, are enraptured, but Russian poets and artists just smile half-suspiciously. As if they know something that no Zeppelin knows" (Chukovskii, "Letuchie listki ... "). It is telling that during the initial shock at hearing the news of the air disaster in May 1911 at Issy-les-Moulineaux, it was on the pages of the periodical press, not in belles-lettres, that an anonymous article containing a commonplace allusion to Shakespeare appeared:

For the first minute attention was absorbed by the details of the accident itself and the stunned impression it left. But only for the first minute, for

---

[4]Another flight at 500 meters over St. Isaac's Cathedral, Nevskii Prospekt, and Troitskii Bridge was made twenty months later by Sikorskii (1889–1972) on a C-6A that he assembled himself. See *Sankt-peterburgskie vedomosti*. June 25, 1912.

ours is the age of the conquering of air. The fact that aviators perish as victims of their bold attempts is something to which we have seemingly become accustomed; these fatalities seem almost normal, making up a part of the professional risk. But in this case the disaster affected not the aviators but the audience, and among these it fell upon those whose safety generally is given the greatest concern [the airplane flew into a group of officials, including the popular government minister, Berteaux —Y.L.]; the victims were people who had everything that makes an enviable life, people on whom life had smiled in all its brightest aspects. Was not the late Berteaux one of God's most beloved in the eyes of his countrymen? He was wealthy ... he was still relatively young ... ambitious ... Berteaux was not the apparent head of the cabinet, but he was one of its cornerstones, and what would have kept him from becoming the president of the council of ministers in an upcoming configuration of them? Why not president of the whole republic? But blind fate blew on this life, rich with acquisitions and with expectations, and Berteaux's life was extinguished, the star of his ambition extinguished. In such a disaster there is so much that is universal that partisan strife vanishes straightaway ... and all that remains is a striking *memento mori*, a reminder of how pitiful and weak man is in the face of death, which inevitably turns man and all his noble, and ignoble, strivings into dust. During such disasters even the most thickheaded observer is visited by the same contemplations that Prince Hamlet submits to in the cemetery where he meets the gravediggers.

([Anon.] *Katastrofa v Issy. Rech'*. May 12 (25), 1911)

With all the currency of the aviation theme for the Russian periodical press and despite the regular appearance of minor, generally humorous, short stories in newspapers, its existence was not enough to inspire serious literature, functioning instead mainly to produce sensationalist reportage that stimulated the public interest.

"And the Steel Bird Will Fly": The Airplane in Russian Poetry in the Early Twentieth Century

One of the first printed responses in Russian poetry to controlled human flight appeared in 1910. A poem entitled "Man in the Air," was printed in the November edition of a new Moscow newspaper called *Flight, Science, and Sport* (*Vozdukhoplavanie, nauka, i sport*. November 11, 1910). The poem appeared under the name Karboni. In five stanzas Karboni wields a whole array of aviation motifs, which were soon to be richly deployed in Russian symbolism, post-symbolism, and futurism. Given the rarity of

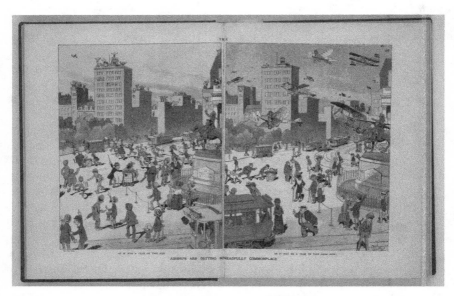

FIGURE 4.3 *"Airships are getting so dreadfully commonplace." Illustration by artist Will Crawford shows a two-panel cartoon with pedestrians looking with amazement at an airplane flying over a city (on the left); and on the right, citizens no longer take notice of all the airplanes crowding the sky above the city. Appeared in* Puck, *vol. 70, no. 1799 (August 23, 1911), centerfold.*

the source and the typological and formative structure of the poem for the genealogy of the flight theme in early-twentieth-century Russian poetry, it seems worthwhile to quote the poem in its entirety:

> The hum of the thousand-strong crowd went silent and vanished.
> The propeller on high sings its song alone.
> The foul, unnecessary world below remained in dust,
> While he aimed his flight beyond the clouds.
>
> Before his eyes the distance ever wider, ever more endless,
> But the proud gaze does not seek beauty:
> To him it all seems more needless and sad
> From his risky careless height.
>
> He reigns. And the king of the conquered elements
> Has enslaved the whole world and taken power.
> And now before an attentive, adoring crowd
> He plunges into a cloud like a royal eagle.
>
> Dark was falling. The dark of night moved over from the east,
> Crept along the stands and spilled around;

Spread a tent high over the stars,
And froze, silent, in the shade of the airfield.

All is quiet. All stays silent in agonizing longing.
But lo! The propeller sings again, full of harmony!
And the cries, and the ecstasy, and the intoxicated joy ...
He is again before the crowd! He is the god of the waves in the air!

The extravagant aviation theme quickly won the attention of the writing and reading public in Europe. Airfields were visited by spectators including Anatole France, Maurice Maeterlinck, Pierre Loti, Emile Verhaeren, Henri Bergson, and Gerhart Hauptmann. Some writers not only sang the praises of the aerial element, but even took the risk of flying themselves: one of the first airplane passengers among European writers was Knut Hamsun, while the name of Aleksandr Kuprin, but for a fortunate combination of events, would have gone down in the annals of Russian literature as the first writer in history to be the victim of an airplane crash.[5]

Kuprin, the rescued passenger, described his feelings in an essay entitled "My Flight" ("Moi polet"; *Sinii zhurnal*. 1911. № 3): "The oncoming air lifts us like the system of a toy snake. It seems to me that we are not moving, but rather that the stands, stone walls, green fields, trees, and factory smokestacks are running backwards beneath us. I look down and everything seems so funny and small as if in a fairy tale. My fear has subsided" (Kuprin, *Sobranie sochinenii*, 9:171–172). Aviation was a favorite theme of the poets Mikhail Zenkevich[6] and Vasilii Kamenskii, who had graduated as a pilot from the Imperial All-Russian Air Club. According to legend, he was inspired to take up flying by a vow made to the Burliuks and Khlebnikov (Kamenskii, *Tango s korovami*, 464), but in the conflict between his Muse and aviation Kamenskii yielded to the latter.

During the early years of aviation the eagerness of writers to embrace this new technology did not correspond to the ceremonial splendor with which it was received in real life. In his article, "Flying Leaves" ("Letuchie listki"), Chukovskii expresses annoyance at the vagueness and absence of any

---

[5]The science and technology magazine, *Vozdushnyi put'* (*Aerial Way*; St. Petersburg. 1911. № 1) reported that on November 12, 1910 in Odessa the aviator I. Zaikin, after several unsuccessful attempts, left the ground together with the writer, but "upon turning, because of the significant weight of the airmen and the steep angle, the plane fell 40 meters. The passengers escaped with bruised legs. The plane was broken." In the same year Kuprin had to defend the pilot, a former circus wrestler, whom the plane's owners were suing for compensation of the cost of the Farman airplane.

[6]Aside from his individual poems on aviation, Zenkevich published a collection in 1928 entitled *A Late Flight* (*Pozdnii polet*) and wrote a biography of the Wright Brothers for a popular Russian biography series in 1933. In 1937 he worked on an unpublished dramatic long poem entitled *The Triumph of Aviation* (*Torzhestvo aviatsii*).

"appetite for propellers" among contemporary writers. Citing Artsybashev's story "At the Last Line" ("U poslednei cherty"), he pokes fun:

> If you fly, you die; if you don't fly, you die; does flying mean anything?! And perhaps all these flights on high are even a bad thing. They just agitate your soul with the impossible dream of some sort of other soaring into some kind of other, unearthly height. They inflame and exhaust you with temptations of some other sky – no, it's better to stagnate in the dust.
>
> (Chukovskii, *Futuristy*)

Chukovskii laments that even Belinskii had to prove to Baratynskii the "usefulness of railroads," that Mitia Karamazov hates Americans because they are "immense machinists," and even Edgar Allen Poe "loves all manner of nuts and bolts," while in Russia plots such as the flight of Hans Pfaall to the moon remained only fit for children's magazines. The reasons for this blindness to urban reality on the part of his compatriots are clear: "The poetry of the struggle with the elements, the poetry of construction, 'technology,' are not even in their infancy yet here" (ibid.). Another "unearthly height" was soon seen, according to Chukovskii, by Valerii Briusov, who included in his book, *Stikhi Nelli* (*Nelly's Poems*),[7] a poem that was experimental not only in thematic terms, but also in rhythmic structure, alternating anapestic trimeter and trochaic pentameter in imitation of the hopping trajectory of the earliest airplane flights (the prose translation below does not reproduce this metric structure):

> If there is anything I like,
> It is a free airplane.
> It would be good, like it, to go
>
> Into the limitlessness of blue countries.
> Far from crowded life,
> High above the flatness of houses,
> The flight of cold clouds will be
> Dear to a tormented soul ...
>
> Let the restaurant outside the city
> Beckon deceptively with lights,
> Do not end your free path
> Into limitlessness, airplane!

Chukovskii's fears proved unfounded, however. From the mid-1910s to the early 1920s interest in flight burgeoned in Russian literature. However, a side effect of

---

[7]Briusov, V. *Stikhi Nelli*. Moscow: Skorpion, 1913.

this interest was a narrow lexicon and a monotony of metaphors in describing the object of praise, which is clearly seen when reading these works today.

Let us take, for example, the abundance of azure (*lazur'*) in aviation-related texts when describing the sky. Although it marked an innovation in poetic description, its popularity ultimately eroded its freshness. Azure at various times infiltrated the aviation texts of Erenburg ("*Through the azure anxiously rushing,* / Drunk from the rays and the air"); Zenkevich ("The *azure*-charred axis of a meteor"); Mandel'shtam ("And you, deep and sated, / *Impregnated by azure*"); Shengeli ("Among my strange dreams is one persistent one / Always repeating: *an azure abyss,* / A whistling in my ears, the spinning blade / Of a propeller, and me, carried into the distance"); Zabolotskii ("Two rabid propellers ... Blades merging with *the splendor of azure,* / Pulled me forward"); and Nabokov:

And a passerby with money out
Froze, his head thrown back,
And watches as gray transparent
Wings slide through the *azure*, where
Large clouds shine.
>   ("Aeroplan," 1926; *Russian Collected Works*, 2:541–542)

In his earthly life the pilot is put into a special class of sky-dwellers and his risk of death is increased a hundredfold. The mysterious azure (*lazur'* is defined in Dal's Russian dictionary as a "deep, bright sky color"; *Dal'* 1996, 2:234), that fills the background with the color of a sky "pregnant with the future," brought the pilot close to reincarnation in a holy azure space: its etymology and phonetic resemblance in Russian (*lazur'*—*Lazar'*) gave the word a symbolic association with "poor Lazarus" (for his earthly suffering Lazarus is rewarded in the next world [Luke 16:19–31]).

From the stock of clichéd aviation images, metaphorical pleonasms included the knife-propeller and wing-sabre. In his poem, "To Somebody" ("Komu-to"; 1909), Briusov addresses the pioneers of flight, Farman and the Wright Brothers, celebrating the "fiery copper" and praising the conquerors of the elements:

Let the mighty whirlwind *be cut*
By the triumphing wings of the ship,
And there below in the cracks of a cloud,
Let the blue earth slip through!
>   (Briusov, *Stikhotvoreniia i poemy*, 322)

Cf. the "cutting" trope in Otsup:
He bent over, looking into the abyss,
Holding death or the wheel in his hand ...

How nicely the sun-glistening circle of the *knife*
Hums in the coolness!

("Aeroplan" ["The Airplane"], 1918;
Otsup, *"Okean vremeni,"* 38)

Soviet poets equated words with wings flying through time and space, as in
the motif of the wings of thought in Gogol: "How the mighty wings carry
me" (*Dead Souls*).

The Magic of Names

The Defense contains a conversation that reconstructs the range of interests
typical to Petersburg residents in the 1910s. Luzhin's aunt is flirting at
breakfast with his father, but the younger Luzhin, concentrating intently
on the unfamiliar foreign names and titles, does not recognize their risqué
amorous game. Filled with realia from the time, the adults' conversation is
presented from the point of view of the young Luzhin, with only the parts
that are understood by and are interesting to his adolescent mind:

> His < ... > sweet copper-haired aunt < ... > threw cake crumbs across the
> table and related that for twenty-five rubles Latham was going to give her a
> ride in his "Antoinette" monoplane, which, by the way, was unable to leave
> the ground for the fifth day, while Voisin on the contrary kept circling the
> aerodrome like clockwork, and moreover so low that when he banked over
> the stands one could even see the cotton wool in the pilot's ears.
>
> (The Defense, 44)

Through indirect speech, the narrator obscures the source of the lines, thus
making it unclear who utters the hyperbole about the cotton in the pilot's
ears—the impressionable child or his aunt who is given to exaggeration. The
conversation takes place in the spring (the table is set with "the remains of
the paschal cream cheese < ... > and a still untouched Easter cake"), and
certain details make it possible to establish the year to which the character's
remembrances relate: the French aviator Hubert Latham (1883–1912)
appeared at the Kolomiazhskii hippodrome in Petersburg in April 1910,[8]
which incidentally inspired Kuzmin to write his poem, "Na sluchai" ("An

---

[8]Blok, who was in the stands, wrote to his mother on April 21, 1910: "a crowd of a million,
a spring day and a most elegant *Antoinette* (the name of his plane)" (Blok, *Pis'ma A. Bloka
k ego rodnym*, 2:74). In 1909 Latham failed in his attempt to cross the English Channel in
a monoplane (*Russian Collected Works*, 2:710, commentary). The Voisin brothers, Gabriel
(1880–1973) and Charles (1882–1912), were French engineers, industrialists, and aviators.

FIGURE 4.4 *Aviators Vsevolod Abramovich (1890–1913) and Russian princess Eugenia Mikhailovna Shakhovskaya (1889–1920). In 1913, the two aviators were in a plane crash in which Abramovich was killed. Glass negative, between c. 1910 and 1913. George Grantham Bain Collection, Library of Congress.*

Incident"), addressed to O. Glebova-Sudeikina after they went to one of the air shows together:

> Can I forget Latham's flight,
> The cars, the dramas of thunder,
> When amid the bustle and din
> We made our way to the hippodrome?
> Let the men walk around in wool,
> The azure is calm and clear,
> And the roses on lavender hats
> Say to me: "Spring has come."
> One loge sheltered us,
> One common table for us two.
> Below, looking like a flower bed,
> The crowd brings a vague hum.[9]

---

[9]Russian State Archive of Literature and Art, f. 232, op. 2, item 1, sheet 31; see Timenchik, "Ol'ga Glebova-Sudeikina," 218.

Another striking example of linguistic strangeness and the influence of the aviation theme on the interpretation of reality by a participant in a dialog is found in *King, Queen, Knave*. After arriving from the provinces, Franz takes part in an unaccustomed worldly discussion on the first evening with his relatives. But the absence of his glasses, the slight dizziness from the wine and the erotic tension between him and Martha shroud him in a fog, and in the epicenter of this fog the "ghostly," but "warm and ruddy" Dreyer is describing

> *a flight he had made two or three years ago from Munich to Vienna in a bad storm; how the plane had tossed and shaken*, and how he had felt like telling the pilot "Do stop for a moment" < ... >. Meanwhile Franz was experiencing fantastic difficulties with the vol-au-vent and then with the dessert. He had the feeling that in another minute *his body would melt completely leaving only his head, which, with its mouth stuffed with a cream puff, would start floating about the room like a balloon.* < ... > Noting the state in which the poor fellow was, he [Dreyer] < ... > did say, however, that < ... > the aviator's principal enemy is not wind but fog, and that, as the salary would not be much at first, he would undertake to pay for the room and would be glad if Franz dropped in every evening if he desired, though he would not be surprised if next year air service were established between Europe and America. The merry-go-round in Franz's head never stopped; *his armchair travelled around the room in gliding circles.*
>
> (*King, Queen, Knave*, 37)

Several topics intertwine in Franz's mind in a complex conglomeration, with the nucleus being Dreyer's story of his flight. A journey in a chair through an imagined country becomes an accustomed literary meditation for Godunov-Cherdyntsev in *The Gift* (where it calls to mind Pushkin's *Journey to Arzrum*); in the *King, Queen, Knave* example, because of the general tone of the story, we would do better to seek Pushkinian subtexts in fairy-tale motifs. The fairy/folk tale (*skazka*) plays a structural role in the novel, independently embodying some of the theoretical models of Propp from the late 1920s. The passage cited above is replete with signs of the "previous century," from the Montgolfier balloon in *The Queen of Spades* to the narrative poem, *Ruslan and Liudmila*, which is parodied by the talking head of Franz and the situation involving the "flying" lovers:

Had swept you off the bridal pillows,
Spun like the whirlwind up and out,
And through black air and foggy billows,
Sped to his mountainous redoubt.[10]

---

[10]Transl. by Jenni Blackwood (Pushkin, *Polnoe sobranie sochinenii*, 4:27).

Literature merges with aviation in Luzhin's fiancée's recollections of youth after seeing a certain famous writer from a distance in rural Finland (the author is not named, but he is later described with a strong resemblance to Leonid Andreev). The observer's gaze is focused on the man's face, and, following the direction of his eyes, moves up to the sky, "which enemy airplanes had begun to haunt" (*Defense*, 90). This is a typically Nabokovian ellipsis, with the view being presented as a ricochet through the eyes of another person (the writer); at the same time, however, the arrangement of the sentence indicates that the description of the airplanes originates with the young woman, who is not well-versed in the technical terminology.

The fashion for aviation in the early twentieth century quickly infiltrated children's games as well as the plots of adventure novels. In *Despair*, Hermann offers Felix money to dress himself in his clothes: "Let me repeat: the job is ridiculously easy; child's play—you know the way *children dress up to represent* soldiers, ghosts, *aviators*" (*Despair*, 87). Felix tries to decline the offer, which he identifies with "picture houses and circuses," citing the example of his cousin who "dashed his brains out by missing a flying swing" (ibid.).

Children's fascination with the first airplane flights and games that featured its hero pilots are preserved in the memoirs of Nabokov's generation. L. V. Uspenskii (1900–78) recalls from St. Petersburg:

> As early as 1908 my earlier passion, locomotives, had become tarnished in my eyes. The shop windows of stationery stores began to display postcards showing the first airplane flights in other countries. Portraits of the intellectual Frenchman in a tin-pot hat, the engineer Louis Blériot, began to appear. Two Americans looked out at me from the pages of *Ogonek* and other illustrated magazines: Wilbur Wright looked like a stereotypical Presbyterian minister with the dry face of a fanatic containing something Indian as we imagined that to be from reading Cooper and Mayne Reid; Orville looked nothing like his brother – a southern European with a black moustache, perhaps a Frenchman or an Italian.
>
> (Uspenskii, *Zapiski starogo peterburzhtsa*, 139)

The names of airplane models gradually eclipsed those of the aviators themselves, whose initial charm was remembered nostalgically by Iurii Olesha in the late 1920s.[11] Spellbound by the magic of foreign sounds, Zenkevich lists a cascade of French names in his 1918 poem, "Aviarekviem" ("Aerorequiem"): Latham, Guynemer, Legagneux, and Pégoud. Maiakovskii

---

[11] In *Envy*: "Ever *since I was a child, the name Lilienthal* – transparent, quivering like insect wings – *has sounded marvelous* to me. ... This name, which flew *as if stretched over light bamboo planks*, was linked in my memory with the dawn of aviation. Otto Lilienthal, an aviator, killed himself" (Olesha, *Envy*, 130).

uses onomatopoeic alliteration to produce repeated variations on the one-syllable name of the first aviators, imitating the sound of a motor: "Ved' na pervom motore i brat'ia Rait / proletali ne bol'she minuty" ("On the first motor the brothers Wright / Flew for no more than a minute").[12] Briusov alternates an eruptive "r" sound with more melodic and sonorous sounds:

Stupiv na pole, shagnuv chrez propast', Poslushny chutko liudzkim umam, V razmernom gule stuchat mashiny, Vzryvaia glyby pod vzmakh edinyi, I, slovno prizrak, kidaiut lopast' S zemli pokornoi, vvys', k oblakam. ("Pust' vechno mily posevy, skaty ...," 1920; Briusov, Stikhotvoreniia i poemy, 554)	Stepping on the field, pacing across the abyss, Obedient to keenly human minds, Machines knock in a dimensional hum, Exploding clods to a single stroke, And, like a phantom, throw a blade From the conquered earth, upwards, to the clouds.

Insects, Birds, and Fish

The earliest mimetic identifications of a flying machine with an insect in Russian poetry date to 1913 and are found simultaneously in a number of poems by a number of authors, including P. S. Solov'eva (1867–1924), the sister of the poet and philosopher Vladimir Solov'ev, in her poem "Polet" ("The Flight"):

Leaving the valleys, and dust, and fog,
To meet the breath of the cool heights,
Airplanes churn like dragonflies,
And proud is the first human flight.
Fly, carried by a new strength,
Fly, spinning into a winged thread,

---

[12]First published in the magazine, Samolet (Moscow, 1925. August. № 8).

Fly, fly, but you will not blow
A wingless life to the sky with cold flight.

(*Poety 1880–1890-kh godov*, 376)

The other example is in Briusov's poem, "V lesu" ("In the forest"): "Like little monoplanes / Blue dragonflies chirr" (Briusov, *Stikhi Nelli*, 19). The dragonfly would continue to be a source of poetic imagery and a calque for the design of airplanes (as in a poem by Aseev: "His plane ... / Jets through the clouds like a dragonfly"; *Segodnia ruskoi poezii*, 1924, 5). In "Opiat' voiny raznogolositsa ..." ("Again the dissonance of war ...") from 1923, Mandel'shtam writes:

Because today the victors
Evaded the graveyard of flight,
Broke the wings of the dragonfly
And executed them with hammers.

(Mandel'shtam, *Sobranie sochinenii*, 1:306)

Poplavskii in his poem "Aviator" also has:

But suddenly a crystal ringing and crackling,
The propeller burst where it may:
Into it, flying across its path,
Fell an earthly dragonfly.

(Poplavskii, *Sochineniia*, 165)

The comparison with a dragonfly is, to a certain extent, synecdoche: those who lived in the first quarter of the twentieth century would have heard the name of the superlight airplane *Demoiselle* (one of the meanings for which in French is dragonfly), designed by the Frenchman Santos-Dumont.[13] After 1908 when a dragonfly was mentioned in a poetic text it was impossible not to associate it with the "dragonflies of death" in Bely's symphony *Kubok Metelei* (*Goblet of Blizzards*), an image which Mandel'shtam plays on in his poem written after Bely's death: "O God, how black and blue-eyed / The dragonflies of death, like black azure" (Mandel'shtam, *Sobranie sochinenii*, 1:207).[14]

---

[13]This association applies not only to the outward appearance and name, but also to the movement of flying machines. Shklovskii's suggestion for depicting the dynamics of the earliest flights was the all-encompassing formula: "The airplane *flew like a wounded beetle*" (Shklovskii, *Gamburgskii schet*, 142).

[14]As a bird bringing death, the airplane appears in an opera by Kruchenykh to the music of Matiushin; one of the characters in this opera warns: "Don't cross the firing line / The iron bird is flying" (*Pobeda nad solntsem* [*Victory over the Sun*]; St. Petersburg, 1914, 13).

FIGURE 4.5 *Continental Can hangar, Morristown Airport, New Jersey. April 9, 1952. Gottscho-Schleisner Collection, Library of Congress.*

The introduction of insect or bird imagery into an aviation text enabled a change in the point of view, allowing the poet to change perspective freely:

> If sometime one could dream
> A blown sphere under heaven,
> But not, horrors, that bird,
> In a cloud no larger than a mosquito …
> Now he bent down,
> Looking into the abyss.
>
> ("Aeroplan," 1918; Otsup, "*Okean vremeni,*" 38–39)

Most aviation texts are constructed on the *airplane as steel bird* metaphor (with the bird generally being predatory, but sometimes with pacifistic plumage):

> Late at night, righting his wings,
> An aviator faltered and fell.
> Only a kite flying past
> Cried over the *fallen bird*.
>
> ("Aviator," 1911; Erenburg, *Stikhotvoreniia*, 123)

The desire to embellish descriptions of airplanes and pilots with such imagery led to some interesting consequences, as we see in a note written by a hapless eyewitness to an early air battle, who deployed a whole aviary:

> [T]he machine turned its nose to the earth and began to descend rapidly, cutting through the air like a hawk pouncing on its prey. ... At this point the plane that had been flying head over heels quickly turned to the side and rushed just over the ground, like a swallow before the rain. This was a magnificent spectacle, and though I knew that the enemy was at the helm I could not restrain myself at the sight of his cool nerves. ... The pilot was tall with a flaxen beard. His whole posture, those hunched shoulders, his head extended forward, his bent body, were reminiscent of a predatory bird. His hair was long. ... They [the French planes] flew behind him ... coming closer and closer, like eagles ready to descend upon a heron.
>
> ([B. p.] "Battle in the Air," *Biulleteni literatury i zhizni*. September 1914. № 2, 193–194)

The evolution of the bird motif went through several stages, from the archaeological to the fantastic, and the mythology of flight grew out of misconceptions about contemporary engineering, which were sometimes based more on the trends of the age than on actual physical and mathematical calculations.[15] The metaphor, supported by revolutions in technological thinking, quickly turned into a mere template, however, losing its heights of inspiration: "*Like strange birds*" (V. Briusov, "Monoplanes," 1918); "Not even fluttering their wings, / The bird-monsters fly" (N. Otsup, "The Airplane," 1918); "That cry of the mechanical bird / Leaving the airfield" (D. Tumannyi, "The Pilot," 1924). Parting ways with the winged imagery was painful: Mandel'shtam lamented that "people-birds are worse than beasts / And that we can't help / Trusting vultures and kites more" (Mandel'shtam, "And the sky is pregnant with the future," 1923–29).

Like Mandel'shtam, Blok saw in the development of aviation a process analogous in many ways to the process by which marine animals moved to dry land. During the early stages of aviation symbolism, Blok's poetry provided a concise evolutionary formula: "*As the sea monster into water*, / [The flyer] *Slipped into the currents of air*"—an oxymoronic figuration constructed on a combination of falling and flight: "into water" (downward) = "into air currents" (upward).[16] However, a decade later a regressive tendency had begun. Olesha spoke with disappointment at the outward changes that had

---

[15] An article entitled "The Flexible Wings of Airplanes" (*Vozdukhoplavatel'*. 1914. № 7.), signed with the initials V. O., states that a flexible wing "facilitates the turning of an airplane, as it assists in forming a cross pitch."

[16] "to replace the creeping ways come flying and soaring ways" ("Riav o zheleznykh dorogakh," 1913; Khlebnikov, *Tvoreniia*, 594).

taken place with improvements in airplane design: "Flying machines have ceased to look like birds. Light wings with transparent yellow have been replaced by flippers. One might think they are beating the ground at liftoff. In any case, dust is raised at liftoff. *The flying machine now resembles a heavy fish*. How quickly aviation has become an industry!" (Olesha, *Envy*, 34).[17] Here the airplane returns to its "prehistoric condition" transforming into a fish or reptile. Shklovskii similarly made this analogy between airplane and fish in 1928: "The entire plane, if you don't count the wings, *looks like a blunt-nosed fish*. The pilot and engine technician climb in and out the eyes of this fish" (Shklovskii, *Gamburgskii schet*, 278).

A tentative summary of the dualistic process in the development of Russian aviation literature was given by none other than Vladimir Nabokov, who suggested a compromise in the quarrel between the elements of air and water. In the scene in Grunewald Forest in *The Gift*, Fyodor Konstantinovich observes the sky, "where droned a highflying plane that seemed filmed over with blue dust, the blue essence of the firmament: the plane was bluish, as a fish is wet in water" (*The Gift*, 304). Two pages before this, the forest is described as an underwater kingdom at the bottom of which, like Sadko in the Russian *byliny*, the poet Godunov-Cherdyntsev finds himself: "And still higher above my upturned face, the summits and trunks of the pines participated in a complex exchange of shadows, and their leafage *reminded me of algae swaying in transparent water*" (ibid., 302). At the dawn of the age of flight a skeptic wrote that man will never succeed in replacing the instincts of living creatures and "creating a *flying machine built on the principles of flight in birds and insects*. Locomotives and automobiles do not have jointed legs, nor do steamships and submarines have fins, and thus *a flying machine must not have wings*" (Bubnov, "Mechanized Flight in the Future"). Two decades later, betraying the hopes invested in it by poetry, the airplane finally enters the ranks of soulless machines triumphantly marching over the spiritual life of civilization:

In the watery depths steel fish prowl,
Weighty vessels throw up clumps,
    Propellers sing
      At heights beyond the clouds:
Earth and water, air and fire –
All have joined together against man.
                ("Mashina" ["Machine"] 1922; Voloshin,
                Stikhotvoreniia i poemy, 323)

---

[17]See also Karel Čapek: "Only after looking carefully do I begin to think that in essence the airplane does not so much resemble a bird, not even at all, though it does fly. ... The *plane resembles a bird as little as a torpedo does a trout*" ("On Inventions. [The Airplane]"; Chapek, *Izbrannoe*, 613–614).

On the Genesis and Context of Nabokov's Poem, "The Airplane"

Among more than the one hundred poems in the anthology Nabokov published in 1923 under the title *Gornii put'* (*The Empyrian Path*) is a short poem called "Aeroplan" ("The Airplane"):

> After sliding on the worn grass,
> It lifted resonantly, effortlessly,
> And the wings conceived long ago
> Began shining in the blue.
>
> And proud thoughts flowed
> To the music of the propeller and wind ...
> The bottom of the scarred earth
> Seemed to be the ravings of a geometer.
>
> (Russian Collected Works, 1:511–512)

The poem depicts an airplane's flight and the feelings of a pilot being in the cockpit. The logical rupture, emphasized by an ellipsis, between the second and third lines in the second stanza seems to point to an accident left "behind the scenes" by the author.

Despite the poetic austerity and lack of flamboyant metaphors usually found in the young Sirin's work, the poem has enough semantic density at various levels to enter into intertextual contact with a number of other poems on the same theme, with two of these being especially close. The first is Blok's "Aviator" (1911) and the second is Vladislav Khodasevich's poem of the same name written three years later in 1914.

The concept behind both of these works is similar: the accident occurs not because of an equipment failure, but because of a drama endured by the pilot. In formal terms each of the poems has a three-part structure (*a-b-c*): an introduction describing the free flight (*a*), an appeal directly to the man driving the machine (*b*), and a culminating fall and attempt to ascertain the reasons for the accident (*c*).

The compositional parallels in the situations described warrant attention:

The picture of the earth seen from above by the pilots: "In the smoky darkness over the meadow / Hangars, people, all earthly things / Seem to be pressed onto the earth" (Blok) = "Over the fields, forests, swamps, / Over the bends of northern rivers" (Khodasevich).

The flight of the airplane: "slipped into the currents of air" (Blok) = "you pass in flowing ascents" (Khodasevich).

The height attained: "To the blind sun ... / Strives your propeller flight" (Blok) = "Higher, higher draw your spirals" (Khodasevich).

The presence of the public: "above the stands" (Blok) = "where the stands" (Khodasevich).

Characteristics of the *pilot*: "the unwavering pilot ... brave" (Blok) = "Rest from the heights and hazards" (Khodasevich).

Focus on an immobile hand, the symbolic *loss of control* over life: "a hand, more dead than the lever" (Blok) = "on the wheel a hand turns to bone" (Khodasevich).

The condition of the sky: "Only the air, clear as water" (Blok) = "What to you is the clearness above the clouds?" (Khodasevich).

Rhetorical authorial remarks: "Why were you in the sky, brave one, / For your first and last time?" (Blok) = "But remember – think – stop" (Khodasevich).

The finale of the aerial drama: "Too late: on the grass of the plains / The crumpled arc of a wing" (Blok) = "Ah, tear away, and in large zigzags / Fall" (Khodasevich).

From an early poem by Blok ("V neuverennom, zybkom polete ..." ["In an uncertain, shaky flight ..."], 1910) Khodasevich borrows the ending, with an airplane crashing directly over the stands. In Blok:

Let the orchestra play in the stands.
But to the light music of a waltz
The heart and the propeller stop.

And in Khodasevich:

Fall, shattering the ridge,
Where the stands are colored with flags,
Where the people, the orchestra, and the buffet are

Blok's poem first appeared in his 1910 *Sobranie stikhotvorenii* (*Anthology of Poems*) with the title "Aeroplan" ("The Airplane"), which was later removed. Nabokov used the same title in *The Empyrian Path*.[18] Despite a superficial resemblance to the earlier texts, the aviation theme in his work is transformed. The inserted "pilot vs. socialite" plot, hinting at a romantic reason for the pilot's death, is removed. Unlike his predecessors, Nabokov describes a transmigration of the soul, a stage following the plane crash in the poem, with the aviator's spirit being removed from its bodily housing. The symbolic metamorphosis of the soul into a butterfly (see the 1925 story, "Christmas") takes place in accordance with classical myth and with the

---

[18]The memory might have been refreshed by the two-volume edition of Blok's *Sochineniia* (Berlin, 1923), published by "Slovo," which was instigated by Vladimir Dmitrievich Nabokov, among others.

early Nabokov's own poetic vision. The resurrection of the pilot is suggested by the ambiguous clause: "And the wings conceived long ago / Began shining in the blue," where the theme of recognition dovetails with the closing lines of the programmatic 1921 poem, "Babochka" ("The Butterfly"): "Yes, I will recognize you among the Seraphim at the wondrous meeting, / *I will recognize your wings*, that sacred pattern!"

In the religious context of the anthology (Nabokov later tried to understate his attempt to "develop Byzantine imagery" and his "literary stylization" [*Russian Collected Works*, 2:788]), the wings of the angel/ butterfly are synonymous with divine soaring. The spiritual release of the poet—a constant trope in the poetics of flight—enters into various poems in the "angel cycle." In the poem, "Prestoly" ("Thrones"), the landscape that opens up before the winged creature accompanying the earthly church reproduces the opening of Khodasevich's "Aviator" almost verbatim:

Magically before the mountain
the plain unfurled.
And the dark groves and the bright fields,
And the bends of rivers ...
And the angel sang resonantly ... flying away without success

Cf. Khodasevich:

Over the fields, forests, swamps,
Over the bends of northern rivers
You pass in flowing ascents
Heaven-dweller

In the poem, "Dvizhen'e" ("Movement"), from *The Empyrean Path*, the leitmotifs (rushing, music, science, and myth), which had hitherto been seen separately, are gathered into a polyphonic statement:

A slope, a substantiated calculation,
and a concise, repeating burst –
and there it is, the dream of Daedalus,
flying up, its stringed wings outstretched!

(*Russian Collected Works*, 1:531)

Daedalus will have his own chapter later (3.8), so here it will suffice to note the echo of the mathematical theme from poems written by Briusov in 1907–08 ("His [Daedalus's] stern gaze rose / And with a dead compass he measured / The possibility of impossible dreams"). Briusov's "Sluzhitel' muz" ("Servant of the Muses") provides a likely source for Nabokov's rhyming of the genitive case forms of "wind" ("*vetra*") and "geometer" ("*geometra*"):

> When the fury of the wind
> Blows in our face the enemy's banners,
> Smash your geometer's compass,
> Take armor on your shoulders!
>
> (Briusov, *Stikhotvoreniia i poemy*, 319)

This poem in turn is a reference to Blok's "Na ostrovakh" ("On the Islands," 1909), which contains the same rhyme.

The story of Blok's "Aviator" was touched on in correspondence between Nabokov and Mark Aldanov. In a letter dated May 13, 1942 Aldanov consulted with Nabokov on editorial policy:

> Lednitskii gave us an article on *Retribution*. There were two poems "where it reeks of *Novoe vremia*, where only the Yid is sovereign" (I'm not citing the second line verbatim, but the basic sense and the word "Yid" are there). We tossed out these two lines, out of respect for the talent and memory of Blok. This half-clever, half-drunk, half-educated man was a great poet, but to state that in Petersburg in 1909 the Jews were sovereign is not logical even when one is in desperate need of a rhyme for "reek" [the rhyme in question is *smerdit-zhid* in Russian].[19] How would you proceed?
>
> (Nabokov, "Kak redko teper' pishu po-russki ...," 133).

A week later Nabokov responded:

> I would print Blok's reeking rhyme without concern, but then I would indicate to Pan Lednitskii that *Retribution* is an entirely insignificant, phony, and tasteless poem ("turbid verses," as my wife called it). Blok was a reed that sang but did not think at all. Poor Lednitskii was worried that not all of his diarrhea would be poured out in this issue and that he would have to hold the better part of the peas and boiled water to the next one. "That's where the main feeling gathers for me!" he cried in despair. It's a horribly repellent poem, but I would certainly not get rid of "Yid"; this is typical for Blok's mentality. I'm in complete agreement with your wonderful assessment, but I would add "half-shaman" ("or has the terrible sight of coming wars/struck your unhappy brain/*a night* flyer, in inclement *darkness*/carrying dynamite to the earth." Blok's poem "The Airplane" from, I think, 1911).
>
> (ibid., 134; italics in the original)

---

[19]The beginning of Lednitskii's article, "Blok's Polish Poem," was printed in issue № 2 of *Novyi zhurnal* (1942, 309).

Twenty years after entering the literary field, after shedding Sirin's complexes about influence and poetic ambition, Nabokov quotes Blok from memory. This is apparent from the incorrect verb ("struck" should be "poisoned"), and from the fact that instead of the original title "Aviator" he inserts the name of his own poem. Aldanov, unaware of the internal back story regarding the "aviation hypertext," reacts hesitantly:

> However, you cite his [Blok's] sonorous lines about the airplane as "half-prophetic." In fact there was nothing prophetic there at all. You might not remember this, but I remember quite well that not only in 1911, but even much earlier, after Blériot's flight, all the feuilleton writers in newspapers were describing future nighttime flights over cities with dynamite and fire bombs and so on. Similarly, *The Scythians*, with all its ingenious thoughts ("you stab each other's bellies, and we will see") was a retelling of articles in the publications of the Bolsheviks and left socialist revolutionaries after Brest-Litovsk. And the blasphemous vulgarity of Christ leading the red army soldiers I heard from Lunacharskii long before *The Twelve*, and Lunacharskii had taken it from some Polish romantic writer. Unfortunately, however, none of this keeps Blok from being a great poet.
>
> (ibid., 134)

The Music of Flight

In the second poem by Nabokov entitled "The Airplane," written three years after the first, which praised "the music of the propeller and wind," the echo of Blok's "Aviator" remains audible:

Nabokov: "its heavenly *hum* is wondrous ... *Unearthly* sounds soar"
Blok: "Its *propellers sing like strings*"; "the propeller keeps *singing*"; "But once again in the golden haze / As if an *unearthly chord*"

It is noteworthy that when the original newspaper publication (*Rul'*. June 25, 1926) was reprinted in the anthology *Vozvrashchenie Chorba* (1930) one single word was changed. "Its heavenly *hum* is wondrous" was revised to read "its heavenly *shine* is wondrous" (*Russian Collected Works*, 2:541–542). Evidently, the revision was not made so much to improve the original semantic carelessness[20] as it was to produce a camouflage effect: it meant

---

[20]The Russian word is *gul*, for which one of the dictionary definitions is "a booming noise, a knocking sound" (Dal', *Tolkovyi slovar' zhivogo velikorusskogo iazyka* v 4 tomakh, 1:406), which contradicts the harmony of the *unearthly sounds*.

a shading of the religious pathos of the heavenly message that, by the 1930s, Nabokov found unacceptable and undesirable to demonstrate. The wondrous (*chudnyi*, here bordering on the meaning "miraculous") dialog was removed, and the phenomenon was returned to the realm of a trivial optical aberration.

Blok and Nabokov were not the only authors to interpret the revving of a motor as an industrial symphony. Zabolotskii calls the hum of an airplane an "agreeable chorus of propellers,"[21] Kirillov an "iron bass,"[22] Gerasimov listens as a "propeller sang of our victory,"[23] and Mandel'shtam hears Bach fugues in the noise:

> Let us listen to the preaching of thunder,
> Like the grandsons of Sebastian Bach,
> Both in the east and in the west
> Put on organ wings!
>   (Mandel'shtam, "Again the dissonance of war …," 1923)

The curtain of noise from the symbolists and acmeists was inherited by Soviet fantasy writers, but Nabokov refused to depict flight with the characteristic array of sounds and visual effects. In the novel, *Letters from Terra*, written by Van Veen who "quietly < … > borrowed what his greatest forerunners < … > had imagined in the way of a manned capsule's propulsion" (*Ada*, 339), discredits the poetics of space, laying bare the nature of time. The refined idea of acceleration is embodied in the description of a utopian aircraft that flies more than 1,000 miles per hour and that, acted on by "intermediate environment" combining sibling galaxies, grows to several trillion light years per second, only to descend later to the speed of "dwindling harmlessly to a parachute's indolent descent" (ibid.).

Flight and Performance

The public keenly felt the festive and carnivalesque aesthetic surrounding aviation in the earliest years of its rapid development. The stadiums where aviators put on demonstrations in front of huge crowds of spectators from all social strata gave rise to comparisons with ancient spectacles. A report from the first international aviation week at the Kolomiazhskii airfield by N. Breshko-Breshkovskii compared the aerial competitions with

---

[21]Zabolotskii, *Polnoe sobranie*, 216.
[22]"Letchik" ("The Pilot"), 1923; *Proletarskie poety*, 253.
[23]Cf. the ending of the same poem: "*The stars sang us a victory marsh*, / Light, laughing, cascaded into a whirlwind, / And spirits – flamed with the sun / Under the rich whistling of iron wings" ("Letim" ("We Fly"); *Let. Aviastikhi*, 10).

FIGURE 4.6 *South American aviator Juan Domenjos with his wife, 1915. Harris &*
Ewing photograph collection, Library of Congress.

a bullfight: "Everyone was captivated by flight. There was a kind of nervous, elevated mood. *Just like Madrid before a bullfight*" (*Birzhevye vedomosti.* April 20, 1910. № 11671, 3 [evening edition]). Another contemporary described the general scene surrounding public air shows in Petersburg thusly:

I will never forget the bright spring sun over the endlessly broad and green racing field; I will never forget the high, multi-layered stands at the southwestern edge, capped by joyous flags and simmering with a whole sea of heads ... I will never forget the brass of several orchestras disjointedly playing, here "On the Hills of Manchuria," there "Cakewalk," and somewhere else "Viking" or "Seagull," and the red-faced Kapellmeisters in officer's greatcoats directing these orchestras. ... The overfilled stands buzzed like an apiary full of titanic hives. Throughout the lower rows the ice cream vendors, elated at such unexpected commercial success, rolled their sky-blue, green, and dark blue wheeled boxes. Peddlers of lemonade and baked goods with their baskets, and candy sellers, were reaping an abundant harvest.

(Uspenskii, *Zapiski starogo peterburzhtsa*, 141–143)

Clearly these public flights were interpreted as an event akin to a circus show. Newspapers printed announcements of the flight programs as a type of sports match.[24]

Generally speaking, the competitive element in aviation was *in statu nascendi* of fundamental importance; it is noted by Blok ("He is close, a moment of applause / *And the pitiful world record*!"; "Aviator," 1912) and Zenkevich ("In set world records prozes / For the circus balancing act in the heavens"; "Aerorequiem," 1918). Anna Akhmatova recalled that Amadeo Modigliani was interested in pilots, but when the artist met one of them he was disappointed: "they seemed to be no more than sportsmen (what had he expected?)" ("Amadeo Modil'iani," 1965; Akhmatova, *Sochineniia*, 2:148).

Removed from its historical context, the internal logic of this metonymy is not entirely clear. Meanwhile, the poetic tradition reminds us that in ancient cultures competitions were part of religious holidays and were essential as sacred rites. By the twentieth century this connection had been lost in sports and, as Huizinga states, the high level at which modern societal mechanisms reinforce the external effects of mass spectacles does nothing to change the fact that neither the Olympic games nor any other international competition can make sports into an activity that creates styles and cultures (Huizinga, *Homo Ludens*, 188). It is quite likely that flight was the basis for the symbolists and their followers to hope (with the hope being only partially realized) for a resurrection of the refined spirit of games and clashes of honor ("Sailors of aerial flight, / *Gladiators of solar battles*. / Your harbors are / Myriads of planetary orbits"; A. Zharov, "Gladiators of the Air," *Let. Aviastikhi*, 15). The pilot's struggle with the element of air was constructed based on a set schematic:

Festive flags waved proudly.
All gathered at the square to see

---

[24] *Vozdukhoplavanie, nauka i sport.* October 10, 1910. № 1.

How much boldness and strength
Were needed to overcome this sky.
He stood there cold and calm
Before the untrusting crowd,
That unusually hot mid-day,
Beginning his battle with the heavens
      (Erenburg, "Aviator," 1911; Erenburg, *Stikhotvoreniia*, 122–123)

The canons of performance presume an unbreakable connection between sporting passion and spectacle. Khodasevich directed his attention to the atmosphere of aviation competitions: "*Where the stands are colored with flags, / Where the people, the orchestra, and the buffet are*" ("To an Aviator," 1914; Khodasevich, *Sobranie sochinenii*, 1:183). Mass culture and the theatricalization of events in turn had their effect on the commercial aspect, the cost of tickets and the amount of prize money available. Aviation quickly became quite profitable, though still a dangerous enterprise.

The Aesthetics of Public Death

The risk of death made it impossible for competition organizers to play tricks. In the sporting hierarchy, flight moved from the sphere of magical illusions to the plane of relations between heaven and earth, with the accompanying metaphysical connotations. Something that was fundamentally new in flight, as compared with the reception of circus shows, was overcoming the boundaries of what was possible. The enraptured viewer saw the conquering of space in an apparent *transgression* (*prestuplenie*), in the etymological sense. Over time this semantic intonation dissipated and the demonic element faded into the background, but the theme of the ominous human experiment remained, periodically returning in instances when audience members died, and later being resurrected with new force after the dawn of aerial attacks and bombings of cities.

It is difficult to discern any psychological underpinnings in the string of clearly technological accidents that occurred in the 1910s, but poetry does have a tendency to "deduce" from the facts its own version of the motivations. When V. F. Smit's plane crashed in 1911 the crowd of stunned onlookers included the pilot's young wife, whom he had married five days before. Poetry projected the pilot's death onto the knightly plot of a death in a duel with the Beautiful Lady present:

Why were you in the sky, *brave one*,
For your first and last time?

FIGURE 4.7 *A photograph of Louis Blériot's aeroplane after an accident at Reims, August 1909. George Grantham Bain Collection, Library of Congress.*

So that the *worldly, procurable lioness*
Would raise to you the violets of her eyes?
                    (A. Blok, "Aviator," 1910–12; Blok,
                    Polnoe sobranie sochinenii v 8 tt., 3:34)

The rhetoric of love in this poem originates in a loose Russian translation of Baudelaire's poem, "Les Plaintes d'un Icare," which, back-translated into English, reads as follows:

In the embraces of procurable love
Life is carefree and easy,
While I – mad and brave –
Once again embrace the clouds.
                    (translated by Ellis; Baudelaire [Bodler], *Tsvety zla*, 130)

Erotic flare is of great importance in aviation literature. In the overwhelming majority of instances the sky takes on feminine features; it is often associated with a giant bed[25] with biblical silks and byssus (calling to mind

---

[25]Which can be reduced to the space of the airplane as well, as in Severianin's poem "Nelly" (July 1911): "Oh, when could a couch fit into a Bleriot!" (*Poeziia russkogo futurizma*, 340).

the amorous games in the "Song of Solomon"), where coitus takes place ("And to somersault in spasms on a biplane, / Two wildly roaring machines of chance / In the air in frenzied copulation"; Zenkevich, *Skazochnaia era*, 152). Meanwhile, the phallic force is clearly embodied by the male pilot ("I trod / With a biplane on the skirt of the waltzing clouds! ... / And *my torment is long, like the trunk of an elephant*"; "Faster"; Shershenevich, *Listy imazhinista*, 118–119). The male pilot in turn can be ruined by the embraces of the insidious sky, who takes the form of a seductive coquette ("And the ghost of a girl, bowing, wiped / The pre-death sweat from the face of the pale man"; Zenkevich, *Skazochnaia era*, 151). Thus in *Ada* we see that the airplane is a striking detail in the amorous correspondence between Ada and Veen. In a letter dated 1890 Ada requests that the recipient use the most advanced possible technology to come to her immediately:

> Take the fastest flying machine you can rent straight to El Paso, your Ada will be waiting for you there, waving like mad, and we'll continue, by the New World Express, in a suite I'll obtain, to the burning tip of Patagonia, Captain Grant's Horn, a Villa in Verna, my jewel, my agony.
>
> (*Ada*, 334)

Love for the nearby feminine was succeeded by love for the nearby masculine: flight provided the notion of an aerial baptism (based in part on the superficial resemblance of the propeller and the cross; due to the perpendicular structure of the wings, the airplane itself looks like a cross in the sky from the ground). It comes as no surprise that the symbolism of *christening* and its protective functions are preserved even after the Christian connotations, associated with Christians fighting wild animals in the pagan arenas of Rome, had long been removed from the poetics of aviation:

> And, amid the burning heavens,
> Yellow like gold,
> The singing crosses
> Of people flying into the dawn.
>
> ("Winged," 1912; Gippius, *Stikhotvoreniia*, 195)[26]

---

[26]It was traditional for a propeller to be affixed to the grave of a pilot, e.g.: "That on the grave the broken propeller / Would lay its stormy blade like a cross" (Zenkevich, *Skazochnaia era*, 137). The religious component of airplane symbolism was remarked on by Lawrence Goldstein who maintained that once "human beings accomplished heavier-than-air flight a new order of religious feeling evolved in which elect members of the community who participated in the mysteries of the winged life experienced the ecstasy resulting from an immediate apprehension of the infinite. Inevitably, the new forms of magical flight began to challenge the icons which preceded them – the Romantic bird, the risen Christ – for cultural dominance" (Goldstein, *The Flying Machine*, 3).

The first flights staged at horse tracks, as no other type of public competition, invited comparisons with the romantic image of the lone hero, the poet/tightrope walker elevated above the crowd. This is even more true if we consider the fact that the aerial space required a right of way. The rupture between the high and the low, the insignificant everyday life of the townspeople and the world of the heavenly firmament, was grotesquely emphasized by the "poet of the sky," Kamenskii:

> What kind of public are you – strange and rough –
> I know that I bore you with Height –
> Borne on an airplane I Warsaw I
> Often saw below the ant-like pile.
>
> ("Vasilii Kamenskii – A Living Monument," 1916;
> *Poeziia russkogo futurizma*, 254)

This contemptuous view is opposed by the point of view of the pedestrian, with whom the "earthly" poets were concerned, from Briusov[27] to Nabokov: "There over the roofs, in the deep / Sky" ("The Airplane," 1926).

The semantics of the ontological conflict between heaven and earth were weakened as the aviation theme and its symbolic weight moved from the headlines of newspapers to the current events and crossword sections, i.e., as the flying machine became a part of everyday life. The protagonist of Nabokov's short story, "A Dashing Fellow," is unable to remember the name of the father of aviation (*Stories*, 259); in *The Gift* Godunov-Cherdyntsev is entirely indifferent in noting "the exact spot where a small airplane fell the other day: someone who was taking his girl for a morning ride in the blue got overexuberant, lost control of his joystick, and plunged with a screech and a crackle straight into the pines" (*The Gift*, 302).

By the time Fyodor arrives,

> they had had time to clear up the wreckage, < ... > but one could still see the imprint of a daring death beneath the pines, one of which had been shaved from top to bottom by a wing < ... >; but a few days later all traces had disappeared (there was only the yellow wound on the pine tree), and already in complete ignorance an old man and his old woman facing each other—she in her bodice and he in his underpants—were doing uncomplicated gymnastics on the same spot.
>
> (ibid.)

The lightning-fast death rhymes with the transience of oblivion, and the aerial acrobatics of the pilot and his femme fatale are travestied in the unpretentious exercises of the elderly couple.

---

[27]"High above the city, / In a proud flight crossing, / Like strange birds, / Monoplanes soar" ("Monoplanes," 1918; Briusov, *Sobranie sochinenii*, 3:504).

Death of the Pilot

The disturbing growth in the number of aviation-related deaths in the early years of flight forced one critic to state that "along with the rapid increase in the successes of aviation, along with the continuing increase in world records, the numbers of victims left on the field of humanity's battle with the element of air also, unfortunately, continues to grow" (*Ezhegodnik gazety* Rech' *na 1912*, St. Petersburg, 513). Statistics show that during the first three years of global aviation (1908–10), there were thirty-four deaths, while in 1911 alone the number increased to ninety-seven. As A. Monoszon wrote in his analytical article: "the months of May–August [1911] were particularly unlucky: on average, an air crash with a human victim occurred almost every other day" (ibid.). As for Russia, the picture of the fateful year for the history of domestic aviation was vividly conveyed by Blok in the introduction to *Retribution* (1919), where he wrote that 1911, when aviation "was particularly fashionable," stuck in his memory as a series of "beautiful aerial loops, upside-down flights, falls and deaths of talented and untalented aviators" (Blok, *Polnoe sobranie sochinenii v 8 tt.*, 3:296–297). The Russian aviation martyr list, which in 1910 contained just a single name (captain L. M. Matsievich), in 1911 swelled to six: the brothers Matyevich-Matseevich, V. F. Smit, G. Shimanskii, Zolotukhin, and Rudnev. A significant number of Russian pilots, including Vasil'ev, Segno, Utochkin, Kotin, Lerkhe, and others, sustained serious injuries in crashes.

During the early years of flight a crash was essentially part of the spectacle, the dramatic climax of the event, and also an entirely predictable occurrence.[28] Accidents took on heroic and mythical connotations, and the abundantly detailed descriptions shocked the salon-reared public of the 1910s. The naturalist literary tendencies in aviation texts appeared in a jocular manner in the poetry of Zenkevich,[29] while Kruchenykh attempted to transfer the shock therapy of the airfield to the theatrical stage.[30]

---

[28]The author of an article entitled "Reasons for Airplane Crashes," who signed simply as "O," admits that "accidents involving flying machines, due to deficiencies in their design, are a *normal phenomenon* at present" and also calls for more stringent standards for candidates to earn the title of pilot or aviator, pointing out that "it is highly desirable for individuals designated to undergo training for airplane flight to *first take the exam required to become a bicyclist or a chauffeur*: bicycling teaches people to instinctively sense and avoid danger, while the automobile teaches one to sense speed and provides the opportunity to quickly control the machine with a steering wheel, levers, and pedals" (*Vozdukhoplavatel'. Organ Imperatorskogo vserossiiskogo aerokluba*. 1911. № 3).

[29]"After the speed of lightning in motionless calm / He lay in a crater in the debris of the motor, / A smoking kebab of human meat" ("Death of an Aviator," 1922; Zenkevich, *Skazochnaia era*, 137).

[30]Planning how to mimic an air crash on stage, Kruchenykh wrote the following stage directions for his opera, *Victory over the Sun*: "Deafening noise. An airplane falls. A broken wing is visible on the stage. Cries: "Z ... Z ... Knocking ... knocking ... A woman has been crushed" (*Russkii futurism*, 256).

FIGURE 4.8 *"The discovery of the law of gravitation." Illustration by artist Louis Glackens shows a Wright Brothers airplane crashed into a tree with Sir Isaac Newton and another man in the wreckage on the ground. Published on the cover of* Puck, *vol. 68, no. 1753 (October 5, 1910).*

On aggregate, shocking inventions prepared the ground for the *language of violence* in which the Russian avant-garde began to speak after the First World War. We see this clearly in the response garnered in Russian literature by the feat of military pilot P. N. Nesterov (1887–1914), who in 1913 was the first to complete the "loop of death," and on September 8, 1914 was the first to use a battering ram in an aerial battle.

Although not every crash resulted in the death of the pilot, the event of the crash in the eyes of the everyday public was steeped in the same mythological aura, which Nabokov subsequently demythologizes. In *Ada*, Van Veen's father, Demon, dies in an airplane crash. Van finds out about the March 1905 tragedy while reading a newspaper in Nice, but for some time he remains unaware that his father is among the dead: "In the fourth or fifth worst airplane disaster of the young century, a gigantic flying machine had inexplicably disintegrated at fifteen thousand feet above the Pacific" (*Ada*, 504). Nabokov focuses on the "odd fascination" with which Van delves into the inventory "of labeled lives" (ibid., 505). Among the victims are presidents, vice presidents, and managers of large companies, industrialists, professors, and reporters:

> The names of those big shots, as well as those of some eighty other men, women, and silent children who perished in blue air, were being withheld until all relatives had been reached; but the tabulatory preview of commonplace abstractions had been thought to be too imposing not to be given at once as an appetizer; and only on the following morning did Van learn that a bank president lost in the closing garble was his father.
>
> (ibid.)

While the character interestedly analyzes the "labeled lives," his creation seems to be captivated by the scale of the catastrophe and the seeming lack of causality and predictability. The reasons for the accident "above the smiling ocean" (ibid., 506) do not stem from natural causes or the psychological or familial vicissitudes in the lives of those involved. The victims include typical passengers and the powerful,[31] regardless of social origin, including a person of royal blood, as is also the case in *Pale Fire*. King Alfin had a passion for "mechanical things, especially for flying apparatuses" (*Pale Fire*, 84), which he passed on to his son (who with his father, "the melancholy, riding-breeched aviator" [ibid., 83] in a 1918 Christmas photograph is holding "the little monoplane of chocolate"). In 1912 the king flew in an umbrella-shaped "Fabre 'hydroplane'" and almost drowned in the sea. Over the course of his career as a pilot he managed to destroy two Farmans, three Zembla machines, and his beloved Santos-Dumont Demoiselle. But his "bird of doom," as Kinbote calls it, was the original "Blenda IV" monoplane built in 1916 by the "aerial adjutant" Peter Gusev (the plane was named

---

[31]Cf. the story with a happy ending, told in *Other Shores*, of Konstantin Dmitrievich Nabokov at the last minute returning his ticket for the *Titanic* and thus avoiding the fate of the 1,503 remaining passengers who perished on April 15, 1912 when the ship sank (*Russian Collected Works*, 5:177).

after the queen of Zembla, while the name of the "pioneer parachutist" Gusev [from the Russian word for "goose"] seems to be a parody of the happenstance clustering of "bird" surnames among Russian aviators, such as the real pilots Utochkin [from *utka*, duck] and Lebedev [from *lebed'*, swan]):

> On the serene, and not too cold, December morning that the angels chose to net his mild pure soul, King Alfin was in the act of trying solo a tricky vertical loop that Prince Andrey Kachurin, the famous Russian stunter and War One hero, had shown him in Gatchina. Something went wrong, and the little Blenda was seen to go into an uncontrolled dive. Behind and above him, in a Caudron biplane, Colonel Gusev (by then Duke of Rahl) and the Queen snapped several pictures of what seemed at first a noble and graceful evolution but then turned into something else. At the last moment, King Alfin managed to straighten out his machine and was again master of gravity when, immediately afterwards, he flew smack into the scaffolding of a huge hotel which was being constructed in the middle of a coastal heath as if for the special purpose of standing in a king's way.
>
> (ibid., 84–85)

Nabokov devises a special constructivist monument that the queen erects at the site of the accident: she orders the frame of the building taken down, replacing it with "a tasteless monument of granite surmounted by an improbable type of aircraft made of bronze" (ibid., 85). It is unclear just to what extent the mythology of Zembla reflects the Russian realia of Nabokov's youth, but at least King Alfin's interest in the experiments of Prince Kachurin cannot help but call to mind the excitement of the Romanovs with early flight in Russia. In 1909–10 Grand Prince Aleksandr Mikhailovich allocated 2 million rubles for aviation, and when planning the ministerial budget for 1913, owing to his influence, the decision was made to reserve an additional 15 million rubles for aircraft in the military (Dimitroff, *Give Russia Wings*, 452). In May 1913 Sikorskii executed the first flight on the largest four-engine plane at the time, the "Grand," which held fifteen passengers, was equipped with a kitchen, and could remain aloft without refueling for twenty hours. After some hesitation, Nikolai II decided to view the craft himself and was photographed next to the plane on August 8 that year (Finne, *Igor Sikorsky*, 28). The royal visit was accompanied by the renaming of the plane in a more patriotic manner: the "Russian Knight." The tsar liked the invention, and signified this fact a month later by giving the resourceful aviator a gold case with the Russian coat of arms decorated in diamonds (*Sankt-peterburgskie vedomosti*. September 23, 1913; Dimitroff, *Give Russia Wings*, 456). The improved version of the gargantuan airplane, now renamed the *Il'ia Muromets* after the legendary

Russian hero, completed a flight from St. Petersburg to Kiev on June 30, 1914. After landing in Petersburg on the return trip, Sikorskii was met by the tsar himself, who awarded the pilot with the Order of St. Vladimir and a gift of 100,000 rubles (Cochrane et al., *The Aviation Careers*, 42–43).

The tragedy involving members of a royal family may have been described by Nabokov based on his childhood recollections of an aviation disaster that occurred in May 1911 at the Issy-les-Moulineaux airfield near Paris in front of more than a hundred thousand spectators. The newspaper *Rech'*, edited by Nabokov's father, devoted an unprecedented number of reports (dozens) and articles to the drama in France, and all Russians who were even remotely interested in the future of aviation were talking about the details of the event. The accident occurred at the start of an international flight from Paris to Madrid involving twenty planes. A pilot named Train reached a height of 10 meters, but decided to turn back due to engine trouble. After making an incomplete circle, Train began to descend, but the wing blocked his view of the runway and he cut through a group of officials standing right in the take-off area. Among the high-ranking observers were the French Prime Minister Monis, the war minister Berteaux, generals Maunoury and Roques, the nephew of a former minister and publisher of *Le Petit Parisien*, Dupuis, as well as members of the jury. Russian journalists, writing before the development of an ethical self-censorship on such matters, reveled in the details of the gruesome injuries, particularly the mutilation of Berteaux, who died on site. The war minister inadvertently

> raised his hand, and the propeller of the monoplane seized it, tore it off, and tossed it to the side. The propeller simultaneously broke his spine, then shattered it into pieces. The wing of the plane took hold of Monis and the Prime Minister sustained the following injuries: both tibiae were broken, his femur and nose were injured, and his eyelids were torn off; the eyes, fortunately, remained unharmed.
>
> ([Unsigned] "Aviatsionnaia katastrofa vo Frantsii." *Rech'*. May 9 (22), 1911. № 125)

A more humane correspondent reported that Monis has been transported to the Ministry of Internal Affairs and had sustained a "broken leg and a completely mutilated face." The competition was immediately called off and the stunned crowd began to disperse. After receiving the tragic news, Berteaux's wife, according to a wire report, "fell into a deep swoon. She was soon visited by President of the Republic Fallières and Grand Prince Aleksandr Mikhailovich. All events in honor of the arrival of King Peter of Serbia have been cancelled" (ibid.). The chilling details were retold based on the words of Antoine Monis, the son of the minister, who "seeing the plane approaching him at dizzying speed ... pushed his father hard; the latter fell and, perhaps for this reason, remained alive. When A. Monis looked, he *saw the severed arm of Berteaux floating in a pool of blood, and Berteaux's body several paces away from it"* (ibid.).

The focus on the hand as the "strong point" is brought about by a number of things, not the least of which is the stylistics of film that had become entrenched by the 1910s. Semantic perspective (a term used in avant-garde art theory to indicate that the size of an object in a picture is determined by its symbolic importance rather than its actual proportions) captures the attention of the viewer, distorting the diction of the Russian correspondent who reverses the primary and secondary objects, as if the body is part of the arm rather than vice versa.

Analyzing the fictional list of victims in the air disaster in *Ada*, which also includes presidents and vice presidents, we notice that the basis of Nabokov's methods for working with a literary extract is a confluence of quotations and concentration of facts. Nabokov's work with documentary insertions corresponds to how Shklovskii in 1929 described Tolstoy's use of historical materials to achieve the desired effect through an accumulation and rearrangement of details and by silencing motivations and "tossing out psychology" (Shklovskii, *Mater'ial i stil'*, 180), which Nabokov also pushes aside to the margins of his drafts. Right through to his old age, Nabokov had nightmares about airplane crashes, as we see in a diary entry from October 19, 1964:

> I was able to recall only one image, at the edge of waking, hardly a proper dream, unconnected unrealities, rudiments or remnants – specifically, a vague image of something white and resembling a propeller on a chair, in a dark alley; and the words "kars" (or "kans") and "Etan" in another part of the dream. Webster says that "Etana" was a Babylonian astronaut who, trying to reach the sky on an eagle, got scared, fell, and was killed.

In the entry for the next day, Nabokov connects this dream with a report he read later: "In the *New York Times* I read about the death of several Red Army officers in a plane crash near Belgrade. The plane crashed into a mountain in the fog, and one engine fell onto the forest road leading to the top of Avala mountain. Cf. yesterday's dream. Not bad?"[32]

War in the Air

By the middle of the 1910s it would no longer have occurred to anyone, as a reader of *Rech'*, to dispute the opinion of the pessimists with regard to the

---

[32]Berg Collection. "Notes for a Work in Progress." Remarks regarding: Dunne J. W. *An Experiment With Time* [1927]. London: Faber Ltd., 1973.

new mode of transportation, avowing that "aviation is no longer a toy or an amusement, but a serious thing with a great future, which we must think about and work on" (A. Monozson, "Flight." *Ezhegodnik gazety* Rech' *na 1912*, St. Petersburg, 511). Successful attempts had been made to use the airplane in marine contexts, with wireless telegraphs, and for carrying mail, but many in the military were particularly interested in its application, initially as a reconnaissance tool, and later as a weapon for surprise attacks. In 1914, the journal, *Vozdukhoplavatel'* (*Flyer*), № 6, reprinted an article from the German *Flugsport* entitled "The Flying Machine as a Weapon of Attack," which specifically stated that arming a plane with machine guns would create "the entirely natural need to outfit the latter with armor." H. G. Wells's recent predictions in his book *Anticipations* (see chapter 6, "War in the Twentieth Century"), which Zamiatin tells us was followed closely by the Russian intelligentsia, had seemingly begun to come true:

> By day the victor's aeroplanes will sweep down upon the apparatus of all sorts in the adversary's rear, and will drop explosives and incendiary matters upon them, so that no apparatus or camp or shelter will any longer be safe. < ... > A general advance will occur under the aerial van, ironclad road fighting-machines may perhaps play a considerable part in this. < ... > Under the moonlight and the watching balloons there will be swift noiseless rushes of cycles.
>
> (Wells, *Anticipations of the Reaction*, 196–197)

Subsequent issues of the magazine vividly described the battle between German and English pilots: a scene almost straight out of a fairy-tale speaks to the early stage at which aviation happenings coalesced into a topos, embellished by tall tales, so-called "events from life" (*sluchai iz zhizni*). The memoirs of Russian general Baron Kaul'bars provide a unique retrospective on the real-world difficulties faced during the First World War by both pilots and military design engineers.[33]

The fatal shift in aviation, rapidly grown out of its circus net, was reacted to by poetry with an ambivalent mixture of horror and naïve fascination. The catastrophic potential of flight was both frightening and captivating. Blok, an aesthete by nature, wrote in a letter to his wife (August 7, 1916)

---

[33]In the chapter "War in the Air" in an unpublished work prepared as a history and training aid for military pilots, Kaul'bars writes: "At the beginning of the Great War only a few brave pilots in one-seater planes dared to engage in battle in the air, and it was not infrequent for both combatants to die when their own planes crashed" (Kaul'bars, *Vozdushnaia voina*, 60–62).

FIGURE 4.9 *Russian poster showing fighter plane in flight, with man standing to fire mounted machine gun. The caption reads: "Sign up for a military loan, help achieve victory!" Petrograd, 1916. Color Lithograph.*

about aerial attacks that he had witnessed: "In the evening and the next morning ... airplanes were fired on – *beautiful explosions of shrapnel around the plane.* Both times it was driven off and dropped no bombs." A few days later he wrote to his mother: "An airplane sometimes circles over the field, shining yellow, and around it a haze of shrapnel, quite beautiful"

(Blok, *Pis'ma A. Bloka k ego rodnym*, 2:468; 472).[34] The tonality of the interpretation changed over time: "From the heights of a plane / Will I really engage in aesthetics?" is the exclamation from a character in a dialog with the devil, pointing from the clouds at a pile of fresh corpses on the ground (T. Podkuz'mikhin [F. F. Syromolotov]; "On a Plane"; *Proletarskie poety*, 2). The roar of a plane is unambiguously interpreted as a "terrible phantom on high … forging death day and night" (Blok, *Polnoe sobranie sochinenii v 8 tt.*, 3:305–306). This becomes particularly noticeable after the Russian Civil War and during the Second World War, when a rigidly destructive meaning is attached to the airplane in poetry.[35]

Prompted by popular fads for space exploration and militarism in the 1920s, the mood revived the futurists' old "airplane myths" in their memories, while the future air war apocalypse described by Maiakovskii in "Flying Proletariat" (with pilots in place of warring angels) was in its own way a response to the aviation agitprop of the time (Vaiskopf, *Vo ves' logos*, 141). In a poem by Dits, what stands out apart from the banal rhyming in the Russian original is the imperative, beset with a forceful threat, towards an astral unity of all peoples:

> The proletariat is measuring the air,
> The rhythm of engines is keenly clear.
> The winged have no accidents,
> Strong wind does not frighten them!
> We will command the distances of the sky,
> Our wings will cut the air.
> We will bind the threads of brotherhood.
> The squadron boldly soars!
>
> (*Vozdushnyi flot.* 1923. № 1–2)

The air fleet, placed by the Party into the service of revolutionary ideology, not only confirmed the might of the new Soviet republic, but also assured that it would spread to a planetary scale. The basic provisions of the new direction were quickly shifted to the realm of religious rhetoric. In painting and graphic arts, Rodchenko completed a series of advertising posters and design materials ordered by the "Dobrolet" government corporation from

---

[34]See G. Apolliner's war cycle entitled *Calligrams. Poems of Peace and War* (1918): "German grenades bloomed in a constellation / In a magical forest where we now live a ball / The machine gun stopped its furious staccato / They're finally signaling for the dances to start … / Throwing a thousand fragments from the heights" ("April Night 1915"; Apolliner, *Esteticheskaia khirurgiia*, 115). In statistical terms: Russia had 263 military planes at the start of the First World War, Germany had 232, and France had 156.

[35]"Now the heavy rumble of planes – / A distant threat, closer and more audible, / And the sky gives a wide path / Under a flock of deadly cranes" (T. Ratgauz, "First Year of the Second World War," 1939–40; *Antologiia poezii russkogo zarubezh'ia*, 3:351–352).

1923–5. In poetry Maiakovskii and his numerous proletarian imitators approached the energy of mantras as they conjured the future:

> From the proud cities: airplanes,
> A steel flock of solar dragonflies,
> To worlds above the stars, to unknown lands
> A living, quivering bridge.
>   (A. P. Kraiskii, "Borders of the Future," 1920; *Proletarskie poety*, 407)

The Russian word *nebozhitel'* ("sky/heaven-dweller") lost its religious exclusiveness,[36] transformed from the meaning given in Dal's nineteenth-century dictionary of "one resurrected in eternity" to a meaning of "temporary inhabitant of the sky." The word gradually recoded its own semantics into a complete negation (*ne bozhitel'*: "not a godder"), supplanted into aviation nomenclature (cf. Khodasevich: "You are carried in smooth ascents / A sky-dweller – a hero – a man" ["To an Aviator," 1914; Khodasevich, *Sobranie sochinenii*, 1:183], and Sel'vinskii's verse novel: "The pilot, hanging in a loop in a biplane, / For an instant became a *sky-dweller*"). Certain changes reflected in the poetic lexicon also speak to shifts in artistic and societal awareness.

The Futurist Thesaurus

Along with the emergence of the technical slang of pilots in the 1910s there was a shift of futurist language away from standard Russian. The airplane made it possible to look at the earth as a carte blanche:

> They let me fly in an airplane to the Don. ... *From above the river looks like a signature flourish. Nothing is written in the margins* [also "fields" in Russian]. *The Moscow River was signed on the whole page.*
>   (Shklovskii, *Gamburgskii schet*, 142)

The first issue of the aviation magazine, *Sportivnaia zhizn'* (*Sporting Life*), in 1910 included a special article entitled "On Words," in which an anonymous author called for logical order in the use of aviation terminology. For example, he believed the use of the word *vozdukhoplan* (based on the Russian root *vozdukh*, for air) instead of *aeroplan* was absurd. Why, the author wonders,

---

[36]Cf. Iazykov's 1825 "Elegy": "In vain from the heaven-dwellers / Did I ask for a simple share" (Iazykov, *Stikhotvoreniia i poemy*, 140); and Tiutchev's "Cicero": "He is the viewer of their lofty spectacles, / He was admitted to their council, / And alive as a *heaven-dweller*, / He drank from the cup of their immortality!" (Tiutchev, *Polnoe sobranie stikhotvorenii*, 105).

FIGURE 4.10 *Farman airplane, 1908. George Grantham Bain Collection, Library of Congress.*

should the "classic word" *aviator* (cognate with the identical English word) be replaced by words with Slavic roots for flight such as *letun, letchik,* or *letatel'*? The editors of *Novoe vremia* are also singled out for publishing material that opened with a short story about a "new pilot-aviator" (both words identical to the English equivalents), who six sentences later is referred to as a "bold *letun*" (see Dimitroff, *Give Russia Wings,* 36–37). As the anonymous observer rightly notes, if the word "aviator" is expunged from the Russian language merely because of its foreign origin, then one also has to get rid of a number of nouns that are already part of everyday conversation, including *aeroplan* (airplane), *aerodrom* (airfield/aerodrome), *magneto,* and *monoplan* (monoplane), but also the very word *aviatsiia* (aviation). Such verbal purges, the author continues, would in the end inevitably result in replacing the universally accepted Russian word *Aero-Klub* with *Vozdukhosobranie,* a bizarre neologism based on the analogous Slavic roots. And yet there were suggestions to go even further and establish official instructions for the use of words in the new field of aviation, which would then be distributed to the editorial boards of periodical publications ("Terminology in the Field of Russian Flight," *Vozdukhoplavatel'.* 1912. № 5, 335). The editor of the Imperial All-Russian Air Club's publication, *Flyer* (*Vozdukhoplavatel'*), Veigelin correctly predicted in 1912 that *aeroplan* was destined to be forced out by *samolet* ("self-flyer") in the national air fleet, but he also believed that verbs of motion were a far more complicated matter. He proposed that the word *otlet* ("fly-away") be used only for the start of a hot air balloon flight, and *vzlet* ("fly-up") be used to describe an airplane leaving the ground (see Dimitroff, *Give Russia Wings*, 39, 29, notes).

Aviation took on the features of a trademark: the airplane represented the final word in technology and destroyer of mundaneness, influencing mores and stocking the thesaurus with metaphors;[37] the pilot in turn was looked on as all but the legislator of verbal fashions.[38] Kamenskii gave a talk entitled "Airplanes and Futurist Poetry" about "the influence of technological innovations on contemporary poetry" and how airplanes, "by making the earth smaller, provide a new conception of the modern world" (Kamenskii, *Tango s korovami*, 471; on the elimination of space and time as elements of the "colonizing spirit," see Goldstein, *The Flying Machine*, 145). On May 25, 1916 in the House of Arts and Sciences in Tsarytsin, the futurist poet Petrovskii, accompanied by V. Tatlin (whom Velimir Khlebnikov would ultimately call "the seer of blades / And the stern singer of the propeller, / From the ranks of the suncatchers") delivered a talk entitled "Iron Wings," with the first section called "The Days of Icarus." Khlebnikov was interested in aviation primarily from the standpoint of lexical creation. Trying to stall foreign language expansion and the inevitable pollution of the native Russian with technological calques, Khlebnikov suggested alternative terms based on the native Slavic *-let-* lexeme for flight: for aviator he proposed *letailo*, and instead of *prazdnik aviatsii* ("aviation holiday") he offered *letina*, and by analogy with *strel'bishche* (a shooting ground): *letalishche*. Even after many years, the treatment of flight in poetry, according to Nabokov, who acerbically cited the ending of Evgenii Shakh's poem in a review, required increased tact and attentiveness both to words and to the rules for combining them: "The same arduous, fateful, reasoned turmoil as his colleagues, and the syntax is the same, the techniques are the same, and the boredom is the same. His poem 'The Aviator,' which ends with the line 'He does not take off his leather helmet, so nobody will see his face,' is simply very bad" (*Russian Collected Works*, 3:694).

It is difficult to imagine what Russian neologisms Nabokov himself would have chosen to adequately translate the aviation terms he invents in *Ardor*. In the made-up world of Terra and Antiterra, Van and Ada fly on something between a magic carpet and a primitive little plane stored in the attic:

Rolled up in its case was an old "jikker" or skimmer, a blue magic rug with Arabian designs, faded but still enchanting, which Uncle Daniel's father had used in his boyhood and later flown when drunk. Because of

---

[37]Which quickly turned into official administrative terms: postal services invented a special word for envelopes delivered by air: *aeropis'mo* (aeroletter) (*Rech'*. February 18, 1912, 112).

[38]Cf. Elena Guro: "Wind-racer, raver, flyer, / creator of spring storms, / sculptor of tumultuous thoughts, / chasing the azure" (*Russkii futurizm*, 140).

the many collisions, collapses and other accidents, especially numerous in sunset skies over idyllic fields, jikkers were banned by the air patrol; but four years later Van who loved that sport bribed a local mechanic to clean the thing, reload its hawking-tubes, and generally bring it back into magic order and many a summer day would they spend, his Ada and he, hanging over grove and river or gliding at a safe ten-foot altitude above surfaces of roads or roofs. How comic the wobbling, ditch-diving cyclist, how weird the arm-flailing and slipping chimney sweep!

(*Ada*, 44)

The overcoming of gravity (the metaphor of flight as artistic inspiration) harks back to passages in Nabokov's *Lectures on Literature* and his private correspondence (Nabokov, *Selected Letters*, 78), wherein Nabokov compares the writer to a magician (the image of the time rug in *Other Shores/Speak, Memory*, which the creator folds in such a way that patterns superimpose; *Speak, Memory*, 139).

Given Nabokov's inclination towards literary hoaxes and his heightened awareness of ancient Russian texts while translating *The Lay of Igor's Campaign* (1952), we might assume that in this novel written from 1963–68 we hear echoes of the ideologically motivated surge of interest in a nineteenth-century forgery in the Soviet Union in the early 1950s. A manuscript entitled "On Aerial Flight in Russia from 906 AD," forged by A. I. Sulakadzev (for more, see Nevskaia, "Slovesnoe vozdukhoplavanie," 1994, 22), described how in Ryazan in 1731 a scrivener named Kriakutnoi made a "furvin" in which "an evil force lifted him to the sky above the birch trees." In 1951, the magazine *Ogonek* devoted much space to marking the 220-year anniversary of Kriakutnoi's flight. In an essay on the occasion, a professor named Anoshchenko stated that, thanks to Sulakadzev, "the whole now knows that our great Motherland should rightly be considered the birthplace of modern flight" (*Ogonek*. 1951. № 39, 9). Anoshchenko blamed Western historians for supposedly intentionally silencing "the remarkable achievements of Russian inventors," despite the fact that "the flight testing of Kriakutnoi's first hot-air balloon was performed in Russia fifty-two years before the Montgolfier brothers' 'invention' of a similar type of aerial flight in France" (ibid., 9).

The conflict of East and West in aviation texts emerged far earlier than was acknowledged by the members of the Soviet anniversary committee: Merezhkovskii's book *Sick Russia* devotes a whole section ("Earth in the Mouth") to the question: "will we fly or will we not?" Merezhkovskii cites Zheliabuzhskii notes on an unsuccessful attempt by a Russian peasant man in spring 1695 to fly on homemade wings of mica (his expenses had been paid from the state treasury, so he was beaten as punishment). The section also recalls Leonardo da Vinci's drawings of flying machines from the Biblioteca Ambrosiana, which Merezhkovskii came to know of at the same time as his own first experience of aviation. The basic point of his question "Will we fly?" concerns not the practice of flight, but the extent to which Russia will participate "in the pan-human freedom that wants to be embodied in wings" (Merezhkovskii, *Bol'naia Rossiia*, 189). The author answers his own question in the negative, but finds consolation in the words of Viacheslav Ivanov: "visionaries in the East and the West agree that in our very time the Slavic world, and especially Russia, have been passed some sort of torch; whether our people will lift it or drop it – that is a question for the fates of the world" (ibid., 190). Merezhkovskii compares the Russian idea with the notion of the harmonious technological and spiritual ascent of America:

> The first inventors of the airplane, Americans, Orville and Wilbur Wright, were sons of a Puritan minister from Dayton, Ohio – the descendants of the puritans who conquered the New World.
>
> True to the faith of their fathers, the Wright Brothers would never fly on Sunday, the day of the Lord: on this day they pray for the Lord to bless their humble and holy work, their humble and holy ascent.
>
> The extreme boundary of ascent, of freedom, is flight. Western culture was able to reach this boundary for the very reason that the Lord appeared to it not in "the form of a servant," but as the Liberator of nations, the King of kings, approaching in the clouds with much glory and strength.
>
> (ibid., 195)

A conceptually similar set of motives is put forth by the Russian aviator poet: "I decided to fly on an airplane. The poet liked this undertaking immediately: he had been sorely missing the Spirit searching for flights – flights of the body above the clouds, missing purposeful freedom in the sky" ("Ego – moia biografiia," 1918; Kamenskii, *Ego – moia biografiia*, 109).

Russians could thus get by without enigmatic technologies, relying on "some sort of torch," a time-tested epic force. During the First World War, when Germany effortlessly took out Imperial Russian Army posts from the air, an optimistic printed circular (*lubok*) appeared:

> The rough and red-haired German
> Scattered in the air over Warsaw,
> And the Cossack Danilo Dikii
> Sharpened his lance,
> And now his wife Polina
> Sews pants out of a Zeppelin.

The poster has two pictures: the first depicts the Cossack poking his spear into the Zeppelin as it soars over the city, and the second shows his wife sewing pants from the fabric that covered the dirigible.[39]

---

[39]From the Hoover Institute collection. RU/SU 154 [1914–18]. Moscow. Color 15 × 22 in.

The crisis that Merezhkovskii outlines was answered by Chukovskii, though perhaps against his own wishes. Arranging Russian literature *facing the East* (that is, demonstrating its indigenous Eastern origins), Chukovskii juxtaposes "flying" (*vzletevshii*) Russian futurism with futurism in Western Europe and shows that the connection between the Italian founders and Russian inheritors of the futurist movement is nominal. In essence, he argues, they are entirely different and dissimilar phenomena with roots in the linguistic, mythological, and religious differences in the collective cultural memory.

The poor things were energized by the same thing: monoplanes, airplanes, biplanes, but as something indifferent, formal, seemingly foreign, learned. Clearly, this was nothing of the feeling of life. Though they endlessly repeat: "Oh, we want the greatest achievements, / And then, we now have the airplane!"; Though even their own poets call themselves "airplane poets" [a reference to Fofanov's collection of that name—*Y.L.*], I repeat, this is not the main thing about them, nor is it even a tertiary thing; their root, their foundation, is elsewhere.

If you take away airplanes, engines, and cars from Marinetti, nothing is left of Marinetti, but Kruchenykh with no engine is still Kruchenykh.

Airplanes, film cameras, skyscrapers, and cars are of course also not high culture; a savage in a pot remains a savage. Futurism abroad is the offspring of such a savage in a pot. But the one from Tambov is even more savage.

In the "Donkey Tail" manifesto the "rayonist"[40] Futurists just, for the millionth time, as if on command, rattled out the same praises to the coming urban newspaper-poster-car-airplane culture, as they suddenly, seeming to lose themselves, exclaimed: "Down with the West! Long live the beautiful East!"

Why the East? Think about it ... What kind of futurism is there in the East? And why do you want airplanes if you are denying the West?

That's just the point: their airplanes are for show, and they themselves look away, as if to be whisked to the "beautiful East." ... Vasilii Kamenskii, as we have seen, is an Asian from head to toe. He sings the praises of streetcars, sewers, and asphalt, but he sings in Tatar:

"Bar Khan Nar
Bishtym
Ek-zurma
Ai-malikem!"

Such is futurism in Russia – Votyak-Persian, Bashkir-Chinese, Assyrian-Babylonian-Egyptian!

(Chukovskii, *Futuristy*, 48–49)

---

[40] Based on the theory of abstract painting formulated by the artists Larionov and Goncharova, "Luchizm" ("Rayonism," 1913).

The subsequent attacks on the Futurists reflect the position that crystallized over the next decade, originally expressed by Chukovskii, who in 1911 had openly mocked Merezhkovskii's "prayer," Fofanov's stylistic clumsiness, and Bal'mont's earthliness:

> *We need wings, but not these wings.*
> *Give us wings, give us wings,*
> *The wings of Your spirit!*[41]

Such is Merezhkovskii's prayer. Does it behoove us to sing the praises of dirigibles! And this insect pride is, if you please, ridiculous.

> *But I find these ventures pitiful,*
> *The ecstasy of human hearts is funny;*
> *On their flying sticks*
> *The Creator looks with a grin.*
> *The proud efforts are in vain.*

This is how K. M. Fofanov expresses it. Even the outward appearance of these "flying sticks" makes him feel nothing but spite. He imagines some sort of skeletons, tombs, something reptilian from a cemetery: "More buzzing rattles / In my ears from their wings, / Skeletal, long, sepulchral." Their confinement to the earth weighs them down, but it is a completely different sort of confinement: "Why did you give me an unearthly soul / And shackle me to the earth?" (Bal'mont). "This is a metaphysical sickness, and it cannot be soothed with a propeller" (Chukovskii, *Futuristy*).

In Fofanov's defense it might be said that the "airplane skeleton" is likely an early manifestation of the image of the pterodactyl fossil (see page 266, Insects, Birds, and Fish), and the comparison of flying machines to graves is more than justified given the mortality statistics at the time. In any case, Fofanov's name in this polemic is lumped in with a group of poets from a different cultural generation, which is in turn juxtaposed to Valerii Briusov, whose celebratory hymns demonstrated that he "along among Russian poets [felt] ... the conquering of the air as *his own, as a personal victory*, as an initiation into the glory of all mankind" (ibid.; italics in the original).

Nabokov sees no fundamental difference between the soaring "Russian idea" and the ascent in the popularity of the "yellow balloon" with Sigmund Freud on board. The latter, in a thinly veiled form, flashes beneath the windows of his rented Biarritz apartment: "in a roped-off section of the square, a huge custard-colored balloon was being inflated by Sigismond

---

[41]An inaccurate citation from the poem, "Prayer for Wings" (1902; Merezhkovskii, *Stikhotvoreniia i poemy*, 527).

Lejoyeux, a local aeronaut" (*Speak, Memory*, 156). On the other hand, the prospect of collective consciousness acquiring spiritual wings is present in the metaphysical landscape of *Glory* in the scene of Martin's Nietzschean trial: at the top of the mountain the protagonist must complete his first feat of glory, overcoming himself and his own fear of heights.

Overcoming Gravity: Hymn to the Airplane

Nabokov was not a fan of "science fiction" and considered it second-rate literature, with the only exception being his childhood fascination with the world of H. G. Wells, which he said was reminiscent of an urban fairy-tale. In Wells one might encounter a helmet of invisibility or a flying carpet, but the difference between his stories and those of his Russian contemporaries was that "the Londoner does not rely on magical formulas, but on himself; he sits at a drafting table, takes up a slide rule, and calculates a flying carpet" (Zamiatin, *Izbrannye*, 2:298). Nabokov, like many of his contemporaries, followed the development of the new technologies (the telephone, electricity, radio, etc.) that were fostering the technological breakthrough into the future with unwavering curiosity but also a respectful distance. Elements that can be definitively categorized as science fiction are found a number of times in Nabokov's American period. According to Nabokov's sister, Elena Sikorskaia, the only time Nabokov rented a television in his rooms at the Montreux Palace Hotel was when the Americans landed on the moon.[42]

The short story "Time and Ebb" takes place in the twenty-first century, whence the ninety-year-old protagonist looks back nostalgically at the previous century. Unlike the committed fantasy writers Wells and Verne, who tried to invent and describe plausible complex futuristic scenarios, Nabokov refrains from depicting the material world of the future. His approach is much simpler: he simply nullifies their existence. A sense of the endless rupture in the movement of civilization over just a few decades is conveyed through a defamiliarized description of phenomena that would have seemed perfectly normal to readers in the 1940s and 1950s. Hinting at the future invention of a means of teleportation that devalues the efforts of aviators, the narrator addresses the psychological and aesthetic consequences of the shift for the post-aviation generation:

> To those who have been born since the staggering discoveries of the seventies, and who thus have seen nothing in the nature of flying things save perhaps a kite or a toy balloon < ... >, it is not easy to imagine airplanes, particularly because *old photographic pictures of those*

---

[42]Letter from Elena Sikorskaia to Yuri Leving, November 22, 1998.

splendid machines in full flight lack the life which only art could have been capable of retaining—and oddly enough no great painter ever chose them as a special subject into which to inject his genius and thus preserve their image from deterioration.

(*Stories*, 585)

The interactions between changing eras and immortal art excites Nabokov much more than the speed at which distances are overcome, as we see in his study of Pushkin. In a French essay entitled "Pushkin, or the True and the Seemingly True" (1937), Nabokov declared that the era of Pushkin was the final epoch in the passage of time where our imaginations can still travel without a passport, giving details from that time that he took from painting. Elsewhere he compares his own childhood to the background of an engraving in a memory that finds a similar picture in old Russian literature (*Russian Collected Works*, 5:176; see also Leving, "Uzor vechnosti," 254–255).

The "inverted telescope" effect, providing a reverse historical perspective ("The future is but the obsolete in reverse," Nabokov writes in "Lance"; *Stories*, 635) poses the problem of interpreting the past and the distortions that inevitably result: how will our world seem to our descendants? The exhaust pipes of defunct airplanes, like fossilized animals, will acquire the status of archaeological treasures ("perhaps it is time, my friend, to view ancient snapshots, *cave drawings of trains and airplanes*, put your toys in the cupboard" [*Other Shores*, in *Russian Collected Works*, 5:324/*Speak, Memory*, 295]); circadian details will become anthropological discoveries:

In those distant days when no spot on earth was more than sixty hours' flying time from one's local airport, a boy would know planes from propeller spinner to rudder trim tab, and could distinguish the species not only by the shape of thewing tip or the jutting of a cockpit, but even by the pattern of exhaust flames in the darkness; thus vying in the recognition of characters with those mad naturesleuths—the post-Linnean systematists.

("Time and Ebb"; *Stories*, 585)

This story was written in September 1944 (published in the *Atlantic Monthly* in January 1945). The above excerpt has an autobiographical component to it, as is clear in a letter from Nabokov to his sister dated November 26, 1945. He tells her that Dmitri is sometimes capable of "forgetting everything else on earth and getting mired in aviation magazines – airplanes are for him what butterflies are for me, and based on a distant silhouette, practically based on the humming sound, he can unfailingly determine the type of plane; he loves building and assembling all manner of models" (Nabokov, *Perepiska s sestroi*, 24). Judging by his paternal pride, his son's fascination with aviation represents the next step in a familial passion for lepidoptery ("airplanes are for him what butterflies are for me") and, in a broader sense, for the study of nature in general. Dmitri's ability to classify airplanes evokes associations with the classification system of Linnaeus and his followers. The middle of the 1940s saw the peak of Nabokov's professional engagement in entomology with his work at the Harvard Museum of Comparative Zoology. Nabokov's biological turn of mind, along with his scientific intuition and synthetic approach to the study of literature, recalls the style and methods used in the early 1930s by Osip Mandel'shtam, whom Nabokov greatly esteemed. In his article, "Around Naturalists" (1932), which Nabokov could hardly have known, Mandel'shtam theorized a connection between the study of the history of views on nature and the patterns of shifts in literary styles.

In *Pnin* the shutdown of the factory pipeline for making a particular airplane model is compared with a physiological process similar to a heart stopping:

> [T]hrough the open door of the schoolroom I could see a map of Russia on the wall, books on a shelf, a stuffed squirrel, and a toy monoplane with linen wings and a rubber motor. I had a similar one but twice bigger, bought in Biarritz. *After one had wound up the propeller for some time, the rubber would change its manner of twist and develop fascinating thick whorls which predicted the end of its tether.*
>
> (*Pnin*, 177)

Nabokov took a skeptical approach to the predictions of scientists and journalists who piqued the imaginations of readers with man-made satellites, stellar runways, and international space stations (which in "Lance" [1952] he calls "strong castles in the air each complete with cookhouse and keep, set up by terrestrial nations in a frenzy of competitive confusion, phony gravitation, and savagely flapping flags"; *Stories*, 633), to a large extent repeating Gumilev's axiom about the ineffability of the ineffable.[43] In this regard, the finale of the short story "Time and Ebb" (1944), a hymn to the era of flight, to nostalgia for a lost civilization of machines, which humanity never adequately valued, shifts to human and lyrical undertones:

> Admirable monsters, great flying machines, they have gone, they have vanished like that flock of swans which passed with a mighty swish of multitudinous wings one spring night above Knights Lake in Maine, from the unknown into the unknown: swans of a by science, never seen before, never seen since—and then nothing but a lone star remained in the sky, like an asterisk leading to an undiscoverable footnote.
>
> (*Stories*, 586)

---

[43] "All of the beauty, all of the sacred meaning of the stars is in the fact that they are infinitely far from the earth and will come no closer regardless of the successes of aviation" ("Nasledie simvolizma i akmeizma" ["The Legacy of Symbolism and Acmeism"]; Gumilev, *Sobranie sochinenii*, 4:174).

Nabokov uses the same device as we saw before with regard to the train and the car: as with the cinematic technique of combining several series of images into a new moving image dense with symbols akin to Eisenstein's montage, the means of transportation imperceptibly dissolves in the text, sinking in a metonymical deck of word-symbols. The airplane is literally replaced by a star and then by a typographical asterisk. But the referent, as later in *Pale Fire*, is absent: the author suddenly annuls all previous conventions, and the unwitting reader is left to contemplate the bared device, the protruding springs of a literary trick.

Flights, Dreaming, and Waking

In the play *The Waltz Invention* (1938), the protagonist demands that the seventeen-year-old daughter of General Berg (General Gump in the English translation) be brought to him immediately: "be so kind as to inform your daughter at once that an aircraft will be sent to fetch her immediately. Where is she?"; The general responds coolly to the ultimatum: "Come, come, my good fellow – why do you frighten me like that? My daughter has never flown and, as long as I live, never shall" (*The Waltz Invention*, 105).

Nabokov's moratorium on flying takes place in a context wherein he, as he also paradoxically did with learning to drive a car, avoided the personal experience of flying. Even at a time when the passenger air fleet had become a part of everyday life for most of the world's travelers, Nabokov, who in the 1920s had celebrated planes in his poetry, still preferred the slow but reliable means of transportation by sea and land. With civilian aviation fully accessible to him as an American citizen, various arguments against it continued to crop up—financial,[44] psychological,[45] aesthetic, and philosophical. Among the reasons for choosing the week-long trip from North America to Europe in the autumn of 1959 on the ocean liner *Liberté*, Brian Bord states that Nabokov always found "the leisurely pace and the uncrowded space of transatlantic liners much more soothing than he imagined air travel must be" (Boyd, *American Years*, 393).

Nabokov took his first European flight when he was more than seventy years old. In the spring of 1971 the noise of reconstruction work at the

---

[44]At the private school Nabokov attended in New Hampshire his parents visited him by car. Cf. the letter sent in the winter of 1949: "To go there (to New Hampshire) takes forever – two days by car, a day by train, *and to fly there is quite expensive if you charter a plane*" (Nabokov, *Perepiska s sestroi*, 54).

[45]"Other venerable professors, no more well-off than I, simply board a plane and think nothing of visiting five central European countries and restaurants and being home a week later. But, like a boulder, I am for some reason difficult to lift" (letter from Nabokov to E. Sikorskaia, January 1, 1958; Nabokov, *Perepiska s sestroi*, 91).

Montreux Palace Hotel made it impossible for him to work, and he left Switzerland for the warm south of Portugal. During the flight Nabokov was captivated by the elevations and the expansive views—impressions that he quickly transferred into the finale of his new novel, *Transparent Things* (ibid., 583). In an interview a year later for *Vogue* magazine (April 1972), Nabokov was asked what he thought about "super-planes," and he answered, honestly, that "those great machines are masterpieces of technology." Nabokov also confessed that he had "never flown across the Atlantic, but [he had] had delightful hops with Swissair and Air France. They serve excellent liquor and the view at low elevations is heartbreakingly lovely" (*Strong Opinions*, 203).

In a short passage in *Transparent Things*, Nabokov uses the idea of flight to convey the "orgasm of art," a power greater than "sexual ecstasy or metaphysical panic" (*Transparent Things*, 102). The narrative is approaching collapse; Eros is merging with Thanatos. The tragedy is anticipated by Person's dream of a plane crash which, judging by the structure of the novel's conclusion, is intended to provide symmetry for the character's death in a hotel fire.

> At this moment of her now indelible dawning through the limpid door of his room he felt the elation a tourist feels, when taking off and – to use a neo-Homeric metaphor – *the earth slants and then regains its horizontal position, and practically in no spacetime we are thousands of feet above land, and the clouds (fleecy light clouds, very white, more or less widely separated) seem to lie on a flat sheet of glass in a celestial laboratory and, through this glass, far below it, bits of gingerbread earth show, a scarred hillside, a round indigo lake, the dark green of pine woods, the incrustations of villages.* Here comes the air hostess bringing bright drinks, and she is Armande who has just accepted his offer of marriage < ... > – and now *the airplane explodes with a roar and a retching cough.*
> (ibid., 102–103)

Comparing this with the author's early excursions into the aviation theme, we see that the range of new physiological sensations in this work does not fundamentally differ from those that Nabokov hypothetically reconstructed. No significant additions are made in his depiction of flight. This conclusion in turn forces us to question whether it is necessary (or, more cautiously, to what extent is it necessary) for an author to participate in the process he describes and for personal experience to influence the quality and/or verisimilitude of the aesthetic reproduced in the text. The poetics of flight perhaps fall outside the realm of personally achievable experience and belong in the world of imagination. The *Let* (*Flight*) compilation from 1923, from which we have already cited a number of works, seems to confirm this. From among the many ideologically irreproachable but artistically weak texts, the ones that stand out are those by poets far from the world of aviation: Osip Mandel'shtam's cycle and the poem "Flight" ("Polet"), by Valentin Kataev:

In a dream he flew.
And in waking
He played hoop with children:
Into poison grass
The wheel settled,
Wasp flew after wasp,
Axle passed for rose,
And a slanting garden fell supine
Under the sun all over the place.
And all over the place Santos-Dumont
Above hundreds of people
Almost fell,
As if going home,
Onto the striped track.
In a dream he flew.

And in waking,
Not like for hoops –
For real,
Bleriot landed on the grass
Near Dover;
The channel smoked from the squadrons,
The plane shifted in the film
And it was hard to find
The flickering monoplane,
There the pilot's helmet became a bullet,
There the flight became a bullet,
And in honor of the paper tail
The pilot cut the engine.

(*Let. Aviastikhi*, 18)

Kataev's monoplane dissolves into its own image on film, which in negative sheds light on the otherworldly delirium of the wounded pilot, and on the recollections of the viewer falling asleep during a silent film. The disjointed speech and montage connection to distant planes in a kind of "shutter kiss" (see the jump from the wasp to the panoramic view of the crowd) are transplanted from the language of film, the medium that definitively canonized the airplane in mass culture.

The lowering of aviation poetics by earthly passions and the petty spirit of commercialism is used as a device in Nabokov's final novel, which starkly expresses his rejection of the commercial aspect of contemporary passenger aviation. Vadim Vadimovich, the narrator of *Look at the Harlequins!* (1974), is faced with the prospect of spending five hours aboard "Aeroflot turboprop to Moscow" (*Look at the Harlequins!*, 206; as we know, the

comedic details of Soviet life in the novel were based on the impressions of
Nabokov's sister, who visited the USSR in the 1970s):

> My mood and mental condition needed strong liquor rather than another
> round of *vzlyotnyy*[46] or some nice reading matter; still I accepted a
> publicity magazine from a stout, unsmiling, bare-armed stewardess in sky
> blue, and was interested to learn that (in contrast to current triumphs)
> Russia had not done so well in the Soccer Olympics of 1912.
>
> (ibid., 207)

Nabokov spoke with annoyance at the growth of advertising in an
interview, objecting both to the inaccuracy of the picture they present and
pushy commercial agenda: "I think [the airline's] publicity department,
when advertising the spaciousness of the seat rows, should stop picturing
impossible children fidgeting between their unperturbed mother and gray-
templed stranger trying to read" (*Strong Opinions*, 203).

The above quote from the novel marks the concluding phase of the
evolution of Nabokov's attitudes toward aviation. After beginning as a
game of chance with fate, a sport for real men, a loner's feat, flight had
over a half century become an industry from which all romanticism was
irretrievably lost. We might say that it was most likely the pragmatism of
the artist that must have kept Nabokov from attempting to fly for so many
years. After living through the triumphal era of Blok's and Khodasevich's
"aviator" poems, breaking the artist's taboo, Nabokov had nothing else to
show besides restrained criticism and a poorly concealed satisfaction.

* * *

The invention and testing of the airplane, the tragic days of early aviation
history, the newspaper reports and oral accounts by eyewitnesses led to a
persistent interest in flight among contemporary spectators, while poetry,
it seemed, found in controlled human flight a material representation of
the spiritual strivings of all prior romantic literature. The niche of Byron's
Childe Harold and Pushkin's Aleko was now occupied by a new "hero of
our time": a man in a leather helmet and a fur-lined jacket. His glory was
truly international, particularly after aviation gained widespread appeal in
Russia in the 1910s and 1920s.

The most prominent representatives of Russian society saw the airplane's
emergence as an undoubted breakthrough into a new cultural dimension, a
qualitative leap in man's consciousness and self-awareness. However, opinions
diverged with regard to the wisdom and potential negative effects of this shift

---

[46]Cf. the paragraph before this one: "hard candy (named *Ledenets vzlyotnyy*, 'take-off caramel,'
on the wrapper) generously distributed to us before the start <206> of the flight."

in the history of ideas and technological thinking, ranging from unquestioning acceptance to a belief that aviation contained signs of the coming apocalypse. The issue of flight as practiced in Russia was set against the background of persistent cultural conflict between East and West, but it was also a concern for Russians long before the actual invention of the airplane, as it was embodied by the locomotive, the potential "aerial steam flyer":

And I pray kind providence,
that the air remain forever inaccessible
to the senseless desires of man.
Why move the iron locomotive
With its avaricious industry?
to there, where this sun glistens,
Let it crawl on earth, like a despised worm,
for its poor, base purpose,
And our market passions
Follow it like a child its mother!
But the sky, let it be free!
There are the spirits of the chosen people –
They ascend to the throne of providence
Without base wings and steam.

> (Dmitrii Struiskii, "The Aerial Steam Flyer,"
> *Moskvitianin*. June 1845. № 5–6, 87–88)

Some made the possibility of developing flight in Russia a function of the degree of participation by the state in "the pan-human freedom that wants to be embodied in wings" ("Sick Russia"; Merezhkovskii, *Bol'naia Rossiia*, 189). For others, the concept of a technological revolution harmonized well with the original "Russian idea," and any possible contradictions were captured on a folkloric[47] and mythological[48] level:

The patterned airplane hums
Over the peaked thicket of fir trees.

---

[47]Cf. the popular books published widely in the USSR: N. Riazanov, *Skazka o zolotom petushke-samolete po A. S. Pushkinu* (*Tale of the Golden Cockerel-Airplane, after A. S. Pushkin*). Moscow: Izdatel'stvo sektsiia ODVF, 1925; Berezov and Glagolev, *O popovskoi zabote, o saranche i o samolete* (*On Popov's Effort, Locusts, and an Airplane*). Moscow: ODVF, 1925; A. Grigorovich, *Udivitel'nye prikliucheniia Petra, Ivana i odnogo aeroplana: Veselaia povest' v stikhakh* (*The Amazing Adventures of Petr, Ivan, and an Airplane: A Happy Story in Verse*). Moscow, Leningrad: GIZ, 1925.
[48]See the poem, "Airplane Carpet" in Gorodetskii's 1909 book, *Rus'* (*Russia*): "Fly away, carry away, my airplane carpet! / Rush on and on in the very heart of the heights, / So the years and wastelands become incalculable" (Gorodetskii, *Stikhotvoreniia*, 2:228).

Now and then it floats over a river,
Startling the quick quail ...
To the place where the foggy crag
Boasts of its regal prey,
Where the eternal whistle and avian rustling,
Where my airplane carried me.
("Airplane Carpet," 1906; Sadovskoi, *Stikhotvoreniia*, 33–34)

In the final analysis, aviation was seen as a feat that overcame the pull of the earth, as the victory of humanity over its physical limitations.[49] The interpretation of this long-awaited upward release was also dictated by the participants in the very process of conquering the elements. For example, the popular Russian aviation pioneer Nikolai Popov sent regular reports back home when traveling across continents, which were printed in *Novoe vremia* in a column entitled "Conquering the Air" ("Zavoevanie vozdukha"). Over the course of two years, the newspaper published more than sixty pieces of correspondence from Popov in the "Foreign News" section, many of which have a certain sense of poetry, as can be seen in this excerpt from a letter sent from Nice in 1911:

There are great joys in flying. Anyone who has boarded a plane, steered it like a toy, and soared high and calm over everything in his path: over the green thickets and fields, over a silver river, the choppy sea, the stern mountains, which had seemed so forbidding, knows the joy borne of moments in flight; the novelty and hitherto unexplored beauty of the world are enchanting. You cannot forget this joy. Everything on earth seems small and distant then. The air whistling as a fresh wind in your ears and the caressing sun seem so familial. The flyer easily climbs up, then dives, flying downwards, as if falling, floats with no road to the right and left – wherever he wants – and is afraid of nothing and no one. His spirit holds the happiness of strength and power over the sea of air.
(Sashonko, *Kolomiazhskii ippodrom*, 185–186)

Naïve but full of enthusiasm and unquestioning faith in the future of aviation, the pilot "floats with no road to the right and left—wherever he wants"—for a

---

[49]For example, in Kuprin's essay, "Liudi-ptitsy" ("Bird People") published in the newspaper, *Petrogradskii listok* (April 1, 1917. № 79): "Aviation will never cease to be engaging and exciting, and will always once again amaze free-thinking minds. There they are high in the air floating over us with a striking hum: Merlin's magic cloaks, flying chests, magic carpets, ships in the air, trained eagles; huge, glimmering with dragon scales – the boldest tale of humanity, its dream for millennia, the symbol of the free spirit and the victory over the dark pull of the earth!" (Kuprin, *Sobranie sochinenii*, 9:263).

time he forgets the destructive power of dynamite or ideological propaganda, attracted only by the enchanting "beauty of the earth." This idyll was soon to change dramatically, however: the romantic pathos in the depiction of flight was extinguished by the brutal reality of the First World War, overshadowed as never before by the high mortality among pilots and the evident fatal design flaws of these early flying machines.

In literature also, the theme of flight was quickly recycled into a new form: the greatest achievement of civilization, igniting a spark of hope for a radical restructuring of material life, was immediately written into the universal pool of mythemes with the fable of Daedalus and Icarus at the center. Although even as late as the end of the 1920s airplanes continued to produce a magical impression and their designs demonstrated great imagination,[50] it would be misguided to believe today that aviation motifs in Russian literature were played out in any key other than that shared with general European trends. In both Russian and world literature the variations on the theme paralleled each other: a tendency to depict the pilot as the analog of the fictional adventure hero; the energetic introduction of the specific vocabulary of aviation technology (which in Russian poetry also included phonetic games with the names of foreign pilots); zoomorphism of flying machines, which generally did not move beyond ornithological fantasy; and reflection on the frivolous associations arising from the brief union of sky and man, where one of these symbolically subdues the other, or takes it by force.

First conceived in Sirin's experimental poetic workshop, the aviation theme seeps through all of Nabokov's work to his late Swiss-period prose, either in the form of a leitmotif or an unremarkable narrative notation (the fragment of a propeller on the wall of a random home rented by the characters in a short story, which causes even the unnamed landlady to remark: "My husband used to work at the airport"; "Perfection"; *Stories*, 342). Due to both the consciously directed orientation and the typological universality of the motif, Nabokov's work at various levels enters into an intertextual dialog with other works on aviation themes. As we have seen in Nabokov's early poem, "The Airplane" (1923), its motifs are borrowed from Blok and Khodasevich in their "Aviator" poems from 1911 and 1914 respectively. Synthesizing these two sources, Nabokov guides the reader to the idea of metempsychosis (the stage in his poem following the airplane

---

[50]The potential of the design engineer was, in the opinion of contemporaries, quite different from the imagination of the poet, though they should be considered of the same ilk: "The wings of Pegasus, the wings of Icarus, the winged sandals of Hermes – all of this in truth is quite poor imagination. The flying carpet is no better, nor is the broom on which witches fly. These are familiar things taken and combined together. Imagination here follows what is given and ready, without distorting it sufficiently" (Toporkov, *Tekhnicheskii byt*, 171–172).

crash as the pilot's spirit departs from its corporeal shell),[51] not so much demonstrating a fidelity to the classical story of the soul's metamorphosis into a butterfly as formulating the basis for a new urban mythology that will later be developed in complex ideas regarding the laws of mimicry in nature and the meaning of evolution in the world of technology.

The Last Station

Chaliapin's voice bellows on the first gramophone, the first telephone rings, the first electric lamp shines over the porch of the house and the first automobile is parked at the entrance, to take us to some field to watch the flight of the first biplane.

—Nina Berberova, *The Italics Are Mine*

Nabokov's works are constructed as palimpsests through which one can see previous works of Russian and world literature that the author selected for reasons of narrative or thematic preference in order to create the optical illusion of texts that reflect and penetrate each other. Perspective in general is an exceptionally capacious concept for Nabokov: "On occasion I allow myself the luxury of imagining today's world, our machines, our fashions, as they will appear to our descendants four or five hundred years hence. I assure you that I feel as ancient as a Renaissance monk" ("La Veneziana"; *Stories*, 98).[52] The writer executes a shift, distancing himself from the object itself, describing 1970, for example, by adding "how they resemble telephone numbers, those distant years!" ("Perfection"; *Stories*, 341). As Karel Čapek, who performed the same sort of thought experiments,[53]

---

[51]Cf. the reminiscences by her son of Véra Nabokov's reaction to her husband's death: "On 2 July 1977, as the nurse came out of the hospital room in tears and tried to hug Vera, the latter drew back and said 'Please, this is not necessary, Madame!' She had no patience for dramatic scenes. In the evening Dmitri drove her to the Montreux Palace. [Dmitri Nabokov:] Mama was silent as we drove. Then she suddenly said in complete calm: 'Let's charter an airplane and crash it'" (Zubtsov & Zubtsova, "Glavnyi roman V. Nabokova" [Interview with D. V. Nabokov]. *Domovoi*. May 2003. № 5).

[52]Cf. "The centuries will roll by, and schoolboys will yawn over the history of our upheavals" ("A Letter That Never Reached Russia"; *Stories*, 140).

[53]Cf.: "Someday they will write about 'grandfather's spacious car,' just as they wrote earlier about the old-fashioned carriages and about old, seasoned chauffeurs just as one now sometimes hears about old, seasoned carriage drivers. We always imagine the future to be full of innovations; but they will also have much that is old, and old-fashioned. Do you want to look into the future? Here's an example: 'A little old organ grinder was playing for children on an old decrepit radio-hurdy-gurdy that had electric lights on it'" ("The Glorious Car"; Chapek, *Izbrannoe*, 615).

put it: reverse perspective is achieved by the effect of "gazing into the future."[54] In his French-language essay entitled "Pushkin, or the True and the Seemingly True," Nabokov expresses his position on settling accounts with time; though he does not cite it or enter into a direct polemic with it, he surely has in mind the lines from Pushkin's 1824 poem, "Conversation Between a Bookseller and a Poet": "Our age is a money-grubber; *in this iron age* / Without money there can even be no freedom" (Pushkin, *Polnoe sobranie sochinenii*, 2:329):

> I do not mean to say that the century in which we live is worse than any other. ... Of course the philistine may have the impression that *the world is going from bad to worse: either it is the old refrain about machines becoming our masters, or else the fear of some catastrophe that our newspapers predict*. But the philosopher's eye surveys the world and sparkles with satisfaction as it notes that the essential things do not change, that goodness and beauty retain their place of honor.
>
> (Nabokov, *Think, Write, Speak*, 131)

Nabokov mercilessly attacks those who forsake moral considerations and get carried away by the iron surface of the new age, as we see in the example of the poet Aleksei Eisner in a review of an issue of the journal, *Volia Rossii* (*Will of Russia*). The reviewer draws our attention to the long poem "Sud" ("Trial"): "Here once again everything is very modern – we start off right away with a newspaper report and a murder in an automobile and it is clear right away that *the poet is in step with his times*, in which, as we know, newspapers and automobiles play such a predominant role" (*Russian Collected Works*, 3:685). This frank approach, Nabokov states, reminds him of the "banal images" with which "Maiakovskii (still appreciated by some) amazed high school students in 1912 or 1913":[55] "good form then required that there be more automobiles," but why does Eisner now approach life "with such stubborn refrains of the old days?" (*Russian Collected Works*, 3:685–686). Freed from condescension to his own youthful weaknesses,[56]

---

[54]In her essay, "Natal'ia Goncharova," Marina Tsvetaeva expressed a thought very close in spirit: "there is a remoteness in innovations ... Rails have been rivers for a long time now, with embankment-shores. Tomorrow the airplane will be just part of the sky; why even speak of tomorrow when today it is already a bird! And who will object to the first car – wheels?" (Tsvetaeva, *Sobranie sochinenii*, 4:124).

[55]Cf.: "Red-haired devils, automobiles rose / Blowing their horns just above the ear" ("Adishche goroda" ["Hellishness of the City"], 1913; Maiakovskii, *Sobranie sochinenii*, 1:84).

[56]L. V. Rosental' (1894–1990), a graduate of the Tenishev Academy who, as a student at Petersburg University in 1916, tutored the younger Nabokov in mathematics, recalled (in 1968) conversations with his former pupil about literature: "I brought him Maiakovskii's just-published *Simple as Mooing* to sample. He approved with snobbish condescension. He felt nothing beyond poetic mischief" (Rosental', "Neprimechatel'nye dostovernosti," 105).

Nabokov in the 1930s monopolizes the right to urban aesthetics, criticizing others while his own characters feel more than comfortable in the world of machines. In Berlin, Franz is intoxicated as he breathes "the sharp autumn air," concluding: "the susurration of tires – this was the life!" (*King, Queen, Knave*, 51). A smitten heroine in a taxi cab doesn't stop smiling "that vague, happy smile < ... > and the sound of the motor and the hiss of the tires blended with the hot humming in her temples" ("Bachmann"; *Stories*, 122). The sentiment is echoed by Fyodor Godunov-Cherdyntsev, who "as usual, was gladdened by the wonderful poetry of railroad banks" (*The Gift*, 299). The elderly narrator of "Time and Ebb" cherishes in his memory "the unforgettable tonality of mixed traffic noises coming from the street—these patterns and melodic figures" of his youth (*Stories*, 583). Humbert longs for the Paris of the 1930s, the city that "suited" him, where he "sat with uranists in the Deux Magots" and "published tortuous essays in obscure journals" (*Lolita*, 16). Stock in the most insignificant thing in the market of cultural assets increases in proportion to the remoteness of the time to which the thing belongs:

> The horse-drawn tram has vanished, and so will the trolley, and some eccentric Berlin writer in the twenties of the twenty-first century, wishing to portray our time, will go to a museum of technological history and locate a hundred-year-old streetcar, yellow, uncouth, with old-fashioned curved seats < ... >. *Everything, every trifle, will be valuable and meaningful: the conductor's purse, the advertisement over the window, that peculiar jolting motion which our great-grandchildren will perhaps imagine— everything will be ennobled and justified by its age.*
>
> ("A Guide to Berlin"; *Stories*, 156)

Nabokov attempts to present a future world without cars, and this world causes him to feel pity and disappointment at the same time that his colleagues are enraptured by the world of the future where they themselves will be absent.[57] One way or another, contemporaries were entirely justified in stating the opinion that "Sirin is undoubtedly a product of modernity."[58]

---

[57]Cf. the poetic fantasy on the theme of "Paris without Russians" (*Illiustrirovannaia Rossiia*. October 1, 1927. № 40), published under the name "Leri," musing on what would become of Paris after the Russians left it: "Imagine the day when in French homes / Not a Russian soul remains, / Left without Russian chauffeurs, / Noisy Clichy will fall silent, / The Russian coutourier shops will be closed, / There will be no Russian chefs, / No more 'culture days' will be held, / No Russian parties, // Russian newspapers will depart ... / Without the shift managers and others / Work at Renault will come to a halt! / And all that now shines will be gone, / And everywhere all will be smooth and quiet, / And it will resemble a desert, / When Paris once again is French."

[58]N. Rezinkova, "Gordost' emigrantskoi literatury – V. Sirin" ("The Pride of Émigré Literature – V. Sirin"). *Zaria* (Kharbin). October 27, 1935 (cited from *Klassik bez retushi*, 203–204).

Vladimir Nabokov belonged to the borderline émigré semiosphere. Mourning the loss of his familiar space during the intensive development of the new mythopoeic worlds of Berlin and Paris in the two decades between the world wars had a profound influence on the creation of this writer during a period that was transitional in every sense of the word.

BIBLIOGRAPHY

1. Vladimir Nabokov's Works

Russian sources

Bongard-Levin, Grigory. "Vladimir Nabokov i russkie uchenye-emigranty v SShA. O pis'makh Nabokova k trem izvestnym russkim istorikam: M. I. Rostovtsevu, G. V. Vernadskomu i M. M. Karpovichu," *Russkaia mysl'* (Paris), (No. 4296), December 9, 1999.

"Doklady Vladimira Nabokova v Berlinskom literaturnom kruzhke (Iz rukopisnykh materialov dvadtsatykh godov)," Publ. by A. Dolinin, A. *Zvezda*, 4, 1999.

"'Dorogoi i milyi Odissei ... ' (Perepiska V.V. Nabokova i V.M. Zenzinova)," Glushanok, G. B. [Vstup. stat'ia, publ. i kommentarii], *Nashe Nasledie*, 53, 2000.

"Kak redko teper' pishu po-russki ... ": Iz perepiski V. Nabokova i M. Aldanova (1940–1956). *Oktiabr'*. № 1. 1996.

"Neskol'ko slov ob ubozhestve sovetskoi belletristiki i popytka ustanovit' prichiny onogo," *Diaspora*. Vol. 2. St. Petersburg, 2001.

"Palestinskoe pis'mo Vladimira Nabokova 1937 goda." Leving, Y. in *V. V. Nabokov: Pro et contra*. Vol. 2. St. Petersburg, 2001.

Perepiska s sestroi. Ann Arbor: Ardis, 1985.

"Postscript to the Russian Edition of *Lolita*," trans. Earl D. Sampson, in *Nabokov's Fifth Arc: Nabokov and Others on his Life's Work*, ed. by J. E. Rivers and Charles Nicol. Austin: University of Texas Press, 1982.

Rozental', Lazar. "Neprimechatel'nye dostovernosti" ["Unremarkable Truths"]. *Nashe Nasledie*. № 1. 1991.

Russian Collected Works. Sobranie sochinenii russkogo perioda [*Collected Works of the Russian Period*]. 5 vols., St. Petersburg: Simpozium, 1999–2000.

Stikhotvoreniia. Vstupit. stat'ia, podgotovka i kommentarii M. E. Malikovoi. St. Petersburg: Akademicheskii proekt, 2002.

Yangirov, Rashit. "Druz'ia, babochki i monstry (Iz perepiski Vladimira i Very Nabokovykh s Romanom Grinbergom (1943–1967))," *Diaspora*. Vol. 1. Paris, 2001.

English sources

Ada, or Ardor: A Family Chronicle. New York: Vintage, 1990.

Bend Sinister. New York: Vintage, 1990.

The Defense. New York: Vintage, 1990.

Despair. New York: Vintage, 1989.

Enchanter. New York: Vintage, 1991.

Glory. New York: Vintage, 1991.

King, Queen, Knave. New York: Vintage, 1989 [1928].

Laughter in the Dark. New York: Vintage, 1989.

Lolita. New York: Vintage, 1989.

Mary. New York: Vintage, 1989.

Nabokov's Butterflies: Unpublished and Uncollected Writings. Ed. and annotated by B. Boyd and R. M. Pyle. Trans. by D. Nabokov. Boston: Beacon Press, 2000.

Nikolai Gogol. New York: New Directions, 1961.

Pale Fire. New York: Vintage, 1989.

Pnin. New York: Vintage, 1989.

The Real Life of Sebastian Knight. New York: Vintage, 1992.

Speak, Memory: An Autobiography Revisited. New York: Vintage, 1989.

Stories: The Stories of Vladimir Nabokov. New York: Vintage, 2008.

Nabokov, V. *Amerikanskoe sobranie sochinenii v 5 tomakh*. St. Petersburg: Simpozium, 1997.

Nabokov, V. *Eugene Onegin. A Novel in Verse by Alexandr Pushkin*. Transl. from the Russian, with a Commentary, in 4 vols. (Bollingen Series LXXII). New York: Pantheon Books, 1964.

Nabokov, V. *The Eye*. New York: Vintage, 1990.

Nabokov, V. *Lectures on Russian Literature*, New York: Harcourt Brace & Company, 1981.

Nabokov, V. *Look at the Harlequins*. New York: Vintage, 1990.

Nabokov, V. *The Nabokov–Wilson Letters: Correspondence Between Vladimir Nabokov and Edmund Wilson, 1941–1971*. Ed. by Simon Karlinsky. New York: Harper and Row, 1979.

Nabokov, V. "On Learning Russian," *The Wellesley Magazine*. April 1945.

Nabokov, V. *Poems and Problems*. New York: McGraw-Hill, 1970.

Nabokov, V. *Selected Letters: 1940–1977*. Ed. by D. Nabokov and M. J. Bruccoli. New York: Harcourt Brace Jovanovich/Bruccoli Clark Layman, 1989.

Nabokov, V. *Strong Opinions*. New York: McGraw-Hill, 1973.

Nabokov, V. *Think, Write, Speak: Uncollected Essays, Reviews, Interviews, and Letters to the Editor*. Ed. by Brian Boyd and Anastasia Tolstoy. New York: Knopf, 2018.

Nabokov, V. *Transparent Things*. New York: Vintage, 1990.

2. Fiction: Other sources

Ageev, M. *Roman s kokainom*. Moscow, 1990.

Akhmatova, Anna. *Sochineniia v 2 tt*. Moscow, 1990.

Akhmatova, Anna. *Stikhotvoreniia i poemy*. Leningrad, 1976.

Andreev, Leonid. *Sobranie sochinenii v 6 tt*. Moscow, 1990–94.

Annenskii, Innokentii. *Stikhotvoreniia i tragedii*. Leningrad, 1990.

Antologiia poezii russkogo zarubezh'ia: "*My zhili togda na planete drugoi ...*": *1920–1990*. V 4 kn. Moscow, 1994.

Apolliner, Gijom. *Esteticheskaia khirurgiia*. St. Petersburg, 1999.

Apukhtin, A. G. *Stikhotvoreniia*. Leningrad, 1991.

Aseev, Nikolai. *Stikhotvoreniia, poemy, vospominaniia, stat'i*. Moscow, 1990.

Averchenko, Arkadii. *Britva v kisele*. Moscow, 1990.

Babel, Isaac. *Isaac Babel's Selected Writings*. Ed. by Gregory Freidin; trans. by Peter Constantine. New York: W. W. Norton & Company, 2010.

Bagritskii, Eduard. *Stikhotvoreniia i poemy*. Perm, 1987.

Bal'zak, Onore. *Sobranie sochinenii v 24 tt*. Moscow, 1960.

Bashkirtseva, Maria. *Dnevnik Marii Bashkirtsevoi*. Moscow, 1991.

Baudelaire [Bodler], Charles. *Tsvety zla*, Moscow, 1970.

Bely, Andrei. *Petersburg*. Trans., annotated, and introduced by Robert A. Maguire and John E. Malmstad. Bloomington: Indiana University Press, 1979.

Bely, Andrei. *Sochineniia: v 2 tt.*, Moscow, 1990.

Benua, Aleksandr. *Moi vospominaniia*. V 2 tt. Moscow, 1990.

Berberova, Nina. *Biiankurskie prazdniki. Rasskazy v izgnanii*. Moscow, 1997.

Berberova, Nina. *The Italics Are Mine [Kursiv moi]*. Moscow, 1996.

Berendgof, Nikolai. *Beg*. Moscow, 1928.

Bezrodnyi, Mikhail. "Rossiia na rel'sakh," *Solnechnoe spletenie*. Vol. 9, 1999.

Blok, Aleksandr. *Pis'ma A. Bloka k ego rodnym*. V 2 tt. Moscow-Leningrad, 1927–32.

Blok, Aleksandr. *Polnoe sobranie sochinenii i pisem v 20 tt*. Moscow, 1997.

Blok, Aleksandr. *Polnoe sobranie sochinenii v 8 tt*. Moscow, 1963.

Boborykin, Pyotr. *Sochineniia v 3 tt*. Moscow, 1993.

Bozhnev, Boris. *Bor'ba za nesushchestvovan'e. Sobranie stikhotvorenii*. St. Petersburg, 1999.

Briusov, Valery. *Sobranie sochinenii v 7 tt*. Moscow, 1973–75.

Briusov, Valery. *Stikhi Nelli*. Moscow, 1913.

Briusov, Valery. *Stikhotvoreniia i poemy*. Leningrad, 1961.

Briusov, Valery. *Urbi et Orbi. Stikhi 1900—1903*. Moscow, 1903.

Bulgakov, Mikhail. *White Guard*. Trans. from the Russian by Michael Glenny. London: Fontana Books, 1973.

Burliuk, David, and Nikolai Burliuk. *Stikhotvoreniia*. St. Petersburg, 2002.

Chapek [Čapek], Karel. *Izbrannoe*. Kishinev, 1974.

Chekhonin, M. *Stikhi*. New York, 1946.

Chekhov, Anton. *Five Plays*. Trans. by Ronald Hingley. Oxford, 1998.

Chekhov, Anton. *Plays: Ivanov; The Seagull; Uncle Vanya; Three Sisters; The Cherry Orchard*. Transl. from Russian by Peter Carson. London: Penguin Classics, 2002.

Chekhov, Anton. *Polnoe sobranie sochinenii i pisem: v 20 tt*. Moscow, 1944–51.

Chernyi, Sasha. *Sobranie sochinenii v 5 tt*. Moscow, 1996.

Chetyrnadtsat'. Kruzhok russkikh poetov v Amerike. New York, 1949.

Chukovskaia, Lidiia. *Zapiski ob Anne Akhmatovoi*. 1938–41. Vol. 1. Moscow, 1997.

Chukovskii, Kornei. *Dnevnik. 1901–1929*. Vol. 1. Moscow, 1991.

Chukovskii, Kornei. *Futuristy. (Severianin. Kruchenykh. Khlebnikov. Kamenskii. Maiakovskii)*. Petrograd, 1922.

Chukovskii, Kornei. *Sobranie sochinenii v 6 tt.* Moscow, 1966.

Churilin, Tikhon. *Vesna posle smerti*. Moscow, 1915.

Dal', Vladimir. *Tolkovyi slovar' zhivogo velikorusskogo iazyka*. V 4 tomakh. Moscow, 1996.

Dekabristy: Estetika i Kritika. Ed. by L. Frizman. Moscow, 1991.

Don-Aminado (Shpolianskii, A. P.). *Poezd na tret'em puti*. Moscow, 2000.

Dostoevsky, Fyodor. *The Brothers Karamazov*. Trans. from the Russian by Constance Garnett. New York: The Lowell Press, 2009.

Dostoevsky, Fyodor. *Demons*. Trans. by Richard Pevear and Larissa Volokhonsky. New York: Alfred A. Knopf, 1994.

Erenburg, Il'ia. *Sobranie sochinenii v 9 tt.* Moscow, 1964.

Erenburg, Il'ia. *Stikhotvoreniia*. St. Petersburg, 2000.

Fet, Afanasii. *Stikhotvoreniia i poemy*. Leningrad, 1986.

Fofanov, Konstantin. *Stikhotvoreniia i poemy*. Moscow, 1962.

Gaidar, Arkadii. *Sobranie sochinenii v 4 tt.*, Moscow, 1964.

Gertsen, Alexander. *Povesti i rasskazy*. Moscow, 1962.

Ginger, Aleksandr. "Vecher na vokzale," *Chisla*. № 2–3. 1930.

Gippius, Zinaida. *Stikhotvoreniia*. St. Petersburg, 1999.

Gogol, Nikolai. "Diary of a Madman," in *Plays and Petersburg Tales*. Trans. by Christopher English. Oxford: Oxford University Press, 1998.

Gogol, Nikolai. *Sobranie khudozhestvennykh proizvedenii v 5 tt.* Moscow, 1959–60.

Goncharov, Ivan. *Oblomov*. St. Petersburg, 1993.

Goncharov, Ivan. *Polnoe sobranie sochinenii v 12 tt.* St. Petersburg, 1899.

Gordon, Lev. *Ottepel'. Pervaia kniga stikhov*. Berlin, 1924.

Gorodetskii, Sergei. *Stikhotvoreniia*. Moscow, 1975.

Gor'kii, Maxim. *Mat'*. Moscow, 1975.

Gumilev, Nikolai. *Izbrannoe*. Moscow, 1991.

Gumilev, Nikolai. *Sobranie sochinenii v 4 tt.* Washington, 1962–68.

Hesse, Herman. *Steppenwolf: A Novel*. Trans. by Basil Creighton. New York: Picador, 2002.

Ianovskii, Vassily. *Sochineniia v 2 tt.* Moscow, 2000.

Iazykov, Nikolai. *Stikhotvoreniia i poemy*. Leningrad, 1988.

Ivanov, Georgii. *Sobranie sochinenii v 3 tt.* Moscow, 1994.

Ivanov, Vsevolod. *Izbrannye proizvedeniia v 2 tt.* Moscow, 1954.

Il'f, Ilya and Evgeny Petrov. *Sobranie sochinenii v 5 tt.* Moscow, 1961.

Il'f, Ilya and Evgeny Petrov. *The Twelve Chairs*. Trans. from the Russian by John H. C. Richardson. New York: Vintage Books, 1961.

Kafka, Franz. *Sochineniia v 3 tomakh*. Moscow, 1995.

Kamenskii, Vasilii. *Ego – moia biografiia*. Moscow, 1918.

Kamenskii, Vasilii. *Tango s korovami. Put' entuziasta. Avtobiograficheskaia kniga*. Moscow, 1990.

Kannegiser, Leonid. *Stat'i. Iz posmertnykh stikhov*. Paris, 1928.

Kellerman, Bernhard. *The Tunnel*. Anon. Trans. from German *Der Tunnel* (1913). London: Hodder and Stoughton, 1915.

Khlebnikov, Velimir. *Tvoreniia*. Moscow, 1987.

Khodasevich, Vladislav. *Sobranie sochinenii v 4 tt.* Moscow, 1996.

Khomiakov, Aleksey. *Polnoe sobranie sochinenii.* Moscow, 1914.

Komarovskii, Vasilii. *Stikhotovoreniia. Proza. Pis'ma.* St. Petersburg, 2000.

Komsomol'skie poety dvadtsatykh godov. Leningrad, 1988.

Kriuchkov, Dmitri. *Tsvety Ledianye. Vtoraia kniga stikhov.* St. Petersburg, 1913.

Kuprin, Aleksandr. *Sobranie sochinenii v 6 tt.* Moscow, 1957.

Kuzmin, Mikhail. *Proza.* Berkeley, 1984.

Kuzmin, Mikhail. *Sochineniia.* Leningrad, 1990.

Leskov, Nikolai. *Satirical Stories.* Selected works. Trans. and ed. by William B. Edgerton. New York: Pegasus, 1969.

Let. Aviastikhi. [Anthology of the Soviet Poetry about Aviation]. Moscow, 1923.

Likhachev, Dmitri. *Vospominaniia.* St. Petersburg, 1995.

Lukash, Ivan. "List'ia," in *List'ia. Literaturnyi sbornik.* Konstantinopol', 1921.

Maiakovskii, Vladimir. *Sobranie sochinenii v 12 tt.* Moscow, 1978.

Malevich, Kazimir. *Chernyi kvadrat.* St. Petersburg, 2001.

Mandel'shtam, Osip. *Kamen'.* Leningrad, 1990.

Mandel'shtam, Osip. *Shary [Balls].* Leningrad, 1926.

Mandel'shtam, Osip. *Sobranie sochinenii v 2 tt.* Moscow, 1990.

Mandel'stam, Osip. *Sobranie sochinenii v 2 tomakh.* Moscow, 1990.

Marshak, Samuil. *Stikhotvoreniia i poemy.* Leningrad, 1973.

Merezhkovskii, Dmitri. *Bol'naia Rossiia. Izbrannoe.* Leningrad, 1991.

Merezhkovskii, Dmitri. *Stikhotvoreniia i poemy.* St. Petersburg, 2000.

Mineeva, E. *Sbornik stikhotovorenii.* Vol. 1. St. Petersburg, 1913.

Na Zapade. Antologiia russkoi zarubezhnoi poezii. Ed. by Iu. Ivask. New York, 1953.

Nadson, Semyon. *Polnoe sobranie stikhotvorenii.* St. Petersburg, 2001.

Nal'ianch [Shovgenov], Sergei. "Stolitsa," *Volia Rossii*, (1) 1928.

Narbut, Vladimir. *Stikhotvoreniia.* Moscow, 1990.

Nizen, Ekaterina. *Sadok sudei.* Moscow, 1914.

Olesha, Yuri. *Envy.* Trans. by Marian Schwartz. New York: New York Review Books, 2004.

Olesha, Yuri. *Izbrannye sochineniia.* Moscow, 1956.

Osorgin, Mikhail. "Subbotnii poezd," *Novyi zhurnal.* № 6. 1943.

Otsup, Nikolai. *"Okean vremeni": Stikhotvoreniia; Dnevnik v stikhakh; stat'i, vospominaniia.* St. Petersburg, 1993.

Pasternak, Boris. *Safe Conduct. An Autobiography and Other Writings.* Trans. from the Russian by Beatrice Scott. New York: New Directions, 1958.

Pasternak, Boris. *Sobranie sochinenii v 5 tt.* Moscow, 1989–92.

Pasternak, Zhozefina. *Koordinaty.* Berlin, 1938.

Paustovskii, Konstantin. *Sobranie sochinenii v 8 tt.* Moscow, 1967–69.

Pertsov, Petr. *Literaturnye vospominaniia 1890–1902.* Moscow, 2002.

Peterburg v russkoi poezii 18 – nachala 20 vv. [Poeticheskaia antologiia]. Leningrad, 1988.

Pilnyak, Boris. *Angliiskie rasskazy.* Moscow, Leningrad, 1924.

Pilnyak, Boris. *The Naked Year.* Trans. from *Golyi god* by Alec Brown. New York: Payson & Clarke Ltd., 1971.

Pilnyak, Boris. *Rasplesnutoe vremia: Romany, povesti, rasskazy.* Moscow, 1990.

Platonov, Andrei. *Chevengur.* Moscow, 1988.

Polonskii, Yakov. *Stikhotvoreniia i poemy*. Leningrad, 1935.

Ponzh, Fransis. *Na storone veshchei*. Moscow, 2000.

Poplavskii, Boris. *Sochineniia*. St. Petersburg, 1999.

Poety-imazhinisty. St. Petersburg, 1997.

Poety 1880–1890-kh godov. Leningrad, 1972.

Poeziia russkogo futurizma. St. Petersburg, 1999.

Proletarskie poety pervykh let sovetskoi epokhi. Leningrad, 1959.

Proust, Marcel. *In Search of Lost Time*. Vol. IV (Modern Library Edition). Trans. by C. K. Scott Moncrieff and Terence Kilmartin. New York: Random House, 1993.

Proust, Marcel. *Sodom and Gomorrah*. (*In Search of Lost Time*). Vol. 4. Trans. by John Sturrock. London: Penguin, 2003.

Pushkin, Alexander. *Polnoe sobranie sochinenii*. Moscow, 1962–66.

Pushkin, Alexander. *The Queen of Spades and Other Stories*. Trans. by Alan Myers. Oxford: Oxford University Press, 1999.

Radishchev, Alexander. *Izbrannye filosofskie i obshchestvenno-politicheskie proizvedeniia*. Moscow, 1952.

Remarque, Erich Maria. *Three Comrades*. Trans. from German by A. W. Wheen. Boston: Little, Brown and Company, 1937.

Rimbaud, Arthur. *Complete Works*. Trans. by Paul Schmidt. New York: Perennial Modern Classics, 2008.

Roshcha. Vtorori sbornik berlinskikh poetov. Berlin, 1932.

Rozanov, Vasily. *"Inaia zemlia, inoe nebo ..." Polnoe sobranie putevykh ocherkov 1899–1913 gg*. Moscow, 1994.

Rozanov, Vasily. *Opavshie list'ia: Liriko-filosofskie zapiski*. Moscow, 1992.

Russkaja poeziia – XX veka: Antologiia. Moscow, 1999.

Russkaia poeziia XX veka: Antologiia russkoi liriki pervoi chetverti XX v. Moscow, 1991.

Russkaia poeziia Serebrianogo veka, 1890–1917. Moscow, 1993.

Russkii futurizm. Teoriia. Praktika. Kritika. Vospominaniia. Ed. by V. Terekhina and A. Zimenkov. Moscow, 2000.

Sadof'ev, Il'ia. *Izbrannoe*. Moscow, 1960.

Sadovskoi, Boris. *Stikhotvoreniia. Rasskazy v stikhah. P'esy*. St. Petersburg, 2001.

Samoilov, David. *Izbrannye proizvedeniia v 2 tt*. Moscow, 1989.

Sashonko, V. N. *Kolomiazhskii ippodrom. Dokumental'naia povest' o russkom aviatore N. E. Popove*. Leningrad, 1983.

Satira i iumor russkoi emigratsii. RAN, Institut Rossiiskoi Istorii, Moscow, 1998.

Sergeev-Tsenskii, Sergei. *Brusilovskii proryv: istoricheskii roman*. Moscow, 1944.

Serebrianyi vek. Peterburgskaia poeziia kontsa XIX – nachala XX v. Ed. by M. F. P'ianykh. Leningrad, 1991.

Shakh, Evgenii. *Gorodskaia vesna*. Paris, 1930.

Shakh, Evgenii. *Semia na kamne. Stikhotvoreniia*. Paris, 1927.

Shefner, Vadim. *Sobranie sochinenii v 4 tt*. Leningrad, 1991.

Shengeli, Georgii. *Inokhodets*. Moscow, 1997.

Shershenevich, Vadim. *Listy imazhinista: Stikhotvoreniia. Poemy. Teoreticheskie raboty*. Iaroslavl', 1996.

Shershenevich, Vadim. *Stikhotvoreniia i poemy*. St. Petersburg, 2000.

Sholem Aleichem. *Tevye the Dairyman and The Railroad Stories*. Trans. from the Yiddish by Hillel Halkin. New York: Schocken Books, 1987.

Shvarts, Evgenii. "*Ia budu pisatelem ...*" *Dnevniki. Pis'ma.* Moscow, 1999.
Shvarts, Evgenii. *Memuary.* Paris, 1982.
Shuvalova, E. "Bessonitsa" ["Insomnia"]. *Novyi zhurnal.* № 18. 1948.
Sobol', Andrei. *Oblomki. Tret'ia kniga rasskazov, 1920–1923 gg.* Moscow, 1923.
Sologub, Fyodor. *Stikhotvoreniia.* St. Petersburg, 2000.
Sovetskaia poeziia. 60 let sovetskoi poezii. Sobranie stikhov. V 4 tt. Ed. by N. Kriukov. Moscow, 1977.
Sovremennye russkie liriki. 1907–1912. Ed. by E. Shtern. St. Petersburg, 1913.
Spengler, Oswald. *The Decline of the West. Form and Actuality.* Authorized trans. with notes by Charles Francis Atkinson. New York: Alfred A. Knopf, 1927.
Stepun, Fyodor. *Sbyvsheesia i nesbyvsheesia.* St. Petersburg, 1994.
Svetlov, Mikhail. *Stikhotvoreniia i poemy.* Moscow, 1966.
Sviatopolk-Mirskii, Dmitry. *Stikhotvoreniia.* 1906–10. St. Petersburg, 1911.
Tan, V. "Wells i sovremennaia utopia," in Wells, H. *Sobranie sochinenii v 9 tt.* St. Petersburg, 1909–11. 1909.
Teffi, Nadezhda. *Smeshnoe v pechal'nom: Razzkasy. Avantiurnyi roman.* Moscow, 1992.
Teffi, Nadezhda. *Sobranie sochinenii v 5 tt.* Moscow, 2000.
Tikhonov, Nikolai. *Sobranie sochinenii v 7 tt.* Moscow, 1973.
Tiutchev, Fyodor. *Polnoe sobranie stikhotvorenii.* Leningrad, 1987.
Tolstoy, Leo. *Anna Karenina.* The Aylmer Maude trans. revised by George Gibian. New York: W. W. Norton & Company, 1995.
Tolstoy, Leo. *The Death of Ivan Ilych and Other Stories.* Trans. by Aylmer Maude and J. D. Duff, with a new afterword by Hugh McLean. New York: Signet Classics, 2003.
Tret'iakov, Sergei. *Zheleznaia pauza.* Vladivostok, 1919.
Tsvetaeva, Marina. *Sobranie sochinenii v 7 tt.* Moscow, 1994.
Tsvetaeva, Marina. *Sochineniia v 2 tt.* Moscow, 1980.
Tsvetaeva, Marina. *Stikhotvoreniia i poemy.* Leningrad, 1990.
Uspenskii, Lev. *Zapiski starogo peterburzhtsa.* Leningrad, 1990.
Utkin, Iosif. *Izbrannye stikhi.* Moscow, 1936.
Vaginov, Konstantin. *Kozlinaia pesn'.* Trudy i dni Svistonova: Romany. Moscow, 2000.
Verlaine, Paul Marie. *Oeuvres poétiques completes.* Paris: Gallimard, Bibliothèque de La Pléiade, 1962.
Viazemskii, Pyotr. *Polnoe sobranie sochinenii kniazia P. A. Viazemskogo.* St. Petersburg, 1879.
Viazemskii, Pyotr. *Stikhotvoreniia.* Leningrad, 1986.
Verhaeren, Émile. *Les Forces tumultueuses.* Paris, 1902.
Virgil. *The Aeneid.* Intr. by Robert Fagles, trans. by Bernard Knox. New York: Penguin Classics (Deluxe Edition), 2008.
Volkov, Boris. *V pyli chuzhikh dorog.* Stikhi. Berlin, 1933.
Voloshin, Maksimilian. *Stikhotvoreniia i poemy.* St. Petersburg, 1995.
Vvedenskii, Alexander. *Polnoe sobranie proizvedenii v 2 tt.* Vstup. stat'ia i prim. M. Meilakha, Moscow, 1993.
Wells, H. G. "A Story of the Days to Come," in *Tales of Space and Time.* London and New York: Harper & Brothers Publishers, 1900.

Wells, H. G. *Anticipations of the Reaction of Mechanical and Scientific Progress upon Human Life and Thought*. London: Chapman & Hall, Ltd., 1902.
Whitman, Walt. *Leaves of Grass*. Philadelphia: David McKay, 1900.
Wolfe, Thomas. *A Stone, A Leaf, A Door*. With a Foreword by Louis Untermeyer. New York: Charles Scribner's Sons, 1945.
Zabolotskii, Nikolai. *Polnoe sobranie stikhotvorenii i poem*. St. Petersburg, 2002.
Zamyatin, Evgeny. *We*. Trans. by Mirra Ginsburg. New York: Eos, 1999.
Zenkevich, Mikhail. *Skazochnaia era*. Moscow, 1994.
Zenzinov, Mikhail. *Zheleznyi skrezhet. Iz amerikanskikh vpechatlenii*. Paris, 1927.
Zhemchuzhnikov, Aleksei. *Stikhotvoreniia*. Moscow, 1988.

3. Scholarship

3.1 General Literature

Russian sources

Ashukin, N. and M. Ashukina. *Krylatye slova. Literaturnye tsitaty*. Moscow. 1987.
Bakhtin, Mikhail. *Problemy Poetiki Dostoevskogo*. Kiev, 1994.
Bakhtin, Mikhail. *Raboty 1920-kh godov*. Kiev, 1994.
Barabtarlo, Gennadii. "Prizrak iz pervogo akta," *Zvezda* (Vladimir Nabokov. Neizdannoe v Rossii). № 11. 1996.
Belousov, Aleksandr. "Akklimatizaciia sireni v russkoi poezii," *Sbornik statei k 70-letiiu prof. Iu. M. Lotmana*. Tartu, 1992.
Berdjis, Nassim Winnie. *Imagery in Vladimir Nabokov's Last Russian Novel ([Dar]), Its English Translation (the Gift), and Other Prose Works of the 1930s*. Frankfurt: Peter Lang Publishing, 1995.
Buks, Nora. *Eshafot v khrustal'nom dvortse: o russkikh romanakh V. Nabokova*. Moscow, 1998.
Connolly, Julian W. "Laughter in the Dark," in *The Garland Companion to Vladimir Nabokov*, ed. by Vladimir E. Alexandrov. New York: Garland, 1995.
De Vries, Gerard and D. Barton Johnson. *Nabokov and the Art of Painting*. With an essay by Liana Ashenden. Amsterdam: Amsterdam University Press, 2006.
Dolinin, Alexander. "Plata za proezd. (Beglye zametki o genezise nekotorykh literaturnykh otsenok Nabokova)," *Nabokovskii vestnik*. Vol. 1. St. Petersburg, 1998.
Dolinin, Alexander. "Tri zametki o romane Vladimira Nabokova *Dar*," *Pro et contra*. Vol. 1, 1997.
Dostoyevsky, Fyodor; *The Idiot*. Trans. by Eva Martin. Auckland, N.Z.: Floating Press, 2009.
Dviniatin, Fyodor. "Nabokov i futuristicheskaia traditsiia," *Vestnik filologicheskogo fakul'teta*. 2/3. St. Petersburg, 1999.
Dviniatin, Fyodor. "Piat' peizazhei s nabokovskoi siren'iu," *Pro et contra*. Vol. 2.
Dzhaginov, Mikhail. "Interv'iu s D. Nabokovym," *Okna: Literaturnoe prilozhenie k gazete* Vesti (*Tel-Aviv*). April 13, 1999.

Faryno, Jerzy. "O semioticheskoi tipologii sredstv sviazi i ikh kontseptualizatsii v literature i iskusstve," Tezisy dokladov konferentsii "Semiotika sredstv sviazi." Warszawa, Institut Slawistyki Polskiej Akademii Nauk, 2001.

Faryno, Jerzy. *Vvedenie v literaturovedenie*. Warszawa, 1991.

Gasparov, Boris. *Literaturnye leitmotivy. Ocherki russkoi literatury XX veka.* Moscow, 1994.

Gershtein, Emma. *Memuary.* Moscow, 2002.

Ginzburg, Lidiia. *O lirike.* Moscow, 1964.

Ginzburg, Lidiia. *O starom i novom.* Leningrad, Sovetskii pisatel', 1982.

Gorelik, L. "Kommunikativnost' kak svoistvo kul'turnogo prostranstva: 'Step' v telegrafnyh provodah'," *Tezisy dokladov Mezhdunarodnoi konferentsii 'Semiotika sredstv sviazi'.* Warsaw, 2001.

Grayson, Jane. *Vladimir Nabokov.* New York: Overlook Press, 2001.

Grishakova, Marina. *The Models of Space, Time and Vision in Vladimir Nabokov's Fiction: Narrative Strategies and Cultural Frames.* Tartu: Tartu University Press, 2006.

Hanzen-Leve, Aage. *Russkii simvolizm. Sistema poeticheskikh motivov. Rannii simvolizm.* St. Petersburg, 1999.

Hazan, Vladimir. "Iz nabliudenii nad semanticheskoi poetikoi radio i telegrafa v russkoi poezii XX veka," *Tezisy dokladov Mezhdunarodnoi konferencii 'Semiotika sredstv sviazi'.* Warsaw, 2001.

Iozha, D. "Avtomobil' versus tramvai," *Russkaia literatura mezhdu Vostokom i Zapadom.* Budapest, 1999.

Ivanov, Viacheslav Vs. *Izbrannye trudy po semiotike i istorii kul'tury.* Moscow, 1998.

Klassik bez retushi. Literaturnyi mir o tvorchestve Vladimira Nabokova: Kriticheskie otzyvy, esse, parodii. Ed. by N. Mel'nikov and O. Korostelev. Moscow, 2000.

Langleben, Maria. "Korobkin i Bashmachkin," *Slavianovedenie.* RAN, Moscow, 1992.

Lenin, Vladimir. *Polnoe Sobranie Sochinenii v 55 tomakh.* Moscow: Izdatel'stvo Politicheskoi literatury, 1967.

Levin, Iurii. *Izbrannye Trudy. Poetika, Semiotika.* Moscow, 1998.

Leving, Yuri. "Antipatiia s predystoriei (Nabokovy i Suvoriny v zhizni i proze)" ["Antipathy with History (The Nabokovs and Suvorins in Life and Prose)"], *Novoe Literaturnoe Obozrenie.* (96) 2009.

Leving, Yuri. *Keys to* The Gift. Boston: Academic Studies Press, 2011.

Leving, Yuri. "Six Notes to *The Gift*," *The Nabokovian.* Lawrence, KS. 45, Fall, 2000.

Leving, Yuri. "Tainy literaturnykh adresatov V. V. Nabokova: Gaito Gazdanov," *Nabokovskii Vestnik.* № 4. 1999.

Leving, Yuri. "Uzor vechnosti: Pushkin-grafik – Nabokov-khudozhnik," *A. S. Pushkin i V. V. Nabokov. Sbornik dokladov mezhdunarodnoi nauchnoi konferentsii.* Institut russkoi literatury RAN. St. Petersburg, 1999.

Likhachev, Dmitrii. *Russkaia kul'tura,* Moscow, 2000.

Likhachev, Dmitrii. "Cherez haos k garmonii," *Russkaia literatura.* № 1. 1996.

Livshits, Benedikt. *Polutoroglazyi strelets.* Leningrad, 1989.

Literatura fakta. Pervyi sbornik materialov rabotnikov Lefa. Moscow, 2000.

Literaturnyi sbornik. Regensburg, № 1. 1948.

Lotman, Iurii. *Pushkin. Biografiia pisatelia. Stat'i i zametki. 1960–1990. "Evgenij Onegin." Kommentarii.* St. Petersburg, 1995.

Lotman, Iurii. *Struktura khudozhestvennogo teksta.* Moscow, 1970.

Lutskii, Semyon. *Sochineniia.* Stanford Slavic Studies. Vol. 23. Stanford, 2002.

Malikova, Maria. *Nabokov: Avto-bio-grafia.* St. Petersburg: Akademicheskii Proekt, 2002.

Maslov, Boris. "Poet Koncheev: Opyt tekstologii personazha," *Novoe literaturnoe obozrenie.* № 47. 2001.

Nabokov, S. S. "Profili," *Nabokovskii vestnik.* № 2. 1998.

Nabokov V. D., "Printsip zakonnosti v administratsii, sude, i Gosudarstvennoi Dume." *Rech'.* № 1224. 1912.

Naiman, Eric. "Litlandiia: allegoricheskaia poetika 'Zashchity Luzhina'," *Novoe literaturnoe obozrenie.* № 54. 2002.

Nekrasov, Nikolai. *Polnoe sobranie stikhotvorenii v 3 tt.* Leningrad, 1967.

Nevskaia, D. "Slovesnoe vozdukhoplavanie," *Philologia.* Riga (1) 1994.

Osorgin, Mikhail. [Review]. "V. Sirin. 'Kamera obskura,' roman." *Sovremennye zapiski.* 1934. Book 45, in *V. Nabokov: Pro et contra.* Vol. 1. St. Petersburg, 1997.

Ospovat, Aleksandr and Roman Timenchik. *"Pechal'nu povest' sokhranit' ...."* Moscow, 1985.

Paperno, Irina. *Samoubiistvo kak kul'turnyi institut.* Moscow, 1999.

Piksanov, Nikolai. *Griboedov i Mol'er.* Moscow, 1922.

Piotrovskii, A. "Kino i pisateli," *Zhizn' iskusstva.* Leningrad, № 3. 1928.

Pisarev, Dmitri. "Bazarov. 'Ottsy i deti'. Roman I. S. Turgeneva," *Literaturnaia kritika v trekh tomakh.* Vol. 1. [Stat'i 1859–64 gg.]. Leningrad, 1981.

Proffer, Carl. *Kliuchi k "Lolite."* St. Petersburg, 2000.

Propp, Vladimir. *Morfologiia volshebnoi skazki. Istoricheskie korni volshebnoi skazki.* Moscow, 1998.

Razbeg [Collection of poetry by the Communist Youth League writers]. Leningrad: Priboi, 1928.

Ronen, Omri. "Puti Shklovskogo v 'Putevoditele po Berlinu'," *Zvezda.* № 4. 1999.

Roper, Robert. *Nabokov in America. On the Road to* Lolita. New York: Bloomsbury, 2015.

Rozanov, Vasily. *Bibleiskaia poeziia.* St. Petersburg, 1912.

Sato, Iu. and V. Sorokina. "'Malen'kii muzhik s vz"eroshennoiu borodoi' (Ob odnom simvolicheskom obraze v 'Anne Kareninoi')," *Philologica.* Vol. 5, № 11/13. 1998.

Shakhovskaia, Zinaida. *V poiskakh Nabokova.* Paris, 1979.

Shapiro, Gavriel. *The Sublime Artist's Studio: Nabokov and Painting.* Evanston: Northwestern University Press, 2009.

Shersher, S. "Poetika otchaianiia," *Russian Literature*, XLV. 1999.

Shifman, A. "V. V. Stasov o kinematografii," *Iskusstvo kino.* № 3. 1957.

Shklovskii, Viktor. *Gamburgskii schet.* St. Petersburg, 2000.

Shklovskii, Viktor. *Lev Tolstoy.* Moscow, 1967.

Shklovskii, Viktor. *Mater'ial i stil' v romane L'va Tolstogo "Vojna i mir."* Moscow, 1929.

Simonov, Konstantin. *Sobranie sochinenii v 10 tt.* Moscow, 1979.

Stark, Vadim. "Nabokov – Tsvetaeva: zaochnye dialogi i 'gornie' vstrechi," *Zvezda.* № 11. 1996.

Stuart, Dabney. *Nabokov: The Dimensions of Parody*. Baton Rouge, 1978.
Tomashevskii, Boris. *Pushkin. Raboty raznykh let*. Moscow, 1990.
Uspenskii, Boris. *Semiotika iskusstva*. Moscow, 1995.
V. Nabokov: Pro et contra. Vol. 1. St. Petersburg, 1997.
V. Nabokov: Pro et contra. Vol. 2. St. Petersburg, 2001.
Vaiskopf, Mikhail. *Siuzhet Gogolia*. Moscow, 1993.
Vaiskopf, Mikhail. *Vo ves' logos: religiia Maiakovskogo*. Moscow, 1997.
Viazemskii, Pyotr. "Predislovie k perevodu romana B. Konstana Adol'f," *Estetika i literaturnaia kritika*. Moscow, 1984.
Wyllie, Barbara. *Nabokov at the Movies: Film Perspectives in Fiction*. Jefferson and London: McFarland, 2003.
Zamiatin, Evgenii. *Izbrannye proizvedeniia v 2 tt*. Moscow, 1990.
Zamiatin, Evgenii. *Litsa*. New York, 1967.
Zholkovskii, Alexander. *Inventsii*. Moscow, 1995.
Zholkovskii, Alexander and Mihail Iampol'skii. *Babel'/Babel*. Moscow, 1994.
Zvezda (Tematicheskii nomer k stoletnemu iubileiu V. V. Nabokova). № 4. 1999.
Yangirov, Rashit. "'Ekran zhizni': versiia Don Aminado," *Novoe literaturnoe obozrenie*. № 16. 1995.

English sources

Allan, Nina. *Madness, Death and Disease in the Fiction of Vladimir Nabokov*. Birmingham Slavonic Monographs, University of Birmingham (No. 23), 1994.
Barabtarlo, Gennady. *Phantom of Fact: A Guide to Nabokov's Pnin*. Ann Arbor: Ardis, 1989.
Barthes, Roland. *Mythologies*. Trans. from the French by Annette Lavers. New York: The Noonday Press, Farrar, Straus & Giroux, 1991.
Boyd, Brian. "The Expected Stress Did Not Come": A Note on "Father's Butterflies," *The Nabokovian*, 45, 2000.
Boyd, Brian. *Vladimir Nabokov: The American Years*. Princeton: Princeton University Press, 1991.
Boyd, Brian. *Vladimir Nabokov: The Russian Years*. Princeton: Princeton University Press, 1990.
Braudy, Leo and Marshall Cohen, eds. *Film Theory And Criticism. Introductory Readings*. 7th Edition. New York, Oxford: Oxford University Press, 2009.
Couterier, Maurice. "Nabokov and Flaubert," *Garland Companion*, 1995.
Derrida, Jacques. *De la grammatologie*. Paris: Les éditions de Menuit, 1967.
Dolinin, Alexander. "Clio laughs last: Nabokov's answer to historicism," *Nabokov and His Fiction: New Perspectives*. Ed. by Julian W. Connolly. Cambridge: Cambridge University Press, 1999.
Foster, J. B. *Nabokov's Art of Memory and European Modernism*. Princeton: Princeton University Press, 1993.
Frazer J. G. *Folk-Lore in the Old Testament*. London: Macmillan and Co. Ltd., 1923.
Freidin, Gregory. *A Coat of Many Colors: Osip Mandelstam and His Mythologies of Self-Presentation*. Berkeley: University of California Press, 1987.
The Garland Companion to Vladimir Nabokov. Ed. by Vladimir E. Alexandrov. New York: Garland Publishing, 1995.

Leving, Yuri. "Come serve the Muse and merge in verse ..., " *The Nabokovian*, 48, 2002.

Leving, Yuri. *Keys to* The Gift. *A Guide to Vladimir Nabokov's Novel*. Boston: Academic Studies Press, 2011.

Leving, Yuri. "Six Notes to *The Gift*," *The Nabokovian*, 45, 2000.

Leving, Yuri. "Vladimir Nabokov's Japan," *Krug*. Vol. II (2), 2001.

Lutwack, Leonard. *The Role of Place in Literature*. Syracuse: Syracuse University Press, 1984.

Nakata, Akiko. "Angels on the Planks: The Workmen in the Two Scenes in Mary," *The Nabokovian*, 42, 1999.

Nesbet, Anne. "Suicide as Literary Fact in the 1920s," *Slavic Review*, 50 (4), 1991.

Ronen, Omry. "Nine Notes to *The Gift*," *The Nabokovian*, 44, 2000.

Ronen, Omry and Irena Ronen. "'Diabolically Evocative': an Inquiry into the Meaning of a Metaphor," *Slavica Hierosolimytana*. Vol. 5–6, 1978.

Schiff, Stacy. *Véra (Mrs. Vladimir Nabokov)*. New York: Random House, 1999.

Schuman, Samuel. *Nabokov's Shakespeare*. New York: Bloomsbury, 2014.

Skonechnaia, Olga. "'People of the Moonlight': Silver Age Parodies in Nabokov's *The Eye* and *The Gift*," *Nabokov Studies*, 3, 1996.

Toker, Leona. *Nabokov: The Mystery of Literary Structures*. Ithaca: Cornell University Press, 1989.

Zimmer, Dieter E. *Nabokovs Berlin*. Berlin: Nicolaische Verlagsbuchhandlung GmbH, 2001.

3.2 Urbanism

Russian sources

Barkovskov B., K. Prohazka and L. Ragozin. *Modeli zheleznykh dorog*. Moscow, 1989.

Bestuzhev, A. A. "Vzgliad na russkuiu slovesnost' v techenie 1824 i nachale 1825 godov," *Dekabristy: Estetika i kritika: Sbornik*. Ed. by L. Frizman. Moscow, 1991.

Bezrodnyi, Mikhail. "Rossiia na rel'sakh," *Solnechnoe spletenie*. Vol. 9, 1999.

Bodriiar, Jean. *Amerika*. Perevod s fr. D. Kalugina. St. Petersburg, 2000.

Broitman, L. I. and E. I. Krasnova. *Bol'shaia Morskaia ulitsa*. St. Petersburg, 1997.

Bubnov, B. "Mechanized Flight in the Future" ["Mekhanicheskii polet budushchego"], *Vozdushnyi put'*. № 2. 1911.

Chukovskii, Kornei. "Letuchie listki (Aviatsiia i poeziia)," *Rech'*. № 124.8 (21). May 1911.

Chursina, L. I. "Blok i aviatsiia (Po materialam periodiki nachala XX v.)," *A. Blok. Issledovaniia i materialy*. AN SSSR, Institut russkoi literatury. Leningrad, 1991.

Dobuzhinskii, Mstislav. *Vospominaniia*. Moscow, 1987.

Huizinga, Johan. *Homo Ludens. Stat'i po istorii kul'tury*. Moscow, 1997.

Kaul'bars, General. *Vozdushnaia voina*. [Manuskript <1918>], Hoover Institution on War, Revolution and Peace. Stanford, California. F. N598 (4).

Laird, David. "Versions of Eden: The Automobile and the American Novel," in David L. Lewis and Laurence Goldstein, eds. *The Automobile and American Culture*. Ann Arbor: University of Michigan Press, 1986.

Leites, A., P. Sdobnev and M. Danilova. *Zheleznodorozhnyi transport v khudozhestvennoi literature.* Moscow, 1939.

Levinson, Aleksei. "Zametki po sotsiologii i antropologii reklamy," *Novoe literaturnoe obozrenie.* № 24. 1997.

Piretto, G. P. "Dorozhnye zhaloby Pushkina v zheleznodorozhnoi perspective," *Studia Russica Budapestinensia,* II–III, 1995.

Povelikhina, A. and E. Kovtun. *Russkaia zhivopisnaia vyveska i khudozhniki avangarda.* Leningrad, 1991.

Russkii futurism. Teoriia. Praktika. Kritika. Vospominaniia. Ed. by V. Terekhina and A. Zimenkov. Moscow, 2000.

Shlegel', Karl. "Vospriiatie goroda: Nabokov i taksisty," *Kul'tura russkoi diaspory: Vladimir Nabokov – 100. Materialy nauchnoi konferentsii.* Tallinnskii pedagogicheskii universitet, Tallinn Tartuskii universitet, 2000.

Shteiner, Evgenii. *Avangard i postroenie novogo cheloveka. Iskusstvo detskoi knigi 1920-kh godov.* Moscow, 2002.

Timenchik, Roman. "Raspisan'e i Pisan'e," *Themes and Variations. In Honor of Lazar Fleishman.* Ed. by K. Polivanov. Stanford, 1994.

Timenchik, Roman. "K simvolike telefona v russkoi poezii," *Trudy po znakovym sistemam.* XXII. Tartu, 1988.

Timenchik, Roman. "K simvolike tramvaia v russkoi poezii," *Uchenye zapiski Tartuskogo universiteta.* Vol. 754. 1987.

Timenchik, Roman. "Ol'ga Glebova-Sudeikina: pervoe priblizhenie," *Novoe literaturnoe obozrenie.* № 7. 1994.

Toporkov, A. *Tekhnicheskii byt i sovremennoe iskusstvo.* Moscow, 1928.

Toporkov, A. L. "Iz mifologii russkogo simvolizma: Gorodskoe osveshchenie," *Mir A. Bloka. Blokovskii sbornik,* 5 (vol. 657). Tartu, 1985.

Zheltova, E. L. "Ob otnoshenii M. Tsvetaevoi k aviatsii," *Vtoraia mezhdunarodnaia nauchno-tematicheskaia konferentsiia 9–10 oktiabria 1994 g.* Moscow, 1995.

Other sources

Baehr, Stephen L. "The Machine in Chekhov's Garden: Progress and Pastoral in The Cherry Orchard," *Slavic and East European Journal,* 43 (1), 1999.

Baehr, Stephen L. "The Troika and the Train: Dialogues between Tradition and Technology in Nineteenth-Century Russian Literature," in J. D. Clayton (ed.), *Issues in Russian Literature before 1917.* Columbus: Slavica, 1989.

Ball, D. W. "Toward Sociology of Telephone and Telephoners," in Marcello Truzzi (ed.), *Sociology and Everyday Life.* Englewood Cliffs, N.J., Prentice-Hall, 1968.

Benjamin, Walter. *Reflections: Essays, Aphorisms, Autobiographical Writings.* New York and London: Harcourt Brace Jovanovich, 1978.

Bobrick, Benson. *Labyrinths of Iron: Subways in History, Myth, Art, Technology and War.* New York: Henry Holt and Company, 1986.

Bowlt, John E. "Here and There: The Question of Space in Blok's Poetry," *Aleksandr Blok. Centennial Conference.* Ed. by Walter Vickey. Columbus, OH: Slavica, 1982.

Buel, Ronald A. *Dead End: The Automobile in Mass Transportation.* Englewood Cliffs, N.J.: Prentice-Hall, Inc., 1972.

Carlson, Pierce: *Toy Trains: A History*. New York: Harper & Row, 1986.

Carter, Ian. *Railways and Culture in Britain The Epitome of Modernity*. New York: Manchester University Press, 2001.

Cochrane, Dorothy, Russell Lee, and Von Hardesty. *The Aviation Careers of Igor Sikorsky*. Seattle: University of Washington, 1989.

Cohen, Phil, *Out of the Melting Pot*, in *Imagining Cities: Scripts, Signs, Memory*. Westwood S. and J. Williams (eds). London: Routledge, 1997.

Dimitroff, James S. *Give Russia Wings: The Confluence of Aviation and Russian Futurism, 1909–1914*. Ann Arbor: UMI Dissertation Services, 1998.

Dodds, John W. *The Age of Paradox*. New York and Toronto: Rinehart & Co., 1952.

Evans, Arthur N. *The Motor Car. The Cambridge Introduction to a History of Mankind*. Cambridge: Cambridge University Press, 1983.

Finne, K. N. *Igor Sikorsky: The Russian Years*. Ed. by Carl Bobrow and Von Hardesty; trans. by Von Hardesty. Washington, D.C.: Smithsonian, 1987.

Fitzgerald, F. S. *The Cruise of the Rolling Junk*. Michigan: Bruccoli Clark, 1976.

Flink, James J. *The Automobile Age*. Cambridge, Massachusetts: MIT Press, 1988.

Freeman, Michael. *Railways and the Victorian Imagination*. New Haven: Yale University Press, 1999.

Goldstein, Laurence. *The Flying Machine and Modern Literature*. London: Macmillian, 1986.

Haywood, Richard M. *The Beginnings of Railway Development in Russia in the Reign of Nicholas I, 1835–1842*. Durham, N.C.: Duke University Press, 1969.

Hey, Kenneth. "Cars and Films in American Culture, 1929–1959," in *The Automobile and American Culture*, 1986.

Ingold, Felix Philipp. *Literatur und Aviatik: Europeische Flugdichtung 1909–1927*. Basel, Stuttgart: Birkhauser, 1978.

Lewis, David L. "Sex and the Automobile: From Rumble Seats to Rockin' Vans," in David L. Lewis and Laurence Goldstein (eds), *The Automobile and American Culture*. Ann Arbor: University of Michigan Press, 1986.

Lewis, David L. and Laurence Goldstein, eds. *The Automobile and American Culture*. Ann Arbor: University of Michigan Press, 1986.

Matthews, J. H. "The Railway in Zola's *La Bête humaine*," *Symposium*. Spring, 1960.

Marvin, Carolyn. *When Old Technologies Were New. Thinking About Electric Communication in the Late Nineteenth Century*. New York: Oxford University Press, 1990.

Moline, Norman T. *Mobility and the Small Town: 1900–1930*. Chicago: The University of Chicago, 1971.

Morgan, Bryan (ed.). *The Railway-Lover's Companion*. London: Eyre and Spottiswoode Ltd., 1963.

Mueller, John. "The Automobile: A Sociological Study," Unpublished Ph.D. dissertation, Departments of Sociology and Anthropology, University of Chicago, 1928.

O'Sullivan, Tim. "Transports of Difference and Delight: Advertising and the Motor Car in Twentieth-Century Britain," in *The Motor Car and Popular Culture in the 20th Century*. Aldershot: Ashgate, 1998.

Pettifer, Julian and Nigel Turner. *Automania: Man and the Motor Car*. Toronto: Little, Brown and Company, 1984.

Pressland, David. *Great Book of Tin Toys*. London, 1995.

The Railway-Lover's Companion. Ed. by Bryan Morgan. London: Eyre and Spottiswoode Ltd., 1963.

Richards, Jeffrey and John M. MacKenzie. *The Railway Station: A Social History*. Oxford: Oxford University Press, 1986.

Scharff, Virginia. *Taking the Wheel. Women and the Coming of the Motor Age*. New York: The Free Press, 1991.

Schivelbusch, Wolfgang. *The Railway Journey: The Industrialization of Time and Space in the 19th Century*. Berkeley: The University of California Press, 1986.

Schmidt, Gerhard. *Automobil-Werbung in Wort und Bild. Untersuchungen zur Semiotik in der Werbung*. Stuttgart Akademischer Verlag, 1989.

Smith, Julian. "A Runaway Match: The Automobile in the American Film, 1900–1920," in *The Automobile and American Culture*, 1986.

Weber, Max. *The City*. Trans. by Don Martindale and Gertrud Neuwirth. New York: Collier Books, 1962.

Wells, Paul. "Atomania: Animated Automobiles 1950–1968," *The Motor Car and Popular Culture in the 20th Century*. Aldershot: Ashgate, 1998.

Westwood, J. N. *A History of Russian Railways*. London: George Allen and Unwin Ltd., 1964.

INDEX

Abramovich, Vsevolod xv, 263
Adamovich, Georgii 7, 10
Ageev, M. (Levi, M. L.) 17n26
Aikhenval'd, Iurii 57, 239n97
Akhmatova, Anna 3, 77, 77n50, 174,
  215, 248, 278
Aldanov, Mark 6, 88, 274, 275
Allan, Nina 243n107
Amburger, A. K. 179
Amburger, Karl 179
Andreev, Leonid 54, 82n11, 154, 155,
  265
Andreev, Nikolai 238
Annenskii, Innokentii 22, 79, 90, 106,
  112, 113
Anoshchenko, N. D. 295
Apolliner (Apollinaire), Guillaume 88,
  291n34
Appel, Jr., Alfred 208n46
Apukhtin, Aleksey 52n6, 90, 90n74,
  92n80, 118, 118n145, 141
Artsybashev, Mikhail 260
Aseev, Nikolai 267, 103n107
Ashukina, M. G. 144n183
Ashukin, N. S. 144n183
Auden, W. H. 139n174
Averchenko, Arkadii 125, 126

Babel, Isaac 23n38, 127, 129,
  130–132, 134n166, 135
Bach, Sebastian 276
Baedeker, Karl 63
Baehr, Stephen L. 173n227
Bagritskii, Eduard 123n156, 201n30
Bakhtin, Mikhail 85, 133, 161
Bakst, Leon 251
Balashov, A. V. 164

Ball, D. W. 36
Bal'mont, Konstantin 13, 298
Balzac, Honoré de 9, 194
Barabtarlo, Gennady 188n15, 199,
  199n26, 200, 200n27, 233
Baratynskii, Evgenii 260
Barkovskov, B. V. 63n22
Barthes, Roland 2, 10, 208,
  241n103
Bashkirtseva, Maria 51n1, 74
Batalin, R. G. 168
Baudelaire, Charles 8n14, 280
Belasco, Warren 176, 177
Belinskii, Vissarion 260
Bell, Alexander Graham 34
Belousov, Aleksandr 151
Bely, Andrei 39n64, 41n67, 89,
  100n101, 102
Benjamin, Walter 8n14
Benua, A. N. 64n26
Benua, N. L. 64n26
Benz, Karl 204n36
Berberova, Nina 40n65, 91, 115n139,
  309
Berdjis, Nassim Winnie 241n102
Berendgof, Nikolai 31n51, 70n36,
  77n49
Bergson, Henri 259
Berezov, L. 306n47
Berkman, S. 98
Berteaux, H. M. 257, 287–288
Bestuzhev, A. A. 48
Bezrodnyi, Mikhail 52n4, 119
Blake, William 67
Blériot, Louis 253, 265, 280n25, 304
Blok, Aleksandr 21, 34, 39, 43, 80,
  82n57, 85, 96n91, 116, 119, 172,

174, 246, 251, 253-256, 262n8, 269, 271–276, 278, 280, 283, 289, 291, 305, 308
Blokh, Andrei 43, 96n93
Boborykin, Pyotr 119, 119n148
Bobrick, Benson 165n218
Bobrov, Sergei 107
Bogdanov, A. A. 91n79
Bongard-Levin, Grigory 29n48
Bowlt, John E. 251
Boyd, Brian 3n3, 53n8, 73, 82n59, 98, 116n141, 181–182, 184, 189, 191, 197–198, 200n27, 205n38, 220n62, 239, 239n27, 302
Bozhnev, Boris 203n32
Breshko-Breshkovskii, N. N. 276
Briullov, Karl 167
Briusov, Valerii 1, 21, 46n74, 52n3, 95, 107, 122n155, 162n213, 174, 197n23, 224, 229
Broitman, L. I. 179
Brook, Rupert 139n174, 250n118, 260–261, 266–267, 269, 273–274, 282, 298
Brothers, Joyce 223
Bubnov, B. 270
Buel, Ronald A. 177n5
Buks, Nora 26
Bulgakov, Mikhail 103
Bunin, Ivan 3, 172
Burliuk, David 78n51, 111, 121n151, 139n172, 218n59, 259
Burliuk, Nikolai 78n51, 97, 218n59, 259
Byron, George Gordon 305

Carter, Ian 53n7
Chapek [Čapek], Karel 270n17, 309n53
Chernyi, Sasha 40, 93n84, 115n138, 167, 170, 212n54, 244–245
Chekhov, Anton 57n15, 101, 111n126, 112n130, 117, 119n147, 125, 131, 147, 153, 172, 173n227, 229, 251
Chekhonin, M. 20n31
Chesterton, Gilbert 71, 139n174
Christie, Agatha 122

Chukovskaia, Lidiia 77n50
Chukovskii, Kornei 173n225, 221, 223, 223n67, 256, 259, 260, 297–298
Churilin, Tikhon 122n152
Chursina, L. I. 254n3, 256
Citroën, André 3n4, 250, 253
Cochrane, Dorothy 287
Cohen, Marshall 215
Cohen, Phil 8, 10
Collignon, Édouard 63
Cooper, James Fennimore 121, 265
Couterier, Maurice 126n161

Dal', Vladimir 261, 275n20, 292
Dali, Salvador 37n61
Dante Alighieri 168, 169, 169n223, 171
Derrida, Jacques 41
Derzhavin, Gavrila 144n183
De Vries, Gerard 167
Diderot, Denis 99n99
Dickens, Charles 9
Dimitroff, James S. 286, 293, 294
Dits, L. 291
Dobroliubov, Nikolai 105
Dobuzhinskii, Mstislav 39n63
Dodds, John W. 121
Dovgard, R. I. 210n49
Dolinin, Alexander 4, 6, 8n14, 88, 153n200, 197n24, 200n28, 204n37, 240, 248
Don-Aminado (Shpolianskii, A. P.) 142, 148n194, 151n198, 248
Dostoevsky, Fyodor 52, 64n25, 87n67, 96, 119, 119n149
Dunne, J. W. 288n32
Dumas, Alexandre 121
Dupuis 287
Dviniatin, Fyodor 150, 248, 248n115
Dzhaginov, Mikhail 33n54
Dzhanumov, Iu. 74n41, 102n102

Efimov, Mikhail 252
Elagin, Ivan 98n98, 142n180, 157n205
El'iashov, Nikolai 170
Ellis [Kobylinskii L. L.] 280

Eisenstein, Sergei 215, 302
Eisner, Aleksei 23n38, 78n52,
    107n117, 146, 310
Erenburg, Il'ia 3n4, 41n68, 43n70,
    91–92, 92n80, 93, 141, 142n181,
    160n210, 210n47, 247, 249, 253,
    261, 268, 279
Erofeev, Venedikt 52n5
Esenin, Sergei 18n27
Evans, Arthur N. 185, 204

Faber 47
Fabergé, Peter Carl 47
Fabre, Henri 285
Fallières, Armand 287
Farman, Henry 256, 259n5, 261, 285,
    293
Faryno, Jerzy 2, 3, 34, 34n56, 106n115
Fel'zen, Iurii 31n52
Fet, Afanasii 56n14, 103, 104, 105
Finne, K. N. 286
Fitzgerald, F. S. 228n79
Flaubert, Gustave 126n161
Fofanov, Konstantin 91, 232, 297, 298
Ford, Henry 225n75
Forshteter, M. A. 146n190
Foster, J. B. 112n132
France, Anatole 259
Frazer, J. G. 234n89
Freeman, Michael 63
Freidin, Gregory 169n224
Freud, Sigmund 3, 6, 223, 298

Gagarin, S. S. 179
Gaidar, Arkadii 111n125, 136n169
Gasparov, Boris 2
Gastev, Aleksei 143n182
Gautier, Theophile 71
Gazdanov, Gaito 84n61, 240n100
Gerasimov, M. 276
Gershtein, Emma 49, 252
Gertsen, Alexander 118, 119n146
Gessen, Iosif 4n6
Ginger, Aleksandr 124
Ginzburg, Lidiia 49, 79, 203
Gippius, Vladimir 34n58
Gippius, Zinaida 22, 52n3, 281
Glagolev, N. P. 306n47

Glebova-Sudeikina, Ol'ga 263
Glushkov, I. F. 144n183
Goethe, Johann Wolfgang von 86, 250,
    250n118
Gogol, Nikolai 14, 29n48, 32, 40, 131,
    151, 194, 206n42, 208, 210, 229,
    262
Goldstein, Laurence 176, 177, 228n78,
    281n26, 294
Golikov, V. M. 145n187
Goncharov, Ivan 47, 126
Goncharova, Natalia 252, 297n40,
    310n54
Gordeev, Ivan 119, 120n150
Gordon, Lev 76
Gorelik, L. 36
Gorianskii, Valentin 211n52
Gor'kii, Maxim 57n15
Gornyi, Sergei (A. A. Otsup) 39n64
Gorodetskii, Sergei 74, 216, 306n48
Grayson, Jane 193n19
Griboedov, Aleksandr 145, 179, 179n7
Grigorovich, A. P. 306n47
Grinberg, Roman 196
Guadanini, Irina 137n170
Gumilev, Nikolai 7, 49, 82n60, 93n85,
    301, 301n43
Guro, Elena 294n38
Guynemer, Georges 265

Hanzen-Leve, Aage 1, 2n1, 13n18
Hardy, Thomas 139n174
Hauptmann, Gerhart 259
Hawthorne, Nathaniel 121
Haywood, Richard M. 71n37
Heine, Heinrich 139n174
Hemingway, Ernest 200
Hesse, Herman 231n83
Hey, Kenneth 228n78
Hoffman, Herbert 223, 224, 224n72
Hoffmann, E. T. A. 40, 46, 194
Homer 144n183, 303
Hugo, Victor 9
Huizinga, Johan 278

Iakobson, Roman 37
Iakubovich, A. I. 179, 179n7
Iampol'skii, Mikhail 127

Ianovskii, Vassily 147n192
Iazykov, Nikolai 292n36
Il'f, Ilya 8, 88, 138n171, 139, 148,
    149, 210, 233n87
Ingold, Felix Philipp 253
Ionov, I. I. 107n117
Iurin, M. P. 141n178
Ivanov, Georgii 6–7, 88, 100, 159
Ivanov, Viacheslav Iv. 296
Ivanov, Viacheslav Vs. 158n207
Ivanov, Vsevolod 141, 142
Ivnev, Riurik 147n191

James, Henry 121
Johnson, Donald Barton 167
Joyce, James 8, 22, 205, 205n38

Kablukov, S. P. 52n3
Kafka, Franz 89, 116n141
Kamenskii, Vasilii 259, 282, 294, 296,
    297
Kannegiser, Leonid 78n51, 132
Kaplan, Fanny 132
Karboni 257
Karpovich, Mikhail 29n48, 189
Kataev, Valentin 303, 304
Kaul'bars, baron 289
Kellerman, Bernhard 169–170
Kerenskii, Aleksandr 220
Kharms, Daniil 69n34
Khazan, Vladimir 159
Khlebnikov, Velimir 11, 106, 107, 259,
    269n16, 294
Khodasevich, Vladislav 55, 168, 230,
    230n81, 231n82, 271–273, 279,
    292, 305, 308
Khomiakov, Aleksey 173
Kipling, Rudyard 139
Kirillov, V. T. 276
Kirsanov, Semyon 109n123
Kliun, Ivan 251
Kochetkov, A. S. 100n101
Kolomeitsev, Nikolai 239n97
Kolomeitseva, Nina 239n97
Komarovskii, Vasilii 87n68
Korinfskii, A. A. 106, 159
Korvin-Piotrovskii, V. L. 189
Kotin, aviator 283

Kovtun, E. F. 44, 81n56
Kraiskii, A. P. 107n119, 292
Krasnova, E. I. 179
Kriakutnoi, a scrivener 295
Kriuchkov, Dmitri 77n48
Kruchenykh, Aleksei 75n42, 93, 251,
    267n14, 283, 297
Kubrick, Stanley 184
Kuprin, Aleksandr 20n32, 56n14,
    66, 104n109, 108n121, 110, 114,
    122n153, 125n157, 259, 259n5,
    307n49
Kuzmin, Mikhail 54, 66, 96n95,
    211n51, 262

Laird, David 177
Lamarck, Jean-Baptiste 169n224
Langleben, Maria 12n17
Lapen, Zhan 6n8
Lapshin, N. F. 205
Larionov, Mikhail 297n40
Latham, Hubert 262, 265
Lavrov, Aleksandr 88n71
Lebedev, V. A. 286
Lebedev, Viacheslav 96
Lednitskii, V. 274
Legagneux, Georges 265
Leites, A. M. 43n9, 105
Lenin, Vladimir (Ul'ianov, Vladimir)
    81n55, 106, 130, 132
Leon, Paul 205n38
Leonardo da Vinci 295
Leri (Klopotovskii, V.) 311n57
Lerkhe, fon M. G., aviator 283
Lermontov, Mikhail 159
Leskov, Nikolai 131, 243n106
Leuthold, Dorothy 178
Levin, Iurii 209, 241
Leving, Yuri 2n1, 4n6, 47, 66n31,
    69n33, 84n61, 153n202, 167, 204,
    243n108, 244n111, 245, 299n42,
    300
Levinson, Aleksei 45–46
Lewis, David L. 176, 177, 223, 224,
    228n78
Likhachev, A. V. 95n89
Likhachev, Dmitri 39, 63n23, 47, 253
Lilli, S. (Lilley) 176n3

Lilienthal, Otto 265n11
Linnaeus, Carl 300, 301
Lisitskii, El' 142n181
Livshits, Benedikt 139n172, 221n65
Loti, Pierre 259
Lotman, Iurii 10, 13, 57
Lourié, Arthur 81n56
Lukash, Ivan 201, 202
Lunacharskii, Anatolii 275
Lunts, Lev 30
Lutskii, Semyon 90n73
Lutwack, Leonard 218n58
Lyne, Adrian 191

MacKenzie, John 65n28, 71, 80, 175
MAD (Drizo M. A.) 189n16
Maiakovskii, Vladimir 3, 4, 18n27,
    23n39, 40n66, 41n68, 96n92,
    201n30, 210, 212n53, 265–266,
    291, 292, 310
Makarov A. A. 111n124
Malevich, Kazimir 75, 76, 212, 213,
    251
Malikova, Maria 8n13, 179
Mandel'shtam, Osip 35n59, 37n61,
    38, 49, 52, 52n3, 59, 60n17, 72, 73,
    113n135, 169, 169n223, 169n224,
    205–206, 206n40, 224n73, 232,
    232n86, 245, 248, 252, 261, 267,
    269, 276, 301, 303
Mann, Thomas 53
Mansurov, Pavel 81n56
Marinetti, Filippo Tommaso 221, 297
Markova, E. 92n81
Marshak, Samuil 6n9, 91n79, 136,
    137, 138
Marvin, Carolyn 34, 201
Maslov, Boris 64n25, 72, 169n223
Matiushin, Mikhail 267n14
Matsievich, L. M. 283
Matthews, J. H. 53n7, 116n143
Matyevich-Matseevich, B. 283
Matyevich-Matseevich, S. 283
Maunoury, general 287
Maupassant, Guy de 221n64
Mayne Reid 265
McAdam, John 196
Merezhkovskii, Dmitri 295–298, 306
Michelangelo 191

Miliukov, Pavel 4n6
Mineeva, E.77, 77n48
Minskii, Nikolai 13
Modigliani, Amedeo 278
Moline, Norman T. 176n2
Monet, Claude 72
Monis, Antoine 287
Monis, Ernest 287
Monoszon A. 283
Montgolfier, Joseph-Michel 264, 295
Montgolfier, Jacques-Étienne 264, 295
Morgunov, A. A. 251
Morini, Simona 109
Musin-Pushkin, A. I. 179

Nabokov, Dmitri Vladimirovich 9,
    33n54, 59, 69, 183, 184, 189–191,
    193, 194, 198, 202, 213, 239, 300,
    309n51
Nabokov, Kirill Vladimirovich 180
Nabokov, Konstantin Dmitrievich 285
Nabokov, Vladimir Dmitrievich 36,
    87n69, 272n18
Nabokova (Sikorskii), Elena
    Vladimirovna 202, 299–300
Nabokova, Véra Evseevna 9, 59, 69,
    98, 182, 184, 186–188, 190, 198,
    202, 309n51
Nadson, Semyon 113, 114
Naiman, Eric 24n40
Nakata, Akiko 207n43
Nal'ianch [Shovgenov], Sergei 41
Napoleon 228
Narbut, Vladimir 59, 139n175, 140,
    157n24, 245
Nartsissov, Boris 111n129
Nellis, K. K. 220
Nekrasov, Nikolai 8, 57n15, 95, 143
Nesbet, Anne 95n89
Nesterov, Pyotr 284
Nevskaia, D. 295
Nietzsche, Friedrich 85, 86, 87, 299
Nikolai I 64n26
Nikolai II 286
Nizen, Ekaterina 93n83

Odarchenko, Yuri 138n171
Oginskii, M. K. 179
Olesha, Iurii 48, 265, 269, 270

Ol'sh-ii, B. S. 221n66
Osorgin, Mikhail 30, 160
Ospovat, Aleksandr 13
O'Sullivan, Tim 223
Otsup, N. A. 3, 78n51, 211, 222,
    261–262, 268, 269
Ovid 144n183

Paperno, Irina 95n89
Pasternak, Boris 2, 51n2, 54, 71, 72,
    77, 77n50, 80, 106n114, 139, 140,
    141, 148, 158n207, 163n214, 230,
    231
Pasternak, Zhozefina 109n122
Pasynok, M. 175n1
Paustovskii, Konstantin 138
Pégoud, Adolphe 265
Peter the Great 13
Peter, King of Serbia 287
Petrov, Evgeny 7, 8, 88, 138n171, 139,
    148, 149, 210, 233
Petrovskii, D. V. 294
Pettifer, Julian 177n6, 180n11,
    185n13, 232n85, 235n92
Pertsov, Petr 174
Piksanov, Nikolai 144n183
Pil'niak, Boris 60, 133, 134, 134n166,
    197, 197n24
Piotrovskii, A. I. 30n50
Piretto, G. 104
Pirogov (chauffeur) 180
Pisarev, Dmitri 105n113
Platonov, Andrei 29n46, 143
Podkuz'mikhin, T. (F. F. Syromolotov)
    291
Poe, Edgar Allen 260
Poletaev, N. G. 141
Polonskii, Iakov 91, 173
Ponge, Francis 75n46
Poplavskii, Boris 6n11, 92n81, 96,
    96n95, 103n106, 267
Popov, Nikolai 307
Povelikhina, A. 44, 81n56
Pressland, David 63
Proffer, Carl 211n50, 223
Propp, Vladimir 52, 180, 180n10,
    264
Proust, Marcel 122n153, 138–139,
    177

Pushkin, Alexander 13, 14, 28, 31,
    51, 57, 90, 91, 102, 112n132, 118,
    136, 179, 179n7, 196, 197, 212,
    238, 244, 244n109, 264, 300, 305,
    306n47, 310

Rabelais, François 133
Radishchev, Alexander 90
Ratgauz, T. D. 295n35, 115n139,
    291n35
Remarque, Erich Maria 15n23
Riazanov, N. 306n47
Richards, Jeffrey 65, 71, 80, 175
Rodzianko, M. V. 81n55
Rodchenko, Alexander 291
Ronen, Omri 15, 47, 235
Roques, general 287
Roper, Robert 184
Rozanov, Vasily 130, 145, 145n186,
    174
Rozhdestvenskii, Vs. A. 90n73
Rozov, Samuil 113n135
Rousseau, Jean-Jacques 221n64
Rudakov, Sergei 49
Rudnev, E. V. 283
Rukavishnikov, Vasilii 69, 94

Sadof'ev, Il'ia 77, 77n49, 103n107,
    203n35
Sadovskoi, Boris 3, 307
Samoilov, David 60
Santos-Dumont, Alberto 267, 285,
    304
Sashonko, V. N. 307
Sato, Iu. 112n131
Scharff, Virginia 188n14
Schiff, Stacy 98, 186, 189
Schivelbusch, Wolfgang 99
Schmidt, Gerhard 223n69
Segno, G. 283
Sel'vinskii, Il'ia 292
Sergeev-Tsenskii, Sergei 54, 54n10
Severianin, Igor 223, 223n67, 224n73,
    280n25
Shakespeare, William 211, 211n50,
    256
Shakh, Evgenii 19n29, 76n47, 80
Shakhovskaia, Zinaida 57, 204
Shapiro, Gavriel 167

Shchusev, A. V. 75n45
Shefner, Vadim 160n211
Shengeli, Georgii 38n62, 107n117, 245, 261
Shershenevich, Vadim 15n24, 25n42, 41, 96, 224n71, 281
Shersher, S. 129
Shevyrev, Stepan 173n225
Shifman, A. V. 172
Shimanskii, G. 283
Shirokov, P. D. 44n71
Shklovskii, Viktor 184, 203, 203n34, 203n35, 211n51, 222, 267n13, 270, 288, 292
Shlegel', Karl 168n220, 239n96, 240n100
Shteiner, Evgenii 174
Shuf, Vladimir 60n18
Shuvalova, E. 52n6
Shvarts, Evgenii 132, 138
Sikorskii, Igor 256n4, 286–287
Sikorskii, Vladimir 202
Simonov, Konstantin 77n50, 90n73
Skonechnaia, Olga 54n12
Smit, V. F. 255, 256, 279, 283
Smith, Julian 228n78, 232n85
Snessarev, Nikolai 4n6
Sobinov, L. V. 179n7
Sobol', Andrei 52n5, 129–132, 134n167, 135n168
Sologub, Fyodor 13, 13n19, 40, 231n84
Solov'ev, Vladimir 95n88
Solov'ev, Sergei 14
Solov'eva, Polyxena 159, 266
Sorokina, V. V. 112n131
Sosinskii, Bronislav 15, 17
Spender, Stephen 139n174
Spengler, Oswald 85, 86, 87
Sredinskii, A. N. 256
Stasov, Vladimir 172, 173
Stepun, Fyodor 145, 172
Stevenson, Robert Louis 139, 167, 168, 181
Struiskii, Dmitrii 306
Stuart, Dabney 236n94
Svetlov, Mikhail 139n173
Sviatopolk-Mirskii, Dmitry 107n120

Svinarenko, Igor 191
Sulakadzev, A. I. 295

Tan, V. G. 17
Tatlin, Vladimir 251, 294
Teffi, Nadezhda 52, 212n55
Terapiano, Iurii 238
Tikhonov, Nikolai 79, 249n117
Timenchik, Roman 4, 13, 36, 80n54, 263n9
Tiutchev, Fyodor 56, 121, 121n151, 251, 292n36
Toker, Leona 207n43
Tolstoi, Lev 13, 34, 38, 51n2, 52, 63, 65n27, 95, 100, 103, 103n105, 112, 112n131, 112n132, 113n133, 119, 144, 155, 172, 243n106, 288
Tomashevskii, Boris 13
Toporkov, A. K. 143, 308n50
Toporkov, A. L. 21n35
Tret'iakov, Sergei 24, 29, 29n45, 247n113
Trotskii, Leon 130
Tsetlin, Mikhail 31n52
Tsvetaeva, Marina 3, 74, 74n40, 77, 85n63, 96, 96n96, 97, 112n132, 132–133, 134n166, 149–151, 157n206, 158, 167, 250n118, 254n3, 310n54
Tumannyi, D. (Panov N. N.) 269
Turgenev, Ivan 172
Turne, F. 99n99
Turner, Nigel 177n6, 180n11, 185n13, 232n85, 235n92
Tynianov, Iurii 203, 237, 52n3

Uritskii, Moisei 132
Uspenskii, Boris 163n214
Uspenskii, Lev 265, 278
Utkin, Iosif 111n127, 140n176
Utochkin, S. I. 283, 286

Vaginov, Konstantin 115n139, 119, 119n149, 237n95
Vaiskopf, Mikhail 214, 291
Vasil'ev A. A., aviator 283
Veigelin, K. E. 293
Vereshchagin, V. V. 21

Verlaine, Paul-Marie 90, 90n73
Verhaeren, Émile 14, 40, 72, 80,
166n219, 259
Verkhovskii, Iu. N. 110
Verne, Jules 2, 299
Vertov, Dziga 113n134
Viazemskii, Pyotr 99, 100, 104n110,
105–106, 144n183, 194, 196
Virgil 180n9
Voisin brothers 262
Volkov, Boris 77n48
Voloshin, Maksimilian 14n22,
40, 66n29, 73–75, 88–89, 110,
166n219, 200–201, 270
Vorontsovskii, V. 147n191
Vrubel', Mikhail 245
Vvedenskii, Alexander 251n1

Weber, Max 38
Wells, H.G. 17, 47, 76, 105n111, 289,
299
Wells, Paul 228n78
Westinghouse, D. 4
Westwood, J. N. 51, 64n24, 95,
115n137, 155n203
Wilson, Edmund 134n166, 197,
197n22, 224–225
Whitman, Walt 66, 67

Wolfe, Thomas 79n53
Wright, Orville 259n6, 261, 266, 284,
296
Wright, Wilbur 259n6, 261, 265, 266,
284, 296

Yangirov, Rashit 2n2, 196n20

Zabolotskii, Nikolai 39, 261, 276
Zaikin, I. M. 259n5
Zamiatin, Evgenii 56, 57, 80n54, 196,
289, 299
Zenkevich, Mikhail 90n77, 159n209,
259, 259n6, 261, 265, 278, 281, 283
Zenzinov, Mikhail 59, 210n47, 249
Zeppelin, Ferdinand von 256, 296
Zharov, A. A. 278
Zheliabuzhskii, I. A. 295
Zheltova, E. L. 254n3
Zhemchuzhnikov, Aleksei 90
Zholkovskii, Alexander 92n82, 127
Zimmer, Dieter E. 144n184, 239n96
Zivert, Svetlana 82
Zolotukhin, aviator 283
Zola, Émile 8, 53, 70, 101, 116n143,
246, 247
Zubtsov, Iu. 309n51
Zubtsova, Ia. 309n51